I0641937

# BEST FRENCH SHORT STORIES

Edited by
Vladimir Orel

# TABLE OF CONTENTS

# From the editor

This collection of French short stories is a logical continuation of our earlier publication, *Best Russian Short Stories*. The present volume reflects — to some extent — the enigmatic universe of French story-telling with its tradition of crisp, clear and stylistically refined language giving an unusual depth and laconism to psychological characteristics of human beings. We hope that English translations render some of the beauty and internal narrative consistency of French originals.

## THE GUILTY SECRET
## BY PAUL DE KOCK

Nathalie De Hauteville was twenty-two years old, and had been a widow for three years. She was one of the prettiest women in Paris; her large dark eyes shone with remarkable brilliancy, and she united the sparkling vivacity of an Italian and the depth of feeling of a Spaniard to the grace which always distinguishes a Parisian born and bred. Considering herself too young to be entirely alone, she had long ago invited M. d'Ablaincourt, an old uncle of hers, to come and live with her.

M. d'Ablaincourt was an old bachelor; he had never loved anything in this world but himself. He was an egotist, too lazy to do any one an ill turn, but at the same time too selfish to do any one a kindness, unless it would tend directly to his own advantage. And yet, with an air of complaisance, as if he desired nothing so much as the comfort of those around him, he consented to his niece's proposal, in the hope that she would do many little kind offices for him, which would add materially to his comfort.

M. d'Ablaincourt accompanied his niece when she resumed her place in society; but sometimes, when he felt inclined to stay at home, he would say to her: "My dear Nathalie, I am afraid you will not be much amused this evening. They will only play cards; besides, I don't think any of your friends will be there. Of course, I am ready to take you, if you wish to go."

And Nathalie, who had great confidence in all her uncle said, would stay at home.

In the same manner, M. d'Ablaincourt, who was a great gourmand, said to his niece: "My dear, you know that I am not at all fond of eating, and am satisfied with the simplest fare; but I must tell you that your cook puts too much salt in everything! It is very unwholesome."

So they changed the cook.

Again, the garden was out of order; the trees before the old gentleman's window must be cut down, because their shade would doubtless cause a dampness in the house prejudicial to Nathalie's health; or the surrey was to be changed for a landau.

Nathalie was a coquette. Accustomed to charm, she listened with smiles to the numerous protestations of admiration which she received. She sent all who aspired to her hand to her uncle, saying: "Before I give you any hope, I must know my uncle's opinion."

It is likely that Nathalie would have answered differently if she had ever felt a real preference for any one; but heretofore she seemed to have preferred her liberty.

The old uncle, for his part, being now master in his niece's house, was very anxious for her to remain as she was. A nephew might be somewhat less submissive than Nathalie. Therefore, he never failed to discover some great fault in each of those who sought an alliance with the pretty widow.

Besides his egotism and his Epicureanism, the dear uncle had another passion — to play backgammon. The game amused him very much; but the difficulty was to find any one to play with. If, by accident, any of Nathalie's visitors understood it, there was no escape from a long siege with the old gentleman; but most people preferred cards.

In order to please her uncle, Nathalie tried to learn this game; but it was almost impossible. She could not give her attention to one thing for so long a time. Her uncle scolded. Nathalie gave up in despair.

"It was only for your own amusement that I wished to teach it to you," said the good M. d'Ablaincourt.

Things were at this crisis when, at a ball one evening, Nathalie was introduced to a M. d'Apremont, a captain in the navy.

Nathalie raised her eyes, expecting to see a great sailor, with a wooden leg and a bandage over one eye; when to her great surprise, she beheld a man of about thirty, tall and finely formed, with two sound legs and two good eyes.

Armand d'Apremont had entered the navy at a very early age, and had arrived, although very young, to the dignity of a captain.

He had amassed a large fortune, in addition to his patrimonial estates, and he had now come home to rest after his labors. As yet, however, he was a single man, and, moreover, had always laughed at love.

But when he saw Nathalie, his opinions underwent a change. For the first time in his life he regretted that he had never learned to dance, and he kept his eyes fixed on her constantly.

His attentions to the young widow soon became a subject of general conversation, and, at last, the report reached the ears of M. d'Ablaincourt. When Nathalie mentioned, one evening, that she expected the captain to spend the evening with her, the old man grew almost angry.

"Nathalie," said he, "you act entirely without consulting me. I have heard that the captain is very rude and unpolished in his manners. To be sure, I have only seen him standing behind your chair; but he has never even asked after my health. I only speak for your interest, as you are so giddy."

Nathalie begged her uncle's pardon, and even offered not to receive the captain's visit; but this he forbore to require — secretly resolving not to allow these visits to become too frequent.

But how frail are all human resolutions — overturned by the merest trifle! In this case, the game of backgammon was the unconscious cause of Nathalie's becoming Mme. d'Apremont. The captain was an excellent hand at backgammon. When the uncle heard this, he proposed a game; and the captain, who understood that it was important to gain the uncle's favor, readily acceded.

This did not please Nathalie. She preferred that he should be occupied with herself. When all the company were gone, she turned to her uncle, saying: "You were right, uncle, after all. I do not admire the captain's manners; I see now that I should not have invited him."

"On the contrary, niece, he is a very well-behaved man. I have invited him to come here very often, and play backgammon with me — that is, to pay his addresses to you."

Nathalie saw that the captain had gained her uncle's heart, and she forgave him for having been less attentive to her. He soon came again, and, thanks to the backgammon, increased in favor with the uncle.

He soon captivated the heart of the pretty widow, also. One morning, Nathalie came blushing to her uncle.

"The captain has asked me to marry him. What do you advise me to do?"

He reflected for a few moments. "If she refuses him, D'Apremont will come here no longer, and then no more backgammon. But if she marries him, he will be here always, and I shall have my games." And the answer was: "You had better marry him."

Nathalie loved Armand; but she would not yield too easily. She sent for the captain.

"If you really love me — "

"Ah, can you doubt it?"

"Hush! do not interrupt me. If you really love me, you will give me one proof of it."

"Anything you ask. I swear — "

"No, you must never swear any more; and, one thing more, you must never smoke. I detest the smell of tobacco, and I will not have a husband who smokes."

Armand sighed, and promised.

The first months of their marriage passed smoothly, but sometimes Armand became thoughtful, restless, and grave. After some time, these fits of sadness became more frequent.

"What is the matter?" asked Nathalie one day, on seeing him stamp with impatience. "Why are you so irritable?"

"Nothing — nothing at all!" replied the captain, as if ashamed of his ill humor.

"Tell me," Nathalie insisted, "have I displeased you in anything?"

The captain assured her that he had no reason to be anything but delighted with her conduct on all occasions, and for a time he was all right. Then soon he was worse than before.

Nathalie was distressed beyond measure. She imparted her anxiety to her uncle, who replied: "Yes, my dear, I know what you mean; I have often remarked it myself, at backgammon. He is very inattentive, and often passes his hand over his forehead, and starts up as if something agitated him."

And one day, when his old habits of impatience and irritability reappeared, more marked than ever, the captain said to his wife: "My dear, an evening walk will do me a world of good; an old sailor like myself cannot bear to sit around the house after dinner. Nevertheless, if you have any objection — "

"Oh, no! What objection can I have?"

He went out, and continued to do so, day after day, at the same hour. Invariably he returned in the best of good humor.

Nathalie was now unhappy indeed. "He loves some other woman, perhaps," she thought, "and he must see her every day. Oh, how wretched I am! But I must let him know that his perfidy is discovered. No, I will wait until I shall have some certain proof wherewith to confront him."

And she went to seek her uncle. "Ah, I am the most unhappy creature in the world!" she sobbed.

"What is the matter?" cried the old man, leaning back in his armchair.

"Armand leaves the house for two hours every evening, after dinner, and comes back in high spirits and as anxious to please me as on the day of our marriage. Oh, uncle, I cannot bear it any longer! If you do not assist me to discover where he goes, I will seek a separation."

"But, my dear niece — "

"My dear uncle, you who are so good and obliging, grant me this one favor. I am sure there is some woman in the secret."

M. d'Ablaincourt wished to prevent a rupture between his niece and nephew, which would interfere very much with the quiet, peaceable life which he led at their house. He pretended to follow Armand; but came back very soon, saying he had lost sight of him.

"But in what direction does he go?"

"Sometimes one way, and sometimes another, but always alone; so your suspicions are unfounded. Be assured, he only walks for exercise."

But Nathalie was not to be duped in this way. She sent for a little errand boy, of whose intelligence she had heard a great deal.

"M. d'Apremont goes out every evening."

"Yes, madame."

"To-morrow, you will follow him; observe where he goes, and come and tell me privately. Do you understand?"

"Yes, madame."

Nathalie waited impatiently for the next day, and for the hour of her husband's departure. At last, the time came — the pursuit is going on — Nathalie counted the moments. After three-quarters of an hour, the messenger arrived, covered with dust.

"Well," exclaimed Nathalie, "speak! Tell me everything that you have seen!"

"Madame, I followed M. d'Apremont, at a distance, as far as the Rue Vieille du Temple, where he entered a small house, in an alley. There was no servant to let him in."

"An alley! No servant! Dreadful!"

"I went in directly after him, and heard him go up-stairs and unlock a door."

"Open the door himself, without knocking! Are you sure of that?"

"Yes, madame."

"The wretch! So he has a key! But, go on."

"When the door shut after him, I stole softly up-stairs, and peeped through the keyhole."

"You shall have twenty francs more."

"I peeped through the keyhole, and saw him drag a trunk along the floor."

"A trunk?"

"Then he undressed himself, and — "

"Undressed himself!"

"Then, for a few seconds, I could not see him, and directly he appeared again, in a sort of gray blouse, and a cap on his head."

"A blouse! What in the world does he want with a blouse? What next?"

"I came away, then, madame, and made haste to tell you; but he is there still."

"Well, now run to the corner and get me a cab, and direct the coachman to the house where you have been."

While the messenger went for the cab, Nathalie hurried on her hat and cloak, and ran into her uncle's room.

"I have found him out — he loves another. He's at her house now, in a gray blouse. But I will go and confront him, and then you will see me no more."

The old man had no time to reply. She was gone, with her messenger, in the cab. They stopped at last.

"Here is the house."

Nathalie got out, pale and trembling.

"Shall I go up-stairs with you, madame?" asked the boy.

"No, I will go alone. The third story, isn't it?"

"Yes, madame; the left-hand door, at the head of the stairs."

It seemed that now, indeed, the end of all things was at hand.

Nathalie mounted the dark, narrow stairs, and arrived at the door, and, almost fainting, she cried: "Open the door, or I shall die!"

The door was opened, and Nathalie fell into her husband's arms. He was alone in the room, clad in a gray blouse, and — smoking a Turkish pipe.

"My wife!" exclaimed Armand, in surprise.

"Your wife — who, suspecting your perfidy, has followed you, to discover the cause of your mysterious conduct!"

"How, Nathalie, my mysterious conduct? Look, here it is!" (Showing his pipe.) "Before our marriage, you forbade me to smoke, and I promised to obey you. For some months I kept my promise; but you know what it cost me; you remember how irritable and sad I became. It was my pipe, my beloved pipe, that I regretted. One day, in the country, I discovered a little cottage, where a peasant was smoking. I asked him if he could lend me a blouse and cap; for I should like to smoke with him, but it was necessary to conceal it from you, as the smell of smoke, remaining in my clothes, would have betrayed me. It was soon settled between us. I returned thither every afternoon, to indulge in my favorite occupation; and, with the precaution of a cap to keep the smoke from remaining in my hair, I contrived to deceive you. This is all the mystery. Forgive me."

Nathalie kissed him, crying: "I might have known it could not be! I am happy now, and you shall smoke as much as you please, at home."

And Nathalie returned to her uncle, saying: "Uncle, he loves me! He was only smoking, but hereafter he is to smoke at home."

"I can arrange it all," said D'Ablaincourt; "he shall smoke while he plays backgammon."

"In that way," thought the old man, "I shall be sure of my game."

# THE ELIXIR OF LIFE
## BY HONORE DE BALZAC

In a sumptuous palace of Ferrara, one winter evening, Don Juan Belvidéro was entertaining a prince of the house of Este. In those days a banquet was a marvelous affair, which demanded princely riches or the power of a nobleman. Seven pleasure-loving women chatted gaily around a table lighted by perfumed candles, surrounded by admirable works of art whose white marble stood out against the walls of red stucco and contrasted with the rich Turkey carpets. Clad in satin, glittering with gold and laden with gems which sparkled only less brilliantly than their eyes, they all told of passions, intense, but of various styles, like their beauty. They differed neither in their words nor their ideas; but an expression, a look, a motion or an emphasis served as a commentary, unrestrained, licentious, melancholy or bantering, to their words.

One seemed to say: "My beauty has power to rekindle the frozen heart of age." Another: "I love to repose on soft cushions and think with rapture of my adorers." A third, a novice at these fêtes, was inclined to blush. "At the bottom of my heart I feel compunction," she seemed to say. "I am a Catholic and I fear hell; but I love you so — ah, so dearly — that I would sacrifice eternity to you!" The fourth, emptying a cup of Chian wine, cried: "Hurrah, for pleasure! I begin a new existence with each dawn. Forgetful of the past, still intoxicated with the violence of yesterday's pleasures, I embrace a new life of happiness, a life filled with love."

The woman sitting next to Belvidéro looked at him with flashing eyes. She was silent. "I should have no need to call on a bravo to kill my lover if he abandoned me." Then she had laughed; but a comfit dish of marvelous workmanship was shattered between her nervous fingers.

"When are you to be grand duke?" asked the sixth of the prince, with an expression of murderous glee on her lips and a look of Bacchanalian frenzy in her eyes.

"And when is your father going to die?" said the seventh, laughing and throwing her bouquet to Don Juan with maddening coquetry. She was an innocent young girl who was accustomed to play with sacred things.

"Oh, don't speak of it!" cried the young and handsome Don Juan. "There is only one immortal father in the world, and unfortunately he is mine!"

The seven women of Ferrara, the friends of Don Juan, and the prince himself gave an exclamation of horror. Two hundred years later, under Louis XV, well-bred persons would have laughed at this sally. But perhaps at the beginning of an orgy the mind had still an unusual degree of lucidity. Despite the heat of the candles, the intensity of the emotions, the gold and silver vases, the fumes of wine, despite the vision of ravishing women, perhaps there still lurked in the depths of the heart a little of that respect for things human and divine which struggles until the revel has drowned it in floods of sparkling wine. Nevertheless, the flowers were already crushed, the eyes were steeped with drink, and intoxication, to quote Rabelais, had reached even to the sandals. In the pause that followed a door opened, and, as at the feast of Balthazar, God manifested himself. He seemed to command recognition now in the person of an old, white-haired servant with unsteady gait and drawn brows; he entered with gloomy mien and his look seemed to blight the garlands, the ruby cups, the pyramids of fruits, the brightness of the feast, the glow of the astonished faces and the colors of the cushions dented by the white arms of the women; then he cast a pall over this folly by saying, in a hollow voice, the solemn words: "Sir, your father is dying!"

Don Juan rose, making a gesture to his guests, which might be translated: "Excuse me, this does not happen every day."

Does not the death of a parent often overtake young people thus in the fullness of life, in the wild enjoyment of an orgy? Death is as unexpected in her caprices as a woman in her fancies, but more faithful — Death has never duped any one.

When Don Juan had closed the door of the banquet hall and walked down the long corridor, which was both cold and dark, he compelled himself to assume a mask, for, in thinking of his role of son, he had cast off his merriment as he threw down his napkin. The night was black. The silent servant who conducted the young man to the death chamber, lighted the way so insufficiently that Death, aided by the cold, the silence, the gloom, perhaps by a reaction of intoxication, was able to force some reflections into the soul of the spendthrift; he examined his life, and became thoughtful, like a man involved in a lawsuit when he sets out for the court of justice.

Bartholomeo Belvidéro, the father of Don Juan, was an old man of ninety, who had devoted the greater part of his life to business. Having traveled much in Oriental countries he had acquired there great wealth and learning more precious, he said, than gold or diamonds, to which he no longer gave more than a passing thought. "I value a tooth more than a ruby," he used to say, smiling, "and power more than knowledge." This good father loved to hear Don Juan relate his youthful adventures, and would say, banteringly, as he lavished money upon him: "Only amuse yourself, my dear child!" Never did an old man find such pleasure in watching a young man. Paternal love robbed age of its terrors in the delight of contemplating so brilliant a life.

At the age of sixty, Belvidéro had become enamored of an angel of peace and beauty. Don Juan was the sole fruit of this late love. For fifteen years the good man had mourned the loss of his dear Juana. His many servants and his son attributed the strange habits he had contracted to this grief. Bartholomeo lodged himself in the most uncomfortable wing of his palace and rarely went out, and even Don Juan could not intrude into his father's apartment without first obtaining permission. If this voluntary recluse came or went in the palace or in the streets of Ferrara he seemed to be searching for something which he could not find. He walked dreamily, undecidedly, preoccupied like a man battling with an idea or with a memory. While the young man gave magnificent entertainments and the palace re-echoed his mirth, while the horses pawed the ground in the courtyard and the pages quarreled at their game of dice on the stairs, Bartholomeo ate seven ounces of bread a day and drank water. If he asked for a little poultry it was merely that he might give the bones to a black spaniel, his faithful companion. He never complained of the noise. During his illness if the blast of horns or the barking of dogs interrupted his sleep, he only said: "Ah, Don Juan has come home." Never before was so untroublesome and indulgent a father to be found on this earth; consequently young Belvidéro, accustomed to treat him without ceremony, had all the faults of a spoiled child. His attitude toward Bartholomeo was like that of a capricious woman toward an elderly lover, passing off an impertinence with a smile, selling his good humor and submitting to be loved. In calling up the picture of his youth, Don Juan recognized that it would be difficult to find an instance in which his father's goodness had failed him. He felt a newborn remorse while he traversed the corridor, and he very nearly forgave his father for having lived so long. He reverted to feelings of filial piety, as a thief returns to honesty in the prospect of enjoying a well-stolen million.

Soon the young man passed into the high, chill rooms of his father's apartment. After feeling a moist atmosphere and breathing the heavy air and the musty odor which is given forth by old tapestries and furniture covered with dust, he found himself in the antique room of the old man, in front of a sick bed and near a dying fire. A lamp standing on a table of Gothic shape shed its streams of uneven light sometimes more, sometimes less strongly upon the bed and showed the form of the old man in ever-varying aspects. The cold air whistled through the insecure windows, and the snow beat with a dull sound against the panes.

This scene formed so striking a contrast to the one which Don Juan had just left that he could not help shuddering. He felt cold when, on approaching the bed, a sudden flare of light, caused by a gust of wind, illumined his father's face. The features were distorted; the skin, clinging tightly to the bones, had a greenish tint, which was made the more horrible by the whiteness of the pillows on which the old man rested; drawn with pain, the mouth, gaping and toothless, gave breath to sighs which the howling of the tempest took Tip and drew out into a dismal wail. In spite of these signs of dissolution an incredible expression of power shone in the face. The eyes, hallowed by disease, retained a singular steadiness. A superior spirit was fighting there with death. It seemed as if Bartholomeo sought to kill with his dying look some enemy seated at the foot of his bed. This gaze, fixed and cold, was made the more appalling by the immobility of the head, which was like a skull standing on a doctor's table. The body, clearly outlined by the coverlet, showed that the dying man's limbs preserved the same rigidity. All was dead, except the eyes. There was something mechanical in the sounds which came from the mouth. Don Juan felt a certain shame at having come to the deathbed of his father with a courtesan's bouquet on his breast, bringing with him the odors of a banquet and the fumes of wine.

"You were enjoying yourself!" cried the old man, on seeing his son.

At the same moment the pure, high voice of a singer who entertained the guests, strengthened by the chords of the viol by which she was accompanied, rose above the roar of the storm and penetrated the chamber of death. Don Juan would gladly have shut out this barbarous confirmation of his father's words.

Bartholomeo said: "I do not grudge you your pleasure, my child."

These words, full of tenderness, pained Don Juan, who could not forgive his father for such goodness.

"What, sorrow for me, father!" he cried.

"Poor Juanino," answered the dying man, "I have always been so gentle toward you that you could not wish for my death?"

"Oh!" cried Don Juan, "if it were possible to preserve your life by giving you a part of mine!" ("One can always say such things," thought the spendthrift; "it is as if I offered the world to my mistress.")

The thought had scarcely passed through his mind when the old spaniel whined. This intelligent voice made Don Juan tremble. He believed that the dog understood him.

"I knew that I could count on you, my son," said the dying man. "There, you shall be satisfied. I shall live, but without depriving you of a single day of your life."

"He raves," said Don Juan to himself.

Then he said, aloud: "Yes, my dearest father, you will indeed live as long as I do, for your image will be always in my heart."

"It is not a question of that sort of life," said the old nobleman, gathering all his strength to raise himself to a sitting posture, for he was stirred by one of those suspicions which are only born at the bedside of the dying. "Listen, my son," he continued in a voice weakened by this last effort. "I have no more desire to die than you have to give up your lady loves, wine, horses, falcons, hounds and money —— "

"I can well believe it," thought his son, kneeling beside the pillow and kissing one of Bartholomeo's cadaverous hands. "But, father," he said aloud, "my dear father, we must submit to the will of God!"

"God! I am also God!" growled the old man.

"Do not blaspheme!" cried the young man, seeing the menacing expression which was overspreading his father's features. "Be careful what you say, for you have received extreme unction and I should never be consoled if you were to die in a state of sin."

"Are you going to listen to me?" cried the dying man, gnashing his toothless jaws.

Don Juan held his peace. A horrible silence reigned. Through the dull wail of the snowstorm came again the melody of the viol and the heavenly voice, faint as the dawning day.

The dying man smiled.

"I thank you for having brought singers and music! A banquet, young and beautiful women, with dark locks, all the pleasures of life. Let them remain. I am about to be born again."

"The delirium is at its height," said Don Juan to himself.

"I have discovered a means of resuscitation. There, look in the drawer of the table — you open it by pressing a hidden spring near the griffin."

"I have it, father."

"Good! Now take out a little flask of rock crystal."

"Here it is."

"I have spent twenty years in — — "

At this point the old man felt his end approaching, and collected all his energy to say:

"As soon as I have drawn my last breath rub me with this water and I shall come to life again."

"There is very little of it," replied the young man.

Bartholomeo was no longer able to speak, but he could still hear and see. At these words he turned his head toward Don Juan with a violent wrench. His neck remained twisted like that of a marble statue doomed by the sculptor's whim to look forever sideways, his staring eyes assumed a hideous fixity. He was dead, dead in the act of losing his only, his last illusion. In seeking a shelter in his son's heart he had found a tomb more hollow than those which men dig for their dead. His hair, too, had risen with horror and his tense gaze seemed still to speak. It was a father rising in wrath from his sepulchre to demand vengeance of God.

"There, the good man is done for!" exclaimed Don Juan.

Intent upon taking the magic crystal to the light of the lamp, as a drinker examines his bottle at the end of a repast, he had not seen his father's eye pale. The cowering dog looked alternately at his dead master and at the elixir, as Don Juan regarded by turns his father and the phial. The lamp threw out fitful waves of light. The silence was profound, the viol was mute. Belvidéro thought he saw his father move, and he trembled. Frightened by the tense expression of the accusing eyes, he closed them, just as he would have pushed down a window-blind on an autumn night. He stood motionless, lost in a world of thought.

Suddenly a sharp creak, like that of a rusty spring, broke the silence. Don Juan, in his surprise, almost dropped the flask. A perspiration, colder than the steel of a dagger, oozed out from his pores. A cock of painted wood came forth from a clock and crowed three times. It was one of those ingenious inventions by which the savants of that time were awakened at the hour fixed for their work. Already the daybreak reddened the casement. The old timepiece was more faithful in its master's service than Don Juan had been in his duty to Bartholomeo. This instrument was composed of wood, pulleys, cords and wheels, while he had that mechanism peculiar to man, called a heart.

In order to run no further risk of losing the mysterious liquid the skeptical Don Juan replaced it in the drawer of the little Gothic table. At this solemn moment he heard a tumult in the corridor. There were confused voices, stifled laughter, light footsteps, the rustle of silk, in short, the noise of a merry troop trying to collect itself in some sort of order. The door opened and the prince, the seven women, the friends of Don Juan and the singers, appeared, in the fantastic disorder of dancers overtaken by the morning, when the sun disputes the paling light of the candles. They came to offer the young heir the conventional condolences.

"Oh, oh, is poor Don Juan really taking this death seriously?" said the prince in la Brambilla's ear.

"Well, his father was a very good man," she replied.

Nevertheless, Don Juan's nocturnal meditations had printed so striking an expression upon his face that it commanded silence. The men stopped, motionless. The women, whose lips had been parched with wine, threw themselves on their knees and began to pray. Don Juan could not help shuddering as he saw this splendor, this joy, laughter, song, beauty, life personified, doing homage thus to Death. But in this adorable Italy religion and revelry were on such good terms that religion was a sort of debauch and debauch religion. The prince pressed Don Juan's hand affectionately, then all the figures having given expression to the same look, half-sympathy, half-indifference, the phantasmagoria disappeared, leaving the chamber empty. It was, indeed, a faithful image of life! Going down the stairs the prince said to la Rivabarella:

22

"Heyho! who would have thought Don Juan a mere boaster of impiety? He loved his father, after all!"

"Did you notice the black dog?" asked la Brambilla.

"He is immensely rich now," sighed Bianca Cavatolini.

"What is that to me?" cried the proud Veronese, she who had broken the comfit dish.

"What is that to you?" exclaimed the duke. "With his ducats he is as much a prince as I am!"

At first Don Juan, swayed by a thousand thoughts, wavered toward many different resolutions. After having ascertained the amount of the wealth amassed by his father, he returned in the evening to the death chamber, his soul puffed up with a horrible egoism. In the apartment he found all the servants of the household busied in collecting the ornaments for the bed of state on which "feu monseigneur" would lie to-morrow — a curious spectacle which all Ferrara would come to admire. Don Juan made a sign and the servants stopped at once, speechless and trembling.

"Leave me alone," he said in an altered voice, "and do not return until I go out again."

When the steps of the old servant, who was the last to leave, had died away on the stone flooring, Don Juan locked the door hastily, and, sure that he was alone, exclaimed:

"Now, let us try!"

The body of Bartholomeo lay on a long table. To hide the revolting spectacle of a corpse whose extreme decrepitude and thinness made it look like a skeleton, the embalmers had drawn a sheet over the body, which covered all but the head. This mummy-like figure was laid out in the middle of the room, and the linen, naturally clinging, outlined the form vaguely, but showing its stiff, bony thinness. The face already had large purple spots, which showed the urgency of completing the embalming. Despite the skepticism with which Don Juan was armed, he trembled as he uncorked the magic phial of crystal. When he stood close to the head he shook so that he was obliged to pause for a moment. But this young man had allowed himself to be

23

corrupted by the customs of a dissolute court. An idea worthy of the Duke of Urbino came to him, and gave him a courage which was spurred on by lively curiosity. It seemed as if the demon had whispered the words which resounded in his heart: "Bathe an eye!" He took a piece of linen and, after having moistened it sparingly with the precious liquid, he passed it gently over the right eyelid of the corpse. The eye opened!

"Ah!" said Don Juan, gripping the flask in his hand as we clutch in our dreams the branch by which we are suspended over a precipice.

He saw an eye full of life, a child's eye in a death's head, the liquid eye of youth, in which the light trembled. Protected by beautiful black lashes, it scintillated like one of those solitary lights which travelers see in lonely places on winter evenings. It seemed as if the glowing eye would pierce Don Juan. It thought, accused, condemned, threatened, judged, spoke — it cried, it snapped at him! There was the most tender supplication, a royal anger, then the love of a young girl imploring mercy of her executioners. Finally, the awful look that a man casts upon his fellow-men on his way to the scaffold. So much life shone in this fragment of life that Don Juan recoiled in terror. He walked up and down the room, not daring to look at the eye, which stared back at him from the ceiling and from the hangings. The room was sown with points full of fire, of life, of intelligence. Everywhere gleamed eyes which shrieked at him.

"He might have lived a hundred years longer!" he cried involuntarily when, led in front of his father by some diabolical influence, he contemplated the luminous spark.

Suddenly the intelligent eye closed, and then opened again abruptly, as if assenting. If a voice had cried, "Yes," Don Juan could not have been more startled.

"What is to be done?" he thought

He had the courage to try to close this white eyelid, but his efforts were in vain.

"Shall I crush it out? Perhaps that would be parricide?" he asked himself.

"Yes," said the eye, by means of an ironical wink.

"Ah!" cried Don Juan, "there is sorcery in it!"

He approached the eye to crush it. A large tear rolled down the hollow cheek of the corpse and fell on Belvidéro's hand.

"It is scalding!" he cried, sitting down.

This struggle had exhausted him, as if, like Jacob, he had battled with an angel.

At last he arose, saying: "So long as there is no blood — "

Then, collecting all the courage needed for the cowardly act, he crushed out the eye, pressing it in with the linen without looking at it. A deep moan, startling and terrible, was heard. It was the poor spaniel, who died with a howl.

"Could he have been in the secret?" Don Juan wondered, surveying the faithful animal.

Don Juan was considered a dutiful son. He raised a monument of white marble over his father's tomb, and employed the most prominent artists of the time to carve the figures. He was not altogether at ease until the statue of his father, kneeling before Religion, imposed its enormous weight on the grave, in which he had buried the only regret that had ever touched his heart, and that only in moments of physical depression.

On making an inventory of the immense wealth amassed by the old Orientalist, Don Juan became avaricious. Had he not two human lives in which he should need money? His deep, searching gaze penetrated the principles of social life, and he understood the world all the better because he viewed it across a tomb. He analyzed men and things that he might have done at once with the past, represented by history, with the present, expressed by the law, and with the future revealed by religion. He took soul and matter, threw them into a crucible, and found nothing there, and from that time forth he became Don Juan.

Master of the illusions of life he threw himself — young and beautiful — into life; despising the world, but seizing the world. His happiness could never be of that bourgeois type which is satisfied by boiled beef, by a welcome warming-pan in winter, a lamp at night and new slippers at each quarter. He grasped existence as a monkey seizes a nut, peeling off the coarse shell to enjoy the savory kernel. The poetry and sublime transports of human passion touched no higher than his instep. He never made the mistake of those strong men who, imagining that little Souls believe in the great, venture to exchange noble thoughts of the future for the small coin of our ideas of life. He might, like them, have walked with his feet on earth and his head among the clouds, but he preferred to sit at his ease and sear with his kisses the lips of more than one tender, fresh and sweet woman. Like Death, wherever he passed, he devoured all without scruple, demanding a passionate, Oriental love and easily won pleasure. Loving only woman in women, his soul found its natural trend in irony.

When his inamoratas mounted to the skies in an ecstasy of bliss, Don Juan followed, serious, unreserved, sincere as a German student. But he said "I" while his lady love, in her folly, said "we." He knew admirably how to yield himself to a woman's influence. He was always clever enough to make her believe that he trembled like a college youth who asks his first partner at a ball: "Do you like dancing?" But he could also be terrible when necessary; he could draw his sword and destroy skilled soldiers. There was banter in his simplicity and laughter in his tears, for he could weep as well as any woman who says to her husband: "Give me a carriage or I shall pine to death."

For merchants the world means a bale of goods or a quantity of circulating notes; for most young men it is a woman; for some women it is a man; for certain natures it is society, a set of people, a position, a city; for Don Juan the universe was himself! Noble, fascinating and a model of grace, he fastened his bark to every bank; but he allowed himself to be carried only where he wished to go. The more he saw the more skeptical he became. Probing human nature he soon guessed that courage was rashness; prudence, cowardice; generosity, shrewd calculation; justice, a crime; delicacy, pusillanimity; honesty, policy; and by a singular fatality he perceived that the persons who were really honest, delicate, just, generous, prudent and courageous received no consideration at the hands of their fellows.

26

"What a cheerless jest!" he cried. "It does not come from a god!"

And then, renouncing a better world, he showed no mark of respect to holy things and regarded the marble saints in the churches merely as works of art. He understood the mechanism of human society, and never offended too much against the current prejudices, for the executioners had more power than he; but he bent the social laws to his will with the grace and wit that are so well displayed in his scene with M. Dimanche. He was, in short, the embodiment of Molière's Don Juan, Goethe's Faust, Byron's Manfred, and Maturin's Melmoth — grand pictures drawn by the greatest geniuses of Europe, and to which neither the harmonies of Mozart nor the lyric strains of Rossini are lacking. Terrible pictures in which the power of evil existing in man is immortalized, and which are repeated from one century to another, whether the type come to parley with mankind by incarnating itself in Mirabeau, or be content to work in silence, like Bonaparte; or to goad on the universe by sarcasm, like the divine Rabelais; or again, to laugh at men instead of insulting things, like Maréchal de Richelieu; or, still better, perhaps, if it mock both men and things, like our most celebrated ambassador.

But the deep genius of Don Juan incorporated in advance all these. He played with everything. His life was a mockery, which embraced men, things, institutions, ideas. As for eternity, he had chatted for half an hour with Pope Julius II., and at the end of the conversation he said, laughing:

"If it were absolutely necessary to choose, I should rather believe in God than in the devil; power combined with goodness has always more possibilities than the spirit of evil."

"Yes; but God wants one to do penance in this world."

"Are you always thinking of your indulgences?" replied Belvidéro. "Well, I have a whole existence in reserve to repent the faults of my first life."

"Oh, if that is your idea of old age," cried the Pope, "you are in danger of being canonized."

"After your elevation to the papacy, one may expect anything."

And then they went to watch the workmen engaged in building the huge basilica consecrated to St. Peter.

"St. Peter is the genius who gave us our double power," said the Pope to Don Juan, "and he deserves this monument. But sometimes at night I fancy that a deluge will pass a sponge over all this, and it will need to be begun over again."

Don Juan and the Pope laughed. They understood each other. A fool would have gone next day to amuse himself with Julius II at Raphael's house or in the delightful Villa Madama; but Belvidéro went to see him officiate in his pontifical capacity, in order to convince himself of his suspicions. Under the influence of wine della Rovere would have been capable of forgetting himself and criticizing the Apocalypse.

When Don Juan reached the age of sixty he went to live in Spain. There, in his old age, he married a young and charming Andalusian. But he was intentionally neither a good father nor a good husband. He had observed that we are never so tenderly loved as by the women to whom we scarcely give a thought. Doña Elvira, piously reared by an old aunt in the heart of Andalusia in a castle several leagues from San Lucas, was all devotion and meekness. Don Juan saw that this young girl was a woman to make a long fight with a passion before yielding to it, so he hoped to keep from her any love but his until after his death. It was a serious jest, a game of chess which he had reserved for his old age.

Warned by his father's mistakes, he determined to make the most trifling acts of his old age contribute to the success of the drama which was to take place at his deathbed. Therefore, the greater part of his wealth lay buried in the cellars of his palace at Ferrara, whither he seldom went. The rest of his fortune was invested in a life annuity, so that his wife and children might be interested in keeping him alive. This was a species of cleverness which his father should have practiced; but this Machiavellian scheme was unnecessary in his case. Young Philippe Belvidéro, his son, grew up a Spaniard as conscientiously religious as his father was impious, on the principle of the proverb: "A miserly father, a spendthrift son."

The Abbot of San Lucas was selected by Don Juan to direct the consciences of the Duchess of Belvidéro and of Philippe. This ecclesiastic was a holy man, of fine carriage, well proportioned, with beautiful black eyes and a head like Tiberius. He was wearied with fasting, pale and worn, and continually battling with temptation, like all recluses. The old nobleman still hoped perhaps to be able to kill a monk before finishing his first lease of life. But, whether the Abbot was as clever as Don Juan, or whether Doña Elvira had more prudence or virtue than Spain usually accords to women, Don Juan was obliged to pass his last days like a country parson, without scandal. Sometimes he took pleasure in finding his wife and son remiss in their religious duties, and insisted imperiously that they should fulfill all the obligations imposed upon the faithful by the court of Rome. He was never so happy as when listening to the gallant Abbot of San Lucas, Doña Elvira and Philippe engaged in arguing a case of conscience.

Nevertheless, despite the great care which the lord of Belvidéro bestowed upon his person, the days of decrepitude arrived. With this age of pain came cries of helplessness, cries made the more piteous by the remembrance of his impetuous youth and his ripe maturity. This man, for whom the last jest in the farce was to make others believe in the laws and principles at which he scoffed, was compelled to close his eyes at night upon an uncertainty. This model of good breeding, this duke spirited in an orgy, this brilliant courtier, gracious toward women, whose hearts he had wrung as a peasant bends a willow wand, this man of genius, had an obstinate cough, a troublesome sciatica and a cruel gout. He saw his teeth leave him, as, at the end of an evening, the fairest, best dressed women depart one by one, leaving the ballroom deserted and empty. His bold hands trembled, his graceful limbs tottered, and then one night apoplexy turned its hooked and icy fingers around his throat. From this fateful day he became morose and harsh. He accused his wife and son of being insincere in their devotion, charging that their touching and gentle care was showered upon him so tenderly only because his money was all invested. Elvira and Philippe shed bitter tears, and redoubled their caresses to this malicious old man, whose broken voice would become affectionate to say:

"My friends, my dear wife, you will forgive me, will you not? I torment you sometimes. Ah, great God, how canst Thou make use of me thus to prove these two angelic creatures! I, who should be their joy, am their bane!"

It was thus that he held them at his bedside, making them forget whole months of impatience and cruelty by one hour in which he displayed to them the new treasures of his favor and a false tenderness. It was a paternal system which succeeded infinitely better than that which his father had formerly employed toward him. Finally he reached such a state of illness that maneuvers like those of a small boat entering a dangerous canal were necessary in order to pus him to bed.

Then the day of death came. This brilliant and skeptical man, whose intellect only was left unimpaired by the general decay, lived between a doctor and a confessor, his two antipathies. But he was jovial with them. Was there not a bright light burning for him behind the veil of the future? Over this veil, leaden and impenetrable to others, transparent to him, the delicate and bewitching delights of youth played like shadows.

It was on a beautiful summer evening that Don Juan felt the approach of death. The Spanish sky was gloriously clear, the orange trees perfumed the air and the stars cast a fresh glowing light. Nature seemed to give pledges of his resurrection. A pious and obedient son regarded him with love and respect. About eleven o'clock he signified his wish to be left alone with this sincere being.

"Philippe," he began, in a voice so tender and affectionate that the young man trembled and wept with happiness, for his father had never said "Philippe" like this before. "Listen to me, my son," continued the dying man. "I have been a great sinner, and all my life I have thought about death. Formerly I was the friend of the great Pope Julius II. This illustrious pontiff feared that the excessive excitability of my feelings would cause me to commit some deadly sin at the moment of my death, after I had received the blessed ointment. He made me a present of a flask of holy water that gushed forth from a rock in the desert. I kept the secret of the theft of the Church's treasure, but I am authorized to reveal the mystery to my son 'in articulo mortis.' You will find the flask in the drawer of the Gothic table which always stands at my bedside. The precious crystals may be of service to you also, my dearest Philippe. Will you swear to me by your eternal salvation that you will carry out my orders faithfully?"

Philippe looked at his father. Don Juan was too well versed in human expression not to know that he could die peacefully in perfect faith in such a look, as his father had died in despair at his own expression.

"You deserve a different father," continued Don Juan. "I must acknowledge that when the estimable Abbot of San Lucas was administering the viaticum' I was thinking of the incompatibility of two so wide-spreading powers as that of the devil and that of God."

"Oh, father!"

"And I said to myself that when Satan makes his peace he will be a great idiot if he does not bargain for the pardon of his followers. This thought haunted me. So, my child, I shall go to hell if you do not carry out my wishes."

"Oh, tell them to me at once, father!"

"As soon as I have closed my eyes," replied Don Juan, "and that may be in a few minutes, you must take my body, still warm, and lay it on a table in the middle of the room. Then put out the lamp — the light of the stars will be sufficient. You must take off my clothes, and while you recite 'Paters' and 'Aves' and uplift your soul to God, you must moisten my eyes, my lips, all my head first, and then my body, with this holy water. But, my dear son, the power of God is great. You must not be astonished at anything."

At this point Don Juan, feeling the approach of death, added in a terrible voice: "Be careful of the flask!"

Then he died gently in the arms of his son, whose tears fell upon his ironical and sallow face.

It was nearly midnight when Don Philippe Belvidéro placed his father's corpse on the table. After kissing the stern forehead and the gray hair he put out the lamp. The soft rays of the moonlight which cast fantastic reflections over the scenery allowed the pious Philippe to discern his father's body dimly, as something white in the midst of the darkness. The young man moistened a cloth in the liquid and then, deep in prayer, he faithfully anointed the revered head. The silence was intense. Then he heard indescribable rustlings, but he attributed them to the wind among the tree-tops. When he had bathed the right arm he felt himself rudely seized at the back of the neck by an arm, young and vigorous — the arm of his father! He gave a piercing cry, and dropped the phial, which fell on the floor and broke. The liquid flowed out.

The whole household rushed in, bearing torches. The cry had aroused and frightened them as if the trumpet of the last judgment had shaken the world. The room was crowded with people. The trembling throng saw Don Philippe, fainting, but held up by the powerful arm of his father, which clutched his neck. Then they saw a supernatural sight, the head of Don Juan, young and beautiful as an Antinoüs, a head with black hair, brilliant eyes and crimson lips, a head that moved in a blood-curdling manner without being able to stir the skeleton to which it belonged.

An old servant cried: "A miracle!"

And all the Spaniards repeated: "A miracle!"

Too pious to admit the possibility of magic, Doña Elvira sent for the Abbot of San Lucas. When the priest saw the miracle with his own eyes he resolved to profit by it, like a man of sense, and like an abbot who asked nothing better than to increase his revenues. Declaring that Don Juan must inevitably be canonized, he appointed his monastery for the ceremony of the apotheosis. The monastery, he said, should henceforth be called "San Juan de Lucas." At these words the head made a facetious grimace.

The taste of the Spaniards for this sort of solemnities is so well known that it should not be difficult to imagine the religious spectacle with which the abbey of San Lucas celebrated the translation of "the blessed Don Juan Belvidéro" in its church. A few days after the death of this illustrious nobleman, the miracle of his partial resurrection had been so thoroughly spread from village to village throughout a circle of more than fifty leagues round San Lucas that it was as good as a play to see the curious people on the road. They came from all sides, drawn by the prospect of a "Te Deum" chanted by the light of burning torches. The ancient mosque of the monastery of San Lucas, a wonderful building, erected by the Moors, which for three hundred years had resounded with the name of Jesus Christ instead of Allah, could not hold the crowd which was gathered to view the ceremony. Packed together like ants, the hidalgos in velvet mantles and armed with their good swords stood round the pillars, unable to find room to bend their knees, which they never bent elsewhere. Charming peasant women, whose dresses set off the beautiful lines of their figures, gave their arms to white-haired old men. Youths with glowing eyes found themselves beside old women decked out in gala dress. There were couples trembling with pleasure, curious-fiancées, led thither by their sweethearts, newly married couples and frightened children, holding one another by the hand. All this throng was there, rich in colors, brilliant in contrast, laden with flowers, making a soft tumult in the silence of the night. The great doors of the church opened.

Those who, having come too late, were obliged to stay outside, saw in the distance, through the three open doors, a scene of which the tawdry decorations of our modern operas can give but a faint idea. Devotees and sinners, intent upon winning the favor of a new saint, lighted thousands of candles in his honor inside the vast church, and these scintillating lights gave a magical aspect to the edifice. The black arcades, the columns with their capitals, the recessed chapels glittering with gold and silver, the galleries, the Moorish fretwork, the most delicate features of this delicate carving, were all revealed in the dazzling brightness like the fantastic figures which are formed in a glowing fire. It was a sea of light, surmounted at the end of the church by the gilded choir, where the high altar rose in glory, which rivaled the rising sun. But the magnificence of the golden lamps, the silver candlesticks, the banners, the tassels, the saints and the "ex voto" paled before the reliquary in which Don Juan lay. The body of the blasphemer was resplendent with gems, flowers, crystals, diamonds, gold, and plumes as white as the wings of a seraphim; it replaced a picture of Christ on the altar. Around him burned wax candles, which threw out waves of light. The good Abbot of San Lucas, clad in his pontifical robes, with his jeweled mitre, his surplice and his golden crosier reclined, king of the choir, in a large armchair, amid all his clergy, who were impassive men with silver hair, and who surrounded him like the confessing saints whom the painters group round the Lord. The precentor and the dignitaries of the order, decorated with the glittering insignia of their ecclesiastical vanities, came and went among the clouds of incense like planets revolving in the firmament.

When the hour of triumph was come the chimes awoke the echoes of the countryside, and this immense assembly raised its voice to God in the first cry of praise which begins the "Te Deum."

Sublime exultation! There were voices pure and high, ecstatic women's voices, blended with the deep sonorous tones of the men, thousands of voices so powerful that they drowned the organ in spite of the bellowing of its pipes. The shrill notes of the choir-boys and the powerful rhythm of the basses inspired pretty thoughts of the combination of childhood and strength in this delightful concert of human voices blended in an outpouring of love.

"Te Deum laudamus!"

In the midst of this cathedral, black with kneeling men and women, the chant burst forth like a light which gleams suddenly in the night, and the silence was broken as by a peal of thunder. The voices rose with the clouds of incense which threw diaphanous, bluish veils over the quaint marvels of the architecture. All was richness, perfume, light and melody.

At the moment at which this symphony of love and gratitude rolled toward the altar, Don Juan, too polite not to express his thanks and too witty not to appreciate a jest, responded by a frightful laugh, and straightened up in his reliquary. But, the devil having given him a hint of the danger he ran of being taken for an ordinary man, for a saint, a Boniface or a Pantaléon, he interrupted this harmony of love by a shriek in which the thousand voices of hell joined. Earth lauded, heaven condemned. The church trembled on its ancient foundations.

"Te Deum laudamus!" sang the crowd.

"Go to the devil, brute beasts that you are! 'Carajos demonios!' Beasts! what idiots you are with your God!"

And a torrent of curses rolled forth like a stream of burning lava at an eruption of Vesuvius.

"'Deus sabaoth! sabaoth'!" cried the Christians.

Then the living arm was thrust out of the reliquary and waved threateningly over the assembly with a gesture full of despair and irony.

"The saint is blessing us!" said the credulous old women, the children and the young maids.

It is thus that we are often deceived in our adorations. The superior man mocks those who compliment him, and compliments those whom he mocks in the depths of his heart.

When the Abbot, bowing low before the altar, chanted: "'Sancte Johannes, ora pro nobis'!" he heard distinctly: "'O coglione'!"

"What is happening up there?" cried the superior, seeing the reliquary move.

"The saint is playing devil!" replied the Abbot.

At this the living head tore itself violently away from the dead body and fell upon the yellow pate of the priest.

"Remember, Doña Elvira!" cried the head, fastening its teeth in the head of the Abbot.

The latter gave a terrible shriek, which threw the crowd into a panic. The priests rushed to the assistance of their chief.

"Imbecile! Now say that there is a God!" cried the voice, just as the Abbot expired.

## SOLANGE
## DR. LEDRU'S STORY OF THE REIGN OF TERROR
## BY ALEXANDRE DUMAS

Leaving l'Abbaye, I walked straight across the Place Turenne to the Rue Tournon, where I had lodgings, when I heard a woman scream for help.

It could not be an assault to commit robbery, for it was hardly ten o'clock in the evening. I ran to the corner of the place whence the sounds proceeded, and by the light of the moon, just then breaking through the clouds, I beheld a woman in the midst of a patrol of sans-culottes.

The lady observed me at the same instant, and seeing, by the character of my dress, that I did not belong to the common order of people, she ran toward me, exclaiming:

"There is M. Albert! He knows me! He will tell you that I am the daughter of Mme. Ledieu, the laundress."

With these words the poor creature, pale and trembling with excitement, seized my arm and clung to me as a shipwrecked sailor to a spar.

"No matter whether you are the daughter of Mme. Ledieu or some one else, as you have no pass, you must go with us to the guard-house."

The young girl pressed my arm. I perceived in this pressure the expression of her great distress of mind. I understood it.

"So it is you, my poor Solange?" I said. "What are you doing here?"

"There, messieurs!" she exclaimed in tones of deep anxiety; "do you believe me now?"

"You might at least say 'citizens!'"

"Ah, sergeant, do not blame me for speaking that way," said the pretty young girl; "my mother has many customers among the great people, and taught me to be polite. That's how I acquired this bad habit — the habit of the aristocrats; and, you know, sergeant, it's so hard to shake off old habits!"

This answer, delivered in trembling accents, concealed a delicate irony that was lost on all save me. I asked myself, who is this young woman? The mystery seemed complete. This alone was clear; she was not the daughter of a laundress.

"How did I come here, Citizen Albert?" she asked. "Well, I will tell you. I went to deliver some washing. The lady was not at home, and so I waited; for in these hard times every one needs what little money is coming to him. In that way it grew dark, and so I fell among these gentlemen — beg pardon, I would say citizens. They asked for my pass. As I did not have it with me, they were going to take me to the guard-house. I cried out in terror, which brought you to the scene; and as luck would have it, you are a friend. I said to myself, as M. Albert knows my name to be Solange Ledieu, he will vouch for me; and that you will, will you not, M. Albert?"

"Certainly, I will vouch for you."

"Very well," said the leader of the patrol; "and who, pray, will vouch for you, my friend?"

"Danton! Do you know him? Is he a good patriot?"

"Oh, if Danton will vouch for you, I have nothing to say."

"Well, there is a session of the Cordeliers to-day. Let us go there."

"Good," said the leader. "Citizens, let us go to the Cordeliers."

The club of the Cordeliers met at the old Cordelier monastery in the Rue l'Observance. We arrived there after scarce a minute's walk. At the door I tore a page from my note-book, wrote a few words upon it with a lead pencil, gave it to the sergeant, and requested him to hand it to Danton, while I waited outside with the men.

The sergeant entered the clubhouse and returned with Danton.

"What!" said he to me; "they have arrested you, my friend? You, the friend of Camilles — you, one of the most loyal republicans? Citizens," he continued, addressing the sergeant, "I vouch for him. Is that sufficient?"

"You vouch for him. Do you also vouch for her?" asked the stubborn sergeant.

"For her? To whom do you refer?"

"This girl."

"For everything; for everybody who may be in his company. Does that satisfy you?"

"Yes," said the man; "especially since I have had the privilege of seeing you."

With a cheer for Danton, the patrol marched away. I was about to thank Danton, when his name was called repeatedly within.

"Pardon me, my friend," he said; "you hear? There is my hand; I must leave you — the left. I gave my right to the sergeant. Who knows, the good patriot may have scrofula?"

"I'm coming!" he exclaimed, addressing those within in his mighty voice with which he could pacify or arouse the masses. He hastened into the house.

I remained standing at the door, alone with my unknown.

"And now, my lady," I said, "whither would you have me escort you? I am at your disposal."

"Why, to Mme. Ledieu," she said with a laugh. "I told you she was my mother."

"And where does Mme. Ledieu reside?"

"Rue Ferou, 24."

"Then, let us proceed to Rue Ferou, 24."

On the way neither of us spoke a word. But by the light of the moon, enthroned in serene glory in the sky, I was able to observe her at my leisure. She was a charming girl of twenty or twenty-two — brunette, with large blue eyes, more expressive of intelligence than melancholy — a finely chiseled nose, mocking lips, teeth of pearl, hands like a queen's, and feet like a child's; and all these, in spite of her costume of a laundress, betokened an aristocratic air that had aroused the sergeant's suspicions not without justice.

Arrived at the door of the house, we looked at each other a moment in silence.

"Well, my dear M. Albert, what do you wish?" my fair unknown asked with a smile.

"I was about to say, my dear Mlle. Solange, that it was hardly worth while to meet if we are to part so soon."

"Oh, I beg ten thousand pardons! I find it was well worth the while; for if I had not met you, I should have been dragged to the guard-house, and there it would have been discovered that I am not the daughter of Mme. Ledieu — in fact, it would have developed that I am an aristocrat, and in all likelihood they would have cut off my head."

"You admit, then, that you are an aristocrat?"

"I admit nothing."

"At least you might tell me your name."

"Solange."

"I know very well that this name, which I gave you on the inspiration of the moment, is not your right name."

"No matter; I like it, and I am going to keep it — at least for you."

"Why should you keep it for me? if we are not to meet again?"

"I did not say that. I only said that if we should meet again it will not be necessary for you to know my name any more than that I should know yours. To me you will be known as Albert, and to you I shall always be Solange."

"So be it, then; but I say, Solange," I began.

"I am listening, Albert," she replied.

"You are an aristocrat — that you admit."

"If I did not admit it, you would surmise it, and so my admission would be divested of half its merit."

"And you were pursued because you were suspected of being an aristocrat?"

"I fear so."

"And you are hiding to escape persecution?"

"In the Rue Ferou, No. 24, with Mme. Ledieu, whose husband was my father's coachman. You see, I have no secret from you."

"And your father?"

"I shall make no concealment, my dear Albert, of anything that relates to me. But my fathers secrets are not my own. My father is in hiding, hoping to make his escape. That is all I can tell you."

"And what are you going to do?"

"Go with my father, if that be possible. If not, allow him to depart without me until the opportunity offers itself to me to join him."

"Were you coming from your father when the guard arrested you to-night?"

"Yes."

"Listen, dearest Solange."

"I am all attention."

"You observed all that took place to-night?"

"Yes. I saw that you had powerful influence."

"I regret my power is not very great. However, I have friends."

"I made the acquaintance of one of them."

"And you know he is not one of the least powerful men of the times."

"Do you intend to enlist his influence to enable my father to escape?"

"No, I reserve him for you."

"But my father?"

"I have other ways of helping your father."

"Other ways?" exclaimed Solange, seizing my hands and studying me with an anxious expression.

"If I serve your father, will you then sometimes think kindly of me?"

"Oh, I shall all my life hold you in grateful remembrance!"

She uttered these words with an enchanting expression of devotion. Then she looked at me beseechingly and said:

"But will that satisfy you?"

"Yes," I said.

"Ah, I was not mistaken. You are kind, generous. I thank you for my father and myself. Even if you should fail, I shall be grateful for what you have already done!"

"When shall we meet again, Solange?"

"When do you think it necessary to see me again?"

"To-morrow, when I hope to have good news for you."

"Well, then, to-morrow."

"Where?"

"Here."

"Here in the street?"

"Well, mon Dieu!" she exclaimed. "You see, it is the safest place. For thirty minutes, while we have been talking here, not a soul has passed."

"Why may I not go to you, or you come to me?"

"Because it would compromise the good people if you should come to me, and you would incur serious risk if I should go to you."

"Oh, I would give you the pass of one of my relatives."

"And send your relative to the guillotine if I should be accidentally arrested!"

"True. I will bring you a pass made out in the name of Solange."

"Charming! You observe Solange is my real name."

"And the hour?"

"The same at which we met to-night — ten o'clock, if you please."

"All right; ten o'clock. And how shall we meet?"

"That is very simple. Be at the door at five minutes of ten, and at ten I will come down."

"Then, at ten to-morrow, dear Solange."

"To-morrow at ten, dear Albert."

I wanted to kiss her hand; she offered me her brow.

The next day I was in the street at half past nine. At a quarter of ten Solange opened the door. We were both ahead of time.

With one leap I was by her side.

"I see you have good news," she said.

"Excellent! First, here is a pass for you."

"First my father!"

She repelled my hand.

"Your father is saved, if he wishes."

"Wishes, you say? What is required of him?"

"He must trust me."

"That is assured."

"Have you seen him?"

"Yes."

"You have discussed the situation with him?"

"It was unavoidable. Heaven will help us."

"Did you tell your father all?"

"I told him you had saved my life yesterday, and that you would perhaps save his to-morrow."

"To-morrow! Yes, quite right; to-morrow I shall save his life, if it is his will."

"How? What? Speak! Speak! If that were possible, how fortunately all things have come to pass!"

"However — " I began hesitatingly.

"Well?"

"It will be impossible for you to accompany him."

"I told you I was resolute."

"I am quite confident, however, that I shall be able later to procure a passport for you."

"First tell me about my father; my own distress is less important."

"Well, I told you I had friends, did I not?"

"Yes."

"To-day I sought out one of them."

"Proceed."

"A man whose name is familiar to you; whose name is a guarantee of courage and honor."

"And this man is?"

"Marceau."

"General Marceau?"

"Yes."

"True, he will keep a promise."

"Well, he has promised."

"Mon Dieu! How happy you make me! What has he promised? Tell me all."

"He has promised to help us."

"In what manner?"

"In a very simple manner. Kléber has just had him promoted to the command of the western army. He departs to-morrow night."

"To-morrow night! We shall have no time to make the smallest preparation."

"There are no preparations to make."

"I do not understand."

"He will take your father with him."

"My father?"

"Yes, as his secretary. Arrived in the Vendée, your father will pledge his word to the general to undertake nothing against France. From there he will escape to Brittany, and from Brittany to England. When he arrives in London, he will inform you; I shall obtain a passport for you, and you will join him in London."

"To-morrow," exclaimed Solange; "my father departs tomorrow!"

"There is no time to waste."

"My father has not been informed."

"Inform him."

"To-night?"

"To-night."

"But how, at this hour?"

"You have a pass and my arm."

"True. My pass."

I gave it to her. She thrust it into her bosom.

"Now? your arm?"

I gave her my arm, and we walked away. When we arrived at the Place Turenne — that is, the spot where we had met the night before — she said: "Await me here."

I bowed and waited.

She disappeared around the corner of what was formerly the Hôtel Malignon. After a lapse of fifteen minutes she returned.

"Come," she said, "my father wishes to receive and thank you."

She took my arm and led me up to the Rue St. Guillaume, opposite the Hôtel Mortemart. Arrived here, she took a bunch of keys from her pocket, opened a small, concealed door, took me by the hand, conducted me up two flights of steps, and knocked in a peculiar manner.

A man of forty-eight or fifty years opened the door. He was dressed as a working man and appeared to be a bookbinder. But at the first utterance that burst from his lips, the evidence of the seigneur was unmistakable.

"Monsieur," he said, "Providence has sent you to us. I regard you an emissary of fate. Is it true that you can save me, or, what is more, that you wish to save me?"

I admitted him completely to my confidence. I informed him that Marceau would take him as his secretary, and would exact no promise other than that he would not take up arms against France.

"I cheerfully promise it now, and will repeat it to him."

"I thank you in his name as well as in my own."

"But when does Marceau depart?"

"To-morrow."

"Shall I go to him to-night?"

"Whenever you please; he expects you."

Father and daughter looked at each other.

"I think it would be wise to go this very night," said Solange.

"I am ready; but if I should be arrested, seeing that I have no permit?"

"Here is mine."

"But you?"

45

"Oh, I am known."

"Where does Marceau reside?"

"Rue de l'Université, 40, with his sister, Mlle. Dégraviers-Marceau."

"Will you accompany me?"

"I shall follow you at a distance, to accompany mademoiselle home when you are gone."

"How will Marceau know that I am the man of whom you spoke to him?"

"You will hand him this tri-colored cockade; that is the sign of identification."

"And how shall I reward my liberator?"

"By allowing him to save your daughter also."

"Very well."

He put on his hat and extinguished the lights, and we descended by the gleam of the moon which penetrated the stair-windows.

At the foot of the steps he took his daughter's arm, and by way of the Rue des Saints Pères we reached Rue de l'Université. I followed them at a distance of ten paces. We arrived at No. 40 without having met any one. I rejoined them there.

"That is a good omen," I said; "do you wish me to go up with you?"

"No. Do not compromise yourself any further. Await my daughter here."

I bowed.

"And now, once more, thanks and farewell," he said, giving me his hand. "Language has no words to express my gratitude. I pray that heaven may some day grant me the opportunity of giving fuller expression to my feelings."

I answered him with a pressure of the hand.

He entered the house. Solange followed him; but she, too, pressed my hand before she entered.

In ten minutes the door was reopened.

"Well?" I asked.

"Your friend," she said, "is worthy of his name; he is as kind and considerate as yourself. He knows that it will contribute to my happiness to remain with my father until the moment of departure. His sister has ordered a bed placed in her room. To-morrow at three o'clock my father will be out of danger. To-morrow evening at ten I shall expect you in the Rue Ferou, if the gratitude of a daughter who owes her father's life to you is worth the trouble."

"Oh, be sure I shall come. Did your father charge you with any message for me?"

"He thanks you for your pass, which he returns to you, and begs you to join him as soon as possible."

"Whenever it may be your desire to go," I said, with a strange sensation at my heart.

"At least, I must know where I am to join him," she said. "Ah, you are not yet rid of me!"

I seized her hand and pressed it against my heart, but she offered me her brow, as on the previous evening, and said: "Until to-morrow."

I kissed her on the brow; but now I no longer strained her hand against my breast, but her heaving bosom, her throbbing heart.

I went home in a state of delirious ecstasy such as I had never experienced. Was it the consciousness of a generous action, or was it love for this adorable creature? I know not whether I slept or woke. I only know that all the harmonies of nature were singing within me; that the night seemed endless, and the day eternal; I know that though I wished to speed the time, I did not wish to lose a moment of the days still to come.

The next day I was in the Rue Ferou at nine o'clock. At half-past nine Solange made her appearance.

She approached me and threw her arms around my neck.

"Saved!" she said; "my father is saved! And this I owe you. Oh, how I love you!"

Two weeks later Solange received a letter announcing her father's safe arrival in England.

47

The next day I brought her a passport.

When Solange received it she burst into tears.

"You do not love me!" she exclaimed.

"I love you better than my life," I replied; "but I pledged your father my word, and I must keep it."

"Then, I will break mine," she said. "Yes, Albert; if you have the heart to let me go, I have not the courage to leave you."

Alas, she remained!

Three months had passed since that night on which we talked of her escape, and in all that time not a word of parting had passed her lips.

Solange had taken lodgings in the Rue Turenne. I had rented them in her name. I knew no other, while she always addressed me as Albert. I had found her a place as teacher in a young ladies' seminary solely to withdraw her from the espionage of the revolutionary police, which had become more scrutinizing than ever.

Sundays we passed together in the small dwelling, from the bedroom of which we could see the spot where we had first met. We exchanged letters daily, she writing to me under the name of Solange, and I to her under that of Albert.

Those three months were the happiest of my life.

In the meantime I was making some interesting experiments suggested by one of the guillotiniers. I had obtained permission to make certain scientific tests with the bodies and heads of those who perished on the scaffold. Sad to say, available subjects were not wanting. Not a day passed but thirty or forty persons were guillotined, and blood flowed so copiously on the Place de la Révolution that it became necessary to dig a trench three feet deep around the scaffolding. This trench was covered with deals. One of them loosened under the feet of an eight-year-old lad, who fell into the abominable pit and was drowned.

For self-evident reasons I said nothing to Solange of the studies that occupied my attention during the day. In the beginning my occupation had inspired me with pity and loathing, but as time wore on I said: "These studies are for the good of humanity," for I hoped to convince the lawmakers of the wisdom of abolishing capital punishment.

The Cemetery of Clamart had been assigned to me, and all the heads and trunks of the victims of the executioner had been placed at my disposal. A small chapel in one corner of the cemetery had been converted into a kind of laboratory for my benefit. You know, when the queens were driven from the palaces, God was banished from the churches.

Every day at six the horrible procession filed in. The bodies were heaped together in a wagon, the heads in a sack. I chose some bodies and heads in a haphazard fashion, while the remainder were thrown into a common grave.

In the midst of this occupation with the dead, my love for Solange increased from day to day; while the poor child reciprocated my affection with the whole power of her pure soul.

Often I had thought of making her my wife; often we had mutually pictured to ourselves the happiness of such a union. But in order to become my wife, it would be necessary for Solange to reveal her name; and this name, which was that of an emigrant, an aristocrat, meant death.

Her father had repeatedly urged her by letter to hasten her departure, but she had informed him of our engagement. She had requested his consent, and he had given it, so that all had gone well to this extent.

The trial and execution of the queen, Marie Antoinette, had plunged me, too, into deepest sadness. Solange was all tears, and we could not rid ourselves of a strange feeling of despondency, a presentiment of approaching danger, that compressed our hearts. In vain I tried to whisper courage to Solange. Weeping, she reclined in my arms, and I could not comfort her, because my own words lacked the ring of confidence.

We passed the night together as usual, but the night was even more depressing than the day. I recall now that a dog, locked up in a room below us, howled till two o'clock in the morning. The next day we were told that the dog's master had gone away with the key in his pocket, had been arrested on the way, tried at three, and executed at four.

The time had come for us to part. Solange's duties at the school began at nine o'clock in the morning. Her school was in the vicinity of the Botanic Gardens. I hesitated long to let her go; she, too, was loath to part from me. But it must be. Solange was prone to be an object of unpleasant inquiries.

I called a conveyance and Accompanied her as far as the Rue des Fosses-Saint-Bernard, where I got out and left her to pursue her way alone. All the way we lay mutely wrapped in each other's arms, mingling tears with our kisses.

After leaving the carriage, I stood as if rooted to the ground. I heard Solange call me, but I dared not go to her, because her face, moist with tears, and her hysterical manner were calculated to attract attention.

Utterly wretched, I returned home, passing the entire day in writing to Solange. In the evening I sent her an entire volume of love-pledges.

My letter had hardly gone to the post when I received one from her.

She had been sharply reprimanded for coming late; had been subjected to a severe cross-examination, and threatened with forfeiture of her next holiday. But she vowed to join me even at the cost of her place. I thought I should go mad at the prospect of being parted from her a whole week. I was more depressed because a letter which had arrived from her father appeared to have been tampered with.

I passed a wretched night and a still more miserable day.

The next day the weather was appalling. Nature seemed to be dissolving in a cold, ceaseless rain — a rain like that which announces the approach of winter. All the way to the laboratory my ears were tortured with the criers announcing the names of the condemned, a large number of men, women, and children. The bloody harvest was over-rich. I should not lack subjects for my investigations that day.

The day ended early. At four o'clock I arrived at Clamart; it was almost night.

The view of the cemetery, with its large, new-made graves; the sparse, leafless trees that swayed in the wind, was desolate, almost appalling.

A large, open pit yawned before me. It was to receive to-day's harvest from the Place de la Révolution. An exceedingly large number of victims was expected, for the pit was deeper than usual.

Mechanically I approached the grave. At the bottom the water had gathered in a pool; my feet slipped; I came within an inch of falling in. My hair stood on end. The rain had drenched me to the skin. I shuddered and hastened into the laboratory.

It was, as I have said, an abandoned chapel. My eyes searched — I know not why — to discover if some traces of the holy purpose to which the edifice had once been devoted did not still adhere to the walls or to the altar; but the walls were bare, the altar empty.

I struck a light and deposited the candle on the operating-table on which lay scattered a miscellaneous assortment of the strange instruments I employed. I sat down and fell into a reverie. I thought of the poor queen, whom I had seen in her beauty, glory, and happiness, yesterday carted to the scaffold, pursued by the execrations of a people, to-day lying headless on the common sinners' bier — she who had slept beneath the gilded canopy of the throne of the Tuileries and St. Cloud.

As I sat thus, absorbed in gloomy meditation, wind and rain without redoubled in fury. The rain-drops dashed against the window-panes, the storm swept with melancholy moaning through the branches of the trees. Anon there mingled with the violence of the elements the sound of wheels.

It was the executioner's red hearse with its ghastly freight from the Place de la Révolution.

The door of the little chapel was pushed ajar, and two men, drenched with rain, entered, carrying a sack between them.

"There, M. Ledru," said the guillotinier; "there is what your heart longs for! Be in no hurry this night! We'll leave you to enjoy their society alone. Orders are not to cover them up till to-morrow, and so they'll not take cold."

With a horrible laugh, the two executioners deposited the sack in a corner, near the former altar, right in front of me. Thereupon they sauntered out, leaving open the door, which swung furiously on its hinges till my candle flashed and flared in the fierce draft.

I heard them unharness the horse, lock the cemetery, and go away.

I was strangely impelled to go with them, but an indefinable power fettered me in my place. I could not repress a shudder. I had no fear; but the violence of the storm, the splashing of the rain, the whistling sounds of the lashing branches, the shrill vibration of the atmosphere, which made my candle tremble — all this filled me with a vague terror that began at the roots of my hair and communicated itself to every part of my body.

Suddenly I fancied I heard a voice! A voice at once soft and plaintive; a voice within the chapel, pronouncing the name of "Albert!"

I was startled.

"Albert!"

But one person in all the world addressed me by that name!

Slowly I directed my weeping eyes around the chapel, which, though small, was not completely lighted by the feeble rays of the candle, leaving the nooks and angles in darkness, and my look remained fixed on the blood-soaked sack near the altar with its hideous contents.

At this moment the same voice repeated the same name, only it sounded fainter and more plaintive.

"Albert!"

I bolted out of my chair, frozen with horror.

The voice seemed to proceed from the sack!

I touched myself to make sure that I was awake; then I walked toward the sack with my arms extended before me, but stark and staring with horror. I thrust my hand into it. Then it seemed to me as if two lips, still warm, pressed a kiss upon my fingers!

I had reached that stage of boundless terror where the excess of fear turns into the audacity of despair. I seized the head and collapsing in my chair, placed it in front of me.

Then I gave vent to a fearful scream. This head, with its lips still warm, with the eyes half closed, was the head of Solange!

I thought I should go mad.

Three times I called:

"Solange! Solange! Solange!"

At the third time she opened her eyes and looked at me. Tears trickled down her cheeks; then a moist glow darted from her eyes, as if the soul were passing, and the eyes closed, never to open again.

I sprang to my feet a raving maniac, I wanted to fly; I knocked against the table; it fell. The candle was extinguished; the head rolled upon the floor, and I fell prostrate, as if a terrible fever had stricken me down — an icy-shudder convulsed me, and, with a deep sigh, I swooned.

The following morning at six the grave-diggers found me, cold as the flagstones on which I lay.

Solange, betrayed by her father's letter, had been arrested the same day, condemned, and executed.

The head that had called me, the eyes that had looked at me, were the head, the eyes, of Solange!

# A FIGHT WITH A CANNON
## BY VICTOR HUGO

La vieuville was suddenly cut short by a cry of despair, and a the same time a noise was heard wholly unlike any other sound. The cry and sounds came from within the vessel.

The captain and lieutenant rushed toward the gun-deck but could not get down. All the gunners were pouring up in dismay.

Something terrible had just happened.

One of the carronades of the battery, a twenty-four pounder, had broken loose.

This is the most dangerous accident that can possibly take place on shipboard. Nothing more terrible can happen to a sloop of was in open sea and under full sail.

A cannon that breaks its moorings suddenly becomes some strange, supernatural beast. It is a machine transformed into a monster. That short mass on wheels moves like a billiard-ball, rolls with the rolling of the ship, plunges with the pitching goes, comes, stops, seems to meditate, starts on its course again, shoots like an arrow from one end of the vessel to the other, whirls around, slips away, dodges, rears, bangs, crashes, kills, exterminates. It is a battering ram capriciously assaulting a wall. Add to this the fact that the ram is of metal, the wall of wood.

It is matter set free; one might say, this eternal slave was avenging itself; it seems as if the total depravity concealed in what we call inanimate things has escaped, and burst forth all of a sudden; it appears to lose patience, and to take a strange mysterious revenge; nothing more relentless than this wrath of the inanimate. This enraged lump leaps like a panther, it has the clumsiness of an elephant, the nimbleness of a mouse, the obstinacy of an ox, the uncertainty of the billows, the zigzag of the lightning, the deafness of the grave. It weighs ten thousand pounds, and it rebounds like a child's ball. It spins and then abruptly darts off at right angles.

And what is to be done? How put an end to it? A tempest ceases, a cyclone passes over, a wind dies down, a broken mast can be replaced, a leak can be stopped, a fire extinguished, but what will become of this enormous brute of bronze. How can it be captured? You can reason with a bulldog, astonish a bull, fascinate a boa, frighten a tiger, tame a lion; but you have no resource against this monster, a loose cannon. You can not kill it, it is dead; and at the same time it lives. It lives with a sinister life which comes to it from the infinite. The deck beneath it gives it full swing. It is moved by the ship, which is moved by the sea, which is moved by the wind. This destroyer is a toy. The ship, the waves, the winds, all play with it, hence its frightful animation. What is to be done with this apparatus? How fetter this stupendous engine of destruction? How anticipate its comings and goings, its returns, its stops, its shocks? Any one of its blows on the side of the ship may stave it in. How foretell its frightful meanderings? It is dealing with a projectile, which alters its mind, which seems to have ideas, and changes its direction every instant. How check the course of what must be avoided? The horrible cannon struggles, advances, backs, strikes right, strikes left, retreats, passes by, disconcerts expectation, grinds up obstacles, crushes men like flies. All the terror of the situation is in the fluctuations of the flooring. How fight an inclined plane subject to caprices? The ship has, so to speak, in its belly, an imprisoned thunderstorm, striving to escape; something like a thunderbolt rumbling above an earthquake.

In an instant the whole crew was on foot. It was the fault of the gun captain, who had neglected to fasten the screw-nut of the mooring-chain, and had insecurely clogged the four wheels of the gun carriage; this gave play to the sole and the framework, separated the two platforms, and the breeching. The tackle had given way, so that the cannon was no longer firm on its carriage. The stationary breeching, which prevents recoil, was not in use at this time. A heavy sea struck the port, the carronade, insecurely fastened, had recoiled and broken its chain, and began its terrible course over the deck.

To form an idea of this strange sliding, let one imagine a drop of water running over a glass.

At the moment when the fastenings gave way, the gunners were in the battery, some in groups, others scattered about, busied with the customary work among sailors getting ready for a signal for action. The carronade, hurled forward by the pitching of the vessel, made a gap in this crowd of men and crushed four at the first blow; then sliding back and shot out again as the ship rolled, it cut in two a fifth unfortunate, and knocked a piece of the battery against the larboard side with such force as to unship it. This caused the cry of distress just heard. All the men rushed to the companion-way. The gun-deck was vacated in a twinkling.

The enormous gun was left alone. It was given up to itself. It was its own master and master of the ship. It could do what it pleased. This whole crew, accustomed to laugh in time of battle, now trembled. To describe the terror is impossible.

Captain Boisberthelot and Lieutenant la Vieuville, although both dauntless men, stopped at the head of the companion-way and, dumb, pale, and hesitating, looked down on the deck below. Some one elbowed past and went down.

It was their passenger, the peasant, the man of whom they had just been speaking a moment before.

Reaching the foot of the companion-way, he stopped.

The cannon was rushing back and forth on the deck. One might have supposed it to be the living chariot of the Apocalypse. The marine lantern swinging overhead added a dizzy shifting of light and shade to the picture. The form of the cannon disappeared in the violence of its course, and it looked now black in the light, now mysteriously white in the darkness.

It went on in its destructive work. It had already shattered four other guns and made two gaps in the side of the ship, fortunately above the water-line, but where the water would come in, in case of heavy weather. It rushed frantically against the framework; the strong timbers withstood the shock; the curved shape of the wood gave them great power of resistance; but they creaked beneath the blows of this huge club, beating on all sides at once, with a strange sort of ubiquity. The percussions of a grain of shot shaken in a bottle are not swifter or more senseless.

The four wheels passed back and forth over the dead men, cutting them, carving them, slashing them, till the five corpses were a score of stumps rolling across the deck; the heads of the dead men seemed to cry out; streams of blood curled over the deck with the rolling of the vessel; the planks, damaged in several places, began to gape open. The whole ship was filled with the horrid noise and confusion.

The captain promptly recovered his presence of mind and ordered everything that could check and impede the cannon's mad course to be thrown through the hatchway down on the gun-deck — mattresses, hammocks, spare sails, rolls of cordage, bags belonging to the crew, and bales of counterfeit assignats, of which the corvette carried a large quantity — a characteristic piece of English villainy regarded as legitimate warfare.

But what could these rags do? As nobody dared to go below to dispose of them properly, they were reduced to lint in a few minutes.

There was just sea enough to make the accident as bad as possible. A tempest would have been desirable, for it might have upset the cannon, and with its four wheels once in the air there would be some hope of getting it under control. Meanwhile, the havoc increased.

There were splits and fractures in the masts, which are set into the framework of the keel and rise above the decks of ships like great, round pillars. The convulsive blows of the cannon had cracked the mizzenmast, and had cut into the mainmast.

The battery was being ruined. Ten pieces out of thirty were disabled; the breaches in the side of the vessel were increasing, and the corvette was beginning to leak.

The old passenger having gone down to the gun-deck, stood like a man of stone at the foot of the steps. He cast a stern glance over this scene of devastation. He did not move. It seemed impossible to take a step forward. Every movement of the loose carronade threatened the ship's destruction. A few moments more and shipwreck would be inevitable.

They must perish or put a speedy end to the disaster; some course must be decided on; but what? What an opponent was this carronade! Something must be done to stop this terrible madness — to capture this lightning — to overthrow this thunderbolt.

Boisberthelot said to La Vieuville:

"Do you believe in God, chevalier?"

La Vieuville replied:

"Yes — no. Sometimes."

"During a tempest?"

"Yes, and in moments like this."

"God alone can save us from this," said Boisberthelot.

Everybody was silent, letting the carronade continue its horrible din.

Outside, the waves beating against the ship responded with their blows to the shocks of the cannon. It was like two hammers alternating.

Suddenly, in the midst of this inaccessible ring, where the escaped cannon was leaping, a man was seen to appear, with an iron bar in his hand. He was the author of the catastrophe, the captain of the gun, guilty of criminal carelessness, and the cause of the accident, the master of the carronade. Having done the mischief, he was anxious to repair it. He had seized the iron bar in one hand, a tiller-rope with a slip-noose in the other, and jumped, down the hatchway to the gun-deck.

Then began an awful sight; a Titanic scene; the contest between gun and gunner; the battle of matter and intelligence; the duel between man and the inanimate.

The man stationed himself in a corner, and, with bar and rope in his two hands, he leaned against one of the riders, braced himself on his legs, which seemed two steel posts; and livid, calm, tragic, as if rooted to the deck, he waited.

He waited for the cannon to pass by him.

The gunner knew his gun, and it seemed to him as if the gun ought to know him. He had lived long with it. How many times he had thrust his hand into its mouth! It was his own familiar monster. He began to speak to it as if it were his dog.

58

"Come!" he said. Perhaps he loved it.

He seemed to wish it to come to him.

But to come to him was to come upon him. And then he would be lost. How could he avoid being crushed? That was the question. All looked on in terror.

Not a breast breathed freely, unless perhaps that of the old man, who was alone in the battery with the two contestants, a stern witness.

He might be crushed himself by the cannon. He did not stir.

Beneath them the sea blindly directed the contest.

At the moment when the gunner, accepting this frightful hand-to-hand conflict, challenged the cannon, some chance rocking of the sea caused the carronade to remain for an instant motionless and as if stupefied. "Come, now!" said the man.

It seemed to listen.

Suddenly it leaped toward him. The man dodged the blow.

The battle began. Battle unprecedented. Frailty struggling against the invulnerable. The gladiator of flesh attacking the beast of brass. On one side, brute force; on the other, a human soul.

All this was taking place in semi-darkness. It was like the shadowy vision of a miracle.

A soul — strange to say, one would have thought the cannon also had a soul; but a soul full of hatred and rage. This sightless thing seemed to have eyes. The monster appeared to lie in wait for the man. One would have at least believed that there was craft in this mass. It also chose its time. It was a strange, gigantic insect of metal, having or seeming to have the will of a demon. For a moment this colossal locust would beat against the low ceiling overhead, then it would come down on its four wheels like a tiger on its four paws, and begin to run at the man. He, supple, nimble, expert, writhed away like an adder from all these lightning movements. He avoided a collision, but the blows which he parried fell against the, vessel, and continued their work of destruction.

An end of broken chain was left hanging to the carronade. This chain had in some strange way become twisted about the screw of the cascabel. One end of the chain was fastened to the gun-carriage. The other, left loose, whirled desperately about the cannon, making all its blows more dangerous.

The screw held it in a firm grip, adding a thong to a battering-ram, making a terrible whirlwind around the cannon, an iron lash in a brazen hand. This chain complicated the contest.

However, the man went on fighting. Occasionally, it was the man who attacked the cannon; he would creep along the side of the vessel, bar and rope in hand; and the cannon, as if it understood, and as though suspecting some snare, would flee away. The man, bent on victory, pursued it.

Such things can not long continue. The cannon seemed to say to itself, all of a sudden, "Come, now! Make an end of it!" and it stopped. One felt that the crisis was at hand. The cannon, as if in suspense, seemed to have, or really had — for to all it was a living being — a ferocious malice prepense. It made a sudden, quick dash at the gunner. The gunner sprang out of the way, let it pass by, and cried out to it with a laugh, "Try it again!" The cannon, as if enraged, smashed a carronade on the port side; then, again seized by the invisible sling which controlled it, it was hurled to the starboard side at the man, who made his escape. Three carronades gave way under the blows of the cannon; then, as if blind and not knowing what more to do, it turned its back on the man, rolled from stern to bow, injured the stern and made a breach in the planking of the prow. The man took refuge at the foot of the steps, not far from the old man who was looking on. The gunner held his iron bar in rest. The cannon seemed to notice it, and without taking the trouble to turn around, slid back on the man, swift as the blow of an axe. The man, driven against the side of the ship, was lost. The whole crew cried out with horror.

But the old passenger, till this moment motionless, darted forth more quickly than any of this wildly swift rapidity. He seized a package of counterfeit assignats, and, at the risk of being crushed, succeeded in throwing it between the wheels of the carronade. This decisive and perilous movement could not have been made with more exactness and precision by a man trained in all the exercises described in Durosel's "Manual of Gun Practice at Sea."

The package had the effect of a clog. A pebble may stop a log, the branch of a tree turn aside an avalanche. The carronade stumbled. The gunner, taking advantage of this critical opportunity, plunged his iron bar between the spokes of one of the hind wheels. The cannon stopped. It leaned forward. The man, using the bar as a lever, held it in equilibrium. The heavy mass was overthrown, with the crash of a falling bell, and the man, rushing with all his might, dripping with perspiration, passed the slip noose around the bronze neck of the subdued monster.

It was ended. The man had conquered. The ant had control over the mastodon; the pygmy had taken the thunderbolt prisoner.

The mariners and sailors clapped their hands.

The whole crew rushed forward with cables and chains, and in an instant the cannon was secured.

The gunner saluted the passenger.

"Sir," he said, "you have saved my life."

The old man had resumed his impassive attitude, and made no reply.

The man had conquered, but the cannon might be said to have conquered as well. Immediate shipwreck had been avoided, but the corvette was not saved. The damage to the vessel seemed beyond repair. There were five breaches in her sides, one, very large, in the bow; twenty of the thirty carronades lay useless in their frames. The one which had just been captured and chained again was disabled; the screw of the cascabel was sprung, and consequently leveling the gun made impossible. The battery was reduced to nine pieces. The ship was leaking. It was necessary to repair the damages at once, and to work the pumps.

The gun-deck, now that one could look over it, was frightful to behold. The inside of an infuriated elephant's cage would not be more completely demolished.

However great might be the necessity of escaping observation, the necessity of immediate safety was still more imperative to the corvette. They had been obliged to light up the deck with lanterns hung here and there on the sides.

However, all the while this tragic play was going on, the crew were absorbed by a question of life and death, and they were wholly ignorant of what was taking place outside the vessel. The fog had grown thicker; the weather had changed; the wind had worked its pleasure with the ship; they were out of their course, with Jersey and Guernsey close at hand, further to the south than they ought to have been, and in the midst of a heavy sea. Great billows kissed the gaping wounds of the vessel — kisses full of danger. The rocking of the sea threatened destruction. The breeze had become a gale. A squall, a tempest, perhaps, was brewing. It was impossible to see four waves ahead.

While the crew were hastily repairing the damages to the gun-deck, stopping the leaks, and putting in place the guns which had been uninjured in the disaster, the old passenger had gone on deck again.

He stood with his back against the mainmast.

He had not noticed a proceeding which had taken place on the vessel. The Chevalier de la Vieuville had drawn up the marines in line on both sides of the mainmast, and at the sound of the boatswain's whistle the sailors formed in line, standing on the yards.

The Count de Boisberthelot approached the passenger.

Behind the captain walked a man, haggard, out of breath, his dress disordered, but still with a look of satisfaction on his face.

It was the gunner who had just shown himself so skilful in subduing monsters, and who had gained the mastery over the cannon.

The count gave the military salute to the old man in peasant's dress, and said to him:

"General, there is the man."

The gunner remained standing, with downcast eyes, in military attitude.

The Count de Boisberthelot continued:

"General, in consideration of what this man has done, do you not think there is something due him from his commander?"

"I think so," said the old man.

"Please give your orders," replied Boisberthelot.

"It is for you to give them, you are the captain."

"But you are the general," replied Boisberthelot.

The old man looked at the gunner.

"Come forward," he said.

The gunner approached.

The old man turned toward the Count de Boisberthelot, took off the cross of Saint-Louis from the captain's coat and fastened it on the gunner's jacket.

"Hurrah!" cried the sailors.

The mariners presented arms.

And the old passenger, pointing to the dazzled gunner, added:

"Now, have this man shot."

Dismay succeeded the cheering.

Then in the midst of the death-like stillness, the old man raised his voice and said:

"Carelessness has compromised this vessel. At this very hour it is perhaps lost. To be at sea is to be in front of the enemy. A ship making a voyage is an army waging war. The tempest is concealed, but it is at hand. The whole sea is an ambuscade. Death is the penalty of any misdemeanor committed in the face of the enemy. No fault is reparable. Courage should be rewarded, and negligence punished."

These words fell one after another, slowly, solemnly, in a sort of inexorable metre, like the blows of an axe upon an oak.

And the man, looking at the soldiers, added:

"Let it be done."

The man on whose jacket hung the shining cross of Saint-Louis bowed his head.

At a signal from Count de Boisberthelot, two sailors went below and came back bringing the hammock-shroud; the chaplain, who since they sailed had been at prayer in the officers' quarters, accompanied the two sailors; a sergeant detached twelve marines from the line and arranged them in two files, six by six; the gunner, without uttering a word, placed himself between the two files. The chaplain, crucifix in hand, advanced and stood beside him. "March," said the sergeant. The platoon marched with slow steps to the bow of the vessel. The two sailors, carrying the shroud, followed. A gloomy silence fell over the vessel. A hurricane howled in the distance.

A few moments later, a light flashed, a report sounded through the darkness, then all was still, and the sound of a body falling into the sea was heard.

The old passenger, still leaning against the mainmast, had crossed his arms, and was buried in thought.

Boisberthelot pointed to him with the forefinger of his left hand, and said to La Vieuville in a low voice:

"La Vendée has a head."

# MATEO FALCONE
## BY PROSPER MERIMEE

On leaving Porto-Vecchio from the northwest and directing his steps towards the interior of the island, the traveler will notice that the land rises rapidly, and after three hours' walking over tortuous paths obstructed by great masses of rock and sometimes cut by ravines, he will find himself on the border of a great mâquis. The mâquis is the domain of the Corsican shepherds and of those who are at variance with justice. It must be known that, in order to save himself the trouble of manuring his field, the Corsican husbandman sets fire to a piece of woodland. If the flame spread farther than is necessary, so much the worse! In any case he is certain of a good crop from the land fertilized by the ashes of the trees which grow upon it. He gathers only the heads of his grain, leaving the straw, which it would be unnecessary labor to cut. In the following spring the roots that have remained in the earth without being destroyed send up their tufts of sprouts, which in a few years reach a height of seven or eight feet. It is this kind of tangled thicket that is called a mâquis. They are made up of different kinds of trees and shrubs, so crowded and mingled together at the caprice of nature that only with an axe in hand can a man open a passage through them, and mâquis are frequently seen so thick and bushy that the wild sheep themselves cannot penetrate them.

If you have killed a man, go into the mâquis of Porto-Vecchio. With a good gun and plenty of powder and balls, you can live there in safety. Do not forget a brown cloak furnished with a hood, which will serve you for both cover and mattress. The shepherds will give you chestnuts, milk and cheese, and you will have nothing to fear from justice nor the relatives of the dead except when it is necessary for you to descend to the city to replenish your ammunition.

When I was in Corsica in 18 — , Mateo Falcone had his house half a league from this mâquis. He was rich enough for that country, living in noble style — that is to say, doing nothing —

65

on the income from his flocks, which the shepherds, who are a kind of nomads, lead to pasture here and there on the mountains. When I saw him, two years after the event that I am about to relate, he appeared to me to be about fifty years old or more. Picture to yourself a man, small but robust, with curly hair, black as jet, an aquiline nose, thin lips, large, restless eyes, and a complexion the color of tanned leather. His skill as a marksman was considered extraordinary even in his country, where good shots are so common. For example, Mateo would never fire at a sheep with buckshot; but at a hundred and twenty paces, he would drop it with a ball in the head or shoulder, as he chose. He used his arms as easily at night as during the day. I was told this feat of his skill, which will, perhaps, seem impossible to those who have not traveled in Corsica. A lighted candle was placed at eighty paces, behind a paper transparency about the size of a plate. He would take aim, then the candle would be extinguished, and, at the end of a moment, in the most complete darkness, he would fire and hit the paper three times out of four.

With such a transcendent accomplishment, Mateo Falcone had acquired a great reputation. He was said to be as good a friend as he was a dangerous enemy; accommodating and charitable, he lived at peace with all the world in the district of Porto-Vecchio. But it is said of him that in Corte, where he had married his wife, he had disembarrassed himself very vigorously of a rival who was considered as redoubtable in war as in love; at least, a certain gun-shot which surprised this rival as he was shaving before a little mirror hung in his window was attributed to Mateo. The affair was smoothed over and Mateo was married. His wife Giuseppa had given him at first three daughters (which infuriated him), and finally a son, whom he named Fortunato, and who became the hope of his family, the inheritor of the name. The daughters were well married: their father could count at need on the poignards and carbines of his sons-in-law. The son was only ten years old, but he already gave promise of fine attributes.

On a certain day in autumn, Mateo set out at an early hour with his wife to visit one of his flocks in a clearing of the mâquis.

The little Fortunato wanted to go with them, but the clearing was too far away; moreover, it was necessary some one should stay to watch the house; therefore the father refused: it will be seen whether or not he had reason to repent.

He had been gone some hours, and the little Fortunato was tranquilly stretched out in the sun, looking at the blue mountains, and thinking that the next Sunday he was going to dine in the city with his uncle, the Caporal, when he was suddenly interrupted in his meditations by the firing of a musket. He got up and turned to that side of the plain whence the noise came. Other shots followed, fired at irregular intervals, and each time nearer; at last, in the path which led from the plain to Mateo's house, appeared a man wearing the pointed hat of the mountaineers, bearded, covered with rags, and dragging himself along with difficulty by the support of his gun. He had just received a wound in his thigh.

This man was an outlaw, who, having gone to the town by night to buy powder, had fallen on the way into an ambuscade of Corsican light-infantry. After a vigorous defense he was fortunate in making his retreat, closely followed and firing from rock to rock. But he was only a little in advance of the soldiers, and his wound prevented him from gaining the mâquis before being overtaken.

He approached Fortunato and said: "You are the son of Mateo Falcone?" — "Yes."

"I am Gianetto Saupiero. I am followed by the yellow-collars. Hide me, for I can go no farther."

"And what will my father say if I hide you without his permission?"

"He will say that you have done well."

"How do you know?"

"Hide me quickly; they are coming."

"Wait till my father gets back."

"How can I wait? Malediction! They will be here in five minutes. Come, hide me, or I will kill you."

Fortunato answered him with the utmost coolness:

"Your gun is empty, and there are no more cartridges in your belt."

"I have my stiletto."

"But can you run as fast as I can?"

He gave a leap and put himself out of reach.

"You are not the son of Mateo Falcone! Will you then let me be captured before your house?"

The child appeared moved.

"What will you give me if I hide you?" said he, coming nearer.

The outlaw felt in a leather pocket that hung from his belt, and took out a five-franc piece, which he had doubtless saved to buy ammunition with. Fortunato smiled at the sight of the silver piece; he snatched it, and said to Gianetto:

"Fear nothing."

Immediately he made a great hole in a pile of hay that was near the house. Gianetto crouched down in it and the child covered him in such a way that he could breathe without it being possible to suspect that the hay concealed a man. He bethought himself further, and, with the subtlety of a tolerably ingenious savage, placed a cat and her kittens on the pile, that it might not appear to have been recently disturbed. Then, noticing the traces of blood on the path near the house, he covered them carefully with dust, and, that done, he again stretched himself out in the sun with the greatest tranquillity.

A few moments afterwards, six men in brown uniforms with yellow collars, and commanded by an Adjutant, were before Mateo's door. This Adjutant was a distant relative of Falcone's. (In Corsica the degrees of relationship are followed much further than elsewhere.) His name was Tiodoro Gamba; he was an active man, much dreaded by the outlaws, several of whom he had already entrapped.

"Good day, little cousin," said he, approaching Fortunato; "how tall you have grown. Have you seen a man go past here just now?"

"Oh! I am not yet so tall as you, my cousin," replied the child with a simple air.

"You soon will be. But haven't you seen a man go by here, tell me?"

"If I have seen a man go by?"

"Yes, a man with a pointed hat of black velvet, and a vest embroidered with red and yellow."

"A man with a pointed hat, and a vest embroidered with red and yellow?"

"Yes, answer quickly, and don't repeat my questions?"

"This morning the curé passed before our door on his horse, Piero. He asked me how papa was, and I answered him — "

"Ah, you little scoundrel, you are playing sly! Tell me quickly which way Gianetto went? We are looking for him, and I am sure he took this path."

"Who knows?"

"Who knows? It is I know that you have seen him."

"Can any one see who passes when they are asleep?"

"You were not asleep, rascal; the shooting woke you up."

"Then you believe, cousin, that your guns make so much noise? My father's carbine has the advantage of them."

"The devil take you, you cursed little scapegrace! I am certain that you have seen Gianetto. Perhaps, even, you have hidden him. Come, comrades, go into the house and see if our man is there. He could only go on one foot, and the knave has too much good sense to try to reach the mâquis limping like that. Moreover, the bloody tracks stop here."

"And what will papa say?" asked Fortunato with a sneer; "what will he say if he knows that his house has been entered while he was away?"

"You rascal!" said the Adjutant, taking him by the ear, "do you know that it only remains for me to make you change your tone? Perhaps you will speak differently after I have given you twenty blows with the flat of my sword."

Fortunato continued to sneer.

"My father is Mateo Falcone," said he with emphasis.

"You little scamp, you know very well that I can carry you off to Corte or to Bastia. I will make you lie in a dungeon, on straw, with your feet in shackles, and I will have you guillotined if you don't tell me where Gianetto is."

The child burst out laughing at this ridiculous menace. He repeated:

"My father is Mateo Falcone."

"Adjutant," said one of the soldiers in a low voice, "let us have no quarrels with Mateo."

Gamba appeared evidently embarrassed. He spoke in an undertone with the soldiers who had already visited the house. This was not a very long operation, for the cabin of a Corsican consists only of a single square room, furnished with a table, some benches, chests, housekeeping utensils and those of the chase. In the meantime, little Fortunato petted his cat and seemed to take a wicked enjoyment in the confusion of the soldiers and of his cousin.

One of the men approached the pile of hay. He saw the cat, and gave the pile a careless thrust with his bayonet, shrugging his shoulders as if he felt that his precaution was ridiculous. Nothing moved; the boy's face betrayed not the slightest emotion.

The Adjutant and his troop were cursing their luck. Already they were looking in the direction of the plain, as if disposed to return by the way they had come, when their chief, convinced that menaces would produce no impression on Falcone's son, determined to make a last effort, and try the effect of caresses and presents.

"My little cousin," said he, "you are a very wide-awake little fellow. You will get along. But you are playing a naughty game with me; and if I wasn't afraid of making trouble for my cousin, Mateo, the devil take me! but I would carry you off with me."

"Bah!"

"But when my cousin comes back I shall tell him about this, and he will whip you till the blood comes for having told such lies."

"You don't say so!"

"You will see. But hold on! — be a good boy and I will give you something."

"Cousin, let me give you some advice: if you wait much longer Gianetto will be in the mâquis and it will take a smarter man than you to follow him."

The Adjutant took from his pocket a silver watch worth about ten crowns, and noticing that Fortunato's eyes sparkled at the sight of it, said, holding the watch by the end; of its steel chain:

"Rascal! you would like to have such a watch as that hung around your neck, wouldn't you, and to walk in the streets of Porto-Vecchio proud as a peacock? People would ask you what time it was, and you would say: 'Look at my watch.'"

"When I am grown up, my uncle, the Caporal, will give me a watch."

"Yes; but your uncle's little boy has one already; not so fine as this either. But then, he is younger than you."

The child sighed.

"Well! Would you like this watch, little cousin?"

Fortunato, casting sidelong glances at the watch, resembled a cat that has been given a whole chicken. It feels that it is being made sport of, and does not dare to use its claws; from time to time it turns its eyes away so as not to be tempted, licking its jaws all the while, and has the appearance of saying to its master, "How cruel your joke is!"

However, the Adjutant seemed in earnest in offering his watch. Fortunato did not reach out his hand for it, but said with a bitter smile:

"Why do you make fun of me?"

"Good God! I am not making fun of you. Only tell me where Gianetto is and the watch is yours."

Fortunato smiled incredulously, and fixing his black eyes on those of the Adjutant tried to read there the faith he ought to have had in his words.

"May I lose my epaulettes," cried the Adjutant, "if I do not give you the watch on this condition. These comrades are witnesses; I can not deny it."

While speaking he gradually held the watch nearer till it almost touched the child's pale face, which plainly showed the struggle that was going on in his soul between covetousness and respect for hospitality. His breast swelled with emotion; he seemed about to suffocate. Meanwhile the watch was slowly swaying and turning, sometimes brushing against his cheek. Finally, his right hand was gradually stretched toward it; the ends of his fingers touched it; then its whole weight was in his hand, the Adjutant still keeping hold of the chain. The face was light blue; the cases newly burnished. In the sunlight it seemed to be all on fire. The temptation was too great. Fortunato raised his left hand and pointed over his shoulder with his thumb at the hay against which he was reclining. The Adjutant understood him at once. He dropped the end of the chain and Fortunato felt himself the sole possessor of the watch. He sprang up with the agility of a deer and stood ten feet from the pile, which the soldiers began at once to overturn.

There was a movement in the hay, and a bloody man with a poignard in his hand appeared. He tried to rise to his feet, but his stiffened leg would not permit it and he fell. The Adjutant at once grappled with him and took away his stiletto. He was immediately secured, notwithstanding his resistance.

Gianetto, lying on the earth and bound like a fagot, turned his head towards Fortunato, who had approached.

"Son of — !" said he, with more contempt than anger.

The child threw him the silver piece which he had received, feeling that he no longer deserved it; but the outlaw paid no attention to the movement, and with great coolness said to the Adjutant:

"My dear Gamba, I cannot walk; you will be obliged to carry me to the city."

"Just now you could run faster than a buck," answered the cruel captor; "but be at rest. I am so pleased to have you that I would carry you a league on my back without fatigue. Besides, comrade, we are going to make a litter for you with your cloak and some branches, and at the Crespoli farm we shall find horses."

"Good," said the prisoner, "You will also put a little straw on your litter that I may be more comfortable."

While some of the soldiers were occupied in making a kind of stretcher out of some chestnut boughs and the rest were dressing Gianetto's wound, Mateo Falcone and his wife suddenly appeared at a turn in the path that led to the mâquis. The woman was staggering under the weight of an enormous sack of chestnuts, while her husband was sauntering along, carrying one gun in his hands, while another was slung across his shoulders, for it is unworthy of a man to carry other burdens than his arms.

At the sight of the soldiers Mateo's first thought was that they had come to arrest him. But why this thought? Had he then some quarrels with justice? No. He enjoyed a good reputation. He was said to have a particularly good name, but he was a Corsican and a highlander, and there are few Corsican highlanders who, in scrutinizing their memory, can not find some peccadillo, such as a gun-shot, dagger-thrust, or similar trifles. Mateo more than others had a clear conscience; for more than ten years he had not pointed his carbine at a man, but he was always prudent, and put himself into a position to make a good defense if necessary. "Wife," said he to Giuseppa, "put down the sack and hold yourself ready."

She obeyed at once. He gave her the gun that was slung across his shoulders, which would have bothered him, and, cocking the one he held in his hands, advanced slowly towards the house, walking among the trees that bordered the road, ready at the least hostile demonstration, to hide behind the largest, whence he could fire from under cover. His wife followed closely behind, holding his reserve weapon and his cartridge-box. The duty of a good housekeeper, in case of a fight, is to load her husband's carbines.

On the other side the Adjutant was greatly troubled to see Mateo advance in this manner, with cautious steps, his carbine raised, and his finger on the trigger.

"If by chance," thought he, "Mateo should be related to Gianetto, or if he should be his friend and wish to defend him, the contents of his two guns would arrive amongst us as certainly as a letter in the post; and if he should see me, notwithstanding the relationship!"

In this perplexity he took a bold step. It was to advance alone towards Mateo and tell him of the affair while accosting him as an old acquaintance, but the short space that separated him from Mateo seemed terribly long.

"Hello! old comrade," cried he. "How do you do, my good fellow? It is I, Gamba, your cousin."

Without answering a word, Mateo stopped, and in proportion as the other spoke, slowly raised the muzzle of his gun so that it was pointing upward when the Adjutant joined him.

"Good-day, brother," said the Adjutant, holding out his hand. "It is a long time since I have seen you."

"Good-day, brother."

"I stopped while passing, to say good-day to you and to cousin Pepa here. We have had a long journey to-day, but have no reason to complain, for we have captured a famous prize. We have just seized Gianetto Saupiero."

"God be praised!" cried Giuseppa. "He stole a milch goat from us last week."

These words reassured Gamba.

"Poor devil!" said Mateo, "he was hungry."

"The villain fought like a lion," continued the Adjutant, a little mortified. "He killed one of my soldiers, and not content with that, broke Caporal Chardon's arm; but that matters little, he is only a Frenchman. Then, too, he was so well hidden that the devil couldn't have found him. Without my little cousin, Fortunato, I should never have discovered him."

"Fortunato!" cried Mateo.

"Fortunato!" repeated Giuseppa.

"Yes, Gianetto was hidden under the hay-pile yonder, but my little cousin showed me the trick. I shall tell his uncle, the Caporal, that he may send him a fine present for his trouble. Both his name and yours will be in the report that I shall send to the Attorney-general."

"Malediction!" said Mateo in a low voice.

They had rejoined the detachment. Gianetto was already lying on the litter ready to set out. When he saw Mateo and Gamba in company he smiled a strange smile, then, turning his head towards the door of the house, he spat on the sill, saying:

"House of a traitor."

Only a man determined to die would dare pronounce the word traitor to Falcone. A good blow with the stiletto, which there would be no need of repeating, would have immediately paid the insult. However, Mateo made no other movement than to place his hand on his forehead like a man who is dazed.

Fortunato had gone into the house when his father arrived, but now he reappeared with a bowl of milk which he handed with downcast eyes to Gianetto.

"Get away from me!" cried the outlaw, in a loud voice. Then, turning to one of the soldiers, he said:

"Comrade, give me a drink."

The soldier placed his gourd in his hands, and the prisoner drank the water handed to him by a man with whom he had just exchanged bullets. He then asked them to tie his hands across his breast instead of behind his back.

"I like," said he, "to lie at my ease."

They hastened to satisfy him; then the Adjutant gave the signal to start, said adieu to Mateo, who did not respond, and descended with rapid steps towards the plain.

Nearly ten minutes elapsed before Mateo spoke. The child looked with restless eyes, now at his mother, now at his father, who was leaning on his gun and gazing at him with an expression of concentrated rage.

"You begin well," said Mateo at last with a calm voice, but frightful to one who knew the man.

75

"Oh, father!" cried the boy, bursting into tears, and making a forward movement as if to throw himself on his knees. But Mateo cried, "Away from me!"

The little fellow stopped and sobbed, immovable, a few feet from his father.

Giuseppa drew near. She had just discovered the watch-chain, the end of which was hanging out of Fortunato's jacket.

"Who gave you that watch?" demanded she in a severe tone.

"My cousin, the Adjutant."

Falcone seized the watch and smashed it in a thousand pieces against a rock.

"Wife," said he, "is this my child?"

Giuseppa's cheeks turned a brick-red.

"What are you saying, Mateo? Do you know to whom you speak?"

"Very well, this child is the first of his race to commit treason."

Fortunato's sobs and gasps redoubled as Falcone kept his lynx-eyes upon him. Then he struck the earth with his gun-stock, shouldered the weapon, and turned in the direction of the mâquis, calling to Fortunato to follow. The boy obeyed. Giuseppa hastened after Mateo and seized his arm.

"He is your son," said she with a trembling voice, fastening her black eyes on those of her husband to read what was going on in his heart.

"Leave me alone," said Mateo, "I am his father."

Giuseppa embraced her son, and bursting into tears entered the house. She threw herself on her knees before an image of the Virgin and prayed ardently. In the meanwhile Falcone walked some two hundred paces along the path and only stopped when he reached a little ravine which he descended. He tried the earth with the butt-end of his carbine, and found it soft and easy to dig. The place seemed to be convenient for his design.

"Fortunato, go close to that big rock there."

The child did as he was commanded, then he kneeled.

"Say your prayers."

"Oh, father, father, do not kill me!"

"Say your prayers!" repeated Mateo in a terrible voice.

The boy, stammering and sobbing, recited the Pater and the Credo. At the end of each prayer the father loudly answered, "Amen!"

"Are those all the prayers you know?"

"Oh! father, I know the Ave Maria and the litany that my aunt taught me."

"It is very long, but no matter."

The child finished the litany in a scarcely audible tone.

"Are you finished?"

"Oh! my father, have mercy! Pardon me! I will never do so again. I will beg my cousin, the Caporal, to pardon Gianetto."

He was still speaking. Mateo raised his gun, and, taking aim, said:

"May God pardon you!"

The boy made a desperate effort to rise and grasp his father's knees, but there was not time. Mateo fired and Fortunato fell dead.

Without casting a glance on the body, Mateo returned to the house for a spade with which to bury his son. He had gone but a few steps when he met Giuseppa, who, alarmed by the shot, was hastening hither.

"What have you done?" cried she.

"Justice."

"Where is he?"

"In the ravine. I am going to bury him. He died a Christian. I shall have a mass said for him. Have my son-in-law, Tiodoro Bianchi, sent for to come and live with us."

CARMEN

BY PROSPER MERIMEE

CHAPTER I

I had always suspected the geographical authorities did not know what they were talking about when they located the battlefield of Munda in the county of the Bastuli-Poeni, close to the modern Monda, some two leagues north of Marbella.

According to my own surmise, founded on the text of the anonymous author of the *Bellum Hispaniense*, and on certain information culled from the excellent library owned by the Duke of Ossuna, I believed the site of the memorable struggle in which Caesar played double or quits, once and for all, with the champions of the Republic, should be sought in the neighbourhood of Montilla.

Happening to be in Andalusia during the autumn of 1830, I made a somewhat lengthy excursion, with the object of clearing up certain doubts which still oppressed me. A paper which I shall shortly publish will, I trust, remove any hesitation that may still exist in the minds of all honest archaeologists. But before that dissertation of mine finally settles the geographical problem on the solution of which the whole of learned Europe hangs, I desire to relate a little tale. It will do no prejudice to the interesting question of the correct locality of Monda.

I had hired a guide and a couple of horses at Cordova, and had started on my way with no luggage save a few shirts, and Caesar's *Commentaries*. As I wandered, one day, across the higher lands of the Cachena plain, worn with fatigue, parched with thirst, scorched by a burning sun, cursing Caesar and Pompey's sons alike, most heartily, my eye lighted, at some distance from the path I was following, on a little stretch of green sward dotted with reeds and rushes. That betokened the neighbourhood of some spring, and, indeed, as I drew nearer I perceived that what had looked like sward was a marsh, into which a stream, which seemed to issue from a narrow gorge between two high spurs of the Sierra di Cabra, ran and disappeared.

If I rode up that stream, I argued, I was likely to find cooler water, fewer leeches and frogs, and mayhap a little shade among the rocks.

At the mouth of the gorge, my horse neighed, and another horse, invisible to me, neighed back. Before I had advanced a hundred paces, the gorge suddenly widened, and I beheld a sort of natural amphitheatre, thoroughly shaded by the steep cliffs that lay all around it. It was impossible to imagine any more delightful halting place for a traveler. At the foot of the precipitous rocks, the stream bubbled upward and fell into a little basin, lined with sand that was as white as snow. Five or six splendid evergreen oaks, sheltered from the wind, and cooled by the spring, grew beside the pool, and shaded it with their thick foliage. And round about it a close and glossy turf offered the wanderer a better bed than he could have found in any hostelry for ten leagues round.

The honour of discovering this fair spot did not belong to me. A man was resting there already — sleeping, no doubt — before I reached it. Roused by the neighing of the horses, he had risen to his feet and had moved over to his mount, which had been taking advantage of its master's slumbers to make a hearty feed on the grass that grew around. He was an active young fellow, of middle height, but powerful in build, and proud and sullen-looking in expression. His complexion, which may once have been fine, had been tanned by the sun till it was darker than his hair. One of his hands grasped his horse's halter. In the other he held a brass blunderbuss.

At the first blush, I confess, the blunderbuss, and the savage looks of the man who bore it, somewhat took me aback. But I had heard so much about robbers, that, never seeing any, I had ceased to believe in their existence. And further, I had seen so many honest farmers arm themselves to the teeth before they went out to market, that the sight of firearms gave me no warrant for doubting the character of any stranger. "And then," quoth I to myself, "what could he do with my shirts and my Elzevir edition of Caesar's *Commentaries*?" So I bestowed a friendly nod on the man with the blunderbuss, and inquired, with a smile, whether I had disturbed his nap. Without any answer, he looked me over from head to foot. Then, as if the scrutiny had satisfied him, he looked as closely at my guide, who was just coming up. I saw the guide turn pale, and pull up with an air of evident alarm. "An unlucky meeting!" thought I to myself. But prudence instantly counseled me not to let any symptom of anxiety escape me. So I dismounted. I told the guide to take off the horses' bridles, and kneeling down beside the spring, I laved my head and hands and then drank a long draught, lying flat on my belly, like Gideon's soldiers.

Meanwhile, I watched the stranger, and my own guide. This last seemed to come forward unwillingly. But the other did not appear to have any evil designs upon us. For he had turned his horse loose, and the blunderbuss, which he had been holding horizontally, was now dropped earthward.

Not thinking it necessary to take offence at the scant attention paid me, I stretched myself full length upon the grass, and calmly asked the owner of the blunderbuss whether he had a light about him. At the same time I pulled out my cigar-case. The stranger, still without opening his lips, took out his flint, and lost no time in getting me a light. He was evidently growing tamer, for he sat down opposite to me, though he still grasped his weapon. When I had lighted my cigar, I chose out the best I had left, and asked him whether he smoked.

"Yes, senor," he replied. These were the first words I had heard him speak, and I noticed that he did not pronounce the letter $s$[1] in the Andalusian fashion, whence I concluded he was a traveler, like myself, though, maybe, somewhat less of an archaeologist.

"You'll find this a fairly good one," said I, holding out a real Havana regalia.

He bowed his head slightly, lighted his cigar at mine, thanked me with another nod, and began to smoke with a most lively appearance of enjoyment.

"Ah!" he exclaimed, as he blew his first puff of smoke slowly out of his ears and nostrils. "What a time it is since I've had a smoke!"

In Spain the giving and accepting of a cigar establishes bonds of hospitality similar to those founded in Eastern countries on the partaking of bread and salt. My friend turned out more talkative than I had hoped. However, though he claimed to belong to the

---

[1] The Andalusians aspirate the $s$, and pronounce it like the soft $c$ and the $z$, which Spaniards pronounce like the English $th$. An Andalusian may always be recognized by the way in which he says $senor$.

*partido* of Montilla, he seemed very ill-informed about the country. He did not know the name of the delightful valley in which we were sitting, he could not tell me the names of any of the neighbouring villages, and when I inquired whether he had not noticed any broken-down walls, broad-rimmed tiles, or carved stones in the vicinity, he confessed he had never paid any heed to such matters. On the other hand, he showed himself an expert in horseflesh, found fault with my mount — not a difficult affair — and gave me a pedigree of his own, which had come from the famous stud at Cordova. It was a splendid creature, indeed, so tough, according to its owner's claim, that it had once covered thirty leagues in one day, either at the gallop or at full trot the whole time. In the midst of his story the stranger pulled up short, as if startled and sorry he had said so much. "The fact is I was in a great hurry to get to Cordova," he went on, somewhat embarrassed. "I had to petition the judges about a lawsuit." As he spoke, he looked at my guide Antonio, who had dropped his eyes.

The spring and the cool shade were so delightful that I bethought me of certain slices of an excellent ham, which my friends at Montilla had packed into my guide's wallet. I bade him produce them, and invited the stranger to share our impromptu lunch. If he had not smoked for a long time, he certainly struck me as having fasted for eight-and-forty hours at the very least. He ate like a starving wolf, and I thought to myself that my appearance must really have been quite providential for the poor fellow. Meanwhile my guide ate but little, drank still less, and spoke never a word, although in the earlier part of our journey he had proved himself a most unrivalled chatterer. He seemed ill at ease in the presence of our guest, and a sort of mutual distrust, the cause of which I could not exactly fathom, seemed to be between them.

The last crumbs of bread and scraps of ham had disappeared. We had each smoked our second cigar; I told the guide to bridle the horses, and was just about to take leave of my new friend, when he inquired where I was going to spend the night.

Before I had time to notice a sign my guide was making to me I had replied that I was going to the Venta del Cuervo.

"That's a bad lodging for a gentleman like you, sir! I'm bound there myself, and if you'll allow me to ride with you, we'll go together."

"With pleasure!" I replied, mounting my horse. The guide, who was holding my stirrup, looked at me meaningly again. I answered by shrugging my shoulders, as though to assure him I was perfectly easy in my mind, and we started on our way.

Antonio's mysterious signals, his evident anxiety, a few words dropped by the stranger, above all, his ride of thirty leagues, and the far from plausible explanation he had given us of it, had already enabled me to form an opinion as to the identity of my fellow-traveler. I had no doubt at all I was in the company of a smuggler, and possibly of a brigand. What cared I? I knew enough of the Spanish character to be very certain I had nothing to fear from a man who had eaten and smoked with me. His very presence would protect me in case of any undesirable meeting. And besides, I was very glad to know what a brigand was really like. One doesn't come across such gentry every day. And there is a certain charm about finding one's self in close proximity to a dangerous being, especially when one feels the being in question to be gentle and tame.

I was hoping the stranger might gradually fall into a confidential mood, and in spite of my guide's winks, I turned the conversation to the subject of highwaymen. I need scarcely say that I spoke of them with great respect. At that time there was a famous brigand in Andalusia, of the name of Jose-Maria, whose exploits were on every lip. "Supposing I should be riding along with Jose-Maria!" said I to myself. I told all the stories I knew about the hero — they were all to his credit, indeed, and loudly expressed my admiration of his generosity and his valour.

"Jose-Maria is nothing but a blackguard," said the stranger gravely.

"Is he just to himself, or is this an excess of modesty?" I queried, mentally, for by dint of scrutinizing my companion, I

82

had ended by reconciling his appearance with the description of Jose-Maria which I read posted up on the gates of various Andalusian towns. "Yes, this must be he — fair hair, blue eyes, large mouth, good teeth, small hands, fine shirt, a velvet jacket with silver buttons on it, white leather gaiters, and a bay horse. Not a doubt about it. But his *incognito* shall be respected!" We reached the *venta*. It was just what he had described to me. In other words, the most wretched hole of its kind I had as yet beheld. One large apartment served as kitchen, dining-room, and sleeping chamber. A fire was burning on a flat stone in the middle of the room, and the smoke escaped through a hole in the roof, or rather hung in a cloud some feet above the soil. Along the walls five or six mule rugs were spread on the floor. These were the travelers' beds. Twenty paces from the house, or rather from the solitary apartment which I have just described, stood a sort of shed, that served for a stable.

The only inhabitants of this delightful dwelling visible at the moment, at all events, were an old woman, and a little girl of ten or twelve years old, both of them as black as soot, and dressed in loathsome rags. "Here's the sole remnant of the ancient populations of Munda Boetica," said I to myself. "O Caesar! O Sextus Pompeius, if you were to revisit this earth how astounded you would be!"

When the old woman saw my traveling companion an exclamation of surprise escaped her. "Ah! Senor Don Jose!" she cried.

Don Jose frowned and lifted his hand with a gesture of authority that forthwith silenced the old dame.

I turned to my guide and gave him to understand, by a sign that no one else perceived, that I knew all about the man in whose company I was about to spend the night. Our supper was better than I expected. On a little table, only a foot high, we were served with an old rooster, fricasseed with rice and numerous peppers, then more peppers in oil, and finally a *gaspacho* — a sort of salad made of peppers. These three highly spiced dishes involved our frequent recourse to a goatskin filled with Montella wine, which struck us as being delicious.

After our meal was over, I caught sight of a mandolin hanging up against the wall — in Spain you see mandolins in every corner — and I asked the little girl, who had been waiting on us, if she knew how to play it.

"No," she replied. "But Don Jose does play well!"

"Do me the kindness to sing me something," I said to him, "I'm passionately fond of your national music."

"I can't refuse to do anything for such a charming gentleman, who gives me such excellent cigars," responded Don Jose gaily, and having made the child give him the mandolin, he sang to his own accompaniment. His voice, though rough, was pleasing, the air he sang was strange and sad. As to the words, I could not understand a single one of them.

"If I am not mistaken," said I, "that's not a Spanish air you have just been singing. It's like the *zorzicos* I've heard in the Provinces,[2] and the words must be in the Basque language."

"Yes," said Don Jose, with a gloomy look. He laid the mandolin down on the ground, and began staring with a peculiarly sad expression at the dying fire. His face, at once fierce and noble-looking, reminded me, as the firelight fell on it, of Milton's Satan. Like him, perchance, my comrade was musing over the home he had forfeited, the exile he had earned, by some misdeed. I tried to revive the conversation, but so absorbed was he in melancholy thought, that he gave me no answer.

The old woman had already gone to rest in a corner of the room, behind a ragged rug hung on a rope. The little girl had followed her into this retreat, sacred to the fair sex. Then my guide rose, and suggested that I should go with him to the stable. But at the word Don Jose, waking, as it were, with a start, inquired sharply whither he was going.

"To the stable," answered the guide.

---

[2] The *privileged Provinces*, Alava, Biscay, Guipuzcoa, and a part of Navarre, which all enjoy special *fueros*. The Basque language is spoken in these countries.

84

"What for? The horses have been fed! You can sleep here. The senor will give you leave."

"I'm afraid the senor's horse is sick. I'd like the senor to see it. Perhaps he'd know what should be done for it."

It was quite clear to me that Antonio wanted to speak to me apart.

But I did not care to rouse Don Jose's suspicions, and being as we were, I thought far the wisest course for me was to appear absolutely confident.

I therefore told Antonio that I knew nothing on earth about horses, and that I was desperately sleepy. Don Jose followed him to the stable, and soon returned alone. He told me there was nothing the matter with the horse, but that my guide considered the animal such a treasure that he was scrubbing it with his jacket to make it sweat, and expected to spend the night in that pleasing occupation. Meanwhile I had stretched myself out on the mule rugs, having carefully wrapped myself up in my own cloak, so as to avoid touching them. Don Jose, having begged me to excuse the liberty he took in placing himself so near me, lay down across the door, but not until he had primed his blunderbuss afresh and carefully laid it under the wallet, which served him as a pillow.

I had thought I was so tired that I should be able to sleep even in such a lodging. But within an hour a most unpleasant itching sensation roused me from my first nap. As soon as I realized its nature, I rose to my feet, feeling convinced I should do far better to spend the rest of the night in the open air than beneath that inhospitable roof. Walking tiptoe I reached the door, stepped over Don Jose, who was sleeping the sleep of the just, and managed so well that I got outside the building without waking him. Just beside the door there was a wide wooden bench. I lay down upon it, and settled myself, as best I could, for the remainder of the night. I was just closing my eyes for a second time when I fancied I saw the shadow of a man and then the shadow of a horse moving absolutely noiselessly, one behind the other. I sat upright, and then I thought I recognized Antonio. Surprised to see him outside the stable at such an hour, I got up and went toward him. He had seen me first, and had stopped to wait for me.

"Where is he?" Antonio inquired in a low tone.

"In the *venta*. He's asleep. The bugs don't trouble him. But what are you going to do with that horse?" I then noticed that, to stifle all noise as he moved out of the shed, Antonio had carefully muffled the horse's feet in the rags of an old blanket.

"Speak lower, for God's sake," said Antonio. "You don't know who that man is. He's Jose Navarro, the most noted bandit in Andalusia. I've been making signs to you all day long, and you wouldn't understand."

"What do I care whether he's a brigand or not," I replied. "He hasn't robbed us, and I'll wager he doesn't want to."

"That may be. But there are two hundred ducats on his head. Some lancers are stationed in a place I know, a league and a half from here, and before daybreak I'll bring a few brawny fellows back with me. I'd have taken his horse away, but the brute's so savage that nobody but Navarro can go near it."

"Devil take you!" I cried. "What harm has the poor fellow done you that you should want to inform against him? And besides, are you certain he is the brigand you take him for?"

"Perfectly certain! He came after me into the stable just now, and said, 'You seem to know me. If you tell that good gentleman who I am, I'll blow your brains out!' You stay here, sir, keep close to him. You've nothing to fear. As long as he knows you are there, he won't suspect anything."

As we talked, we had moved so far from the *venta* that the noise of the horse's hoofs could not be heard there. In a twinkling Antonio snatched off the rags he had wrapped around the creature's feet, and was just about to climb on its back. In vain did I attempt with prayers and threats to restrain him.

"I'm only a poor man, senor," quoth he, "I can't afford to lose two hundred ducats — especially when I shall earn them by ridding the country of such vermin. But mind what you're about! If Navarro wakes up, he'll snatch at his blunderbuss, and then look out for yourself! I've gone too far now to turn back. Do the best you can for yourself!"

The villain was in his saddle already, he spurred his horse smartly, and I soon lost sight of them both in the darkness.

I was very angry with my guide, and terribly alarmed as well. After a moment's reflection, I made up my mind, and went back to the *venta*. Don Jose was still sound asleep, making up, no doubt, for the fatigue and sleeplessness of several days of adventure. I had to shake him roughly before I could wake him up. Never shall I forget his fierce look, and the spring he made to get hold of his blunderbuss, which, as a precautionary measure, I had removed to some distance from his couch.

"Senor," I said, "I beg your pardon for disturbing you. But I have a silly question to ask you. Would you be glad to see half a dozen lancers walk in here?"

He bounded to his feet, and in an awful voice he demanded:

"Who told you?"

"It's little matter whence the warning comes, so long as it be good."

"Your guide has betrayed me — but he shall pay for it! Where is he?"

"I don't know. In the stable, I fancy. But somebody told me — "

"Who told you? It can't be the old hag — "

"Some one I don't know. Without more parleying, tell me, yes or no, have you any reason for not waiting till the soldiers come? If you have any, lose no time! If not, good-night to you, and forgive me for having disturbed your slumbers!"

"Ah, your guide! Your guide! I had my doubts of him at first — but — I'll settle with him! Farewell, senor. May God reward you for the service I owe you! I am not quite so wicked as you think me. Yes, I still have something in me that an honest man may pity. Farewell, senor! I have only one regret — that I can not pay my debt to you!"

"As a reward for the service I have done you, Don Jose, promise me you'll suspect nobody — nor seek for vengeance.

Here are some cigars for your journey. Good luck to you." And I held out my hand to him.

He squeezed it, without a word, took up his wallet and blunderbuss, and after saying a few words to the old woman in a lingo that I could not understand, he ran out to the shed. A few minutes later, I heard him galloping out into the country.

As for me, I lay down again on my bench, but I did not go to sleep again. I queried in my own mind whether I had done right to save a robber, and possibly a murderer, from the gallows, simply and solely because I had eaten ham and rice in his company. Had I not betrayed my guide, who was supporting the cause of law and order? Had I not exposed him to a ruffian's vengeance? But then, what about the laws of hospitality?

"A mere savage prejudice," said I to myself. "I shall have to answer for all the crimes this brigand may commit in future." Yet is that instinct of the conscience which resists every argument really a prejudice? It may be I could not have escaped from the delicate position in which I found myself without remorse of some kind. I was still tossed to and fro, in the greatest uncertainty as to the morality of my behaviour, when I saw half a dozen horsemen ride up, with Antonio prudently lagging behind them. I went to meet them, and told them the brigand had fled over two hours previously. The old woman, when she was questioned by the sergeant, admitted that she knew Navarro, but said that living alone, as she did, she would never have dared to risk her life by informing against him. She added that when he came to her house, he habitually went away in the middle of the night. I, for my part, was made to ride to a place some leagues away, where I showed my passport, and signed a declaration before the *Alcalde*. This done, I was allowed to recommence my archaeological investigations. Antonio was sulky with me; suspecting it was I who had prevented his earning those two hundred ducats. Nevertheless, we parted good friends at Cordova, where I gave him as large a gratuity as the state of my finances would permit.

# CHAPTER II

I spent several days at Cordova. I had been told of a certain manuscript in the library of the Dominican convent which was likely to furnish me with very interesting details about the ancient Munda. The good fathers gave me the most kindly welcome. I spent the daylight hours within their convent, and at night I walked about the town. At Cordova a great many idlers collect, toward sunset, in the quay that runs along the right bank of the Guadalquivir. Promenaders on the spot have to breathe the odour of a tan yard which still keeps up the ancient fame of the country in connection with the curing of leather. But to atone for this, they enjoy a sight which has a charm of its own. A few minutes before the Angelus bell rings, a great company of women gathers beside the river, just below the quay, which is rather a high one. Not a man would dare to join its ranks. The moment the Angelus rings, darkness is supposed to have fallen. As the last stroke sounds, all the women disrobe and step into the water. Then there is laughing and screaming and a wonderful clatter. The men on the upper quay watch the bathers, straining their eyes, and seeing very little. Yet the white uncertain outlines perceptible against the dark-blue waters of the stream stir the poetic mind, and the possessor of a little fancy finds it not difficult to imagine that Diana and her nymphs are bathing below, while he himself runs no risk of ending like Acteon.

I have been told that one day a party of good-for-nothing fellows banded themselves together, and bribed the bell-ringer at the cathedral to ring the Angelus some twenty minutes before the proper hour. Though it was still broad daylight, the nymphs of the Guadalquivir never hesitated, and putting far more trust in the Angelus bell than in the sun, they proceeded to their bathing toilette — always of the simplest — with an easy conscience. I was not present on that occasion. In my day, the bell-ringer was incorruptible, the twilight was very dim, and nobody but a cat could have distinguished the difference between the oldest orange woman, and the prettiest shop-girl, in Cordova.

One evening, after it had grown quite dusk, I was leaning over the parapet of the quay, smoking, when a woman came up the steps leading from the river, and sat down near me. In her hair she wore a great bunch of jasmine — a flower which, at night, exhales a most intoxicating perfume. She was dressed simply, almost poorly, in black, as most work-girls are dressed in the evening. Women of the richer class only wear black in the daytime, at night they dress *a la francesa*. When she drew near me, the woman let the mantilla which had covered her head drop on her shoulders, and "by the dim light falling from the stars" I perceived her to be young, short in stature, well-proportioned, and with very large eyes. I threw my cigar away at once. She appreciated this mark of courtesy, essentially French, and hastened to inform me that she was very fond of the smell of tobacco, and that she even smoked herself, when she could get very mild *papelitos*. I fortunately happened to have some such in my case, and at once offered them to her. She condescended to take one, and lighted it at a burning string which a child brought us, receiving a copper for its pains. We mingled our smoke, and talked so long, the fair lady and I, that we ended by being almost alone on the quay. I thought I might venture, without impropriety, to suggest our going to eat an ice at the *neveria*.[3] After a moment of modest demur, she agreed. But before finally accepting, she desired to know what o'clock it was. I struck my repeater, and this seemed to astound her greatly.

"What clever inventions you foreigners do have! What country do you belong to, sir? You're an Englishman, no doubt!"[4]

"I'm a Frenchman, and your devoted servant. And you, senora, or senorita, you probably belong to Cordova?"

"No."

"At all events, you are an Andalusian? Your soft way of speaking makes me think so."

---

[3] A *café* to which a depot of ice, or rather of snow, is attached. There is hardly a village in Spain without its *neveria*.

[4] Every traveler in Spain who does not carry about samples of calicoes and silks is taken for an Englishman (*inglesito*). It is the same thing in the East.

"If you notice people's accent so closely, you must be able to guess what I am."

"I think you are from the country of Jesus, two paces out of Paradise."

I had learned the metaphor, which stands for Andalusia, from my friend Francisco Sevilla, a well-known *picador.*

"Pshaw! The people here say there is no place in Paradise for us!"

"Then perhaps you are of Moorish blood — or — — " I stopped, not venturing to add "a Jewess."

"Oh come! You must see I'm a gypsy! Wouldn't you like me to tell you *la baji?*[5] Did you never hear tell of Carmencita? That's who I am!"

I was such a miscreant in those days — now fifteen years ago — that the close proximity of a sorceress did not make me recoil in horror. "So be it!" I thought. "Last week I ate my supper with a highway robber. To-day I'll go and eat ices with a servant of the devil. A traveler should see everything." I had yet another motive for prosecuting her acquaintance. When I left college — I acknowledge it with shame — I had wasted a certain amount of time in studying occult science, and had even attempted, more than once, to exorcise the powers of darkness. Though I had been cured, long since, of my passion for such investigations, I still felt a certain attraction and curiosity with regard to all superstitions, and I was delighted to have this opportunity of discovering how far the magic art had developed among the gypsies.

Talking as we went, we had reached the *nevería,* and seated ourselves at a little table, lighted by a taper protected by a glass globe. I then had time to take a leisurely view of my *gitana,* while several worthy individuals, who were eating their ices, stared open-mouthed at beholding me in such gay company.

I very much doubt whether Senorita Carmen was a pure-blooded gypsy. At all events, she was infinitely prettier than any other woman of her race I have ever seen. For a women to be

---

[5] Your fortune.

beautiful, they say in Spain, she must fulfill thirty *ifs*, or, if it please you better, you must be able to define her appearance by ten adjectives, applicable to three portions of her person.

For instance, three things about her must be black, her eyes, her eyelashes, and her eyebrows. Three must be dainty, her fingers, her lips, her hair, and so forth. For the rest of this inventory, see Brantome. My gypsy girl could lay no claim to so many perfections. Her skin, though perfectly smooth, was almost of a copper hue. Her eyes were set obliquely in her head, but they were magnificent and large. Her lips, a little full, but beautifully shaped, revealed a set of teeth as white as newly skinned almonds. Her hair — a trifle coarse, perhaps — was black, with blue lights on it like a raven's wing, long and glossy. Not to weary my readers with too prolix a description, I will merely add, that to every blemish she united some advantage, which was perhaps all the more evident by contrast. There was something strange and wild about her beauty. Her face astonished you, at first sight, but nobody could forget it. Her eyes, especially, had an expression of mingled sensuality and fierceness which I had never seen in any other human glance. "Gypsy's eye, wolf's eye!" is a Spanish saying which denotes close observation. If my readers have no time to go to the "Jardin des Plantes" to study the wolf's expression, they will do well to watch the ordinary cat when it is lying in wait for a sparrow.

It will be understood that I should have looked ridiculous if I had proposed to have my fortune told in a *cafe*. I therefore begged the pretty witch's leave to go home with her. She made no difficulties about consenting, but she wanted to know what o'clock it was again, and requested me to make my repeater strike once more.

"Is it really gold?" she said, gazing at it with rapt attention.

When we started off again, it was quite dark. Most of the shops were shut, and the streets were almost empty. We crossed the bridge over the Guadalquivir, and at the far end of the suburb we stopped in front of a house of anything but palatial appearance. The door was opened by a child, to whom the gypsy spoke a few words in a language unknown to me, which I afterward understood to be *Romany*, or *chipe calli* — the gypsy idiom. The child instantly disappeared, leaving us in sole possession of a tolerably spacious room, furnished with a small table, two stools, and a chest. I must not forget to mention a jar of water, a pile of oranges, and a bunch of onions.

As soon as we were left alone, the gypsy produced, out of her chest, a pack of cards, bearing signs of constant usage, a magnet, a dried chameleon, and a few other indispensable adjuncts of her art. Then she bade me cross my left hand with a silver coin, and the magic ceremonies duly began. It is unnecessary to chronicle her predictions, and as for the style of her performance, it proved her to be no mean sorceress.

Unluckily we were soon disturbed. The door was suddenly burst open, and a man, shrouded to the eyes in a brown cloak, entered the room, apostrophizing the gypsy in anything but gentle terms. What he said I could not catch, but the tone of his voice revealed the fact that he was in a very evil temper. The gypsy betrayed neither surprise nor anger at his advent, but she ran to meet him, and with a most striking volubility, she poured out several sentences in the mysterious language she had already used in my presence. The word *payllo*, frequently reiterated, was the only one I understood. I knew that the gypsies use it to describe all men not of their own race. Concluding myself to be the subject of this discourse, I was prepared for a somewhat delicate explanation. I had already laid my hand on the leg of one of the stools, and was studying within myself to discover the exact moment at which I had better throw it at his head, when, roughly pushing the gypsy to one side, the man advanced toward me. Then with a step backward he cried:

"What, sir! Is it you?"

I looked at him in my turn and recognized my friend Don Jose. At that moment I did feel rather sorry I had saved him from the gallows.

"What, is it you, my good fellow?" I exclaimed, with as easy a smile as I could muster. "You have interrupted this young lady just when she was foretelling me most interesting things!"

"The same as ever. There shall be an end to it!" he hissed between his teeth, with a savage glance at her.

Meanwhile the *gitana* was still talking to him in her own tongue. She became more and more excited. Her eyes grew fierce and bloodshot, her features contracted, she stamped her foot. She seemed to me to be earnestly pressing him to do something he was unwilling to do. What this was I fancied I understood only too well, by the fashion in which she kept drawing her little hand backward and forward under her chin. I was inclined to think she wanted to have somebody's throat cut, and I had a fair suspicion the throat in question was my own. To all her torrent of eloquence Don Jose's only reply was two or three shortly spoken words. At this the gypsy cast a glance of the most utter scorn at him, then, seating herself Turkish-fashion in a corner of the room, she picked out an orange, tore off the skin, and began to eat it.

Don Jose took hold of my arm, opened the door, and led me into the street. We walked some two hundred paces in the deepest silence. Then he stretched out his hand.

"Go straight on," he said, "and you'll come to the bridge."

That instant he turned his back on me and departed at a great pace. I took my way back to my inn, rather crestfallen, and considerably out of temper. The worst of all was that, when I undressed, I discovered my watch was missing.

Various considerations prevented me from going to claim it next day, or requesting the *Corregidor* to be good enough to have a search made for it. I finished my work on the Dominican manuscript, and went on to Seville. After several months spent wandering hither and thither in Andalusia, I wanted to get back to Madrid, and with that object I had to pass through Cordova. I had no intention of making any stay there, for I had taken a dislike to that fair city, and to the ladies who bathed in the Guadalquivir. Nevertheless, I had some visits to pay, and certain errands to do, which must detain me several days in the old capital of the Mussulman princes.

The moment I made my appearance in the Dominican convent, one of the monks, who had always shown the most lively interest in my inquiries as to the site of the battlefield of Munda, welcomed me with open arms, exclaiming:

"Praised be God! You are welcome! My dear friend. We all thought you were dead, and I myself have said many a *pater* and *ave* (not that I regret them!) for your soul. Then you weren't murdered, after all? That you were robbed, we know!"

"What do you mean?" I asked, rather astonished.

"Oh, you know! That splendid repeater you used to strike in the library whenever we said it was time for us to go into church. Well, it has been found, and you'll get it back."

"Why," I broke in, rather put out of countenance, "I lost it — "

"The rascal's under lock and key, and as he was known to be a man who would shoot any Christian for the sake of a *peseta*, we were most dreadfully afraid he had killed you. I'll go with you to the *Corregidor*, and he'll give you back your fine watch. And after that, you won't dare to say the law doesn't do its work properly in Spain."

"I assure you," said I, "I'd far rather lose my watch than have to give evidence in court to hang a poor unlucky devil, and especially because — because — — "

"Oh, you needn't be alarmed! He's thoroughly done for; they might hang him twice over. But when I say hang, I say wrong. Your thief is an *Hidalgo*. So he's to be garroted the day after to-morrow, without fail.[6] So you see one theft more or less won't affect his position. Would to God he had done nothing but steal! But he has committed several murders, one more hideous than the other."

"What's his name?"

---

[6] In 1830, the noble class still enjoyed this privilege. Nowadays, under the constitutional *regime*, commoners have attained the same dignity.

"In this country he is only known as Jose Navarro, but he has another Basque name, which neither your nor I will ever be able to pronounce. By the way, the man is worth seeing, and you, who like to study the peculiar features of each country, shouldn't lose this chance of noting how a rascal bids farewell to this world in Spain. He is in jail, and Father Martinez will take you to him."

So bent was my Dominican friend on my seeing the preparations for this "neat little hanging job" that I was fain to agree. I went to see the prisoner, having provided myself with a bundle of cigars, which I hoped might induce him to forgive my intrusion.

I was ushered into Don Jose's presence just as he was sitting at table. He greeted me with a rather distant nod, and thanked me civilly for the present I had brought him. Having counted the cigars in the bundle I had placed in his hand, he took out a certain number and returned me the rest, remarking that he would not need any more of them.

I inquired whether by laying out a little money, or by applying to my friends, I might not be able to do something to soften his lot. He shrugged his shoulders, to begin with, smiling sadly. Soon, as by an after-thought, he asked me to have a mass said for the repose of his soul.

Then he added nervously: "Would you — would you have another said for a person who did you a wrong?"

"Assuredly I will, my dear fellow," I answered. "But no one in this country has wronged me so far as I know."

He took my hand and squeezed it, looking very grave. After a moment's silence, he spoke again.

"Might I dare to ask another service of you? When you go back to your own country perhaps you will pass through Navarre. At all events you'll go by Vittoria, which isn't very far off."

"Yes," said I, "I shall certainly pass through Vittoria. But I may very possibly go round by Pampeluna, and for your sake, I believe I should be very glad to do it."

"Well, if you do go to Pampeluna, you'll see more than one thing that will interest you. It's a fine town. I'll give you this medal," he showed me a little silver medal that he wore hung around his neck. "You'll wrap it up in paper" — he paused a moment to master his emotion — "and you'll take it, or send it, to an old lady whose address I'll give you. Tell her I am dead — but don't tell her how I died."

I promised to perform his commission. I saw him the next day, and spent part of it in his company. From his lips I learned the sad incidents that follow.

# CHAPTER III

"I was born," he said, "at Elizondo, in the valley of Baztan. My name is Don Jose Lizzarrabengoa, and you know enough of Spain, sir, to know at once, by my name, that I come of an old Christian and Basque stock. I call myself Don, because I have a right to it, and if I were at Elizondo I could show you my parchment genealogy. My family wanted me to go into the church, and made me study for it, but I did not like work. I was too fond of playing tennis, and that was my ruin. When we Navarrese begin to play tennis, we forget everything else. One day, when I had won the game, a young fellow from Alava picked a quarrel with me. We took to our *maquilas*,[7] and I won again. But I had to leave the neighbourhood. I fell in with some dragoons, and enlisted in the Almanza Cavalry Regiment. Mountain folks like us soon learn to be soldiers. Before long I was a corporal, and I had been told I should soon be made a sergeant, when, to my misfortune, I was put on guard at the Seville Tobacco Factory. If you have been to Seville you have seen the great building, just outside the ramparts, close to the Guadalquivir; I can fancy I see the entrance, and the guard room just beside it, even now. When Spanish soldiers are on duty, they either play cards or go to sleep. I, like an honest Navarrese, always tried to keep myself busy. I was making a chain to hold my priming-pin, out of a bit of wire: all at once, my comrades said, 'there's the bell ringing, the girls are coming back to work.' You must know, sir, that there are quite four or five hundred women employed in the factory. They roll the cigars in a great room into which no man can go without a permit from the *Veintiquatro*,[8] because when the weather is hot they make themselves at home, especially the young ones. When the work-girls come back after their dinner, numbers of young men go down to see them pass by, and talk all sorts of nonsense to them. Very few of those young

---

[7] Iron-shod sticks used by the Basques.
[8] Magistrate in charge of the municipal police arrangements, and local government regulations.

ladies will refuse a silk mantilla, and men who care for that sort of sport have nothing to do but bend down and pick their fish up. While the others watched the girls go by, I stayed on my bench near the door. I was a young fellow then — my heart was still in my own country, and I didn't believe in any pretty girls who hadn't blue skirts and long plaits of hair falling on their shoulders.[9] And besides, I was rather afraid of the Andalusian women. I had not got used to their ways yet; they were always jeering one — never spoke a single word of sense. So I was sitting with my nose down upon my chain, when I heard some bystanders say, 'Here comes the *gitanella*! Then I lifted up my eyes, and I saw her! It was that very Carmen you know, and in whose rooms I met you a few months ago.

"She was wearing a very short skirt, below which her white silk stockings — with more than one hole in them — and her dainty red morocco shoes, fastened with flame-coloured ribbons, were clearly seen. She had thrown her mantilla back, to show her shoulders, and a great bunch of acacia that was thrust into her chemise. She had another acacia blossom in the corner of her mouth, and she walked along, swaying her hips, like a filly from the Cordova stud farm. In my country anybody who had seen a woman dressed in that fashion would have crossed himself. At Seville every man paid her some bold compliment on her appearance. She had an answer for each and all, with her hand on her hip, as bold as the thorough gypsy she was. At first I didn't like her looks, and I fell to my work again. But she, like all women and cats, who won't come if you call them, and do come if you don't call them, stopped short in front of me, and spoke to me.

"'*Compadre*,' said she, in the Andalusian fashion, 'won't you give me your chain for the keys of my strong box?'

"'It's for my priming-pin,' said I.

"'Your priming-pin!' she cried, with a laugh. 'Oho! I suppose the gentleman makes lace, as he wants pins!'

---

[9] The costume usually worn by peasant women in Navarre and the Basque Provinces.

"Everybody began to laugh, and I felt myself getting red in the face, and couldn't hit on anything in answer.

"'Come, my love!' she began again, 'make me seven ells of lace for my mantilla, my pet pin-maker!'

"And taking the acacia blossom out of her mouth she flipped it at me with her thumb so that it hit me just between the eyes. I tell you, sir, I felt as if a bullet had struck me. I didn't know which way to look. I sat stock-still, like a wooden board. When she had gone into the factory, I saw the acacia blossom, which had fallen on the ground between my feet. I don't know what made me do it, but I picked it up, unseen by any of my comrades, and put it carefully inside my jacket. That was my first folly.

"Two or three hours later I was still thinking about her, when a panting, terrified-looking porter rushed into the guard-room. He told us a woman had been stabbed in the great cigar-room, and that the guard must be sent in at once. The sergeant told me to take two men, and go and see to it. I took my two men and went upstairs. Imagine, sir, that when I got into the room, I found, to begin with, some three hundred women, stripped to their shifts, or very near it, all of them screaming and yelling and gesticulating, and making such a row that you couldn't have heard God's own thunder. On one side of the room one of the women was lying on the broad of her back, streaming with blood, with an X newly cut on her face by two strokes of a knife. Opposite the wounded woman, whom the best-natured of the band were attending, I saw Carmen, held by five or six of her comrades. The wounded woman was crying out, 'A confessor, a confessor! I'm killed!' Carmen said nothing at all. She clinched her teeth and rolled her eyes like a chameleon. 'What's this?' I asked. I had hard work to find out what had happened, for all the work-girls talked at once. It appeared that the injured girl had boasted she had money enough in her pocket to buy a donkey at the Triana Market. 'Why,' said Carmen, who had a tongue of her own, 'can't you do with a broom?' Stung by this taunt, it may be because she felt herself rather unsound in that particular, the other girl replied

100

that she knew nothing about brooms, seeing she had not the honour of being either a gypsy or one of the devil's godchildren, but that the Senorita Carmen would shortly make acquaintance with her donkey, when the *Corregidor* took her out riding with two lackeys behind her to keep the flies off. 'Well,' retorted Carmen, 'I'll make troughs for the flies to drink out of on your cheeks, and I'll paint a draught-board on them!'[10] And thereupon, slap, bank! She began making St. Andrew's crosses on the girl's face with a knife she had been using for cutting off the ends of the cigars.

"The case was quite clear. I took hold of Carmen's arm. 'Sister mine,' I said civilly, 'you must come with me.' She shot a glance of recognition at me, but she said, with a resigned look: 'Let's be off. Where is my mantilla?' She put it over her head so that only one of her great eyes was to be seen, and followed my two men, as quiet as a lamb. When we got to the guardroom the sergeant said it was a serious job, and he must send her to prison. I was told off again to take her there. I put her between two dragoons, as a corporal does on such occasions. We started off for the town. The gypsy had begun by holding her tongue. But when we got to the *Calle de la Serpiente* — you know it, and that it earns its name by its many windings — she began by dropping her mantilla on to her shoulders, so as to show me her coaxing little face, and turning round to me as well as she could, she said:

"'*Oficial mio*, where are you taking me to?'

"'To prison, my poor child,' I replied, as gently as I could, just as any kind-hearted soldier is bound to speak to a prisoner, and especially to a woman.

"'Alack! What will become of me! Senor Oficial, have pity on me! You are so young, so good-looking.' Then, in a lower tone, she said, 'Let me get away, and I'll give you a bit of the *bar lachi*, that will make every woman fall in love with you!'

---

[10] *Pintar un javeque*, "paint a xebec," a particular type of ship. Most Spanish vessels of this description have a checkered red and white stripe painted around them.

"The *bar lachi*, sir, is the loadstone, with which the gypsies declare one who knows how to use it can cast any number of spells. If you can make a woman drink a little scrap of it, powdered, in a glass of white wine, she'll never be able to resist you. I answered, as gravely as I could:

"'We are not here to talk nonsense. You'll have to go to prison. Those are my orders, and there's no help for it!'

"We men from the Basque country have an accent which all Spaniards easily recognize; on the other hand, not one of them can ever learn to say *Bai, jaona!*[11]

"So Carmen easily guessed I was from the Provinces. You know, sir, that the gypsies, who belong to no particular country, and are always moving about, speak every language, and most of them are quite at home in Portugal, in France, in our Provinces, in Catalonia, or anywhere else. They can even make themselves understood by Moors and English people. Carmen knew Basque tolerably well.

"'*Laguna ene bihotsarena*, comrade of my heart,' said she suddenly. 'Do you belong to our country?'

"Our language is so beautiful, sir, that when we hear it in a foreign country it makes us quiver. I wish," added the bandit in a lower tone, "I could have a confessor from my own country."

After a silence, he began again.

"'I belong to Elizondo,' I answered in Basque, very much affected by the sound of my own language.

"'I come from Etchalar,' said she (that's a district about four hours' journey from my home). 'I was carried off to Seville by the gypsies. I was working in the factory to earn enough money to take me back to Navarre, to my poor old mother, who has no support in the world but me, besides her little *barratcea*[12] with twenty cider-apple trees in it. Ah! if I were only back in my own country, looking up at the white mountains! I have been insulted here, because I don't belong to this land of rogues and sellers of rotten oranges; and those hussies are all banded together against

---

[11] Yes, sir.
[12] Field, garden.

me, because I told them that not all their Seville *jacques*,[13] and all their knives, would frighten an honest lad from our country, with his blue cap and his *maquila*! Good comrade, won't you do anything to help your own countrywoman?'

"She was lying then, sir, as she has always lied. I don't know that that girl ever spoke a word of truth in her life, but when she did speak, I believed her — I couldn't help myself. She mangled her Basque words, and I believed she came from Navarre. But her eyes and her mouth and her skin were enough to prove she was a gypsy. I was mad, I paid no more attention to anything, I thought to myself that if the Spaniards had dared to speak evil of my country, I would have slashed their faces just as she had slashed her comrade's. In short, I was like a drunken man, I was beginning to say foolish things, and I was very near doing them.

"'If I were to give you a push and you tumbled down, good fellow-countryman,' she began again in Basque, 'those two Castilian recruits wouldn't be able to keep me back.'

"Faith, I forgot my orders, I forgot everything, and I said to her, 'Well, then, my friend, girl of my country, try it, and may our Lady of the Mountain help you through.'

"Just at that moment we were passing one of the many narrow lanes one sees in Seville. All at once Carmen turned and struck me in the chest with her fist. I tumbled backward, purposely. With a bound she sprang over me, and ran off, showing us a pair of legs! People talk about a pair of Basque legs! but hers were far better — as fleet as they were well-turned. As for me, I picked myself up at once, but I stuck out my lance[14] crossways and barred the street, so that my comrades were checked at the very first moment of pursuit. Then I started to run myself, and they after me — but how were we to catch her? There was no fear of that, what with our spurs, our swords, and our lances.

"In less time than I have taken to tell you the story the prisoner had disappeared. And besides, every gossip in the quarter

---

[13] Bravos, boasters.
[14] All Spanish cavalry soldiers carry lances.

103

covered her flight, poked scorn at us, and pointed us in the wrong direction. After a good deal of marching and countermarching, we had to go back to the guard-room without a receipt from the governor of the jail.

"To avoid punishment, my men made known that Carmen had spoken to me in Basque; and to tell the truth, it did not seem very natural that a blow from such a little creature should have so easily overthrown a strong fellow like me. The whole thing looked suspicious, or, at all events, not over-clear. When I came off guard I lost my corporal's stripes, and was condemned to a month's imprisonment. It was the first time I had been punished since I had been in the service. Farewell, now, to the sergeant's stripes, on which I had reckoned so surely!

"The first days in prison were very dreary. When I enlisted I had fancied I was sure to become an officer, at all events. Two of my compatriots, Longa and Mina, are captains-general, after all. Chapalangarra was a colonel, and I have played tennis a score of times with his brother, who was just a needy fellow like myself. 'Now,' I kept crying to myself, 'all the time you served without being punished has been lost. Now you have a bad mark against your name, and to get yourself back into the officers' good graces you'll have to work ten times as hard as when you joined as a recruit.' And why have I got myself punished? For the sake of a gypsy hussy, who made game of me, and who at this moment is busy thieving in some corner of the town. Yet I couldn't help thinking about her. Will you believe it, sir, those silk stockings of hers with the holes in them, of which she had given me such a full view as she took to her heels, were always before my eyes? I used to look through the barred windows of the jail into the street, and among all the women who passed I never could see one to compare with that minx of a girl — and then, in spite of myself, I used to smell the acacia blossom she had thrown at me, and which, dry as it was, still kept its sweet scent. If there are such things as witches, that girl certainly was one.

"One day the jailer came in, and gave me an Alcala roll.[15]

"'Look here,' said he, 'this is what your cousin has sent you.'

"I took the loaf, very much astonished, for I had no cousin in Seville. It may be a mistake, thought I, as I looked at the roll, but it was so appetizing and smelt so good, that I made up my mind to eat it, without troubling my head as to whence it came, or for whom it was really intended.

"When I tried to cut it, my knife struck on something hard. I looked, and found a little English file, which had been slipped into the dough before the roll had been baked. The roll also contained a gold piece of two piastres. Then I had no further doubt — it was a present from Carmen. To people of her blood, liberty is everything, and they would set a town on fire to save themselves one day in prison. The girl was artful, indeed, and armed with that roll, I might have snapped my fingers at the jailers. In one hour, with that little file, I could have sawn through the thickest bar, and with the gold coin I could have exchanged my soldier's cloak for civilian garb at the nearest shop. You may fancy that a man who has often taken the eaglets out of their nests in our cliff would have found no difficulty in getting down to the street out of a window less than thirty feet above it. But I didn't choose to escape. I still had a soldier's code of honour, and desertion appeared to me in the light of a heinous crime. Yet this proof of remembrance touched me. When a man is in prison he likes to think he has a friend outside who takes an interest in him. The gold coin did rather offend me; I should have very much liked to return it; but where was I to find my creditor? That did not seem a very easy task.

"After the ceremony of my degradation I had fancied my sufferings were over, but I had another humiliation before me. That came when I left prison, and was told off for duty, and put on sentry, as a private soldier. You can not conceive what a proud man endures at such a moment. I believe I would have just as

---

[15] *Alcala de los Panaderos*, a village two leagues from Seville, where the most delicious rolls are made. They are said to owe their quality to the water of the place, and great quantities of them are brought to Seville every day.

soon been shot dead — then I should have marched alone at the head of my platoon, at all events; I should have felt I was somebody, with the eyes of others fixed upon me.

"I was posted as sentry on the door of the colonel's house. The colonel was a young man, rich, good-natured, fond of amusing himself. All the young officers were there, and many civilians as well, besides ladies — actresses, as it was said. For my part, it seemed to me as if the whole town had agreed to meet at that door, in order to stare at me. Then up drove the colonel's carriage, with his valet on the box. And who should I see get out of it, but the gypsy girl! She was dressed up, this time, to the eyes, togged out in golden ribbons — a spangled gown, blue shoes, all spangled too, flowers and gold lace all over her. In her hand she carried a tambourine. With her there were two other gypsy women, one young and one old. They always have one old woman who goes with them, and then an old man with a guitar, a gypsy too, to play alone, and also for their dances. You must know these gypsy girls are often sent for to private houses, to dance their special dance, the *Romalis*, and often, too, for quite other purposes.

"Carmen recognized me, and we exchanged glances. I don't know why, but at that moment I should have liked to have been a hundred feet beneath the ground.

"'*Agur laguna*,'[16] said she. 'Oficial mio! You keep guard like a recruit,' and before I could find a word in answer, she was inside the house.

"The whole party was assembled in the *patio*, and in spite of the crowd I could see nearly everything that went on through the lattice.[17] I could hear the castanets and the tambourine, the laughter and applause. Sometimes I caught a glimpse of her head

---

[16] Good-day, comrade!

[17] In most of the houses in Seville there is an inner court surrounded by an arched portico. This is used as a sitting-room in summer. Over the court is stretched a piece of tent cloth, which is watered during the day and removed at night. The street door is almost always left open, and the passage leading to the court (*zaguan*) is closed by an iron lattice of very elegant workmanship.

as she bounded upward with her tambourine. Then I could hear the officers saying many things to her which brought the blood to my face. As to her answers, I knew nothing of them. It was on that day, I think, that I began to love her in earnest — for three or four times I was tempted to rush into the *patio*, and drive my sword into the bodies of all the coxcombs who were making love to her. My torture lasted a full hour; then the gypsies came out, and the carriage took them away. As she passed me by, Carmen looked at me with those eyes you know, and said to me very low, 'Comrade, people who are fond of good *fritata* come to eat it at Lillas Pastia's at Triana!'

"Then, light as a kid, she stepped into the carriage, the coachman whipped up his mules, and the whole merry party departed, whither I know not.

"You may fancy that the moment I was off guard I went to Triana; but first of all I got myself shaved and brushed myself up as if I had been going on parade. She was living with Lillas Pastia, an old fried-fish seller, a gypsy, as black as a Moor, to whose house a great many civilians resorted to eat *fritata*, especially, I think, because Carmen had taken up her quarters there.

"'Lillas,' she said, as soon as she saw me. 'I'm not going to work any more to-day. To-morrow will be a day, too.[18] Come, fellow-countryman, let us go for a walk!'

"She pulled her mantilla across her nose, and there we were in the street, without my knowing in the least whither I was bound.

"'Senorita,' said I, 'I think I have to thank you for a present I had while I was in prison. I've eaten the bread; the file will do for sharpening my lance, and I keep it in remembrance of you. But as for the money, here it is.'

"'Why, he's kept the money!' she exclaimed, bursting out laughing. 'But, after all, that's all the better — for I'm decidedly

[18] *Manana sera otro dia.* — A Spanish proverb.

107

hard up! What matter! The dog that runs never starves![19] Come, let's spend it all! You shall treat.'

"We had turned back toward Seville. At the entrance of the *Calle de la Serpiente* she bought a dozen oranges, which she made me put into my handkerchief. A little farther on she bought a roll, a sausage, and a bottle of manzanilla. Then, last of all, she turned into a confectioner's shop. There she threw the gold coin I had returned to her on the counter, with another she had in her pocket, and some small silver, and then she asked me for all the money I had. All I possessed was one peseta and a few cuartos, which I handed over to her, very much ashamed of not having more. I thought she would have carried away the whole shop. She took everything that was best and dearest, *yemas, turon,* preserved fruits — as long as the money lasted. And all these, too, I had to carry in paper bags. Perhaps you know the *Calle del Candilejo,* where there is a head of Don Pedro the Avenger.[20] That head

---

[19] *Chuquel sos pirela, cocal terela.* "The dog that runs finds a bone." — Gypsy proverb.

[20] This king, Don Pedro, whom we call "the Cruel," and whom Queen Isabella, the Catholic, never called anything but "the Avenger," was fond of walking about the streets of Seville at night in search of adventures, like the Caliph Haroun al Raschid. One night, in a lonely street, he quarreled with a man who was singing a serenade. There was a fight, and the king killed the amorous *caballero.* At the clashing of their swords, an old woman put her head out of the window and lighted up the scene with a tiny lamp (candilejo) which she held in her hand. My readers must be informed that King Don Pedro, though nimble and muscular, suffered from one strange fault in his physical conformation. Whenever he walked his knees cracked loudly. By this cracking the old woman easily recognized him. The next day the *veintiquatro* in charge came to make his report to the king. "Sir, a duel was fought last night in such a street — one of the combatants is dead." "Have you found the murderer?" "Yes, sir." "Why has he not been punished already?" "Sir, I await your orders!" "Carry out the law." Now the king had just published a decree that every duelist was to have his head cut off, and that head was to be set up on the scene of the fight. The *veintiquatro* got out of the difficulty like a clever man. He had the head sawed off a statue of the king, and set that up in a niche in the middle of the street in which the murder had taken place. The king and all the Sevillians thought this a very good joke. The street took its name from the lamp held by the old woman, the only witness of the incident. The above is the

ought to have given me pause. We stopped at an old house in that street. She passed into the entry, and knocked at a door on the ground floor. It was opened by a gypsy, a thorough-paced servant of the devil. Carmen said a few words to her in Romany. At first the old hag grumbled. To smooth her down Carmen gave her a couple of oranges and a handful of sugar-plums, and let her have a taste of wine. Then she hung her cloak on her back, and led her to the door, which she fastened with a wooden bar. As soon as we were alone she began to laugh and caper like a lunatic, singing out, 'You are my *rom*, I'm your *romi*.'[21]

"There I stood in the middle of the room, laden with all her purchases, and not knowing where I was to put them down. She tumbled them all onto the floor, and threw her arms round my neck, saying:

"'I pay my debts, I pay my debts! That's the law of the *Cales*.'[22]

"Ah, sir, that day! that day! When I think of it I forget what to-morrow must bring me!"

For a moment the bandit held his peace, then, when he had relighted his cigar, he began afresh.

"We spent the whole day together, eating, drinking, and so forth. When she had stuffed herself with sugar-plums, like any child of six years old, she thrust them by handfuls into the old woman's water-jar. 'That'll make sherbet for her,' she said. She smashed the *yemas* by throwing them against the walls. 'They'll keep the flies from bothering us.' There was no prank or wild frolic she didn't indulge in. I told her I should have liked to see her dance, only there were no castanets to be had. Instantly she

---

popular tradition. Zuniga tells the story somewhat differently. However that may be, a street called *Calle del Candilejo* still exists in Seville, and in that street there is a bust which is said to be a portrait of Don Pedro. This bust, unfortunately, is a modern production. During the seventeenth century the old one had become very much defaced, and the municipality had it replaced by that now to be seen.

[21] *Rom*, husband. *Romi*, wife.

[22] *Calo*, feminine *calli*, plural *cales*. Literally "black," the name the gypsies apply to themselves in their own language.

seized the old woman's only earthenware plate, smashed it up, and there she was dancing the *Romalis*, and making the bits of broken crockery rattle as well as if they had been ebony and ivory castanets. That girl was good company, I can tell you! Evening fell, and I heard the drums beating tattoo.

"'I must get back to quarters for roll-call,' I said.

"'To quarters!' she answered, with a look of scorn. 'Are you a negro slave, to let yourself be driven with a ramrod like that! You are as silly as a canary bird. Your dress suits your nature.[23] Pshaw! you've no more heart than a chicken.'

"I stayed on, making up my mind to the inevitable guard-room. The next morning the first suggestion of parting came from her.

"'Hark ye, Joseito,' she said. 'Have I paid you? By our law, I owed you nothing, because you're a *payllo*. But you're a good-looking fellow, and I took a fancy to you. Now we're quits. Good-day!'

"I asked her when I should see her again.

"'When you're less of a simpleton,' she retorted, with a laugh. Then, in a more serious tone, 'Do you know, my son, I really believe I love you a little; but that can't last! The dog and the wolf can't agree for long. Perhaps if you turned gypsy, I might care to be your *romi*. But that's all nonsense, such things aren't possible. Pshaw! my boy. Believe me, you're well out of it. You've come across the devil — he isn't always black — and you've not had your neck wrung. I wear a woolen suit, but I'm no sheep.[24] Go and burn a candle to your *majari*,[25] she deserves it well. Come, good-by once more. Don't think any more about *La Carmencita*, or she'll end by making you marry a widow with wooden legs.'[26]

"As she spoke, she drew back the bar that closed the door, and once we were out in the street she wrapped her mantilla about her, and turned on her heel.

---

[23] Spanish dragoons wear a yellow uniform.
[24] *Me dicas vriarda de jorpoy, bus ne sino braco.* — A gypsy proverb.
[25] The Saint, the Holy Virgin.
[26] The gallows, which is the widow of the last man hanged upon it.

"She spoke the truth. I should have done far better never to think of her again. But after that day in the *Calle del Candilejo* I couldn't think of anything else. All day long I used to walk about, hoping I might meet her. I sought news of her from the old hag, and from the fried-fish seller. They both told me she had gone away to *Laloro*, which is their name for Portugal. They probably said it by Carmen's orders, but I soon found out they were lying. Some weeks after my day in the *Calle del Candilejo* I was on duty at one of the town gates. A little way from the gate there was a breach in the wall. The masons were working at it in the daytime, and at night a sentinel was posted on it, to prevent smugglers from getting in. All through one day I saw Lillas Pastia going backward and forward near the guard-room, and talking to some of my comrades. They all knew him well, and his fried-fish and fritters even better. He came up to me, and asked if I had any news of Carmen.

"'No,' said I.

"'Well,' said he, 'you'll soon hear of her, old fellow.'

"He was not mistaken. That night I was posted to guard the breach in the wall. As soon as the sergeant had disappeared I saw a woman coming toward me. My heart told me it was Carmen. Still I shouted:

"'Keep off! Nobody can pass here!'

"'Now, don't be spiteful,' she said, making herself known to me.

"'What! you here, Carmen?'

"'Yes, *mi payllo*. Let us say few words, but wise ones. Would you like to earn a douro? Some people will be coming with bundles. Let them alone.'

"'No,' said I, 'I must not allow them through. These are my orders.'

"'Orders! orders! You didn't think about orders in the *Calle del Candilejo!*'

"'Ah!' I cried, quite maddened by the very thought of that night. 'It was well worth while to forget my orders for that! But I won't have any smuggler's money!'

"'Well, if you won't have money, shall we go and dine together at old Dorotea's?'

"'No,' said I, half choked by the effort it cost me. 'No, I can't.'

"'Very good! If you make so many difficulties, I know to whom I can go. I'll ask your officer if he'll come with me to Dorotea's. He looks good-natured, and he'll post a sentry who'll only see what he had better see. Good-bye, canary-bird! I shall have a good laugh the day the order comes out to hang you!'

"I was weak enough to call her back, and I promised to let the whole of gypsydom pass in, if that were necessary, so that I secured the only reward I longed for. She instantly swore she would keep her word faithfully the very next day, and ran off to summon her friends, who were close by. There were five of them, of whom Pastia was one, all well loaded with English goods. Carmen kept watch for them. She was to warn them with her castanets the instant she caught sight of the patrol. But there was no necessity for that. The smugglers finished their job in a moment.

"The next day I went to the *Calle del Candilejo*. Carmen kept me waiting, and when she came, she was in rather a bad temper.

"'I don't like people who have to be pressed,' she said. 'You did me a much greater service the first time, without knowing you'd gain anything by it. Yesterday you bargained with me. I don't know why I've come, for I don't care for you any more. Here, be off with you. Here's a douro for your trouble.'

"I very nearly threw the coin at her head, and I had to make a violent effort to prevent myself from actually beating her. After we had wrangled for an hour I went off in a fury. For some time I wandered about the town, walking hither and thither like a madman. At last I went into a church, and getting into the darkest corner I could find, I cried hot tears. All at once I heard a voice.

"'A dragoon in tears. I'll make a philter of them!'

"I looked up. There was Carmen in front of me.

"'Well, *mi payllo*, are you still angry with me?' she said. 'I must care for you in spite of myself, for since you left me I don't know what has been the matter with me. Look you, it is I who ask you to come to the *Calle del Candilejo*, now!'

"So we made it up: but Carmen's temper was like the weather in our country. The storm is never so close, in our mountains, as when the sun is at its brightest. She had promised to meet me again at Dorotea's, but she didn't come.

"And Dorotea began telling me again that she had gone off to Portugal about some gypsy business.

"As experience had already taught me how much of that I was to believe, I went about looking for Carmen wherever I thought she might be, and twenty times in every day I walked through the *Calle del Candilejo*. One evening I was with Dorotea, whom I had almost tamed by giving her a glass of anisette now and then, when Carmen walked in, followed by a young man, a lieutenant in our regiment.

"'Get away at once,' she said to me in Basque. I stood there, dumfounded, my heart full of rage.

"'What are you doing here?' said the lieutenant to me. 'Take yourself off — get out of this.'

"I couldn't move a step. I felt paralyzed. The officer grew angry, and seeing I did not go out, and had not even taken off my forage cap, he caught me by the collar and shook me roughly. I don't know what I said to him. He drew his sword, and I unsheathed mine. The old woman caught hold of my arm, and the lieutenant gave me a wound on the forehead, of which I still bear the scar. I made a step backward, and with one jerk of my elbow I threw old Dorotea down. Then, as the lieutenant still pressed me, I turned the point of my sword against his body and he ran upon it. Then Carmen put out the lamp and told Dorotea, in her own language, to take to flight. I fled into the street myself, and began running along, I knew not whither. It seemed to me that some one was following me. When I came to myself I discovered that Carmen had never left me.

"'Great stupid of a canary-bird!' she said, 'you never make anything but blunders. And, indeed, you know I told you I should bring you bad luck. But come, there's a cure for everything when you have a Fleming from Rome[27] for your love. Begin by rolling this handkerchief round your head, and throw me over that belt of yours. Wait for me in this alley — I'll be back in two minutes.

"She disappeared, and soon came back bringing me a striped cloak which she had gone to fetch, I knew not whence. She made me take off my uniform, and put on the cloak over my shirt. Thus dressed, and with the wound on my head bound round with the handkerchief, I was tolerably like a Valencian peasant, many of whom come to Seville to sell a drink they make out of '*chufas.*'[28] Then she took me to a house very much like Dorotea's, at the bottom of a little lane. Here she and another gypsy woman washed and dressed my wounds, better than any army surgeon could have done, gave me something, I know not what, to drink, and finally made me lie down on a mattress, on which I went to sleep.

"Probably the woman had mixed one of the soporific drugs of which they know the secret in my drink, for I did not wake up till very late the next day. I was rather feverish, and had a violent headache. It was some time before the memory of the terrible scene in which I had taken part on the previous night came back to me. After having dressed my wound, Carmen and her friend, squatting on their heels beside my mattress, exchanged a few words of '*chipe calli,*' which appeared to me to be something in the nature of a medical consultation. Then they both of them assured me that I should soon be cured, but that I must get out of Seville at the earliest possible moment, for that, if I was caught there, I should most undoubtedly be shot.

[27] *Flamenco de Roma*, a slang term for the gypsies. Roma does not stand for the Eternal City, but for the nation of the *romi*, or the married folk — a name applied by the gypsies to themselves. The first gypsies seen in Spain probably came from the Low Countries, hence their name of *Flemings*.
[28] A bulbous root, out of which rather a pleasant beverage is manufactured.

"'My boy,' said Carmen to me, 'you'll have to do something. Now that the king won't give you either rice or haddock[29] you'll have to think of earning your livelihood. You're too stupid for stealing *a pastesas*.[30] But you are brave and active. If you have the pluck, take yourself off to the coast and turn smuggler. Haven't I promised to get you hanged? That's better than being shot, and besides, if you set about it properly, you'll live like a prince as long as the *minons*[31] and the coast-guard don't lay their hands on your collar.'

"In this attractive guise did this fiend of a girl describe the new career she was suggesting to me, — the only one, indeed, remaining, now I had incurred the penalty of death. Shall I confess it, sir? She persuaded me without much difficulty. This wild and dangerous life, it seemed to me, would bind her and me more closely together. In future, I thought, I should be able to make sure of her love.

"I had often heard talk of certain smugglers who traveled about Andalusia, each riding a good horse, with his mistress behind him and his blunderbuss in his fist. Already I saw myself trotting up and down the world, with a pretty gypsy behind me. When I mentioned that notion to her, she laughed till she had to hold her sides, and vowed there was nothing in the world so delightful as a night spent camping in the open air, when each *rom* retired with his *romi* beneath their little tent, made of three hoops with a blanket thrown across them.

"'If I take to the mountains,' said I to her, 'I shall be sure of you. There'll be no lieutenant there to go shares with me.'

"'Ha! ha! you're jealous!' she retorted, 'so much the worse for you. How can you be such a fool as that? Don't you see I must love you, because I have never asked you for money?'

"When she said that sort to thing I could have strangled her.

"To shorten the story, sir, Carmen procured me civilian clothes, disguised in which I got out of Seville without being

---

[29] The ordinary food of a Spanish soldier.

[30] *Ustilar a pastesas*, to steal cleverly, to purloin without violence.

[31] *Ustilar a pastesas*, to steal cleverly, to purloin without violence.

recognized. I went to Jerez, with a letter from Pastia to a dealer in anisette whose house was the smugglers' meeting-place. I was introduced to them, and their leader, surnamed *El Dancaire*, enrolled me in his gang. We started for Gaucin, where I found Carmen, who had told me she would meet me there. In all these expeditions she acted as spy for our gang, and she was the best that ever was seen. She had now just returned from Gibraltar, and had already arranged with the captain of a ship for a cargo of English goods which we were to receive on the coast. We went to meet it near Estepona. We hid part in the mountains, and laden with the rest, we proceeded to Ronda. Carmen had gone there before us. It was she again who warned us when we had better enter the town. This first journey, and several subsequent ones, turned out well. I found the smuggler's life pleasanter than a soldier's: I could give presents to Carmen, I had money, and I had a mistress. I felt little or no remorse, for, as the gypsies say, 'The happy man never longs to scratch his itch.' We were made welcome everywhere, my comrades treated me well, and even showed me a certain respect. The reason of this was that I had killed my man, and that some of them had no exploit of that description on their conscience. But what I valued most in my new life was that I often saw Carmen. She showed me more affection than ever; nevertheless, she would never admit, before my comrades, that she was my mistress, and she had even made me swear all sorts of oaths that I would not say anything about her to them. I was so weak in that creature's hands, that I obeyed all her whims. And besides, this was the first time she had revealed herself as possessing any of the reserve of a well-conducted woman, and I was simple enough to believe she had really cast off her former habits.

"Our gang, which consisted of eight or ten men, was hardly ever together except at decisive moments, and we were usually scattered by twos and threes about the towns and villages. Each one of us pretended to have some trade. One was a tinker, another was a groom; I was supposed to peddle haberdashery, but I hardly ever showed myself in large places, on account of my unlucky business at Seville. One day, or rather one night, we were to meet below Veger. *El Dancaire* and I got there before the others.

"'We shall soon have a new comrade,' said he. 'Carmen has just managed one of her best tricks. She has contrived the escape of her *rom*, who was in the *presidio* at Tarifa.'

"I was already beginning to understand the gypsy language, which nearly all my comrades spoke, and this word *rom* startled me.

"'What! her husband? Is she married, then?' said I to the captain.

"'Yes!' he replied, 'married to Garcia *el Tuerto*[32] — as cunning a gypsy as she is herself. The poor fellow has been at the galleys. Carmen has wheedled the surgeon of the *presidio* to such good purpose that she has managed to get her *rom* out of prison. Faith! that girl's worth her weight in gold. For two years she has been trying to contrive his escape, but she could do nothing until the authorities took it into their heads to change the surgeon. She soon managed to come to an understanding with this new one.'

"You may imagine how pleasant this news was for me. I soon saw Garcia *el Tuerto*. He was the very ugliest brute that was ever nursed in gypsydom. His skin was black, his soul was blacker, and he was altogether the most thorough-paced ruffian I ever came across in my life. Carmen arrived with him, and when she called him her *rom* in my presence, you should have seen the eyes she made at me, and the faces she pulled whenever Garcia turned his head away.

"I was disgusted, and never spoke a word to her all night. The next morning we had made up our packs, and had already started, when we became aware that we had a dozen horsemen on our heels. The braggart Andalusians, who had been boasting they would murder every one who came near them, cut a pitiful figure at once. There was a general rout. *El Dancaire*, Garcia, a good-looking fellow from Ecija, who was called *El Remendado*, and

---

[32] One-eyed man.

117

Carmen herself, kept their wits about them. The rest forsook the mules and took to the gorges, where the horses could not follow them. There was no hope of saving the mules, so we hastily unstrapped the best part of our booty, and taking it on our shoulders, we tried to escape through the rocks down the steepest of the slopes. We threw our packs down in front of us and followed them as best we could, slipping along on our heels. Meanwhile the enemy fired at us. It was the first time I had ever heard bullets whistling around me and I didn't mind it very much. When there's a woman looking on, there's no particular merit in snapping one's fingers at death. We all escaped except the poor *Remendado*, who received a bullet wound in the loins. I threw away my pack and tried to lift him up.

"'Idiot!' shouted Garcia, 'what do we want with offal! Finish him off, and don't lose the cotton stockings!'

"'Drop him!' cried Carmen.

"I was so exhausted that I was obliged to lay him down for a moment under a rock. Garcia came up, and fired his blunderbuss full into his face. 'He'd be a clever fellow who recognized him now!' said he, as he looked at the face, cut to pieces by a dozen slugs.

"There, sir; that's the delightful sort of life I've led! That night we found ourselves in a thicket, worn out with fatigue, with nothing to eat, and ruined by the loss of our mules. What do you think that devil Garcia did? He pulled a pack of cards out of his pocket and began playing games with *El Dancaire* by the light of a fire they kindled. Meanwhile I was lying down, staring at the stars, thinking of *El Remendado*, and telling myself I would just as lief be in his place. Carmen was squatting down near me, and every now and then she would rattle her castanets and hum a tune. Then, drawing close to me, as if she would have whispered in my ear, she kissed me two or three times over almost against my will.

"'You are a devil,' said I to her.

"'Yes,' she replied.

"After a few hours' rest, she departed to Gaucin, and the next morning a little goatherd brought us some food. We stayed there all that day, and in the evening we moved close to Gaucin. We were expecting news from Carmen, but none came. After daylight broke we saw a muleteer attending a well-dressed woman with a parasol, and a little girl who seemed to be her servant. Said Garcia, 'There go two mules and two women whom St. Nicholas has sent us. I would rather have had four mules, but no matter. I'll do the best I can with these.'

"He took his blunderbuss, and went down the pathway, hiding himself among the brushwood.

"We followed him, *El Dancaire* and I keeping a little way behind. As soon as the woman saw us, instead of being frightened — and our dress would have been enough to frighten any one — she burst into a fit of loud laughter. 'Ah! the *lillipendi*! They take me for an *erani*!'[33]

"It was Carmen, but so well disguised that if she had spoken any other language I should never have recognized her. She sprang off her mule, and talked some time in an undertone with *El Dancaire* and Garcia. Then she said to me:

"'Canary-bird, we shall meet again before you're hanged. I'm off to Gibraltar on gypsy business — you'll soon have news of me.'

"We parted, after she had told us of a place where we should find shelter for some days. That girl was the providence of our gang. We soon received some money sent by her, and a piece of news which was still more useful to us — to the effect that on a certain day two English lords would travel from Gibraltar to Granada by a road she mentioned. This was a word to the wise. They had plenty of good guineas. Garcia would have killed them, but *El Dancaire* and I objected. All we took from them, besides their shirts, which we greatly needed, was their money and their watches.

---

[33] "The idiots, they take me for a smart lady!

"Sir, a man may turn rogue in sheer thoughtlessness. You lose your head over a pretty girl, you fight another man about her, there is a catastrophe, you have to take to the mountains, and you turn from a smuggler into a robber before you have time to think about it. After this matter of the English lords, we concluded that the neighbourhood of Gibraltar would not be healthy for us, and we plunged into the *Sierra de Ronda*. You once mentioned Jose-Maria to me. Well, it was there I made acquaintance with him. He always took his mistress with him on his expeditions. She was a pretty girl, quiet, modest, well-mannered, you never heard a vulgar word from her, and she was quite devoted to him. He, on his side, led her a very unhappy life. He was always running after other women, he ill-treated her, and then sometimes he would take it into his head to be jealous. One day he slashed her with a knife. Well, she only doted on him the more! That's the way with women, and especially with Andalusians. This girl was proud of the scar on her arm, and would display it as though it were the most beautiful thing in the world. And then Jose-Maria was the worst of comrades in the bargain. In one expedition we made with him, he managed so that he kept all the profits, and we had all the trouble and the blows. But I must go back to my story. We had no sign at all from Carmen. *El Dancaire* said: 'One of us will have to go to Gibraltar to get news of her. She must have planned some business. I'd go at once, only I'm too well known at Gibraltar.' *El Tuerto* said:

"'I'm well known there too. I've played so many tricks on the crayfish[34] — and as I've only one eye, it is not overeasy for me to disguise myself.'

"'Then I suppose I must go,' said I, delighted at the very idea of seeing Carmen again. 'Well, how am I to set about it?'

"The others answered:

"'You must either go by sea, or you must get through by San Rocco, whichever you like the best; once you are in Gibraltar, inquire in the port where a chocolate-seller called *La Rollona*

---

[34] Name applied by the Spanish populace to the British soldiers, on account of the colour of their uniform.

lives. When you've found her, she'll tell you everything that's happening.'

"It was settled that we were all to start for the Sierra, that I was to leave my two companions there, and take my way to Gibraltar, in the character of a fruit-seller. At Ronda one of our men procured me a passport; at Gaucin I was provided with a donkey. I loaded it with oranges and melons, and started forth. When I reached Gibraltar I found that many people knew *La Rollona*, but that she was either dead or had gone *ad finibus terrae*,[35] and, to my mind, her disappearance explained the failure of our correspondence with Carmen. I stabled my donkey, and began to move about the town, carrying my oranges as though to sell them, but in reality looking to see whether I could not come across any face I knew. The place is full of ragamuffins from every country in the world, and it really is like the Tower of Babel, for you can't go ten paces along a street without hearing as many languages. I did see some gypsies, but I hardly dared confide in them. I was taking stock of them, and they were taking stock of me. We had mutually guessed each other to be rogues, but the important thing for us was to know whether we belonged to the same gang. After having spent two days in fruitless wanderings, and having found out nothing either as to *La Rollona* or as to Carmen, I was thinking I would go back to my comrades as soon as I had made a few purchases, when, toward sunset, as I was walking along a street, I heard a woman's voice from a window say, 'Orange-seller!'

"I looked up, and on a balcony I saw Carmen looking out, beside a scarlet-coated officer with gold epaulettes, curly hair, and all the appearance of a rich *milord*. As for her, she was magnificently dressed, a shawl hung on her shoulders, she'd a gold comb in her hair, everything she wore was of silk; and the cunning little wretch, not a bit altered, was laughing till she held her sides.

---

[35] To the galleys, or else to all the devils in hell.

"The Englishman shouted to me in mangled Spanish to come upstairs, as the lady wanted some oranges, and Carmen said to me in Basque:

"'Come up, and don't look astonished at anything!'

"Indeed, nothing that she did ought ever to have astonished me. I don't know whether I was most happy or wretched at seeing her again. At the door of the house there was a tall English servant with a powdered head, who ushered me into a splendid drawing-room. Instantly Carmen said to me in Basque, 'You don't know one word of Spanish, and you don't know me.' Then turning to the Englishman, she added:

"'I told you so. I saw at once he was a Basque. Now you'll hear what a queer language he speaks. Doesn't he look silly? He's like a cat that's been caught in the larder!'

"'And you,' said I to her in my own language, 'you look like an impudent jade — and I've a good mind to scar your face here and now, before your spark.'

"'My spark!' said she. 'Why, you've guessed that all alone! Are you jealous of this idiot? You're even sillier than you were before our evening in the *Calle del Candilejo*! Don't you see, fool, that at this moment I'm doing gypsy business, and doing it in the most brilliant manner? This house belongs to me — the guineas of that crayfish will belong to me! I lead him by the nose, and I'll lead him to a place that he'll never get out of!'

"'And if I catch you doing any gypsy business in this style again, I'll see to it that you never do any again!' said I.

"'Ah! upon my word! Are you my *rom*, pray that you give me orders? If *El Tuerto* is pleased, what have you to do with it? Oughtn't you to be very happy that you are the only man who can call himself my *minchorro*?'[36]

"'What does he say?' inquired the Englishman.

"'He says he's thirsty, and would like a drink,' answered Carmen, and she threw herself back upon a sofa, screaming with laughter at her own translation.

---

[36] My "lover," or rather my "fancy."

"When that girl begins to laugh, sir, it was hopeless for anybody to try and talk sense. Everybody laughed with her. The big Englishman began to laugh too, like the idiot he was, and ordered the servant to bring me something to drink.

"While I was drinking she said to me:

"'Do you see that ring he has on his finger? If you like I'll give it to you.'

"And I answered:

"'I would give one of my fingers to have your *milord* out on the mountains, and each of us with a *maquila* in his fist.'

"'*Maquila*, what does that mean?' asked the Englishman.

"'Maquila,' said Carmen, still laughing, 'means an orange. Isn't it a queer word for an orange? He says he'd like you to eat *maquila*.'

"'Does he?' said the Englishman. 'Very well, bring more *maquila* to-morrow.'

"While we were talking a servant came in and said dinner was ready. Then the Englishman stood up, gave me a piastre, and offered his arm to Carmen, as if she couldn't have walked alone. Carmen, who was still laughing, said to me:

"'My boy, I can't ask you to dinner. But to-morrow, as soon as you hear the drums beat for parade, come here with your oranges. You'll find a better furnished room than the one in the *Calle del Candilejo*, and you'll see whether I am still your *Carmencita*. Then afterwards we'll talk about gypsy business.'

"I gave her no answer — even when I was in the street I could hear the Englishman shouting, 'Bring more *maquila* to-morrow,' and Carmen's peals of laughter.

"I went out, not knowing what I should do; I hardly slept, and next morning I was so enraged with the treacherous creature that I made up my mind to leave Gibraltar without seeing her again. But the moment the drums began to roll, my courage failed me. I took up my net full of oranges, and hurried off to Carmen's house. Her window-shutters had been pulled apart a little, and I saw her great dark eyes watching for me. The powdered servant showed me in at once. Carmen sent him out with a message, and as soon as we were alone she burst into one of her fits of crocodile laughter and threw her arms around my neck. Never had I seen her look so beautiful. She was dressed out like a queen, and scented; she had silken furniture, embroidered curtains — and I togged out like the thief I was!

"'*Minchorro*,' said Carmen, 'I've a good mind to smash up everything here, set fire to the house, and take myself off to the mountains.' And then she would fondle me, and then she would laugh, and she danced about and tore up her fripperies. Never did monkey gambol nor make such faces, nor play such wild tricks, as she did that day. When she had recovered her gravity —

"'Hark!' she said, 'this is gypsy business. I mean him to take me to Ronda, where I have a sister who is a nun' (here she shrieked with laughter again). 'We shall pass by a particular spot which I shall make known to you. Then you must fall upon him and strip him to the skin. Your best plan would be to do for him, but,' she added, with a certain fiendish smile of hers, which no one who saw it ever had any desire to imitate, 'do you know what you had better do? Let *El Tuerto* come up in front of you. You keep a little behind. The crayfish is brave, and skilful too, and he has good pistols. Do you understand?'

"And she broke off with another fit of laughter that made me shiver.

"'No,' said I, 'I hate Garcia, but he's my comrade. Some day, maybe, I'll rid you of him, but we'll settle our account after the fashion of my country. It's only chance that has made me a gypsy, and in certain things I shall always be a thorough Navarrese, as the proverb says.

"'You're a fool,' she rejoined, 'a simpleton, a regular *payllo*. You're just like the dwarf who thinks himself tall because he can spit a long way.[37] You don't love me! Be off with you!'

"Whenever she said to me 'Be off with you,' I couldn't go away. I promised I would start back to my comrades and wait the

---

[37] *Or esorjle de or marsichisle, sin chisnar lachinguel.* "The promise of a dwarf is that he will spit a long way." — A gypsy proverb.

arrival of the Englishman. She, on her side, promised she would be ill until she left Gibraltar for Ronda.

"I remained at Gibraltar two days longer. She had the boldness to disguise herself and come and see me at the inn. I departed, I had a plan of my own. I went back to our meeting-place with the information as to the spot and the hour at which the Englishman and Carmen were to pass by. I found *El Dancaire* and Garcia waiting for me. We spent the night in a wood, beside a fire made of pine-cones that blazed splendidly. I suggested to Garcia that we should play cards, and he agreed. In the second game I told him he was cheating; he began to laugh; I threw the cards in his face. He tried to get at his blunderbuss. I set my foot on it, and said, 'They say you can use a knife as well as the best ruffian in Malaga; will you try it with me?' *El Dancaire* tried to part us. I had given Garcia one or two cuffs, his rage had given him courage, he drew his knife, and I drew mine. We both of us told *El Dancaire* he must leave us alone, and let us fight it out. He saw there was no means of stopping us, so he stood on one side. Garcia was already bent double, like a cat ready to spring upon a mouse. He held his hat in his left hand to parry with, and his knife in front of him — that's their Andalusian guard. I stood up in the Navarrese fashion, with my left arm raised, my left leg forward, and my knife held straight along my right thigh. I felt I was stronger than any giant. He flew at me like an arrow. I turned round on my left foot, so that he found nothing in front of him. But I thrust him in the throat, and the knife went in so far that my hand was under his chin. I gave the blade such a twist that it broke. That was the end. The blade was carried out of the wound by a gush of blood as thick as my arm, and he fell full length on his face.

"'What have you done?' said *El Dancaire* to me.

"'Hark ye,' said I, 'we couldn't live on together. I love Carmen and I mean to be the only one. And besides, Garcia was a villain. I remember what he did to that poor *Remendado*. There are only two of us left now, but we are both good fellows. Come, will you have me for your friend, for life or death?'

"*El Dancaire* stretched out his hand. He was a man of fifty.

"'Devil take these love stories!' he cried. 'If you'd asked him for Carmen he'd have sold her to you for a piastre! There are only two of us now — how shall we manage for to-morrow?'

"'I'll manage it all alone,' I answered. 'I can snap my fingers at the whole world now.'

"We buried Garcia, and we moved our camp two hundred paces farther on. The next morning Carmen and her Englishman came along with two muleteers and a servant. I said to *El Dancaire*:

"'I'll look after the Englishman, you frighten the others — they're not armed!'

"The Englishman was a plucky fellow. He'd have killed me if Carmen hadn't jogged his elbow.

"To put it shortly, I won Carmen back that day, and my first words were to tell her she was a widow.

"When she knew how it had all happened —

"'You'll always be a *lillipendi*,' she said. 'Garcia ought to have killed you. Your Navarrese guard is a pack of nonsense, and he has sent far more skilful men than you into the darkness. It was just that his time had come — and yours will come too.'

"'Ay, and yours too! — if you're not a faithful *romi* to me.'

"'So be it,' said she. 'I've read in the coffee grounds, more than once, that you and I were to end our lives together. Pshaw! what must be, will be!' and she rattled her castanets, as was her way when she wanted to drive away some worrying thought.

"One runs on when one is talking about one's self. I dare say all these details bore you, but I shall soon be at the end of my story. Our new life lasted for some considerable time. *El Dancaire* and I gathered a few comrades about us, who were more trustworthy than our earlier ones, and we turned our attention to smuggling. Occasionally, indeed, I must confess we stopped travelers on the highways, but never unless we were at the last extremity, and could not avoid doing so; and besides, we never ill-treated the travelers, and confined ourselves to taking their money from them.

"For some months I was very well satisfied with Carmen. She still served us in our smuggling operations, by giving us notice of any opportunity of making a good haul. She remained either at Malaga, at Cordova, or at Granada, but at a word from me she would leave everything, and come to meet me at some *venta* or even in our lonely camp. Only once — it was at Malaga — she caused me some uneasiness. I heard she had fixed her fancy upon a very rich merchant, with whom she probably proposed to play her Gibraltar trick over again. In spite of everything *El Dancaire* said to stop me, I started off, walked into Malaga in broad daylight, sought for Carmen and carried her off instantly. We had a sharp altercation.

"'Do you know,' said she, 'now that you're my *rom* for good and all, I don't care for you so much as when you were my *minchorro*! I won't be worried, and above all, I won't be ordered about. I choose to be free to do as I like. Take care you don't drive me too far; if you tire me out, I'll find some good fellow who'll serve you just as you served *El Tuerto*.'

"*El Dancaire* patched it up between us; but we had said things to each other that rankled in our hearts, and we were not as we had been before. Shortly after that we had a misfortune: the soldiers caught us, *El Dancaire* and two of my comrades were killed; two others were taken. I was sorely wounded, and, but for my good horse, I should have fallen into the soldiers' hands. Half dead with fatigue, and with a bullet in my body, I sought shelter in a wood, with my only remaining comrade. When I got off my horse I fainted away, and I thought I was going to die there in the brushwood, like a shot hare. My comrade carried me to a cave he knew of, and then he sent to fetch Carmen.

"She was at Granada, and she hurried to me at once. For a whole fortnight she never left me for a single instant. She never closed her eyes; she nursed me with a skill and care such as no woman ever showed to the man she loved most tenderly. As soon as I could stand on my feet, she conveyed me with the utmost secrecy to Granada. These gypsy women find safe shelter everywhere, and I spent more than six weeks in a house only two doors from that of the *Corregidor* who was trying to arrest me. More than once I saw him pass by, from behind the shutter. At last I recovered, but I had thought a great deal, on my bed of pain, and I had planned to change my way of life. I suggested to Carmen that we should leave Spain, and seek an honest livelihood in the New World. She laughed in my face.

"'We were not born to plant cabbages,' she cried. 'Our fate is to live *payllos*! Listen: I've arranged a business with Nathan Ben-Joseph at Gibraltar. He has cotton stuffs that he can not get through till you come to fetch them. He knows you're alive, and reckons upon you. What would our Gibraltar correspondents say if you failed them?'

"I let myself by persuaded, and took up my vile trade once more.

"While I was hiding at Granada there were bull-fights there, to which Carmen went. When she came back she talked a great deal about a skilful *picador* of the name of Lucas. She knew the name of his horse, and how much his embroidered jacket had cost him. I paid no attention to this; but a few days later, Juanito, the only one of my comrades who was left, told me he had seen Carmen with Lucas in a shop in the Zacatin. Then I began to feel alarmed. I asked Carmen how and why she had made the *picador's* acquaintance.

"'He's a man out of whom we may be able to get something,' said she. 'A noisy stream has either water in it or pebbles. He has earned twelve hundred reals at the bull-fights. It must be one of two things: we must either have his money, or else, as he is a good rider and a plucky fellow, we can enroll him in our gang. We have lost such an one an such an one; you'll have to replace them. Take this man with you!'

"'I want neither his money nor himself,' I replied, 'and I forbid you to speak to him.'

"'Beware!' she retorted. 'If any one defies me to do a thing, it's very quickly done.'

"Luckily the *picador* departed to Malaga, and I set about passing in the Jew's cotton stuffs. This expedition gave me a great

128

deal to do, and Carmen as well. I forgot Lucas, and perhaps she forgot him too — for the moment, at all events. It was just about that time, sir, that I met you, first at Montilla, and then afterward at Cordova. I won't talk about that last interview. You know more about it, perhaps, than I do. Carmen stole your watch from you, she wanted to have your money besides, and especially that ring I see on your finger, and which she declared to be a magic ring, the possession of which was very important to her. We had a violent quarrel, and I struck her. She turned pale and began to cry. It was the first time I had ever seen her cry, and it affected me in the most painful manner. I begged her to forgive me, but she sulked with me for a whole day, and when I started back to Montilla she wouldn't kiss me. My heart was still very sore, when, three days later, she joined me with a smiling face and as merry as a lark. Everything was forgotten, and we were like a pair of honeymoon lovers. Just as we were parting she said, 'There's a *fete* at Cordova; I shall go and see it, and then I shall know what people will be coming away with money, and I can warn you.'

"I let her go. When I was alone I thought about the *fete*, and about the change in Carmen's temper. 'She must have avenged herself already,' said I to myself, 'since she was the first to make our quarrel up.' A peasant told me there was to be bull-fighting at Cordova. Then my blood began to boil, and I went off like a madman straight to the bull-ring. I had Lucas pointed out to me, and on the bench, just beside the barrier, I recognized Carmen. One glance at her was enough to turn my suspicion into certainty. When the first bull appeared Lucas began, as I had expected to play the agreeable; he snatched the cockade off the bull and presented it to Carmen, who put it in her hair at once.[38]

"The bull avenged me. Lucas was knocked down, with his horse on his chest, and the bull on top of both of them. I looked for Carmen, she had disappeared from her place already. I

---

[38] *La divisa.* A knot of ribbon, the colour of which indicates the pasturage from which each bull comes. This knot of ribbon is fastened into the bull's hide with a sort of hook, and it is considered the very height of gallantry to snatch it off the living beast and present it to a woman.

couldn't get out of mine, and I was obliged to wait until the bull-fight was over. Then I went off to that house you already know, and waited there quietly all that evening and part of the night. Toward two o'clock in the morning Carmen came back, and was rather surprised to see me.

"'Come with me,' said I.

"'Very well,' said she, 'let's be off.'

"I went and got my horse, and took her up behind me, and we traveled all the rest of the night without saying a word to each other. When daylight came we stopped at a lonely inn, not far from a hermitage. There I said to Carmen:

"'Listen — I forget everything, I won't mention anything to you. But swear one thing to me — that you'll come with me to America, and live there quietly!'

"'No,' said she, in a sulky voice, 'I won't go to America — I am very well here.'

"'That's because you're near Lucas. But be very sure that even if he gets well now, he won't make old bones. And, indeed, why should I quarrel with him? I'm tired of killing all your lovers; I'll kill you this time.'

"She looked at me steadily with her wild eyes, and then she said:

"'I've always thought you would kill me. The very first time I saw you I had just met a priest at the door of my house. And to-night, as we were going out of Cordova, didn't you see anything? A hare ran across the road between your horse's feet. It is fate.'

"'Carmencita,' I asked, 'don't you love me any more?'

"She gave me no answer, she was sitting cross-legged on a mat, making marks on the ground with her finger.

"'Let us change our life, Carmen,' said I imploringly. 'Let us go away and live somewhere we shall never be parted. You know we have a hundred and twenty gold ounces buried under an oak not far from here, and then we have more money with Ben-Joseph the Jew.'

"She began to smile, and then she said, 'Me first, and then you. I know it will happen like that.'

"'Think about it,' said I. 'I've come to the end of my patience and my courage. Make up your mind — or else I must make up mine.'

"I left her alone and walked toward the hermitage. I found the hermit praying. I waited till his prayer was finished. I longed to pray myself, but I couldn't. When he rose up from his knees I went to him.

"'Father,' I said, 'will you pray for some one who is in great danger?'

"'I pray for every one who is afflicted,' he replied.

"'Can you say a mass for a soul which is perhaps about to go into the presence of its Maker?'

"'Yes,' he answered, looking hard at me.

"And as there was something strange about me, he tried to make me talk.

"'It seems to me that I have seen you somewhere,' said he.

"I laid a piastre on his bench.

"'When shall you say the mass?' said I.

"'In half an hour. The son of the innkeeper yonder is coming to serve it. Tell me, young man, haven't you something on your conscience that is tormenting you? Will you listen to a Christian's counsel?'

"I could hardly restrain my tears. I told him I would come back, and hurried away. I went and lay down on the grass until I heard the bell. Then I went back to the chapel, but I stayed outside it. When he had said the mass, I went back to the *venta*. I was hoping Carmen would have fled. She could have taken my horse and ridden away. But I found her there still. She did not choose that any one should say I had frightened her. While I had been away she had unfastened the hem of her gown and taken out the lead that weighted it; and now she was sitting before a table, looking into a bowl of water into which she had just thrown the lead she had melted. She was so busy with her spells that at first she didn't notice my return. Sometimes she would take out a bit of lead and turn it round every way with a melancholy look. Sometimes she would sing one of those magic songs, which

131

invoke the help of Maria Padella, Don Pedro's mistress, who is said to have been the *Bari Crallisa* — the great gypsy queen.[39]

"'Carmen,' I said to her, 'will you come with me?' She rose, threw away her wooden bowl, and put her mantilla over her head ready to start. My horse was led up, she mounted behind me, and we rode away.

"After we had gone a little distance I said to her, 'So, my Carmen, you are quite ready to follow me, isn't that so?'

"She answered, 'Yes, I'll follow you, even to death — but I won't live with you any more.'

"We had reached a lonely gorge. I stopped my horse.

"'Is this the place?' she said.

"And with a spring she reached the ground. She took off her mantilla and threw it at her feet, and stood motionless, with one hand on her hip, looking at me steadily.

"'You mean to kill me, I see that well,' said she. 'It is fate. But you'll never make me give in.'

"I said to her: 'Be rational, I implore you; listen to me. All the past is forgotten. Yet you know it is you who have been my ruin — it is because of you that I am a robber and a murderer. Carmen, my Carmen, let me save you, and save myself with you.'

"'Jose,' she answered, 'what you ask is impossible. I don't love you any more. You love me still, and that is why you want to kill me. If I liked, I might tell you some other lie, but I don't choose to give myself the trouble. Everything is over between us two. You are my *rom*, and you have the right to kill your *romi*, but Carmen will always be free. A *calli* she was born, and a *calli* she'll die.'

"'Then, you love Lucas?' I asked.

---

[39] Maria Padella was accused of having bewitched Don Pedro. According to one popular tradition she presented Queen Blanche of Bourbon with a golden girdle which, in the eyes of the bewitched king, took on the appearance of a living snake. Hence the repugnance he always showed toward the unhappy princess.

132

"'Yes, I have loved him — as I loved you — for an instant — less than I loved you, perhaps. But now I don't love anything, and I hate myself for ever having loved you.'

"I cast myself at her feet, I seized her hands, I watered them with my tears, I reminded her of all the happy moments we had spent together, I offered to continue my brigand's life, if that would please her. Everything, sir, everything — I offered her everything if she would only love me again.

"She said:

"'Love you again? That's not possible! Live with you? I will not do it!'

"I was wild with fury. I drew my knife, I would have had her look frightened, and sue for mercy — but that woman was a demon.

"I cried, 'For the last time I ask you. Will you stay with me?'

"'No! no! no!' she said, and she stamped her foot.

"Then she pulled a ring I had given her off her finger, and cast it into the brushwood.

"I struck her twice over — I had taken Garcia's knife, because I had broken my own. At the second thrust she fell without a sound. It seems to me that I can still see her great black eyes staring at me. Then they grew dim and the lids closed.

"For a good hour I lay there prostrate beside her corpse. Then I recollected that Carmen had often told me that she would like to lie buried in a wood. I dug a grave for her with my knife and laid her in it. I hunted about a long time for her ring, and I found it at last. I put it into the grave beside her, with a little cross — perhaps I did wrong. Then I got upon my horse, galloped to Cordova, and gave myself up at the nearest guard-room. I told them I had killed Carmen, but I would not tell them where her body was. That hermit was a holy man! He prayed for her — he said a mass for her soul. Poor child! It's the *calle* who are to blame for having brought her up as they did."

CHAPTER IV

Spain is one of the countries in which those nomads, scattered all over Europe, and known as Bohemians, Gitanas,

Gypsies, Ziegeuner, and so forth, are now to be found in the greatest numbers. Most of these people live, or rather wander hither and thither, in the southern and eastern provinces of Spain, in Andalusia, and Estramadura, in the kingdom of Murcia. There are a great many of them in Catalonia. These last frequently cross over into France and are to be seen at all our southern fairs. The men generally call themselves grooms, horse doctors, mule-clippers; to these trades they add the mending of saucepans and brass utensils, not to mention smuggling and other illicit practices. The women tell fortunes, beg, and sell all sorts of drugs, some of which are innocent, while some are not. The physical characteristics of the gypsies are more easily distinguished then described, and when you have known one, you should be able to recognize a member of the race among a thousand other men. It is by their physiognomy and expression, especially, that they differ from the other inhabitants of the same country. Their complexion is exceedingly swarthy, always darker than that of the race among whom they live. Hence the name of *cale* (blacks) which they frequently apply to themselves.[40] Their eyes, set with a decided slant, are large, very black, and shaded by long and heavy lashes. Their glance can only be compared to that of a wild creature. It is full at once of boldness and shyness, and in this respect their eyes are a fair indication of their national character, which is cunning, bold, but with "the natural fear of blows," like Panurge. Most of the men are strapping fellows, slight and active. I don't think I ever saw a gypsy who had grown fat. In Germany the gypsy women are often very pretty; but beauty is very uncommon among the Spanish gitanas. When very young, they may pass as being attractive in their ugliness, but once they have reached motherhood, they become absolutely repulsive. The filthiness of both sexes is incredible, and no one who has not seen a gypsy matron's hair can form any conception of what it is, not even if he conjures up the roughest, the greasiest, and the dustiest heads

---

[40] It has struck me that the German gypsies, though they thoroughly understand the word *cale*, do not care to be called by that name. Among themselves they always use the designation *Romane tchave*.

imaginable. In some of the large Andalusian towns certain of the gypsy girls, somewhat better looking than their fellows, will take more care of their personal appearance. These go out and earn money by performing dances strongly resembling those forbidden at our public balls in carnival time. An English missionary, Mr. Borrow, the author of two very interesting works on the Spanish gypsies, whom he undertook to convert on behalf of the Bible Society, declares there is no instance of any gitana showing the smallest weakness for a man not belonging to her own race. The praise he bestows upon their chastity strikes me as being exceedingly exaggerated. In the first place, the great majority are in the position of the ugly woman described by Ovid, "*Casta quam nemo rogavit.*" As for the pretty ones, they are, like all Spanish women, very fastidious in choosing their lovers. Their fancy must be taken, and their favour must be earned. Mr. Borrow quotes, in proof of their virtue, one trait which does honour to his own, and especially to his simplicity: he declares that an immoral man of his acquaintance offered several gold ounces to a pretty gitana, and offered them in vain. An Andalusian, to whom I retailed this anecdote, asserted that the immoral man in question would have been far more successful if he had shown the girl two or three piastres, and that to offer gold ounces to a gypsy was as poor a method of persuasion as to promise a couple of millions to a tavern wench. However that may be, it is certain that the gitana shows the most extraordinary devotion to her husband. There is no danger and no suffering she will not brave, to help him in his need. One of the names which the gypsies apply to themselves, *Rome*, or "the married couple," seems to me a proof of their racial respect for the married state. Speaking generally, it may be asserted that their chief virtue is their patriotism — if we may thus describe the fidelity they observe in all their relations with persons of the same origin as their own, their readiness to help one another, and the inviolable secrecy which they keep for each other's benefit, in all compromising matters. And indeed something of the same sort may be noticed in all mysterious associations which are beyond the pale of the law.

Some months ago, I paid a visit to a gypsy tribe in the Vosges country. In the hut of an old woman, the oldest member of the tribe, I found a gypsy, in no way related to the family, who was sick of a mortal disease. The man had left a hospital, where he was well cared for, so that he might die among his own people. For thirteen weeks he had been lying in bed in their encampment, and receiving far better treatment than any of the sons and sons-in-law who shared his shelter. He had a good bed made of straw and moss, and sheets that were tolerably white, whereas all the rest of the family, which numbered eleven persons, slept on planks three feet long. So much for their hospitality. This very same woman, humane as was her treatment of her guest said to me constantly before the sick man: "*Singo, singo, homte hi mulo.*" "Soon, soon he must die!" After all, these people live such miserable lives, that a reference to the approach of death can have no terrors for them.

One remarkable feature in the gypsy character is their indifference about religion. Not that they are strong-minded or skeptical. They have never made any profession of atheism. Far from that, indeed, the religion of the country which they inhabit is always theirs; but they change their religion when they change the country of their residence. They are equally free from the superstitions which replace religious feeling in the minds of the vulgar. How, indeed, can superstition exist among a race which, as a rule, makes its livelihood out of the credulity of others? Nevertheless, I have remarked a particular horror of touching a corpse among the Spanish gypsies. Very few of these could be induced to carry a dead man to his grave, even if they were paid for it.

I have said that most gypsy women undertake to tell fortunes. They do this very successfully. But they find a much greater source of profit in the sale of charms and love-philters. Not only do they supply toads' claws to hold fickle hearts, and powdered loadstone to kindle love in cold ones, but if necessity arises, they can use mighty incantations, which force the devil to lend them his aid. Last year the following story was related to me

136

by a Spanish lady. She was walking one day along the *Calle d'Alcala*, feeling very sad and anxious. A gypsy woman who was squatting on the pavement called out to her, "My pretty lady, your lover has played you false!" (It was quite true.) "Shall I get him back for you?" My readers will imagine with what joy the proposal was accepted, and how complete was the confidence inspired by a person who could thus guess the inmost secrets of the heart. As it would have been impossible to proceed to perform the operations of magic in the most crowded street in Madrid, a meeting was arranged for the next day. "Nothing will be easier than to bring back the faithless one to your feet!" said the gitana. "Do you happen to have a handkerchief, a scarf, or a mantilla, that he gave you?" A silken scarf was handed her. "Now sew a piastre into one corner of the scarf with crimson silk — sew half a piastre into another corner — sew a peseta here — and a two-real piece there; then, in the middle you must sew a gold coin — a doubloon would be best." The doubloon and all the other coins were duly sewn in. "Now give me the scarf, and I'll take it to the Campo Santo when midnight strikes. You come along with me, if you want to see a fine piece of witchcraft. I promise you shall see the man you love to-morrow!" The gypsy departed alone for the Campo Santo, since my Spanish friend was too much afraid of witchcraft to go there with her. I leave my readers to guess whether my poor forsaken lady ever saw her lover, or her scarf, again.

In spite of their poverty and the sort of aversion they inspire, the gypsies are treated with a certain amount of consideration by the more ignorant folk, and they are very proud of it. They feel themselves to be a superior race as regards intelligence, and they heartily despise the people whose hospitality they enjoy. "These Gentiles are so stupid," said one of the Vosges gypsies to me, "that there is no credit in taking them in. The other day a peasant woman called out to me in the street. I went into her house. Her stove smoked and she asked me to give her a charm to cure it. First of all I made her give me a good bit of bacon, and then I began to mumble a few words in *Romany*. 'You're a fool,' I said, 'you were born a fool, and you'll die a fool!' When I had got near the door I said to her, in good German, 'The most certain way of keeping your stove from smoking is not to light any fire in it!' and then I took to my heels."

The history of the gypsies is still a problem. We know, indeed, that their first bands, which were few and far between, appeared in Eastern Europe towards the beginning of the fifteenth century. But nobody can tell whence they started, or why they came to Europe, and, what is still more extraordinary, no one knows how they multiplied, within a short time, and in so prodigious a fashion, and in several countries, all very remote from each other. The gypsies themselves have preserved no tradition whatsoever as to their origin, and though most of them do speak of Egypt as their original fatherland, that is only because they have adopted a very ancient fable respecting their race.

Most of the Orientalists who have studied the gypsy language believe that the cradle of the race was in India. It appears, in fact, that many of the roots and grammatical forms of the *Romany* tongue are to be found in idioms derived from the Sanskrit. As may be imagined, the gypsies, during their long wanderings, have adopted many foreign words. In every *Romany* dialect a number of Greek words appear.

At the present day the gypsies have almost as many dialects as there are separate hordes of their race. Everywhere, they speak the language of the country they inhabit more easily than their own idiom, which they seldom use, except with the object of conversing freely before strangers. A comparison of the dialect of the German gypsies with that used by the Spanish gypsies, who have held no communication with each other for several centuries, reveals the existence of a great number of words common to both. But everywhere the original language is notably affected, though in different degrees, by its contact with the more cultivated languages into the use of which the nomads have been forced. German in one case and Spanish in the other have so modified the *Romany* groundwork that it would not be possible for a gypsy from the Black Forest to converse with one of his

138

Andalusian brothers, although a few sentences on each side would suffice to convince them that each was speaking a dialect of the same language. Certain words in very frequent use are, I believe, common to every dialect. Thus, in every vocabulary which I have been able to consult, *pani* means water, *manro* means bread, *mas* stands for meat, and *lon* for salt.

The nouns of number are almost the same in every case. The German dialect seems to me much purer than the Spanish, for it has preserved numbers of the primitive grammatical forms, whereas the Gitanos have adopted those of the Castilian tongue. Nevertheless, some words are an exception, as though to prove that the language was originally common to all. The preterite of the German dialect is formed by adding *ium* to the imperative, which is always the root of the verb. In the Spanish *Romany* the verbs are all conjugated on the model of the first conjugation of the Castilian verbs. From *jamar*, the infinitive of "to eat," the regular conjugation should be *jame*, "I have eaten." From *lillar*, "to take," *lille*, "I have taken." Yet, some old gypsies say, as an exception, *jayon* and *lillon*. I am not acquainted with any other verbs which have preserved this ancient form.

While I am thus showing off my small acquaintance with the *Romany* language, I must notice a few words of French slang which our thieves have borrowed from the gypsies. From *Les Mysteres de Paris* honest folk have learned that the word *chourin* means "a knife." This is pure *Romany* — *tchouri* is one of the words which is common to every dialect. Monsieur Vidocq calls a horse *gres* — this again is a gypsy word — *gras*, *gre*, *graste*, and *gris*. Add to this the word *romanichel*, by which the gypsies are described in Parisian slang. This is a corruption of *romane tchave* — "gypsy lads." But a piece of etymology of which I am really proud is that of the word *frimousse*, "face," "countenance" — a word which every schoolboy uses, or did use, in my time. Note, in the first place, the Oudin, in his curious dictionary, published in 1640, wrote the word *firlimouse*. Now in *Romany*, *firla*, or *fila*, stands for "face," and has the same meaning — it is exactly the *os* of the Latins. The combination of *firlamui* was instantly understood by a genuine gypsy, and I believe it to be true to the spirit of the gypsy language.

I have surely said enough to give the readers of Carmen a favourable idea of my *Romany* studies. I will conclude with the following proverb, which comes in very appropriately: *En retudi panda nasti abela macha.* "Between closed lips no fly can pass."

# COLOMBA
## CHAPTER I

"Pe far la to vendetta,
Sta sigur', vasta anche ella."
— Vocero du Niolo.

Early in the month of October, 181-, Colonel Sir Thomas Nevil, a distinguished Irish officer of the English army, alighted with his daughter at the Hotel Beauveau, Marseilles, on their return from a tour in Italy. The perpetual and universal admiration of enthusiastic travelers has produced a sort of reaction, and many tourists, in their desire to appear singular, now take the *nil admirari* of Horace for their motto. To this dissatisfied class the colonel's only daughter, Miss Lydia, belonged. "The Transfiguration" has seemed to her mediocre, and Vesuvius in eruption an effect not greatly superior to that produced by the Birmingham factory chimneys. Her great objection to Italy, on the whole, was its lack of local colour and character. My readers must discover the sense of these expressions as best they may. A few years ago I understood them very well myself, but at the present time I can make nothing of them. At first, Miss Lydia had flattered herself she had found things on the other side of the Alps which nobody had ever before seen, about which she could converse *avec les honnêtes gens,* as M. Jourdain calls them. But soon, anticipated in every direction by her countrymen, she despaired of making any fresh discoveries, and went over to the party of the opposition. It is really very tiresome not to be able to talk abut the wonders of Italy without hearing somebody say "Of course you know the Raphael in the Palazzo — — at — — ? It is the finest thing in Italy!" and just the thing *you* happen to have overlooked! As it would take too long to see everything, the simplest course is to resort to deliberate and universal censure.

At the Hotel Beauveau Miss Lydia met with a bitter disappointment. She had brought back a pretty sketch of the

Pelasgic or Cyclopean Gate at Segni, which, as she believed, all other artists had completely overlooked. Now, at Marseilles, she met Lady Frances Fenwick, who showed her her album, in which appeared, between a sonnet and a dried flower, the very gate in question, brilliantly touched in with sienna. Miss Lydia gave her drawing to her maid — and lost all admiration for Pelasgic structures.

This unhappy frame of mind was shared by Colonel Nevil, who, since the death of his wife, looked at everything through his daughter's eyes. In his estimation, Italy had committed the unpardonable sin of boring his child, and was, in consequence, the most wearisome country on the face of the earth. He had no fault to find, indeed, with the pictures and statues, but he was in a position to assert that Italian sport was utterly wretched, and that he had been obliged to tramp ten leagues over the Roman Campagna, under a burning sun, to kill a few worthless red-legged partridges.

The morning after his arrival at Marseilles he invited Captain Ellis — his former adjutant, who had just been spending six weeks in Corsica — to dine with him. The captain told Miss Lydia a story about bandits, which had the advantage of bearing no resemblance to the robber tales with which she had been so frequently regaled, on the road between Naples and Rome, and he told it well. At dessert, the two men, left alone over their claret, talked of hunting — and the colonel learned that nowhere is there more excellent sport, or game more varied and abundant, than in Corsica. "There are plenty of wild boars," said Captain Ellis. "And you have to learn to distinguish them from the domestic pigs, which are astonishingly like them. For if you kill a pig, you find yourself in difficulties with the swine-herds. They rush out of the thickets (which they call *maquis*) armed to the teeth, make you pay for their beasts, and laugh at you besides. Then there is the mouflon, a strange animal, which you will not find anywhere else — splendid game, but hard to get — and stags, deer, pheasants, and partridges — it would be impossible to enumerate all the kinds with which Corsica swarms. If you want shooting, colonel, go to Corsica! There, as one of my entertainers said to me, you can get a shot at every imaginable kind of game, from a thrush to a man!"

At tea, the captain once more delighted Lydia with the tale of a *vendetta transversale* (A vendetta in which vengeance falls on a more or less distant relation of the author of the original offence.), even more strange than his first story, and he thoroughly stirred her enthusiasm by his descriptions of the strange wild beauty of the country, the peculiarities of its inhabitants, and their primitive hospitality and customs. Finally, he offered her a pretty little stiletto, less remarkable for its shape and copper mounting than for its origin. A famous bandit had given it to Captain Ellis, and had assured him it had been buried in four human bodies. Miss Lydia thrust it through her girdle, laid it on the table beside her bed, and unsheathed it twice over before she fell asleep. Her father meanwhile was dreaming he had slain a mouflon, and that its owner insisted on his paying for it, a demand to which he gladly acceded, seeing it was a most curious creature, like a boar, with stag's horns and a pheasant's tail.

"Ellis tells me there's splendid shooting in Corsica," said the colonel, as he sat at breakfast, alone with his daughter. "If it hadn't been for the distance, I should like to spend a fortnight there."

"Well," replied Miss Lydia, "why shouldn't we go to Corsica? While you are hunting I can sketch — I should love to have that grotto Captain Ellis talked about, where Napoleon used to go and study when he was a child, in my album."

It was the first time, probably, that any wish expressed by the colonel had won his daughter's approbation. Delighted as he was by the unexpected harmony on their opinions, he was nevertheless wise enough to put forward various objections, calculated to sharpen Miss Lydia's welcome whim. In vain did he dwell on the wildness of the country, and the difficulties of travel there for a lady. Nothing frightened her; she liked traveling on horseback of all things; she delighted in the idea of bivouacking in the open; she even threatened to go as far as Asia Minor — in short, she found an answer to everything. No Englishwoman had ever been to Corsica; therefore she must go. What a pleasure it would be, when she got back to St. James's Place, to exhibit her album! "But, my dear creature, why do you pass over that delightful drawing?" "That's only a trifle — just a sketch I made of a famous Corsican bandit who was our guide." "What! you don't mean to say you have been to Corsica?"

As there were no steamboats between France and Corsica, in those days, inquiries were made for some ship about to sail for the island Miss Lydia proposed to discover. That very day the colonel wrote to Paris, to countermand his order for the suite of apartments in which he was to have made some stay, and bargained with the skipper of a Corsican schooner, just about to set sail for Ajaccio, for two poor cabins, but the best that could be had. Provisions were sent on board, the skipper swore that one of his sailors was an excellent cook, and had not his equal for *bouilleabaisse*; he promised mademoiselle should be comfortable, and have a fair wind and a calm sea.

The colonel further stipulated, in obedience to his daughter's wishes, that no other passenger should be taken on board, and that the captain should skirt the coast of the island, so that Miss Lydia might enjoy the view of the mountains.

On the day of their departure everything was packed and sent on board early in the morning. The schooner was to sail with the evening breeze. Meanwhile, as the colonel and his daughter were walking on the Canebiere, the skipper addressed them, and craved permission to take on board one of his relations, his eldest son's godfather's second cousin, who was going back to Corsica, his native country, on important business, and could not find any ship to take him over.

"He's a charming fellow," added Captain Mattei, "a soldier, an officer in the Infantry of the Guard, and would have been a colonel already if *the other* (meaning Napoleon) had still been emperor!"

"As he is a soldier," began the colonel — he was about to add, "I shall be very glad he should come with us," when Miss Lydia exclaimed in English:

"An infantry officer!" (Her father had been in the cavalry, and she consequently looked down on every other branch of the service.) "An uneducated man, very likely, who would be sea-sick, and spoil all the pleasure of our trip!"

The captain did not understand a word of English, but he seemed to catch what Miss Lydia was saying by the pursing up of her pretty mouth, and immediately entered upon an elaborate panegyric of his relative, which he wound up by declaring him to be a gentleman, belonging to a family of *corporals*, and that he would not be in the very least in the colonel's way, for that he, the skipper, would undertake to stow him in some corner, where they should not be aware of his presence.

The colonel and Miss Nevil thought it peculiar that there should be Corsican families in which the dignity of corporal was handed down from father to son. But, as they really believed the individual in question to be some infantry corporal, they concluded he was some poor devil whom the skipper desired to take out of pure charity. If he had been an officer, they would have been obliged to speak to him and live with him; but there was no reason why they should put themselves out for a corporal — who is a person of no consequence unless his detachment is also at hand, with bayonets fixed, ready to convey a person to a place to which he would rather not be taken.

"Is your kinsman ever sea-sick?" demanded Miss Nevil sharply.

"Never, mademoiselle, he is as steady as a rock, either on sea or land!"

"Very good then, you can take him," said she.

"You can take him!" echoed the colonel, and they passed on their way.

Toward five o'clock in the evening Captain Mattei came to escort them on board the schooner. On the jetty, near the captain's gig, they met a tall young man wearing a blue frock-coat, buttoned up to his chin; his face was tanned, his eyes were black, brilliant, wide open, his whole appearance intelligent and frank. His shoulders, well thrown back, and his little twisted mustache clearly revealed the soldier — for at that period mustaches were by no means common, and the National Guard had not carried the habits and appearance of the guard-room into the bosom of every family.

When the young man saw the colonel he doffed his cap, and thanked him in excellent language, and without the slightest shyness, for the service he was rendering him.

"Delighted to be of use to you, my good fellow!" said the colonel, with a friendly nod, and he stepped into the gig.

"He's not very ceremonious, this Englishman of yours," said the young man in Italian, and in an undertone, to the captain.

The skipper laid his forefinger under his left eye, and pulled down the corners of his mouth. To a man acquainted with the language of signs, this meant that the Englishman understood Italian, and was an oddity into the bargain. The young man smiled slightly and touched his forehead, in answer to Mattei's sign, as though to indicate that every Englishman had a bee in his bonnet. Then he sat down beside them, and began to look very attentively, though not impertinently, at his pretty fellow-traveler.

146

"These French soldiers all have a good appearance," remarked the colonel in English to his daughter, "and so it is easy to turn them into officers." Then addressing the young man in French, he said, "Tell me, my good man, what regiment have you served in?" The young man nudged his second cousin's godson's father gently with his elbow, and suppressing an ironic smile, replied that he had served in the Infantry of the Guard, and that he had just quitted the Seventh Regiment of Light Infantry.

"Were you at Waterloo? You are very young!"

"I beg your pardon, colonel, that was my only campaign."

"It counts as two," said the colonel.

The young Corsican bit his lips.

"Papa," said Miss Lydia in English, "do ask him if the Corsicans are very fond of their Buonaparte."

Before the colonel could translate her question into French, the young man answered in fairly good English, though with a marked accent:

"You know, mademoiselle, that no man is ever a prophet in his own country. We, who are Napoleon's fellow-countrymen, are perhaps less attached to him than the French. As for myself, though my family was formerly at enmity with his, I both love and admire him."

"You speak English!" exclaimed the colonel.

"Very ill, as you may perceive!"

Miss Lydia, though somewhat shocked by the young man's easy tone, could not help laughing at the idea of a personal enmity between a corporal and an emperor. She took this as a foretaste of Corsican peculiarities, and made up her mind to note it down in her journal.

"Perhaps you were a prisoner in England?" asked the colonel.

"No, colonel, I learned English in France, when I was very young, from a prisoner of your nation."

Then, addressing Miss Nevil:

"Mattei tells me you have just come back from Italy. No doubt, mademoiselle, you speak the purest Tuscan — I fear you'll find it somewhat difficult to understand our dialect."

"My daughter understands every Italian dialect," said the colonel. "She has the gift of languages. She doesn't get it from me."

"Would mademoiselle understand, for instance, these lines from one of our Corsican songs in which a shepherd says to his shepherdess:

"S'entrassi 'ndru paradisu santu, santu,

E nun truvassi a tia, mi n'escriria."

("If I entered the holy land of paradise and found thee not, I would depart!")

— *Serenata di Zicavo.*

Miss Lydia did understand. She thought the quotation bold, and the look which accompanied it still bolder, and replied, with a blush, "Capisco."

"And are you going back to your own country on furlough?" inquired the colonel.

"No, colonel, they have put me on half-pay, because I was at Waterloo, probably, and because I am Napoleon's fellow-countryman. I am going home, as the song says, low in hope and low in purse," and he looked up to the sky and sighed.

The colonel slipped his hand into his pocket, and tried to think of some civil phrase with which he might slip the gold coin he was fingering into the palm of his unfortunate enemy.

"And I too," he said good-humouredly, "have been put on half-pay, but your half-pay can hardly give you enough to buy tobacco! Here, corporal!" and he tried to force the gold coin into the young man's closed hand, which rested on the gunwale of the gig.

The young Corsican reddened, drew himself up, bit his lips, and seemed, for a moment, on the brink of some angry reply. Then suddenly his expression changed and he burst out laughing. The colonel, grasping his gold piece still in his hand, sat staring at him.

"Colonel," said the young man, when he had recovered his gravity, "allow me to offer you two pieces of advice — the first is never to offer money to a Corsican, for some of my fellow-

148

countrymen would be rude enough to throw it back in your face; the second is not to give people titles they do not claim. You call me 'corporal,' and I am a lieutenant — the difference is not very great, no doubt, still — — "

"Lieutenant! Lieutenant!" exclaimed Sir Thomas. "But the skipper told me you were a corporal, and that your father and all your family had been corporals before you!"

At these words the young man threw himself back and laughed louder than ever, so merrily that the skipper and his two sailors joined the chorus.

"Forgive me, colonel!" he cried at last. "The mistake is so comical, and I have only just realized it. It is quite true that my family glories in the fact that it can reckon many corporals among its ancestors — but our Corsican corporals never wore stripes upon their sleeves! Toward the year of grace 1100 certain villages revolted against the tyranny of the great mountain nobles, and chose leaders of their own, whom they called *corporals*. In our island we think a great deal of being descended from these tribunes."

"I beg your pardon, sir," exclaimed the colonel, "I beg your pardon a thousand times! As you understand the cause of my mistake, I hope you will do me the kindness of forgiving it!" and he held out his hand.

"It is the just punishment of my petty pride," said the young man, still laughing, and cordially shaking the Englishman's hand. "I am not at all offended. As my friend Mattei has introduced me so unsuccessfully, allow me to introduce myself. My name is Orso della Rebbia; I am a lieutenant on half-pay; and if, as the sight of those two fine dogs of yours leads me to believe, you are coming to Corsica to hunt, I shall be very proud to do you the honours of our mountains and our *maquis* — if, indeed, I have not forgotten them altogether!" he added, with a sigh.

At this moment the gig came alongside the schooner, the lieutenant offered his hand to Miss Lydia, and then helped the colonel to swing himself up on deck. Once there, Sir Thomas, who was still very much ashamed of his blunder, and at a loss to know what he had better do to make the man whose ancestry dated from the year 1100 forget it, invited him to supper, without waiting for his daughter's consent, and with many fresh apologies and handshakes. Miss Lydia frowned a little, but, after all, she was not sorry to know what a corporal really was. She rather liked there guest, and was even beginning to fancy there was something aristocratic about him — only she thought him too frank and merry for a hero of romance.

"Lieutenant della Rebbia," said the colonel, bowing to him, English fashion, over a glass of Madeira, "I met a great many of your countrymen in Spain — they were splendid sharp-shooters."

"Yes, and a great many of them have stayed in Spain," replied the young lieutenant gravely.

"I shall never forget the behaviour of a Corsican battalion at the Battle of Vittoria," said the colonel; "I have good reason to remember it, indeed," he added, rubbing his chest. "All day long they had been skirmishing in the gardens, behind the hedges, and had killed I don't know how many of our horses and men. When the retreat was sounded, they rallied and made off at a great pace. We had hoped to take our revenge on them in the open plain, but the scoundrels — I beg your pardon, lieutenant; the brave fellows, I should have said — had formed a square, and there was no breaking it. In the middle of the square — I fancy I can see him still — rode an officer on a little black horse. He kept close beside the standard, smoking his cigar as coolly as if he had been in a café. Every now and then their bugles played a flourish, as if to defy us. I sent my two leading squadrons at them. Whew! Instead of breaking the front of the square, my dragoons passed along the sides, wheeled, and came back in great disorder, and with several riderless horses — and all the time those cursed bugles went on playing. When the smoke which had hung over the battalion cleared away, I saw the officer still puffing at his cigar beside his eagle. I was furious, and led a final charge myself. Their muskets, foul with continual firing, would not go off, but the men had drawn up, six deep, with their bayonets pointed at the noses of our horses; you might have taken them for a wall. I was shouting, urging on my dragoons, and spurring my horse forward, when the officer I have mentioned, at length throwing away his cigar, pointed me out to one of his men, and I heard him say something like *'Al capello bianco!'* — I wore a white plume. Then I did not hear any more, for a bullet passed through my chest. That was a splendid battalion, M. della Rebbia, that first battalion of the Eighteenth — all of them Corsicans, as I was afterward told!"

"Yes," said Orso, whose eyes had shone as he listened to the story. "They covered the retreat, and brought back their eagle. Two thirds of those brave fellows are sleeping now on the plains of Vittoria!"

"And, perhaps, you can tell me the name of the officer in command?"

"It was my father — he was then a major in the Eighteenth, and was promoted colonel for his conduct on that terrible day."

"Your father! Upon my word, he was a brave man! I should be glad to see him again, and I am certain I should recognize him. Is he still alive?"

"No, colonel," said the young man, turning slightly pale.

"Was he at Waterloo?"

"Yes, colonel; but he had not the happiness of dying on the field of battle. He died in Corsica two years ago. How beautiful the sea is! It is ten years since I have seen the Mediterranean! Don't you think the Mediterranean much more beautiful than the ocean, mademoiselle?"

"I think it too blue, and its waves lack grandeur."

"You like wild beauty then, mademoiselle! In that case, I am sure you will be delighted with Corsica."

"My daughter," said the colonel, "delights in everything that is out of the common, and for that reason she did not care much for Italy."

"The only place in Italy that I know," said Orso, "is Pisa, where I was at school for some time. But I can not think, without admiration, of the Campo-Santo, the Duomo, and the Leaning Tower — especially of the Campo-Santo. Do you remember

Orcagna's 'Death'? I think I could draw every line of it — it is so graven on my memory."

Miss Lydia was afraid the lieutenant was going to deliver an enthusiastic tirade.

"It is very pretty," she said, with a yawn. "Excuse me, papa, my head aches a little; I am going down to my cabin."

She kissed her father on the forehead, inclined her head majestically to Orso, and disappeared. Then the two men talked about hunting and war. They discovered that at Waterloo they had been posted opposite each other, and had no doubt exchanged many a bullet. This knowledge strengthened their good understanding. Turning about, they criticized Napoleon, Wellington, and Blucher, and then they hunted buck, boar, and mountain sheep in company. At last, when night was far advanced, and the last bottle of claret had been emptied, the colonel wrung the lieutenant's hand once more and wished him good-night, expressing his hope that an acquaintance, which had begun in such ridiculous fashion, might be continued. They parted, and each went to bed.

# CHAPTER III

It was a lovely night. The moonlight was dancing on the waves, the ship glided smoothly on before a gentle breeze. Miss Lydia was not sleepy, and nothing but the presence of an unpoetical person had prevented her from enjoying those emotions which every human being possessing a touch of poetry must experience at sea by moonlight. When she felt sure the young lieutenant must be sound asleep, like the prosaic creature he was, she got up, took her cloak, woke her maid, and went on deck. Nobody was to be seen except the sailor at the helm, who was singing a sort of dirge in the Corsican dialect, to some wild and monotonous tune. In the silence of the night this strange music had its charm. Unluckily Miss Lydia did not understand perfectly what the sailor was singing. Amid a good deal that was commonplace, a passionate line would occasionally excite her liveliest curiosity. But just at the most important moment some words of *patois* would occur, the sense of which utterly escaped her. Yet she did make out that the subject was connected with a murder. Curses against the assassin, threats of vengeance, praise of the dead were all mingled confusedly. She remembered some of the lines. I will endeavour to translate them here.

. . . "Neither cannon nor bayonets . . . Brought pallor to his brow. . . As serene on the battlefield . . . as a summer sky. He was the falcon — the eagle's friend . . . Honey of the sand to his friends . . . To his enemies, a tempestuous sea. . . . . . . Prouder than the sun . . . gentler than the moon . . . He for whom the enemies of France . . . never waited . . . Murderers in his own land . . . struck him from behind . . . As Vittolo slew Sampiero Corso . . . Never would they have dared to look him in The face . . . Set up on the wall Before my bed . . . my well-earned cross of honour . . . red is its ribbon . . . redder is my shirt! . . . For my son, my son in a far country . . . keep my cross and my blood-stained shirt!
. . .

". . . He will see two holes in it . . . For each hole a hole in another shirt! . . . But will that accomplish the vengeance? . . . I

153

must have the hand that fired, the eye that aimed . . . the heart that planned!" . . .

Suddenly the sailor stopped short.

"Why don't you go on, my good man?" inquired Miss Nevil.

The sailor, with a jerk of his head, pointed to a figure appearing through the main hatchway of the schooner: it was Orso, coming up to enjoy the moonlight. "Pray finish your song," said Miss Lydia. "It interests me greatly!"

The sailor leaned toward her, and said, in a very low tone, "I don't give the *rimbecco* to anybody!"

"The what?"

The sailor, without replying, began to whistle.

"I have caught you admiring our Mediterranean, Miss Nevil," said Orso, coming toward her. "You must allow you never see a moon like this anywhere else!"

"I was not looking at it, I was altogether occupied in studying Corsican. That sailor, who has been singing a most tragic dirge, stopped short at the most interesting point."

The sailor bent down, as if to see the compass more clearly, and tugged sharply at Miss Nevil's fur cloak. It was quite evident his lament could not be sung before Lieutenant Orso.

"What were you singing, Paolo France?" said Orso. "Was it a *ballata* or a *vocero*? Mademoiselle understands you, and would like to hear the end."

"I have forgotten it, Ors' Anton'," said the sailor.

And instantly he began a hymn to the Virgin, at the top of his voice.

Miss Lydia listened absent-mindedly to the hymn, and did not press the singer any further — though she was quite resolved, in her own mind, to find out the meaning of the riddle later. But her maid, who, being a Florentine, could not understand the Corsican dialect any better than her mistress, was as eager as Miss Lydia for information, and, turning to Orso, before the English lady could warn her by a nudge, she said: "Captain what does *giving the rimbecco* mean?"

"The rimbecco!" said Orso. "Why, it's the most deadly insult that can be offered to a Corsican. It means reproaching him with not having avenged his wrong. Who mentioned the rimbecco to you?"

"Yesterday, at Marseilles," replied Miss Lydia hurriedly, "the captain of the schooner used the word."

"And whom was he talking about?" inquired Orso eagerly.

"Oh, he was telling us some odd story about the time — yes, I think it was about Vannina d'Ornano."

"I suppose, mademoiselle, that Vannina's death has not inspired you with any great love for our national hero, the brave Sampiero?"

"But do you think his conduct was so very heroic?"

"The excuse for his crime lies in the savage customs of the period. And then Sampiero was waging deadly war against the Genoese. What confidence could his fellow-countrymen have felt in him if he had not punished his wife, who tried to treat with Genoa?"

"Vannina," said the sailor, "had started off without her husband's leave. Sampiero did quite right to wring her neck!"

"But," said Miss Lydia, "it was to save her husband, it was out of love for him, that she was going to ask his pardon from the Genoese."

"To ask his pardon was to degrade him!" exclaimed Orso.

"And then to kill her himself!" said Miss Lydia. "What a monster he must have been!"

"You know she begged as a favour that she might die by his hand. What about Othello, mademoiselle, do you look on him, too, as a monster?"

"There is a difference; he was jealous. Sampiero was only vain!"

"And after all is not jealousy a kind of vanity? It is the vanity of love; will you not excuse it on account of its motive?"

Miss Lydia looked at him with an air of great dignity, and turning to the sailor, inquired when the schooner would reach port.

"The day after to-morrow," said he, "if the wind holds."

"I wish Ajaccio were in sight already, for I am sick of this ship." She rose, took her maid's arm, and walked a few paces on the deck. Orso stood motionless beside the helm, not knowing whether he had better walk beside her, or end a conversation which seemed displeasing to her.

"Blood of the Madonna, what a handsome girl!" said the sailor. "If every flea in my bed were like her, I shouldn't complain of their biting me!"

Miss Lydia may possibly have overheard this artless praise of her beauty and been startled by it; for she went below almost immediately. Shortly after Orso also retired. As soon as he had left the deck the maid reappeared, and, having cross-questioned the sailor, carried back the following information to her mistress. The *ballata* which had been broken off on Orso's appearance had been composed on the occasion of the death of his father, Colonel della Rebbia, who had been murdered two years previously. The sailor had no doubt at all that Orso was coming back to Corsica *per fare la vendetta*, such was his expression, and he affirmed that before long there would be *fresh meat* to be seen in the village of Pietranera. This national expression, being interpreted, meant that Signor Orso proposed to murder two or three individuals suspected of having assassinated his father — individuals who had, indeed, been prosecuted on that account, but had come out of the trial as white as snow, for they were hand and glove with the judges, lawyers, prefect, and gendarmes.

"There is no justice in Corsica," added the sailor, "and I put much more faith in a good gun than in a judge of the Royal Court. If a man has an enemy he must choose one of the three S's." (A national expression meaning *schioppetto, stiletto, strada* — that is, *gun, dagger,* or *flight.*)

These interesting pieces of information wrought a notable change in Miss Lydia's manner and feeling with regard to Lieutenant della Rebbia. From that moment he became a person of importance in the romantic Englishwoman's eyes.

His careless air, his frank and good humour, which had at first impressed her so unfavourably, now seemed to her an additional merit, as being proofs of the deep dissimulation of a strong nature, which will not allow any inner feeling to appear upon the surface. Orso seemed to her a sort of Fieschi, who hid mighty designs under an appearance of frivolity, and, though it is less noble to kill a few rascals than to free one's country, still a fine deed of vengeance is a fine thing, and besides, women are rather glad to find their hero is not a politician. Then Miss Nevil remarked for the first time that the young lieutenant had large eyes, white teeth, an elegant figure, that he was well-educated, and possessed the habits of good society. During the following day she talked to him frequently, and found his conversation interesting. He was asked many questions about his own country, and described it well. Corsica, which he had left when young, to go first to college, and then to the Ecole militaire, had remained in his imagination surrounded with poetic associations. When he talked of its mountains, its forests, and the quaint customs of its inhabitants he grew eager and animated. As may be imagined, the word *vengeance* occurred more than once in the stories he told — for it is impossible to speak of the Corsicans without either attacking or justifying their proverbial passion. Orso somewhat surprised Miss Nevil by his general condemnation of the undying hatreds nursed by his fellow-countrymen. As regarded the peasants, however, he endeavoured to excuse them, and claimed that the *vendetta* is the poor man's duel. "So true is this," he said, "that no assassination takes place till a formal challenge has been delivered. 'Be on your guard yourself, I am on mine!' are the sacramental words exchanged, from time immemorial, between two enemies, before they begin to lie in wait for each other. There are more assassinations among us," he added, "than anywhere else. But you will never discover an ignoble cause for any of these crimes. We have many murderers, it is true, but not a single thief."

When he spoke about vengeance and murder Miss Lydia looked at him closely, but she could not detect the slightest trace of emotion on his features. As she had made up her mind, however, that he possessed sufficient strength of mind to be able to hide his thoughts from every eye (her own, of course, excepted), she continued in her firm belief that Colonel della Rebbia's shade would not have to wait long for the atonement it claimed.

The schooner was already within sight of Corsica. The captain pointed out the principal features of the coast, and, though all of these were absolutely unknown to Miss Lydia, she found a certain pleasure in hearing their names; nothing is more tiresome than an anonymous landscape. From time to time the colonel's telescope revealed to her the form of some islander clad in brown cloth, armed with a long gun, bestriding a small horse, and galloping down steep slopes. In each of these Miss Lydia believed she beheld either a brigand or a son going forth to avenge his father's death. But Orso always declared it was some peaceful denizen of a neighbouring village traveling on business, and that he carried a gun less from necessity than because it was the fashion, just as no dandy ever takes a walk without an elegant cane. Though a gun is a less noble and poetic weapon than a stiletto, Miss Lydia thought it much more stylish for a man than any cane, and she remembered that all Lord Byron's heroes died by a bullet, and not by the classic poniard.

After three days' sailing, the ship reached Les Sanguinaires (The Bloody Islands), and the magnificent panorama of the Gulf of Ajaccio was unrolled before our travelers' eyes. It is compared, with justice, to the Bay of Naples, and just as the schooner was entering the harbour a burning *maquis*, which covered the Punta di Girato, brought back memories of Vesuvius and heightened the resemblance. To make it quite complete, Naples should be seen after one of Attila's armies had devastated its suburbs — for round Ajaccio everything looks dead and deserted. Instead of the handsome buildings observable on every side from Castellamare to Cape Misena, nothing is to be seen in the neighbourhood of the Gulf of Ajaccio but gloomy *maquis* with bare mountains rising behind them. Not a villa, not a dwelling of any kind —

158

only here and there, on the heights about the town, a few isolated white structures stand out against a background of green. These are mortuary chapels or family tombs. Everything in this landscape is gravely and sadly beautiful.

The appearance of the town, at that period especially, deepened the impression caused by the loneliness of its surroundings. There was no stir in the streets, where only a few listless idlers — always the same — were to be seen; no women at all, except an odd peasant come in to sell her produce; no loud talk, laughter, and singing, as in the Italian towns. Sometimes, under the shade of a tree on the public promenade, a dozen armed peasants will play at cards or watch each other play; they never shout or wrangle; if they get hot over the game, pistol shots ring out, and this always before the utterance of any threat. The Corsican is grave and silent by nature. In the evening, a few persons come out to enjoy the cool air, but the promenaders on the Corso are nearly all of them foreigners; the islanders stay in front of their own doors; each one seems on the watch, like a falcon over its nest.

# CHAPTER IV

When Miss Lydia had visited the house in which Napoleon was born, and had procured, by means more or less moral, a fragment of the wall-paper belonging to it, she, within two days of her landing in Corsica, began to feel that profound melancholy which must overcome every foreigner in a country whose unsociable inhabitants appear to condemn him or her to a condition of utter isolation. She was already regretting her headstrong caprice; but to go back at once would have been to risk her reputation as an intrepid traveler, so she made up her mind to be patient, and kill time as best she could. With this noble resolution, she brought out her crayons and colours, sketched views of the gulf, and did the portrait of a sunburnt peasant, who sold melons, like any market-gardener on the Continent, but who wore a long white beard, and looked the fiercest rascal that had ever been seen. As all that was not enough to amuse her, she determined to turn the head of the descendant of the corporals, and this was no difficult matter, since, far from being in a hurry to get back to his village, Orso seemed very happy at Ajaccio, although he knew nobody there. Furthermore, Miss Lydia had a lofty purpose in her mind; it was nothing less than to civilize this mountain bear, and induce him to relinquish the sinister design which had recalled him to his island. Since she had taken the trouble to study the young man, she had told herself it would be a pity to let him rush upon his ruin, and that it would be a glorious thing to convert a Corsican.

Our travelers spent the day in the following manner: Every morning the colonel and Orso went out shooting. Miss Lydia sketched or wrote letters to her friends, chiefly for the sake of dating them from Ajaccio. Toward six o'clock the gentlemen came in, laden with game. Then followed dinner. Miss Lydia sang, the colonel went to sleep, and the young people sat talking till very late.

Some formality or other, connected with his passports, had made it necessary for Colonel Nevil to call on the prefect. This gentleman, who, like most of his colleagues, found his life very dull, had been delighted to hear of the arrival of an Englishman who was rich, a man of the world, and the father of a pretty daughter. He had, therefore, given him the most friendly reception, and overwhelmed him with offers of service; further, within a very few days, he came to return his visit. The colonel, who had just dined, was comfortably stretched out upon his sofa, and very nearly asleep. His daughter was singing at a broken-down piano; Orso was turning over the leaves of her music, and gazing at the fair singer's shoulders and golden hair. The prefect was announced, the piano stopped, the colonel got up, rubbed his eyes, and introduced the prefect to his daughter.

"I do not introduce M. della Rebbia to you," said he, "for no doubt you know him already."

"Is this gentleman Colonel della Rebbia's son?" said the prefect, looking a trifle embarrassed.

"Yes, monsieur," replied Orso.

"I had the honour of knowing your father."

The ordinary commonplaces of conversation were soon exhausted. The colonel, in spite of himself, yawned pretty frequently. Orso, as a liberal, did not care to converse with a satellite of the Government. The burden of the conversation fell on Miss Lydia. The prefect, on his side, did not let it drop, and it was clear that he found the greatest pleasure in talking of Paris, and of the great world, to a woman who was acquainted with all the foremost people in European society. As he talked, he now and then glanced at Orso, with an expression of singular curiosity.

"Was it on the Continent that you made M. della Rebbia's acquaintance?" he inquired.

Somewhat embarrassed, Miss Lydia replied that she had made his acquaintance on the ship which had carried them to Corsica.

"He is a very gentlemanly young fellow," said the prefect, in an undertone; "and has he told you," he added, dropping his voice still lower, "why he has returned to Corsica?"

Miss Lydia put on her most majestic air and answered:

"I have not asked him," she said. "You may do so."

The prefect kept silence, but, an instant later, hearing Orso speak a few words of English to the colonel, he said:

"You seem to have traveled a great deal, monsieur. You must have forgotten Corsica and Corsican habits."

"It is quite true that I was very young when I went away."

"You still belong to the army?"

"I am on half-pay, monsieur."

"You have been too long in the French army not to have become a thorough Frenchman, I have no doubt?"

The last words of the sentence were spoken with marked emphasis.

The Corsicans are not particularly flattered at being reminded that they belong to the "Great Nations." They claim to be a people apart, and so well do they justify their claim that it may very well be granted them.

Somewhat nettled, Orso replied: "Do you think, M. le Prefet, that a Corsican must necessarily serve in the French army to become an honourable man?"

"No, indeed," said the prefect, "that is not my idea at all; I am only speaking of certain *customs* belonging to this country, some of which are not such as a Government official would like to see."

He emphasized the word *customs*, and put on as grave an expression as his features could assume. Soon after he got up and took his leave, bearing with him Miss Lydia's promise that she would go and call on his wife at the prefecture.

When he had departed: "I had to come to Corsica," said Miss Lydia, "to find out what a prefect is like. This one strikes me as rather amiable."

"For my part," said Orso, "I can't say as much. He strikes me as a very queer individual, with his airs of emphasis and mystery."

The colonel was extremely drowsy. Miss Lydia cast a glance in his direction, and, lowering her voice:

"And I," she said, "do not think him so mysterious as you pretend; for I believe I understood him!"

"Then you are clear-sighted indeed, Miss Nevil. If you have seen any wit in what he has just said you must certainly have put it there yourself."

"It is the Marquis de Mascarille, I think, who says that, M. della Rebbia. But would you like me to give you a proof of my clear-sightedness? I am something of a witch, and I can read the thoughts of people I have seen only twice."

"Good heavens! you alarm me. If you really can read my thoughts I don't know whether I should be glad or sorry."

"M. della Rebbia," went on Miss Lydia, with a blush, "we have only known each other for a few days. But at sea, and in savage countries (you will excuse me, I hope) — in savage countries friendships grow more quickly than they do in society . . . so you must not be astonished if I speak to you, as a friend, upon private matters, with which, perhaps, a stranger ought not to interfere."

"Ah, do not say that word, Miss Nevil. I like the other far better."

"Well, then, monsieur, I must tell you that without having tried to find out your secrets, I have learned some of them, and they grieve me. I have heard, monsieur, of the misfortune which has overtaken your family. A great deal has been said to me about the vindictive nature of your fellow-countrymen, and the fashion in which they take their vengeance. Was it not to that the prefect was alluding?"

"Miss Lydia! Can you believe it!" and Orso turned deadly pale.

"No, M. della Rebbia," she said, interrupting him, "I know you to be a most honourable gentleman. You have told me yourself that it was only the common people in your country who still practiced the *vendetta* — which you are pleased to describe as a kind of duel."

"Do you, then, believe me capable of ever becoming a murderer?"

"Since I have mentioned the subject at all, Monsieur Orso, you must clearly see that I do not suspect you, and if I have spoken to you at all," she added, dropping her eyes, "it is because I have realized that surrounded, it may be, by barbarous prejudices on your return home, you will be glad to know that there is somebody who esteems you for having the courage to resist them. Come!" said she, rising to her feet, "don't let us talk again of such horrid things, they make my head ache, and besides it's very late. You are not angry with me, are you? Let us say good-night in the English fashion," and she held out her hand.

Orso pressed it, looking grave and deeply moved.

"Mademoiselle," he said, "do you know that there are moments when the instincts of my country wake up within me. Sometimes, when I think of my poor father, horrible thoughts assail me. Thanks to you, I am rid of them forever. Thank you! thank you!"

He would have continued, but Miss Lydia dropped a teaspoon, and the noise woke up the colonel.

"Della Rebbia, we'll start at five o'clock to-morrow morning. Be punctual!"

"Yes, colonel."

# CHAPTER V

The next day, a short time before the sportsmen came back, Miss Nevil, returning with her maid from a walk along the seashore, was just about to enter the inn, when she noticed a young woman, dressed in black, riding into the town on a small but strong horse. She was followed by a sort of peasant, also on horseback, who wore a brown cloth jacket cut at the elbows. A gourd was slung over his shoulder and a pistol was hanging at his belt, his hand grasped a gun, the butt of which rested in a leathern pocket fastened to his saddle-bow — in short, he wore the complete costume of a brigand in a melodrama, or of the middle-class Corsican on his travels. Miss Nevil's attention was first attracted by the woman's remarkable beauty. She seemed about twenty years of age; she was tall and pale, with dark blue eyes, red lips, and teeth like enamel. In her expression pride, anxiety, and sadness were all legible. On her head she wore a black silk veil called a *mezzaro*, which the Genoese introduced into Corsica, and which is so becoming to women. Long braids of chestnut hair formed a sort of turban round her head. Her dress was neat, but simple in the extreme.

Miss Nevil had plenty of time to observe her, for the lady in the *mezzaro* had halted in the street, and was questioning somebody on a subject which, to judge from the expression of her eyes, must have interested her exceedingly. Then, as soon as she received an answer, she touched her mount with her riding-switch, and, breaking into a quick trot, never halted till she reached the door of the hotel in which Sir Thomas Nevil and Orso were staying. There, after exchanging a few words with the host, the girl sprang nimbly from her saddle and seated herself on a stone bench beside the entrance door, while her groom led the horses away to the stable. Miss Lydia, in her Paris gown, passed close beside the stranger, who did not raise her eyes. A quarter of an hour later she opened her window, and saw the lady in the *mezzaro* still sitting in the same place and in the same attitude. Not long afterward the colonel and Orso returned from hunting.

Then the landlord said a few words to the young lady in mourning, and pointed to della Rebbia with his finger. She coloured deeply, rose eagerly, went a few paces forward, and then stopped short, apparently much confused. Orso was quite close to her, and was looking at her curiously.

"Are you Orso Antonio della Rebbia?" said she in a tremulous voice. "I am Colomba."

"Colomba!" cried Orso.

And taking her in his arms he kissed her tenderly, somewhat to the surprise of the colonel and his daughter — but in England people do not kiss each other in the street.

"Brother," said Colomba, "you must forgive me for having come without your permission. But I heard from our friends that you had arrived, and it is such a great consolation to me to see you."

Again Orso kissed her. Then, turning to the colonel:

"This is my sister," said he, "whom I never should have recognized if she had not told me her name — Colomba — Colonel Sir Thomas Nevil — colonel, you will kindly excuse me, but I can not have the honour of dining with you to-day. My sister — "

"But, my dear fellow, where the devil do you expect to dine? You know very well there is only one dinner in this infernal tavern, and we have bespoken it. It will afford my daughter great pleasure if this young lady will join us."

Colomba looked at her brother, who did not need much pressing, and they all passed together into the largest room in the inn, which the colonel used as his sitting and dining room. Mademoiselle della Rebbia, on being introduced to Miss Nevil, made her a deep courtesy, but she did not utter a single word. It was easy to see that she was very much frightened at finding herself, perhaps for the first time in her life, in the company of strangers belonging to the great world. Yet there was nothing provincial in her manners. The novelty of her position excused her awkwardness. Miss Nevil took a liking to her at once, and, as there was no room disengaged in the hotel, the whole of which was occupied by the colonel and his attendants, she offered, either out of condescension or curiosity, to have a bed prepared in her own room for Mademoiselle della Rebbia.

Colomba stammered a few words of thanks, and hastened after Miss Nevil's maid, to make such changes in her toilet as were rendered necessary by a journey on horseback in the dust and heat.

When she re-entered the sitting-room, she paused in front of the colonel's guns, which the hunters had left in a corner.

"What fine weapons," said she. "Are they yours, brother?"

"No, they are the colonel's English guns — and they are as good as they are handsome."

"How much I wish you had one like them!" said Colomba.

"One of those three certainly does belong to della Rebbia," exclaimed the colonel. "He really shoots almost too well! To-day he fired fourteen shots, and brought down fourteen head of game."

A friendly dispute at once ensued, in which Orso was vanquished, to his sister's great satisfaction, as it was easy to perceive from the childish expression of delight which illumined her face, so serious a moment before.

"Choose, my dear fellow," said the colonel; but Orso refused.

"Very well, then. Your sister shall choose for you."

Colomba did not wait for a second invitation. She took up the plainest of the guns, but it was a first-rate Manton of large calibre.

"This one," she said, "must carry a ball a long distance."

Her brother was growing quite confused in his expressions of gratitude, when dinner appeared, very opportunely, to help him out of his embarrassment.

Miss Lydia was delighted to notice that Colomba, who had shown considerable reluctance to sit down with them, and had yielded only at a glance from her brother, crossed herself, like a good Catholic, before she began to eat.

"Good!" said she to herself, "that is primitive!" and she anticipated acquiring many interesting facts by observing this youthful representative of ancient Corsican manners. As for Orso, he was evidently a trifle uneasy, fearing, doubtless, that his sister might say or do something which savoured too much of her native village. But Colomba watched him constantly, and regulated all her own movements by his. Sometimes she looked at him fixedly, with a strange expression of sadness, and then, if Orso's eyes met hers, he was the first to turn them away, as though he would evade some question which his sister was mentally addressing to him, the sense of which he understood only too well. Everybody talked French, for the colonel could only express himself very badly in Italian. Colomba understood French, and even pronounced the few words she was obliged to exchange with her entertainers tolerably well.

After dinner, the colonel, who had noticed the sort of constraint which existed between the brother and sister, inquired of Orso, with his customary frankness, whether he did not wish to be alone with Mademoiselle Colomba, offering, in that case, to go into the next room with his daughter. But Orso hastened to thank him, and to assure him they would have plenty of time to talk at Pietranera — this was the name of the village where he was to take up his abode.

The colonel then resumed his customary position on the sofa, and Miss Nevil, after attempting several subjects of conversation, gave up all hope of inducing the fair Colomba to talk, and begged Orso to read her a canto out of Dante, her favourite poet. Orso chose the canto of the Inferno, containing the episode of Francesca da Rimini, and began to read, as impressively as he was able, the glorious tercets which so admirably express the risk run by two young persons who venture to read a love-story together. As he read on Colomba drew nearer to the table, and raised her head, which she had kept lowered. Her wide-open eyes, shone with extraordinary fire, she grew red and pale by turns, and stirred convulsively in her chair. How admirable is the Italian organization, which can understand poetry without needing a pedant to explain its beauties!

When the canto was finished:

"How beautiful that is!" she exclaimed. "Who wrote it, brother?"

Orso was a little disconcerted, and Miss Lydia answered with a smile that it was written by a Florentine poet, who had been dead for centuries.

"You shall read Dante," said Orso, "when you are at Pietranera."

"Good heavens, how beautiful it is!" said Colomba again, and she repeated three or four tercets which she had remembered, speaking at first in an undertone; then, growing excited, she declaimed them aloud, with far more expression than her brother had put into his reading.

Miss Lydia was very much astonished.

"You seem very fond of poetry," she said. "How I envy you the delight you will find in reading Dante for the first time!"

"You see, Miss Nevil," said Orso, "what a power Dante's lines must have, when they so move a wild young savage who knows nothing but her *Pater*. But I am mistaken! I recollect now that Colomba belongs to the guild. Even when she was quite a little child she used to try her hand at verse-making, and my father used to write me word that she was the best *voceratrice* in Pietranera, and for two leagues round about."

Colomba cast an imploring glance at her brother. Miss Nevil had heard of the Corsican *improvisatrici*, and was dying to hear one. She begged Colomba, then, to give her a specimen of her powers. Very much vexed now at having made any mention of his sister's poetic gifts, Orso interposed. In vain did he protest that nothing was so insipid as a Corsican *ballata*, and that to recite the Corsican verses after those of Dante was like betraying his country. All he did was to stimulate Miss Nevil's curiosity, and at last he was obliged to say to his sister:

"Well! well! improvise something — but let it be short!"

Colomba heaved a sigh, looked fixedly for a moment, first at the table-cloth, and then at the rafters of the ceiling; at last, covering her eyes with her hand like those birds that gather courage, and fancy they are not seen when they no longer see themselves, she sang, or rather declaimed, in an unsteady voice, the following *serenata*:

### "THE MAIDEN AND THE TURTLE-DOVE

"In the valley, far away among the mountains, the sun only shines for an hour every day. In the valley there stands a gloomy house, and grass grows on its threshold. Doors and windows are always shut. No smoke rises from the roof. But at noon, when the sunshine falls, a window opens, and the orphan girl sits spinning at her wheel. She spins, and as she works, she sings — a song of sadness. But no other song comes to answer hers! One day — a day in spring-time — a turtle-dove settled on a tree hard by, and heard the maiden's song. 'Maiden,' it said, 'thou art not the only mourner! A cruel hawk has snatched my mate from me!' 'Turtle-dove, show me that cruel hawk; were it to soar higher than the clouds I would soon bring it down to earth! But who will restore to me, unhappy that I am, my brother, now in a far country?' 'Maiden, tell me, where thy brother is, and my wings shall bear me to him.'"

"A well-bred turtle-dove, indeed!" exclaimed Orso, and the emotion with which he kissed his sister contrasted strongly with the jesting tone in which he spoke.

"Your song is delightful," said Miss Lydia. "You must write it in my album; I'll translate it into English, and have it set to music."

The worthy colonel, who had not understood a single word, added his compliments to his daughter's and added: "Is this dove you speak of the bird we ate broiled at dinner to-day?"

Miss Nevil fetched her album, and was not a little surprised to see the *improvisatrice* write down her song, with so much care in the matter of economizing space.

170

The lines, instead of being separate, were all run together, as far as the breadth of the paper would permit, so that they did not agree with the accepted definition of poetic composition — "short lines of unequal length, with a margin on each side of them." Mademoiselle Colomba's somewhat fanciful spelling might also have excited comment. More than once Miss Nevil was seen to smile, and Orso's fraternal vanity suffered tortures.

Bedtime came, and the two young girls retired to their room. There, while Miss Lydia unclasped her necklace, ear-rings, and bracelets, she watched her companion draw something out of her gown — something as long as a stay-busk, but very different in shape. Carefully, almost stealthily, Colomba slipped this object under her *mezzaro*, which she laid on the table. Then she knelt down, and said her prayers devoutly. Two minutes afterward she was in her bed. Miss Lydia, naturally very inquisitive, and as slow as every Englishwoman is about undressing herself, moved over to the table, pretended she was looking for a pin, lifted up the *mezzaro*, and saw a long stiletto — curiously mounted in silver and mother-of-pearl. The workmanship was remarkably fine. It was an ancient weapon, and just the sort of one an amateur would have prized very highly.

"Is it the custom here," inquired Miss Nevil, with a smile, "for young ladies to wear such little instruments as these in their bodices?"

"It is," answered Colomba, with a sigh. "There are so many wicked people about!"

"And would you really have the courage to strike with it, like this?" And Miss Nevil, dagger in hand, made a gesture of stabbing from above, as actors do on the stage.

"Yes," said Colomba, in her soft, musical voice, "if I had to do it to protect myself or my friends. But you must not hold it like that, you might wound yourself if the person you were going to stab were to draw back." Then, sitting up in bed, "See," she added, "you must strike like this — upward! If you do so, the thrust is sure to kill, they say. Happy are they who never need such weapons."

She sighed, dropped her head back on the pillow, and closed her eyes. A more noble, beautiful, virginal head it would be impossible to imagine. Phidias would have asked no other model for Minerva.

CHAPTER VI

It is in obedience to the precept of Horace that I have begun by plunging *in media res*. Now that every one is asleep — the beautiful Colomba, the colonel, and his daughter — I will seize the opportunity to acquaint my reader with certain details of which he must not be ignorant, if he desires to follow the further course of this veracious history. He is already aware that Colonel della Rebbia, Orso's father, had been assassinated. Now, in Corsica, people are not murdered, as they are in France, by the first escaped convict who can devise no better means of relieving a man of his silver-plate. In Corsica a man is murdered by his enemies — but the reason he has enemies is often very difficult to discover. Many families hate each other because it has been an old-standing habit of theirs to hate each other; but the tradition of the original cause of their hatred may have completely disappeared.

The family to which Colonel della Rebbia belonged hated several other families, but that of the Barricini particularly. Some people asserted that in the sixteenth century a della Rebbia had seduced a lady of the Barricini family, and had afterward been poniarded by a relative of the outraged damsel. Others, indeed, told the story in a different fashion, declaring that it was a della Rebbia who had been seduced, and a Barricini who had been poniarded. However that may be, there was, to use the time-honoured expression, "blood between the two houses." Nevertheless, and contrary to custom, this murder had not resulted in others; for the della Rebbia and the Barricini had been equally persecuted by the Genoese Government, and as the young men had all left the country, the two families were deprived, during several generations, of their more energetic representatives. At the close of the last century, one of the della Rebbias, an officer in the Neapolitan service, quarreled, in a gambling hell,

172

with some soldiers, who called him a Corsican goatherd, and other insulting names. He drew his sword, but being only one against three, he would have fared very ill if a stranger, who was playing in the same room, had not exclaimed, "I, too, am a Corsican," and come to his rescue. This stranger was one of the Barricini, who, for that matter, was not acquainted with his countryman. After mutual explanations, they interchanged courtesies and vowed eternal friendship. For on the Continent, quite contrary to their practice in their own island, Corsicans quickly become friends. This fact was clearly exemplified on the present occasion. As long as della Rebbia and Barricini remained in Italy they were close friends. Once they were back in Corsica, they saw each other but very seldom, although they both lived in the same village; and when they died, it was reported that they had not spoken to each other for five or six years. Their sons lived in the same fashion — "on ceremony," as they say in the island; one of them Ghilfuccio, Orso's father, was a soldier; the other Giudice Barricini, was a lawyer. Having both become heads of families, and being separated by their professions, they scarcely ever had an opportunity of seeing or hearing of each other.

One day, however, about the year 1809, Giudice read in a newspaper at Bastia that Captain Ghilfuccio had just been decorated, and remarked, before witnesses, that he was not at all surprised, considering that the family enjoyed the protection of General — — -. This remark was reported at Vienna to Ghilfuccio, who told one of his countrymen that, when he got back to Corsica, he would find Giudice a very rich man, because he made more money out of the suits he lost than out of those he won. It was never known whether he meant this as an insinuation that the lawyer cheated his clients, or as a mere allusion to the commonplace truth that a bad cause often brings a lawyer more profit than a good one. However that may have been, the lawyer Barricini heard of the epigram, and never forgot it. In 1812 he applied for the post of mayor of his commune, and had every hope of being appointed, when General — — — wrote to the prefect, to recommend one of Ghilfuccio's wife's relations. The prefect lost no time in carrying out the general's wish, and Barricini felt no doubt that he owed his failure to the intrigues of Ghilfuccio. In 1814, after the emperor's fall, the general's protégé was denounced as a Bonapartist, and his place was taken by Barricini. He, in his turn, was dismissed during the Hundred Days, but when the storm had blown over, he again took possession, with great pomp, of the mayoral seal and the municipal registers.

From this moment his star shone brighter than ever. Colonel della Rebbia, now living on half-pay at Pietranera, had to defend himself against covert and repeated attacks due to the pettifogging malignity of his enemy. At one time he was summoned to pay for the damage his horse had done to the mayor's fences, at another, the latter, under pretence of repairing the floor of the church, ordered the removal of a broken flagstone bearing the della Rebbia arms, which covered the grave of some member of the family. If the village goats ate the colonel's young plants, the mayor always protected their owners. The grocer who kept the post-office at Pietranera, and the old maimed soldier who had been the village policeman — both of them attached to the della Rebbia family — were turned adrift, and their places filled by Barricini's creatures.

The colonel's wife died, and her last wish was that she might be buried in the middle of the little wood in which she had been fond of walking. Forthwith the mayor declared she should be buried in the village cemetery, because he had no authority to permit burial in any other spot. The colonel, in a fury, declared that until the permit came, his wife would be interred in the spot she had chosen. He had her grave dug there. The mayor, on his side, had another grave dug in the cemetery, and sent for the police, that the law, so he declared, might be duly enforced. On the day of the funeral, the two parties came face to face, and, for a moment, there was reason to fear a struggle might ensue for the possession of Signora della Rebbia's corpse. Some forty well-armed peasants, mustered by the dead woman's relatives, forced the priest, when he issued from the church, to take the road to the wood. On the other hand, the mayor, at the head of his two sons, his dependents, and the gendarmes, advanced to oppose their march. When he appeared, and called on the procession to turn back, he was greeted with howls and threats. The advantage of numbers was with his opponents, and they seemed thoroughly determined. At sight of him several guns were loaded, and one shepherd is even said to have leveled his musket at him, but the colonel knocked up the barrel, and said, "Let no man fire without my orders!" The mayor, who, like Panurge, had "a natural fear of blows," refused to give battle, and retired, with his escort. Then the funeral procession started, carefully choosing the longest way, so as to pass in front of the mayor's house. As it was filing by, an idiot, who had joined its ranks, took it into his head to shout, "Vive l'Empereur!" Two or three voices answered him, and the Rebbianites, growing hotter, proposed killing one of the mayor's oxen, which chanced to bar their way. Fortunately the colonel stopped this act of violence.

It is hardly necessary to mention that an official statement was at once drawn up, or that the mayor sent the prefect a report, in his sublimest style, describing the manner in which all laws, human and divine, had been trodden under foot — how the majesty of himself, the mayor, and of the priest had been flouted and insulted, and how Colonel della Rebbia had put himself at the head of a Bonapartist plot, to change the order of succession to the throne, and to excite peaceful citizens to take arms against one another — crimes provided against by Articles 86 and 91 of the Penal Code.

The exaggerated tone of this complaint diminished its effect. The colonel wrote to the prefect and to the public prosecutor. One of his wife's kinsmen was related to one of the deputies of the island, another was cousin to the president of the Royal Court. Thanks to this interest, the plot faded out of sight, Signora della Rebbia was left quiet in the wood, and the idiot alone was sentenced to a fortnight's imprisonment.

Lawyer Barricini, dissatisfied with the result of this affair, turned his batteries in a different direction. He dug out some old claim, whereby he undertook to contest the colonel's ownership of a certain water-course which turned a mill-wheel. A lawsuit began and dragged slowly along. At the end of twelve months, the court was about to give its decision, and according to all appearances in favour of the colonel, when Barricini placed in the hands of the public prosecutor a letter, signed by a certain Agostini, a well-known bandit, threatening him, the mayor, with fire and sword if he did not relinquish his pretensions. It is well known that in Corsica the protection of these brigands is much sought after, and that, to oblige their friends, they frequently intervene in private quarrels. The mayor was deriving considerable advantage from this letter, when the business was further complicated by a fresh incident. Agostini, the bandit, wrote to the public prosecutor, to complain that his handwriting had been counterfeited, and his character aspersed, by some one who desired to represent him as a man who made a traffic of his influence. "If I can discover the forger," he said at the end of his letter, "I will make a striking example of him."

It was quite clear that Agostini did not write the threatening letter to the mayor. The della Rebbia accused the Barricini of it and *vice versa*. Both parties broke into open threats, and the authorities did not know where to find the culprit.

In the midst of all this Colonel Ghilfuccio was murdered. Here are the facts, as they were elicited at the official inquiry. On the 2d of August, 18 — , toward nightfall, a woman named Maddalena Pietri, who was carrying corn to Pietranera, heard two shots fired, very close together, the reports, as it seemed to her, coming from the deep lane leading to the village, about a hundred and fifty paces from the spot on which she stood. Almost immediately afterward she saw a man running, crouching along a footpath among the vines, and making for the village. The man stopped for a minute, and turned round, but the distance prevented the woman Pietri from seeing his features, and besides, he had a vine-leaf in his mouth, which hid almost the whole of his face. He made a signal with his head to some comrade, whom the witness could not see, and then disappeared among the vines.

176

The woman Pietri dropped her burden, ran up the path, and found Colonel della Rebbia, bathed in his own blood from two bullet wounds, but still breathing. Close beside him lay his gun, loaded and cocked, as if he had been defending himself against a person who had attacked him in front, just when another had struck him from behind. Although the rattle was in his throat, he struggled against the grip of death, but he could not utter a word — this the doctors explained by the nature of the wounds, which had cut through his lungs: the blood was choking him, it flowed slowly, like red froth. In vain did the woman lift him up, and ask him several questions. She saw plainly enough that he desired to speak, but he could not make himself understood. Noticing that he was trying to get his hand to his pocket, she quickly drew out of it a little note-book, which she opened and gave to him.

The wounded man took the pencil out of the note-book and tried to write. In fact, the witness saw him form several letters, but with great difficulty. As she could not read, however, she was unable to understand their meaning. Exhausted by the effort, the colonel left the note-book in the woman's hand, which he squeezed tightly, looking at her strangely, as if he wanted to say (these are the witness's own words): "It is important — it is my murderer's name!"

Maddalena Pietri was going up to the village, when she met Barricini, the mayor, with his son Vincentello. It was then almost dark. She told them what she had seen. The mayor took the note-book, hurried up to his house, put on his sash, and fetched his secretary and the gendarmes. Left alone with young Vincentello, Maddalena Pietri suggested that he should go to the colonel's assistance, in case he was still alive, but Vincentello replied that if he were to go near a man who had been the bitter enemy of his family, he would certainly be accused of having killed him. A very short time afterward the mayor arrived, found the colonel dead, had the corpse carried away, and drew up his report.

In spite of the agitation so natural on such an occasion, Monsieur Barricini had hastened to place the colonel's note-book under seal, and to make all the inquiries in his power, but none of them resulted in any discovery of importance.

When the examining magistrate arrived the note-book was opened, and on a blood-stained page were seen letters written in a trembling hand, but still quite legible; the sheet bore the word *Agosti* — and the judge did not doubt that the colonel had intended to point out Agostini as his murderer. Nevertheless, Colomba della Rebbia, who had been summoned by the magistrate, asked leave to examine the note-book. After turning the leaves for a few moments, she stretched out her hand toward the mayor and cried, "There stands the murderer!" Then with a precision and a clearness which were astonishing, considering the passion of sorrow that shook her, she related that, a few days previously, her father had received a letter from his son, which he had burned, but that before doing so he had written Orso's address (he had just changed his garrison) in the note-book with his pencil. Now, his address was no longer in the note-book, and Colomba concluded that the mayor had torn out the leaf on which it was written, which probably was that on which her father had traced the murderer's name, and for that name the mayor, according to Colomba, had substituted Agostini's. The magistrate, in fact, noticed that one sheet was missing from the quire on which the name was written, but he remarked also that leaves were likewise missing from other quires in the same note-book, and certain witnesses testified that the colonel had a habit of tearing out pages when he wanted to light a cigar — therefore nothing was more probable than that, by an oversight, he had burned the address he had copied. Further, it was shown that the mayor could not have read the note-book on receiving it from Maddalena Pietri, on account of the darkness, and it was proved that he had not stopped an instant before he went into his house, that the sergeant of the gendarmes had gone there with him, and had seen him light a lamp and put the note-book into an envelope which he had sealed before his eyes.

When this officer had concluded his deposition, Colomba, half-distracted, cast herself at his feet, and besought him, by all he held most sacred, to say whether he had not left the mayor alone for a single moment. After a certain amount of hesitation, the man, who was evidently affected by the young girl's excitement, admitted that he had gone into the next room to fetch a sheet of foolscap, but that he had not been away a minute, and that the mayor had talked to him all the time he was groping for the paper in a drawer. Moreover, he deposed that when he came back the blood-stained note-book was still on the table, in the very place where the mayor had thrown it when he first came in.

Monsieur Barricini gave his evidence with the utmost coolness. He made allowances, he said, for Mademoiselle della Rebbia's excitement, and was ready to condescend to justify himself. He proved that he had spent his whole evening in the village, that his son Vincentello had been with him in front of the house at the moment when the crime was committed, and that his son Orlanduccio, who had had an attack of fever that very day, had never left his bed. He produced every gun in his house, and not one of them had been recently discharged. He added, that, as regarded the note-book, he had at once realized its importance; that he had sealed it up, and placed it in the hands of his deputy, foreseeing that he himself might be suspected, on account of his quarrel with the colonel. Finally, he reminded the court that Agostini had threatened to kill the man who had written a letter in his name, and he insinuated that this ruffian had probably suspected the colonel, and murdered him. Such a vengeance, for a similar reason, is by no means unprecedented in the history of brigandage.

Five days after Colonel della Rebbia's death, Agostini was surprised by a detachment of riflemen, and killed, fighting desperately to the last. On his person was found a letter from Colomba, beseeching him to declare whether he was guilty of the murder imputed to him, or not. As the bandit had sent no answer, it was pretty generally concluded that he had not the courage to tell a daughter he had murdered her father. Yet those who claimed to know Agostini's nature thoroughly, whispered that if he had killed the colonel, he would have boasted of the deed.

Another bandit, known by the name of Brandolaccio, sent Colomba a declaration in which he bore witness "on his honour" to his comrade's innocence — but the only proof he put forward was that Agostini had never told him that he suspected the colonel.

The upshot was that the Barricini suffered no inconvenience, the examining magistrate was loud in his praise of the mayor, and the mayor, on his side, crowned his handsome behaviour by relinquishing all his claims over the stream, concerning which he had brought the lawsuit against Colonel della Rebbia.

According to the custom of her country, Colomba improvised a *ballata* in presence of her father's corpse, and before his assembled friends. In it she poured out all her hatred against the Barricini, formally charged them with the murder, and threatened them with her brother's vengeance. It was this same *ballata*, which had grown very popular, that the sailor had sung before Miss Lydia. When Orso, who was in the north of France, heard of his father's death, he applied for leave, but failed to obtain it. A letter from his sister led him to believe at first in the guilt of the Barricini, but he soon received copies of all the documents connected with the inquiry and a private letter from the judge, which almost convinced him that the bandit Agostini was the only culprit. Every three months Colomba had written to him, reiterating her suspicions, which she called her "proofs." In spite of himself, these accusations made his Corsican blood boil, and sometimes he was very near sharing his sister's prejudices. Nevertheless, every time he wrote to her he repeated his conviction that her allegations possessed no solid foundation, and were quite unworthy of belief. He even forbade her, but always vainly, to mention them to him again.

Thus two years went by. At the end of that time Orso was placed on half-pay, and then it occurred to him to go back to his own country — not at all for the purpose of taking vengeance on people whom he believed innocent, but to arrange a marriage for his sister, and the sale of his own small property — if its value should prove sufficient to enable him to live on the Continent.

# CHAPTER VII

Whether it was that the arrival of his sister had reminded Orso forcibly of his paternal home, or that Colomba's unconventional dress and manners made him feel shy before his civilized friends, he announced, the very next day, his determination to leave Ajaccio, and to return to Pietranera. But he made the colonel promise that when he went to Bastia he would come and stay in his modest manor-house, and undertook, in return, to provide him with plenty of buck, pheasant, boar, and other game.

On the day before that of his departure Orso proposed that, instead of going out shooting, they should all take a walk along the shores of the gulf. With Miss Lydia on his arm he was able to talk in perfect freedom — for Colomba had stayed in the town to do her shopping, and the colonel was perpetually leaving the young people to fire shots at sea-gulls and gannets, greatly to the astonishment of the passers-by, who could not conceive why any man should waste his powder on such paltry game.

They were walking along the path leading to the Greek Chapel, which commands the finest view to be had of the bay, but they paid no attention to it.

"Miss Lydia," said Orso, after a silence which had lasted long enough to become embarrassing, "tell me frankly, what do you think of my sister?"

"I like her very much," answered Miss Nevil. "Better than you," she added, with a smile; "for she is a true Corsican, and you are rather too civilized a savage!"

"Too civilized! Well, in spite of myself, I feel that I am growing a savage again, since I have set my foot on the island! A thousand horrid thoughts disturb and torment me, and I wanted to talk with you a little before I plunge into my desert!"

"You must be brave, monsieur! Look at your sister's resignation; she sets you an example!"

"Ah! do not be deceived! Do not believe in her resignation. She has not said a word to me as yet, but every look of hers tells me what she expects of me."

"What does she expect of you, then?"

"Oh, nothing! Except that I should try whether your father's gun will kill a man as surely as it kills a partridge."

"What an idea! You can actually believe that, when you have just acknowledged that she has said nothing to you yet? It really is too dreadful of you!"

"If her thoughts were not fixed on vengeance, she would have spoken to me at once about our father; she has never done it. She would have mentioned the names of those she considers — wrongly, I know — to be his murderers. But no; not a word! That is because we Corsicans, you see, are a cunning race. My sister realizes that she does not hold me completely in her power, and she does not choose to startle me while I may still escape her. Once she has led me to the edge of the precipice, and once I turn giddy there, she will thrust me into the abyss."

Then Orso gave Miss Nevil some details of his father's death, and recounted the principal proofs which had culminated in his belief that Agostini was the assassin.

"Nothing," he added, "has been able to convince Colomba. I saw that by her last letter. She has sworn the Barricini shall die, and — you see, Miss Nevil, what confidence I have in you! — they would not be alive now, perhaps, if one of the prejudices for which her uncivilized education must be the excuse had not convinced her that the execution of this vengeance belongs to me, as head of her family, and that my honour depends upon it!"

"Really and truly, Monsieur della Rebbia!" said Miss Nevil, "you slander your sister!"

"No. As you have said it yourself, she is a Corsican; she thinks as they all think. Do you know why I was so sad yesterday?"

"No. But for some time past you have been subject to these fits of sadness. You were much pleasanter in the earlier days of our acquaintance."

"Yesterday, on the contrary, I was more cheery and happy than I generally am. I had seen how kind, how indulgent, you were to my sister. The colonel and I were coming home in a boat. Do you know what one of the boatmen said to me in his infernal *patois*? 'You've killed a deal of game, Ors' Anton', but you'll find Orlanduccio Barricini a better shot than you!'"

"Well, what was there so very dreadful in that remark? Are you so very much set upon being considered a skilful sportsman?"

"But don't you see the ruffian was telling me I shouldn't have courage to kill Orlanduccio!"

"Do you know, M. della Rebbia, you frighten me! The air of this island of yours seems not only to give people fevers, but to drive them mad. Luckily we shall be leaving it soon!"

"Not without coming to Pietranera — you have promised my sister that."

"And if we were to fail in that promise, we should bring down some terrible vengeance on our heads, no doubt!"

"Do you remember that story your father was telling us, the other day, about the Indians who threatened the company's agents that, if they would not grant their prayer, they would starve themselves to death?"

"That means that you would starve yourself to death! I doubt it very much! You would go hungry for one day and then Mademoiselle Colomba would bring you such a tempting *bruccio* that you would quite relinquish your plan."

"Your jests are cruel, Miss Nevil. You might spare me. Listen, I am alone here; I have no one but you to prevent me from going mad, as you call it. You have been my guardian angel, and now — — !"

"Now," said Miss Lydia gravely, "to steady this reason of yours, which is so easily shaken, you have the honour of a soldier and a man, and," she added, turning away to pluck a flower, "if that will be any help to you, you have the memory of your guardian angel, too!"

"Ah, Miss Nevil, if I could only think you really take some interest!"

"Listen, M. della Rebbia," said Miss Nevil, with some emotion. "As you are a child, I will treat you as I would treat a child. When I was a little girl my mother gave me a beautiful necklace, which I had longed for greatly; but she said to me, 'Every time you put on this necklace, remember you do not know French yet.' The necklace lost some of its value in my eyes, it was a source of constant self-reproach. But I wore it, and in the end I knew French. Do you see this ring? It is an Egyptian scarabaeus, found, if you please, in a pyramid. That strange figure, which you may perhaps take for a bottle, stands for '*human life*.' There are certain people in my country to whom this hieroglyphic should appear exceedingly appropriate. This, which comes after it, is a shield upon an arm, holding a lance; that means '*struggle, battle.*' Thus the two characters, together, form this motto, which strikes me as a fine one, '*Life is a battle.*' Pray do not fancy I can translate hieroglyphics at sight! It was a man learned in such matters who explained these to me. Here, I will give you my scarabaeus. Whenever you feel some wicked Corsican thought stir in you, look at my talisman, and tell yourself you must win the battle our evil passions wage against us. Why, really, I don't preach at all badly!"

"I shall think of you, Miss Nevil, and I shall say to myself — — "

"Say to yourself you have a friend who would be in despair at the idea of your being hanged — and besides it would be too distressing for your ancestors the corporals!"

With these words she dropped Orso's arm, laughing and running to her father.

"Papa," she said, "do leave those poor birds alone, and come and make up poetry with us, in Napoleon's grotto!"

CHAPTER VIII

There is always a certain solemnity about a departure, even when the separation is only to be a short one. Orso and his sister were to start very early in the morning, and he had taken his leave of Miss Lydia the night before — for he had no hope that she would disturb her indolent habits on his account. Their farewells had been cold and grave. Since that conversation on the sea-shore, Miss Lydia had been afraid she had perhaps shown too strong an interest in Orso, and on the other hand, her jests, and more especially her careless tone, lay heavy on Orso's heart. At one moment he had thought the young Englishwoman's manner betrayed a budding feeling of affection, but now, put out of countenance by her jests, he told himself she only looked on him as a mere acquaintance, who would be soon forgotten. Great, therefore, was his surprise, next morning, when, as he sat at coffee with the colonel, he saw Miss Lydia come into the room, followed by his sister. She had risen at five o'clock, and for an Englishwoman, and especially for Miss Nevil, the effort was so great that it could not but give him some cause for vanity.

"I am so sorry you should have disturbed yourself so early," said Orso. "No doubt my sister woke you up in spite of my injunctions, and you must hate us heartily! Perhaps you wish I was hanged already!"

"No," said Miss Lydia, very low and in Italian, evidently so that her father might not hear her, "but you were somewhat sulky with me yesterday, because of my innocent jokes, and I would not have you carry away an unpleasant recollection of your humble servant. What terrible people you are, you Corsicans! Well, good-bye! We shall meet soon, I hope."

And she held out her hand.

A sigh was the only answer Orso could find. Colomba came to his side, led him into a window, and spoke to him for a moment in an undertone, showing him something she held under her *mezzaro.*

"Mademoiselle," said Orso to Miss Nevil, "my sister is anxious to give you a very odd present, but we Corsicans have not much to offer — except our affection — which time never wipes out. My sister tells me you have looked with some curiosity at this dagger. It is an ancient possession in our family. It probably hung, once upon a time, at the belt of one of those corporals, to whom I owe the honour of your acquaintance. Colomba thinks it so precious that she has asked my leave to give it to you, and I hardly know if I ought to grant it, for I am afraid you'll laugh at us!"

"The dagger is beautiful," said Miss Lydia. "But it is a family weapon, I can not accept it!"

"It's not my father's dagger," exclaimed Colomba eagerly; "it was given to one of mother's ancestors by King Theodore. If the signorina will accept it, she will give us great pleasure."

"Come, Miss Lydia," said Orso, "don't scorn a king's dagger!"

To a collector, relics of King Theodore are infinitely more precious than those of the most powerful of monarchs. The temptation was a strong one, and already Miss Lydia could see the effect the weapon would produce laid out on a lacquered table in her room at St. James's Place.

"But," said she, taking the dagger with the hesitating air of one who longs to accept, and casting one of her most delightful smiles on Colomba, "dear Signorina Colomba . . . I can not . . . I should not dare to let you depart thus, unarmed."

"My brother is with me," said Colomba proudly, "and we have the good gun your father has given us. Orso, have you put a bullet in it?"

Miss Nevil kept the dagger, and to avert the danger consequent on *giving* instruments that cut or pierce to a friend, Colomba insisted on receiving a soldo in payment.

A start had to be made at last. Yet once again Orso pressed Miss Nevil's hand, Colomba kissed her, and then held up her rosy lips to the colonel, who was enchanted with this Corsican politeness. From the window of the drawing-room Miss Lydia watched the brother and sister mount their horses. Colomba's eyes shone with a malignant joy which she had never remarked in them before. The sight of this tall strong creature, with her fanatical ideas of savage honour, pride written on her forehead, and curled in a sardonic smile upon her lips, carrying off the young man with his weapons, as though on some death-dealing errand, recalled Orso's fears to her, and she fancied she beheld his evil genius dragging him to his ruin. Orso, who was already in the

186

saddle, raised his head and caught sight of her. Either because he had guessed her thought, or desired to send her a last farewell, he took the Egyptian ring, which he had hung upon a ribbon, and carried it to his lips. Blushing, Miss Lydia stepped back from the window, then returning to it almost at once, she saw the two Corsicans cantering their little ponies rapidly toward the mountains. Half an hour later the colonel showed them to her, through his glasses, riding along the end of the bay, and she noticed that Orso constantly turned his head toward the town. At last he disappeared behind the marshes, the site of which is now filled by a flourishing nursery garden.

Miss Lydia glanced at herself in the glass, and thought she looked pale.

"What must that young man think of me," said she, "and what did I think of him? And why did I think about him? . . . A traveling acquaintance! . . . What have I come to Corsica for? . . . Oh! I don't care for him! . . . No! no! and besides the thing is impossible . . . And Colomba . . . Fancy me sister-in-law to a *voceratrice*, who wears a big dagger!"

And she noticed she was still holding King Theodore's dagger in her hand. She tossed it on to her toilette table. "Colomba, in London, dancing at Almacks! . . . Good heavens! what a lion that would be, to show off! . . . Perhaps she'd make a great sensation! . . . He loves me, I'm certain of it! He is the hero of a novel, and I have interrupted his adventurous career. . . . But did he really long to avenge his father in true Corsican fashion? . . . He was something between a Conrad and a dandy . . . I've turned him into nothing but a dandy! . . . And a dandy with a Corsican tailor! . . ."

She threw herself on her bed, and tried to sleep — but that proved an impossibility, and I will not undertake to continue her soliloquy, during which she declared, more than a hundred times over, that Signor della Rebbia had not been, was not, and never should be, anything to her.

187

# CHAPTER IX

Meanwhile Orso was riding along beside his sister. At first the speed at which their horses moved prevented all conversation, but when the hills grew so steep that they were obliged to go at a foot's pace, they began to exchange a few words about the friends from whom they had just parted. Colomba spoke with admiration of Miss Nevil's beauty, of her golden hair, and charming ways. Then she asked whether the colonel was really as rich as he appeared, and whether Miss Lydia was his only child.

"She would be a good match," said she. "Her father seems to have a great liking for you — — "

And as Orso made no response, she added: "Our family was rich, in days gone by. It is still one of the most respected in the island. All these *signori* about us are bastards. The only noble blood left is in the families of the corporals, and as you know, Orso, your ancestors were the chief corporals in the island. You know our family came from beyond the hills, and it was the civil wars that forced us over to this side. If I were you, Orso, I shouldn't hesitate — I should ask Colonel Nevil for his daughter's hand." Orso shrugged his shoulders. "With her fortune, you might buy the Falsetta woods, and the vineyards below ours. I would build a fine stone house, and add a story to the old tower in which Sambucuccio killed so many Moors in the days of Count Henry, *il bel Missere.*"

"Colomba, you're talking nonsense," said Orso, cantering forward.

"You are a man, Ors' Anton', and of course you know what you ought to do better than any woman. But I should very much like to know what objection that Englishman could have to the marriage. Are there any corporals in England?"

After a somewhat lengthy ride, spent in talking in this fashion, the brother and sister reached a little village, not far from Bocognano, where they halted to dine and sleep at a friend's house. They were welcomed with a hospitality which must be experienced before it can be appreciated. The next morning, their host, who had stood godfather to a child to whom Madame della Rebbia had been godmother, accompanied them a league beyond his house.

"Do you see those woods and thickets?" said he to Orso, just as they were parting. "A man who had met with a misfortune might live there peacefully for ten years, and no gendarme or soldier would ever come to look for him. The woods run into the Vizzavona forest, and anybody who had friends at Bocognano or in the neighbourhood would want for nothing. That's a good gun you have there. It must carry a long way. Blood of the Madonna! What calibre! You might kill better game than boars with it!"

Orso answered, coldly, that his gun was of English make, and carried "the lead" a long distance. The friends embraced, and took their different ways.

Our travelers were drawing quite close to Pietranera, when, at the entrance of a little gorge, through which they had to pass, they beheld seven or eight men, armed with guns, some sitting on stones, others lying on the grass, others standing up, and seemingly on the lookout. Their horses were grazing a little way off. Colomba looked at them for a moment, through a spy-glass which she took out of one of the large leathern pockets all Corsicans wear when on a journey.

"Those are our men!" she cried, with a well-pleased air. "Pieruccio had done his errand well!"

"What men?" inquired Orso.

"Our herdsmen," she replied. "I sent Pieruccio off yesterday evening to call the good fellows together, so that they may attend you home. It would not do for you to enter Pietranera without an escort, and besides, you must know the Barricini are capable of anything!"

"Colomba," said Orso, and his tone was severe, "I have asked you, over and over again, not to mention the Barricini and your groundless suspicions to me. I shall certainly not make myself ridiculous by riding home with all these loafers behind me, and I am very angry with you for having sent for them without telling me."

"Brother, you have forgotten the ways of your own country. It is my business to protect you, when your own imprudence exposes you to danger. It was my duty to do what I have done."

Just at that moment the herdsmen, who had caught sight of them, hastened to their horses, and galloped down the hill to meet them.

"Evviva Ors' Anton'!" shouted a brawny, white-bearded old fellow, wrapped, despite the heat, in a hooded cloak of Corsican cloth, thicker than the skins of his own goats. "The image of his father, only taller and stronger! What a splendid gun! There'll be talk about that gun, Ors' Anton'!"

"Evviva Ors' Anton'!" chorused the herdsmen. "We were sure you'd come back, at last!"

"Ah! Ors' Anton'!" cried a tall fellow, with a skin tanned brick red. "How happy your father would be, if he were here to welcome you! The dear, good man! You would have seen him now, if he would have listened to me — if he would have let me settle Guidice's business! . . . But he wouldn't listen to me, poor fellow! He knows I was right, now!"

"Well, well!" said the old man. "Guidice will lose nothing by waiting."

"Evviva Ors' Anton'!" And the reports of a dozen guns capped the plaudit.

Very much put out, Orso sat in the midst of the group of mounted men, all talking at once, and crowding round to shake hands with him. For some time he could not make himself heard. At last, with the air he put on when he used to reprimand the men of his company, or send one of them to the guard-room, he said:

"I thank you, friends, for the affection you show for me, and for that which you felt for my father! But I do not want advice from any of you, and you must not offer it. I know my own duty."

"He's right! He's right!" cried the herdsmen. "You know you may reckon on us!"

190

"Yes, I do reckon on you. But at this moment I need no help, and no personal danger threatens me. Now face round at once, and be off with you to your goats. I know my way to Pietranera, and I want no guides."

"Fear nothing, Ors' Anton'," said the old man. "They would never dare to show their noses to-day. The mouse runs back to its hole when the tom-cat comes out!"

"Tom-cat yourself, old gray-beard!" said Orso. "What's your name?"

"What! don't you remember me, Ors' Anton'? I who have so often taken you up behind me on that biting mule of mine! You don't remember Polo Griffo? I'm an honest fellow, though, and with the della Rebbia, body and soul. Say but the word, and when that big gun of yours speaks, this old musket of mine, as old as its master, shall not be dumb. Be sure of that, Ors' Anton'!"

"Well, well! But be off with you now, in the devil's name, and let us go on our way!"

At last the herdsmen departed, trotting rapidly off toward the village, but they stopped every here and there, at all the highest spots on the road, as though they were looking out for some hidden ambuscade, always keeping near enough to Orso and his sister to be able to come to their assistance if necessary. And old Polo Griffo said to his comrades:

"I understand him! I understand him! He'll not say what he means to do, but he'll do it! He's the born image of his father. Ah! you may say you have no spite against any one, my boy! But you've made your vow to Saint Nega. Bravo! I wouldn't give a fig for the mayor's hide — there won't be the makings of a wineskin in it before the month is out!"

Preceded by this troop of skirmishers, the last descendant of the della Rebbia entered the village, and proceeded to the old mansion of his forefathers, the corporals. The Rebbianites, who had long been leaderless, had gathered to welcome him, and those dwellers in the village who observed a neutral line of conduct all came to their doorsteps to see him pass by. The adherents of the

Barricini remained inside their houses, and peeped out of the slits in their shutters.

The village of Pietranera is very irregularly built, like most Corsican villages — for indeed, to see a street, the traveler must betake himself to Cargese, which was built by Monsieur de Marboeuf. The houses, scattered irregularly about, without the least attempt at orderly arrangement, cover the top of a small plateau, or rather of a ridge of the mountain. Toward the centre of the village stands a great evergreen oak, and close beside it may be seen a granite trough, into which the water of a neighbouring spring is conveyed by a wooden pipe. This monument of public utility was constructed at the common expense of the della Rebbia and Barricini families. But the man who imagined this to be a sign of former friendship between the two families would be sorely mistaken. On the contrary, it is the outcome of their mutual jealousy. Once upon a time, Colonel della Rebbia sent a small sum of money to the Municipal Council of his commune to help to provide a fountain. The lawyer Barricini hastened to forward a similar gift, and to this generous strife Pietranera owes its water supply. Round about the evergreen oak and the fountain there is a clear space, known as "the Square," on which the local idlers gather every night. Sometimes they play at cards, and once a year, in Carnival-time, they dance. At the two ends of the square stands two edifices, of greater height than breadth, built of a mixture of granite and schist. These are the *Towers* of the two opposing families, the Barricini and the della Rebbia. Their architecture is exactly alike, their height is similar, and it is quite evident that the rivalry of the two families has never been absolutely decided by any stroke of fortune in favor of either.

It may perhaps be well to explain what should be understood by this word, "Tower." It is a square building, some forty feet in height, which in any other country would be simply described as a pigeon-house. A narrow entrance-door, eight feet above the level of the ground, is reached by a very steep flight of steps. Above the door is a window, in front of which runs a sort of balcony, the floor of which is pierced with openings, like a machicolation, through which the inhabitants may destroy an unwelcome visitor without any danger to themselves. Between the window and the door are two escutcheons, roughly carved. One of these bears what was originally a Genoese cross, now so battered that nobody but an antiquary could recognize it. On the other are chiseled the arms of the family to whom the Tower belongs. If the reader will complete this scheme of decoration by imagining several bullet marks on the escutcheons and on the window frames, he will have a fair idea of a Corsican mansion, dating from the middle ages. I had forgotten to add that the dwelling-house adjoins the tower, and is frequently connected with it by some interior passage.

The della Rebbia house and tower stand on the northern side of the square at Pietranera. The Barricini house and tower are on the southern side. Since the colonel's wife had been buried, no member of either family had ever been seen on any side of the square, save that assigned by tacit agreement to its own party. Orso was about to ride past the mayor's house when his sister checked him, and suggested his turning down a lane that would take them to their own dwelling without crossing the square at all.

"Why should we go out of our way?" said Orso. "Doesn't the square belong to everybody?" and he rode on.

"Brave heart!" murmured Colomba. ". . . My father! you will be avenged!"

When they reached the square, Colomba put herself between her brother and the Barricini mansion, and her eyes never left her enemy's windows. She noticed that they had been lately barricaded and provided with *archere*. *Archere* is the name given to narrow openings like loopholes, made between the big logs of wood used to close up the lower parts of the windows. When an onslaught is expected, this sort of barricade is used, and from behind the logs the attacked party can fire at its assailants with ease and safety.

"The cowards!" said Colomba. "Look, brother, they have begun to protect themselves! They have put up barricades! But some day or other they'll have to come out."

Orso's presence on the southern side of the square made a great sensation at Pietranera, and was taken to be a proof of boldness savouring of temerity. It was subject of endless comment on the part of the neutrals, when they gathered around the evergreen oak, that night.

"It is a good thing," they said, "that Barricini's sons are not back yet, for they are not so patient as the lawyer, and very likely they would not have let their enemy set his foot on their ground without making him pay for his bravado."

"Remember what I am telling you, neighbour," said an old man, the village oracle. "I watched Colomba's face to-day. She had some idea in her head. I smell powder in the air. Before long, butcher's meat will be cheap in Pietranera!"

# CHAPTER X

Orso had been parted from his father at so early an age that he had scarcely had time to know him. He had left Pietranera to pursue his studies at Pisa when he was only fifteen. Thence he had passed into the military school, and Ghilfuccio, meanwhile, was bearing the Imperial Eagles all over Europe. On the mainland, Orso only saw his father at rare intervals, and it was not until 1815 that he found himself in the regiment he commanded. But the colonel, who was an inflexible disciplinarian, treated his son just like any other sub-lieutenant — in other words, with great severity. Orso's memories of him were of two kinds: He recollected him, at Pietranera, as the father who would trust him with his sword, and would let him fire off his gun when he came in from a shooting expedition, or who made him sit down, for the first time, tiny urchin as he was, at the family dinner-table. Then he remembered the Colonel della Rebbia who would put him under arrest for some blunder, and who never called him anything but Lieutenant della Rebbia.

"Lieutenant della Rebbia, you are not in your right place on parade. You will be confined to barracks three days."

"Your skirmishers are five yards too far from your main body — five days in barracks."

"It is five minutes past noon, and you are still in your forage-cap — a week in barracks."

Only once, at Quatre-Bras, he had said to him, "Well done, Orso! But be cautious!"

But, after all, these later memories were not connected in his mind with Pietranera. The sight of the places so familiar to him in his childish days, of the furniture he had seen used by his mother, to whom he had been fondly attached, filled his soul with a host of tender and painful emotions. Then the gloomy future that lay before him, the vague anxiety he felt about his sister, and, above all other things, the thought that Miss Nevil was coming to his house, which now struck him as being so small, so poor, so unsuited to a person accustomed to luxury — the idea that she might possibly despise it — all these feelings made his brain a chaos, and filled him with a sense of deep discouragement.

At supper he sat in the great oaken chair, blackened with age, in which his father had always presided at the head of the family table, and he smiled when he saw that Colomba hesitated to sit down with him. But he was grateful to her for her silence during the meal, and for her speedy retirement afterward. For he felt he was too deeply moved to be able to resist the attack she was no doubt preparing to make upon him. Colomba, however, was dealing warily with him, and meant to give him time to collect himself. He sat for a long time motionless, with his head on his hand, thinking over the scenes of the last fortnight of his life. He saw, with alarm, how every one seemed to be watching what would be his behaviour to the Barricini. Already he began to perceive that the opinion of Pietranera was beginning to be the opinion of all the world to him. He would have to avenge himself, or be taken for a coward! But on whom was he to take vengeance? He could not believe the Barricini to be guilty of murder. They were his family enemies, certainly, but only the vulgar prejudice of his fellow-countrymen could accuse them of being murderers. Sometimes he would look at Miss Nevil's talisman, and whisper the motto "Life is a battle!" over to himself. At last, in a resolute voice, he said, "I will win it!" Strong in that thought, he rose to his feet, took up the lamp, and was just going up to his room, when he heard a knock at the door of the house. It was a very unusual hour for any visitor to appear. Colomba instantly made her appearance, followed by the woman who acted as their servant.

"It's nothing!" she said, hurrying to the door.

Yet before she opened it she inquired who knocked. A gentle voice answered, "It is I."

Instantly the wooden bar across the door was withdrawn, and Colomba reappeared in the dining-room, followed by a little ragged, bare-footed girl of about ten years old, her head bound with a shabby kerchief, from which escaped long locks of hair, as black as the raven's wing. The child was thin and pale, her skin was sunburnt, but her eyes shone with intelligence. When she saw Orso she stopped shyly, and courtesied to him, peasant fashion — then she said something in an undertone to Colomba, and gave her a freshly killed pheasant.

"Thanks, Chili," said Colomba. "Thank your uncle for me. Is he well?"

"Very well, signorina, at your service. I couldn't come sooner because he was late. I waited for him in the *maquis* for three hours."

"And you've had no supper?"

"Why no, signorina! I've not had time."

"You shall have some supper here. Has your uncle any bread left?"

"Very little, signorina. But what he is most short of is powder. Now the chestnuts are in, the only other thing he wants is powder."

"I will give you a loaf for him, and some powder, too. Tell him to use it sparingly — it is very dear."

"Colomba," said Orso in French, "on whom are you bestowing your charity?"

"On a poor bandit belonging to this village," replied Colomba in the same language. "This little girl is his niece."

"It strikes me you might place your gifts better. Why should you send powder to a ruffian who will use it to commit crimes? But for the deplorable weakness every one here seems to have for the bandits, they would have disappeared out of Corsica long ago."

"The worst men in our country are not those who are 'in the country.'"

"Give them bread, if it so please you. But I will not have you supply them with ammunition."

"Brother," said Colomba, in a serious voice, "you are master here, and everything in this house belongs to you. But I warn you that I will give this little girl my *mezzaro*, so that she may sell it; rather than refuse powder to a bandit. Refuse to give him powder!

I might just as well make him over to the gendarmes! What has he to protect him against them, except his cartridges?"

All this while the little girl was ravenously devouring a bit of bread, and carefully watching Colomba and her brother, turn about, trying to read the meaning of what they were saying in their eyes.

"And what has this bandit of yours done? What crime has driven him into the *maquis?*"

"Brandolaccio has not committed any crime," exclaimed Colomba. "He killed Giovan' Oppizo, who murdered his father while he was away serving in the army!"

Orso turned away his head, took up the lamp, and, without a word, departed to his bedroom. Then Colomba gave the child food and gunpowder, and went with her as far as the house-door, saying over and over again:

"Mind your uncle takes good care of Orso!"

# CHAPTER XI

It was long before Orso fell asleep, and as a consequence he woke late — late for a Corsican, at all events. When he left his bed, the first object that struck his gaze was the house of his enemies, and the *archere* with which they had furnished it. He went downstairs and asked for his sister.

"She is in the kitchen, melting bullets," answered Saveria, the woman-servant.

So he could not take a step without being pursued by the image of war.

He found Colomba sitting on a stool, surrounded by freshly cast bullets, and cutting up strips of lead.

"What the devil are you doing?" inquired her brother.

"You had no bullets for the colonel's gun," she answered, in her soft voice. "I found I had a mould for that calibre, and you shall have four-and-twenty cartridges to-day, brother."

"I don't need them, thank God!"

"You mustn't be taken at a disadvantage, Ors' Anton'. You have forgotten your country, and the people who are about you."

"If I had forgotten, you would soon have reminded me. Tell me, did not a big trunk arrive here some days ago?"

"Yes, brother. Shall I take it up to your room?"

"You take it up! Why, you'd never be strong enough even to lift it! . . . Is there no man about who can do it?"

"I'm not so weak as you think!" said Colomba, turning up her sleeves, and displaying a pair of round white arms, perfect in shape, but looking more than ordinarily strong. "Here, Saveria," said she to the servant; "come and help me!"

She was already lifting the trunk alone, when Orso came hastily to her assistance.

"There is something for you in this trunk, my dear Colomba," said he. "You must excuse the modesty of my gifts. A lieutenant on half-pay hasn't a very well-lined purse!"

As he spoke, he opened the trunk, and took out of it a few gowns, a shawl, and some other things likely to be useful to a young girl.

"What beautiful things!" cried Colomba. "I'll put them away at once, for fear they should be spoiled. I'll keep them for my wedding," she added, with a sad smile, "for I am in mourning now!"

And she kissed her brother's hand.

"It looks affected, my dear sister, to wear your mourning for so long."

"I have sworn an oath," said Colomba resolutely, "I'll not take off my mourning. . . ." And her eyes were riveted on the Barricini mansion.

"Until your wedding day?" said Orso, trying to avoid the end of her sentence.

"I shall never marry any man," said Colomba, "unless he has done three things . . ." And her eyes still rested gloomily on the house of the enemy.

"You are so pretty, Colomba, that I wonder you are not married already! Come, you must tell me about your suitors. And besides, I'm sure to hear their serenades. They must be good ones to please a great *voceratrice* like you."

"Who would seek the hand of a poor orphan girl? . . . And then, the man for whom I would change my mourning-dress will have to make the women over there put on mourning!"

"This is becoming a perfect mania," said Orso to himself. But to avoid discussion he said nothing at all.

"Brother," said Colomba caressingly, "I have something to give you, too. The clothes you are wearing are much too grand for this country. Your fine cloth frock-coat would be in tatters in two days, if you wore it in the *maquis*. You must keep it for the time when Miss Nevil comes."

Then, opening a cupboard, she took out a complete hunting dress.

"I've made you a velvet jacket, and here's a cap, such as our smart young men wear. I embroidered it for you, ever so long ago.

Will you try them on?" And she made him put on a loose green velvet jacket, with a huge pocket at the back. On his head she set a pointed black velvet cap, embroidered with jet and silk of the same colour, and finished with a sort of tassel.

"Here is our father's *carchera*" she said. "His stiletto is in the pocket of the jacket. I'll fetch you his pistol."

"I look like a brigand at the Ambigu-Comique," said Orso, as he looked at himself in the little glass Saveria was holding up for him.

"Indeed, you look first-rate, dressed like that, Ors' Anton'," said the old servant, "and the smartest *pinsuto* in Bocognano or Bastelica is not braver."

Orso wore his new clothes at breakfast, and during that meal he told his sister that his trunk contained a certain number of books, that he was going to send to France and Italy for others, and intended she should study a great deal.

"For it really is disgraceful, Colomba," he added, "that a grown-up girl like you should still be ignorant of things that children on the mainland know as soon as they are weaned."

"You are right, brother," said Colomba. "I know my own shortcomings quite well, and I shall be too glad to learn — especially if you are kind enough to teach me."

Some days went by, and Colomba never mentioned the name of Barricini. She lavished care and attention on her brother, and often talked to him about Miss Nevil. Orso made her read French and Italian books, and was constantly being surprised either by the correctness and good sense of her comments, or by her utter ignorance on the most ordinary subjects.

One morning, after breakfast, Colomba left the room for a moment, and instead of returning as usual, with a book and some sheets of paper, reappeared with her *mezzaro* on her head. The expression of her countenance was even more serious than it generally was.

"Brother," she said, "I want you to come out with me."

"Where do you want me to go with you?" said Orso, holding out his arm.

"I don't want your arm, brother, but take your gun and your cartridge-pouch. A man should never go abroad without his arms."

"So be it. I must follow the fashion. Where are we going?"

Colomba, without answering, drew her *mezzaro* closer about her head, called the watch-dog, and went out followed by her brother. Striding swiftly out of the village, she turned into a sunken road that wound among the vineyards, sending on the dog, to whom she made some gesture, which he seemed to understand, in front of her. He instantly began to run zigzag fashion, through the vines, first on one side and then on the other, always keeping within about fifty paces of his mistress, and occasionally stopping in the middle of the road and wagging his tail. He seemed to perform his duties as a scout in the most perfect fashion imaginable.

"If Muschetto begins to bark, brother," said Colomba, "cock your gun, and stand still."

Half a mile beyond the village, after making many detours, Colomba stopped short, just where there was a bend in the road. On that spot there rose a little pyramid of branches, some of them green, some withered, heaped about three feet high. Above them rose the top of a wooden cross, painted black. In several of the Corsican cantons, especially those among the mountains, a very ancient custom, connected, it may be with some pagan superstition, constrains every passer-by to cast either a stone or a branch on the spot whereon a man has died a violent death. For years and years — as long as the memory of his tragic fate endures — this strange offering goes on accumulating from day to day.

This is called the dead man's *pile* — his "*mucchio.*"

Colomba stopped before the heap of foliage, broke off an arbutus branch, and cast it on the pile.

"Orso," she said, "this is where your father died. Let us pray for his soul!"

And she knelt down. Orso instantly followed her example. At that moment the village church-bell tolled slowly for a man who had died during the preceding night. Orso burst into tears.

After a few minutes Colomba rose. Her eyes were dry, but her face was eager. She hastily crossed herself with her thumb, after the fashion generally adopted by her companions, to seal any solemn oath, then, hurrying her brother with her, she took her way back to the village. They re-entered their house in silence. Orso went up to his room. A moment afterward Colomba followed him, carrying a small casket which she set upon the table. Opening it, she drew out a shirt, covered with great stains of blood.

"Here is your father's shirt, Orso!"

And she threw it across his knees. "Here is the lead that killed him!" And she laid two blackened bullets on the shirt.

"Orso! Brother!" she cried, throwing herself into his arms and clasping him desperately to her. "Orso, you will avenge him!"

In a sort of frenzy she kissed him, then kissed the shirt and the bullets, and went out of the room, leaving her brother sitting on his chair, as if he had been turned to stone. For some time Orso sat motionless, not daring to put the terrible relics away. At last, with an effort, he laid them back in their box, rushed to the opposite end of his room, and threw himself on his bed, with his face turned to the wall, and his head buried in his pillow, as though he were trying to shut out the sight of some ghost. His sister's last words rang unceasingly in his ears, like the words of an oracle, fatal, inevitable, calling out to him for blood, and for innocent blood! I shall not attempt to depict the unhappy young man's sensations, which were as confused as those that overwhelm a madman's brain. For a long time he lay in the same position, without daring to turn his head. At last he got up, closed the lid of the casket, and rushed headlong out of the house, into the open country, moving aimlessly forward, whither he knew not.

By degrees, the fresh air did him good. He grew calmer, and began to consider his position, and his means of escape from it, with some composure. He did not, as my readers already know, suspect the Barricini of the murder, but he did accuse them of having forged Agostini's letter, and this letter, he believed, at any rate, had brought about his father's death. He felt it was impossible to prosecute them for the forgery. Now and then, when the prejudices or the instincts of his race assailed him, and suggested an easy vengeance — a shot fired at the corner of some path — the thought of his brother-officers, of Parisian drawing-rooms, and above all, of Miss Nevil, made him shrink from them in horror. Then his mind dwelt on his sister's reproaches, and all the Corsican within him justified her appeal, and even intensified its bitterness. One hope alone remained to him, in this battle between his conscience and his prejudices — the hope that, on some pretext or other, he might pick a quarrel with one of the lawyer's sons, and fight a duel with him. The idea of killing the young man, either by a bullet or a sword-thrust reconciled his French and Corsican ideas. This expedient adopted, he began to meditate means for its execution, and was feeling relieved already of a heavy burden, when other and gentler thoughts contributed still further to calm his feverish agitation. Cicero, in his despair at the death of his daughter Tullia, forgot his sorrow when he mused over all the fine things he might say about it. Mr. Shandy consoled himself by discourses of the same nature for the loss of his son. Orso cooled his blood by thinking that he would depict his state of mind to Miss Nevil, and that such a picture could not fail to interest that fair lady deeply.

He was drawing near the village, from which he had unconsciously traveled a considerable distance, when he heard the voice of a little girl, who probably believed herself to be quite alone, singing in a path that ran along the edge of the *maquis*. It was one of those slow, monotonous airs consecrated to funeral dirges, and the child was singing the words:

"And when my son shall see again the dwelling of his father, Give him that murdered father's cross; show him my shirt blood-spattered."

"What's that you're singing, child?" said Orso, in an angry voice, as he suddenly appeared before her.

"Is that you, Ors' Anton'?" exclaimed the child, rather startled. "It is Signorina Colomba's song."

"I forbid you to sing it!" said Orso, in a threatening voice.

The child kept turning her head this way and that, as though looking about for a way of escape, and she would certainly have run off had she not been held back by the necessity of taking care of a large bundle which lay on the grass, at her feet.

Orso felt ashamed of his own vehemence. "What are you carrying there, little one?" said he, with all the gentleness he could muster. And as Chilina hesitated, he lifted up the linen that was wrapped round the bundle, and saw it contained a loaf of bread and other food.

"To whom are you bringing the loaf, my dear?" he asked again.

"You know quite well, Ors' Anton': to my uncle."

"And isn't your uncle a bandit?"

"At your service, Ors' Anton'."

"If you met the gendarmes, they would ask you where you were going. . . ."

"I should tell them," the child replied, at once, "that I was taking food to the men from Lucca who were cutting down the *maquis*."

"And if you came across some hungry hunter who insisted on dining at your expense, and took your provisions away from you?"

"Nobody would dare! I would say they are for my uncle!"

"Well! he's not the sort of man to let himself be cheated of his dinner! . . . Is your uncle very fond of you?"

"Oh, yes, Ors' Anton'. Ever since my father died, he has taken care of my whole family — my mother and my little sister, and me. Before mother was ill, he used to recommend her to rich people, who gave her employment. The mayor gives me a frock every year, and the priest has taught me my catechism, and how to read, ever since my uncle spoke to them about us. But your sister is kindest of all to us!"

Just at this moment a dog ran out on the pathway. The little girl put two of her fingers into her mouth and gave a shrill whistle, the dog came to her at once, fawned upon her, and then plunged swiftly into the thicket. Soon two men, ill-dressed, but very well armed, rose up out of a clump of young wood a few paces from where Orso stood. It was as though they had crawled up like snakes through the tangle of cytisus and myrtle that covered the ground.

"Oh, Ors' Anton', you're welcome!" said the elder of the two men. "Why, don't you remember me?"

"No!" said Orso, looking hard at him.

"Queer how a beard and a peaked cap alter a man! Come, monsieur, look at me well! Have you forgotten your old Waterloo men? Don't you remember Brando Savelli, who bit open more than one cartridge alongside of you on that unlucky day?"

"What! Is it you?" said Orso. "And you deserted in 1816!"

"Even so, sir. Faith! soldiering grows tiresome, and besides, I had a job to settle over in this country. Aha, Chili! You're a good girl! Give us our dinner at once, we're hungry. You've no notion what an appetite one gets in the *maquis*. Who sent us this — was it Signorina Colomba or the mayor?"

"No, uncle, it was the miller's wife. She gave me this for you, and a blanket for my mother."

"What does she want of me?"

"She says the Lucchesi she hired to clear the *maquis* are asking her five-and-thirty sous, and chestnuts as well — because of the fever in the lower parts of Pietranera."

"The lazy scamps! . . . I'll see to them! . . . Will you share our dinner, monsieur, without any ceremony? We've eaten worse meals together, in the days of that poor compatriot of ours, whom they have discharged from the army."

"No, I thank you heartily. They have discharged me, too!"

"Yes, so I heard. But I'll wager you weren't sorry for it. You have your own account to settle too. . . . Come along, cure," said the bandit to his comrade. "Let's dine! Signor Orso, let me introduce the cure. I'm not quite sure he is a cure. But he knows as much as any priest, at all events!"

"A poor student of theology, monsieur," quoth the second bandit, "who has been prevented from following his vocation. Who knows, Brandolaccio, I might have been Pope!"

"What was it that deprived the Church of your learning?" inquired Orso.

"A mere nothing — a bill that had to be settled, as my friend Brandolaccio puts it. One of my sisters had been making a fool of herself, while I was devouring book-lore at Pisa University. I had to come home, to get her married. But her future husband was in too great a hurry; he died of fever three days before I arrived. Then I called, as you would have done in my place, on the dead man's brother. I was told he was married. What was I to do?"

"It really was puzzling! What did you do?"

"It was one of those cases in which one has to resort to the gunflint."

"In other words?"

"I put a bullet in his head," said the bandit coolly.

Orso made a horrified gesture. Nevertheless, curiosity, and, it may be, his desire to put off the moment when he must return home, induced him to remain where he was, and continue his conversation with the two men, each of whom had at least one murder on his conscience.

While his comrade was talking, Brandolaccio was laying bread and meat in front of him. He helped himself — then he gave some food to this dog, whom he introduced to Orso under the name of Brusco, as an animal possessing a wonderful instinct for recognizing a soldier, whatever might be the disguise he had assumed. Lastly, he cut off a hunch of bread and a slice of raw ham, and gave them to his niece. "Oh, the merry life a bandit lives!" cried the student of theology, after he had swallowed a few mouthfuls. "You'll try it some day, perhaps, Signor della Rebbia, and you'll find out how delightful it is to acknowledge no master save one's own fancy!"

Hitherto the bandit had talked Italian. He now proceeded in French.

"Corsica is not a very amusing country for a young man to live in — but for a bandit, there's the difference! The women are all wild about us. I, as you see me now, have three mistresses in three different villages. I am at home in every one of them, and one of the ladies is married to a gendarme!"

"You know many languages, monsieur!" said Orso gravely.

"If I talk French, 'tis because, look you, *maxima debetur pueris reverentia!* We have made up our minds, Brandolaccio and I, that the little girl shall turn out well, and go straight."

"When she is turned fifteen," remarked Chilina's uncle, "I'll find a good husband for her. I have one in my eye already."

"Shall you make the proposal yourself?" said Orso.

"Of course! Do you suppose that any well-to-do man in this neighbourhood, to whom I said, 'I should be glad to see a marriage between your son and Michilina Savelli,' would require any pressing?"

"I wouldn't advise him to!" quoth the other bandit. "Friend Brandolaccio has rather a heavy hand!"

"If I were a rogue," continued Brandolaccio, "a blackguard, a forger, I should only have to hold my wallet open, and the five-franc pieces would rain into it."

"Then is there something inside your wallet that attracts them?" said Orso.

"Nothing. But if I were to write to a rich man, as some people have written, 'I want a hundred francs,' he would lose no time about sending them to me. But I'm a man of honour, monsieur."

"Do you know, Signor della Rebbia," said the bandit whom his comrade called the cure, "do you know that in this country, with all its simple habits, there are some wretches who make use of the esteem our passports" (and he touched his gun) "insure us, to draw forged bills in our handwriting?"

"I know it," said Orso, in a gruff tone; "but what bills?"

"Six months ago," said the bandit, "I was taking my walks abroad near Orezza, when a sort of lunatic came up to me, pulling off his cap to me even in the distance, and said: 'Oh, M. le Cure' (they always call me that), 'please excuse me — give me time. I have only been able to get fifty-five francs together! Honour bright, that's all I've been able to scrape up.' I, in my astonishment, said, 'Fifty-five francs! What do you mean, you rascal!' 'I mean sixty-five,' he replied; 'but as for the hundred francs you asked me to give you, it's not possible.' 'What! you villain! I ask you for a hundred francs? I don't know who you are.' Then he showed me a letter, or rather a dirty rag of paper, whereby he was summoned to deposit a hundred francs on a certain spot, on pain of having his house burned and his cows killed by Giocanto Castriconi — that's my name. And they had been vile enough to forge my signature! What annoyed me most was that the letter was written in *patois*, and was full of mistakes in spelling — I who won every prize at the university! I began by giving my rascal a cuff that made him twist round and round. 'Aha! You take me for a thief, blackguard that you are!' I said, and I gave him a hearty kick, you know where. Then feeling rather better, I went on, 'When are you to take the money to the spot mentioned in the letter?' 'This very day.' 'Very good, then take it there!' It was at the foot of a pine-tree, and the place had been exactly described. He brought the money, buried it at the foot of the tree, and came and joined me. I had hidden myself close by. There I stayed, with my man, for six mortal hours, M. della Rebbia. I'd have staid three days, if it had been necessary. At the end of six hours a *Bastiaccio*, a vile money-lender, made his appearance. As he bent down to take up the money, I fired, and I had aimed so well that, as he fell, his head dropped upon the coins he was unearthing. 'Now, rascal,' said I to the peasant, 'take your money, and never dare to suspect Giocanto Castriconi of a mean trick again!'

"The poor devil, all of a tremble, picked up his sixty-five francs without taking the trouble to wipe them. He thanked me, I gave him a good parting kick, and he may be running away still, for all I know."

"Ah, cure!" said Brandolaccio, "I envy you that shot! How you must have laughed!"

"I had hit the money-lender in the temple," the bandit went on, "and that reminded me of Virgil's lines:

. . . "'Liquefacto tempora plumbo Diffidit, ac multa porrectum, extendit arena.'

"*Liquefacto!* Do you think, Signor Orso, that the rapidity with which a bullet flies through the air will melt it? You who have studied projectiles, tell me whether you think that idea is truth or fiction?"

Orso infinitely preferred discussing this question of physics to arguing with the licentiate as to the morality of his action. Brandolaccio, who did not find their scientific disquisition entertaining, interrupted it with the remark that the sun was just going to set.

"As you would not dine with us, Ors' Anton'," he said, "I advise you not to keep Mademoiselle Colomba waiting any longer. And then it is not always wise to be out on the roads after sunset. Why do you come out without a gun? There are bad folk about here — beware of them! You have nothing to fear to-day. The Barricini are bringing the prefect home with them. They have gone to meet him on the road, and he is to stop a day at Pietranera, before he goes on to Corte, to lay what they call a corner-stone — such stupid nonsense! He will sleep to-night with the Barricini; but to-morrow they'll be disengaged. There is Vincentello, who is a good-for-nothing fellow, and Orlanduccio, who is not much better. . . . Try to come on them separately, one to-day, the other to-morrow. . . . But be on the lookout, that's all I have to say to you!"

"Thanks for the warning," said Orso. "But there is no quarrel between us. Until they come to look for me, I shall have nothing to say to them."

The bandit stuck his tongue in his cheek, and smacked it ironically, but he made no reply. Orso got up to go away.

"By the way," said Brandolaccio, "I haven't thanked you for your powder. It came just when I needed it. Now I have everything I want . . . at least I do still want shoes . . . but I'll make myself a pair out of the skin of a moufflon one of these days."

Orso slipped two five-franc pieces into the bandit's hand.

"It was Colomba who sent you the powder. This is to buy the shoes."

"Nonsense, Lieutenant!" cried Brandolaccio, handing him back the two coins. "D'ye take me for a beggar? I accept bread and powder, but I won't have anything else!"

"We are both old soldiers, so I thought we might have given each other a lift. Well, good-bye to you!"

But before he moved away he had slipped the money into he bandit's wallet, unperceived by him.

"Good-bye, Ors' Anton'," quoth the theologian. "We shall meet again in the *maquis*, some day, perhaps, and then we'll continue our study of Virgil."

Quite a quarter of an hour after Orso had parted company with these worthies, he heard a man running after him, as fast as he could go. It was Brandolaccio.

"This is too bad, lieutenant!" he shouted breathlessly, "really it is too bad! I wouldn't overlook the trick, if any other man had played it on me. Here are your ten francs. All my respects to Mademoiselle Colomba. You have made me run myself quite out of breath. Good-night!"

# CHAPTER XII

Orso found Colomba in a state of considerable anxiety because of his prolonged absence. But as soon as she saw him she recovered her usual serene, though sad, expression. During the evening meal the conversation turned on trivial subjects, and Orso, emboldened by his sister's apparent calm, related his encounter with the bandits, and even ventured on a joke or two concerning the moral and religious education that was being imparted to little Chilina, thanks to the care of her uncle and of his worthy colleague Signor Castriconi.

"Brandolaccio is an upright man," said Colomba; "but as to Castriconi, I have heard he is quite unprincipled."

"I think," said Orso, "that he is as good as Brandolaccio, and Brandolaccio is as good as he. Both of them are at open war with society. Their first crime leads them on to fresh ones, every day, and yet they are very likely not half so guilty as many people who don't live in the *maquis.*"

A flash of joy shone in his sister's eyes. "Yes," he continued, "these wretches have a code of honour of their own. It is a cruel prejudice, not a mean instinct of greed, that has forced them into the life they are leading."

There was a silence.

"Brother," said Colomba, as she poured out his coffee, "perhaps you have heard that Carlo-Battista Pietri died last night. Yes, he died of the marsh-fever."

"Who is Pietri?"

"A man belonging to this village, the husband of Maddalena, who took the pocket-book out of our father's hand as he was dying. His widow has been here to ask me to join the watchers, and sing something. You ought to come, too. They are our neighbours, and in a small place like this we can not do otherwise than pay them this civility."

"Confound these wakes, Colomba! I don't at all like my sister to perform in public in this way."

"Orso," replied Colomba, "every country pays honour to its dead after its own fashion. The *ballata* has come down to us from our forefathers, and we must respect it as an ancient custom. Maddalena does not possess the 'gift,' and old Fiordispina, the best *voceratrice* in the country, is ill. They must have somebody for the *ballata*."

"Do you believe Carlo-Battista won't find his way safely into the next world unless somebody sings bad poetry over his bier? Go if you choose, Colomba — I'll go with you, if you think I ought. But don't improvise! It really is not fitting at your age, and — sister, I beg you not to do it!"

"Brother, I have promised. It is the custom here, as you know, and, I tell you again, there is nobody but me to improvise."

"An idiotic custom it is!"

"It costs me a great deal to sing in this way. It brings back all our own sorrows to me. I shall be ill after it, to-morrow. But I must do it. Give me leave to do it. Brother, remember that when we were at Ajaccio, you told me to improvise to amuse that young English lady who makes a mock of our old customs. So why should I not do it to-day for these poor people, who will be grateful to me, and whom it will help to bear their grief?"

"Well, well, as you will. I'll go bail you've composed your *ballata* already, and don't want to waste it."

"No, brother, I couldn't compose it beforehand. I stand before the dead person, and I think about those he has left behind him. The tears spring into my eyes, and then I sing whatever comes into my head."

All this was said so simply that it was quite impossible to suspect Signorina Colomba of the smallest poetic vanity. Orso let himself be persuaded, and went with his sister to Pietri's house. The dead man lay on a table in the largest room, with his face uncovered. All the doors and windows stood open, and several tapers were burning round the table. At the head stood the widow, and behind her a great many women, who filled all one side of the room. On the other side were the men, in rows, bareheaded, with their eyes fixed on the corpse, all in the deepest silence. Each new arrival went up to the table, kissed the dead face, bowed his or her head to the widow and her son, and joined the circle, without uttering a word. Nevertheless, from time to time one of the persons present would break the solemn silence with a few words, addressed to the dead man.

"Why has thou left thy good wife?" said one old crone. "Did she not take good care of thee? What didst thou lack? Why not have waited another month? Thy daughter-in-law would have borne thee a grandson!" A tall young fellow, Pietri's son, pressed his father's cold hand and cried: "Oh! why hast thou not died of the *mala morte?* Then we could have avenged thee!"

These were the first words to fall on Orso's ear as he entered the room. At the sight of him the circle parted, and a low murmur of curiosity betrayed the expectation roused in the gathering by the *voceratrice's* presence. Colomba embraced the widow, took one of her hands, and stood for some moments wrapped in meditation, with her eyelids dropped. Then she threw back her *mezzaro,* gazed fixedly at the corpse, and bending over it, her face almost as waxen as that of the dead man, she began thus:

"Carlo-Battista! May Christ receive thy soul! . . . To live is to suffer! Thou goest to a place . . . where there is neither sun nor cold. . . . No longer dost thou need thy pruning-hook . . . nor thy heavy pick. . . . There is no more work for thee! . . . Henceforward all thy days are Sundays! . . . Carlo-Battista! May Christ receive thy soul! . . . Thy son rules in thy house. . . . I have seen the oak fall, . . . dried up by the *libeccio.* . . . I thought it was dead indeed, . . . but when I passed it again, its root . . . had thrown up a sapling. . . . The sapling grew into an oak . . . of mighty shade. . . . Under its great branches, Maddele, rest thee well! . . . And think of the oak that is no more!"

Here Maddalena began to sob aloud, and two or three men who, on occasion, would have shot at a Christian as coolly as at a partridge, brushed big tears off their sunburnt faces.

For some minutes Colomba continued in this strain, addressing herself sometimes to the corpse, sometimes to the family, and sometimes, by a personification frequently employed in the *ballata*, making the dead man himself speak words of consolation or counsel to his kinsfolk. As she proceeded, her face assumed a sublime expression, a delicate pink tinge crept over her features, heightening the brilliancy of her white teeth and the lustre of her flashing eyes. She was like a Pythoness on her tripod. Save for a sigh here and there, or a strangled sob, not the slightest noise rose from the assembly that crowded about her. Orso, though less easily affected than most people by this wild kind of poetry, was soon overcome by the general emotion. Hidden in a dark corner of the room, he wept as heartily as Pietri's own son.

Suddenly a slight stir was perceptible among the audience. The circle opened, and several strangers entered. The respect shown them, and the eagerness with which room was made for them, proved them to be people of importance, whose advent was a great honour to the household. Nevertheless, out of respect for the *ballata*, nobody said a word to them. The man who had entered first seemed about forty years of age. From his black coat, his red rosette, his confident air, and look of authority, he was at once guessed to be the prefect. Behind him came a bent old man with a bilious-looking complexion, whose furtive and anxious glance was only partially concealed by his green spectacles. He wore a black coat, too large for him, and which, though still quite new, had evidently been made several years previously. He always kept close beside the prefect and looked as though he would fain hide himself under his shadow. Last of all, behind him, came two tall young men, with sunburnt faces, their cheeks hidden by heavy whiskers, proud and arrogant-looking, and showing symptoms of an impertinent curiosity. Orso had had time to forget the faces of his village neighbours; but the sight of the old man in green spectacles instantly called up old memories in his mind. His presence in attendance on the prefect sufficed to insure his recognition. This was Barricini, the lawyer, mayor of Pietranera, who had come, with his two sons, to show the prefect what a *ballata* was. It would be difficult exactly to describe what happened within Orso's soul at that moment, but the presence of his father's foe filled him with a sort of horror, and more than ever he felt inclined to yield to the suspicions with which he had been battling for so long.

As to Colomba, when she saw the man against whom she had sworn a deadly hatred, her mobile countenance assumed a most threatening aspect. She turned pale, her voice grew hoarse, the line she had begun to declaim died on her lips. But soon, taking up her *ballata* afresh, she proceeded with still greater vehemence.

"When the hawk bemoans himself . . . beside his harried nest, . . . the starlings flutter round him . . . insulting his distress."

A smothered laugh was heard. The two young men who had just come in doubtless considered the metaphor too bold.

"The falcon will rouse himself. . . . He will spread his wings. . . . He will wash his beak in blood! . . . Now, to thee, Carlo-Battista, let thy friends . . . bid an eternal farewell! . . . Long enough have their tears flowed! . . . Only the poor orphan girl will not weep for thee! . . . Wherefore should she moan? . . . Thou has fallen asleep, full of years, . . in the midst of thine own kin . . . ready to appear . . . in the presence of the Almighty. . . . The orphan weeps for her father . . . overtaken by vile murderers, . . struck from behind. . . . For her father, whose blood lies red . . . beneath the heaped-up green leaves. . . . But she has gathered up this blood, . . this innocent and noble blood! . . . She has poured it out over Pietranera . . . that it may become a deadly poison. . . . And the mark shall be on Pietranera . . . until the blood of the guilty . . . shall have wiped out the blood of the innocent man!"

As Colomba pronounced the last words, she dropped into a chair, drew her *mezzaro* over her face, and was heard sobbing beneath it. The weeping women crowded round the *improvisatrice*; several of the men were casting savage glances at the mayor and his sons; some of the elders began to protest against the scandal to which their presence had given rise. The dead man's son pushed his way through the throng, and was about to beg the mayor to clear out with all possible speed. But this functionary had not waited for the suggestion. He was on his way to the door, and his two sons were already in the street. The

216

prefect said a few words of condolence to young Pietri, and followed them out, almost immediately. Orso went to his sister's side, took her arm, and drew her out of the room.

"Go with them," said young Pietri to some of his friends. "Take care no harm comes to them!"

Hastily two or three young men slipped their stilettos up the left sleeves of their jackets and escorted Orso and his sister to their own door.

# CHAPTER XIII

Panting, exhausted, Colomba was utterly incapable of uttering a single word. Her head rested on her brother's shoulder, and she clasped one of his hands tightly between her own. Orso, though secretly somewhat annoyed by her peroration, was too much alarmed to reprove her, even in the mildest fashion. He was silently waiting till the nervous attack from which she seemed to be suffering should have passed, when there was a knock at the door, and Saveria, very much flustered, announced the prefect. At the words, Colomba rose, as though ashamed of her weakness, and stood leaning on a chair, which shook visibly beneath her hand.

The prefect began with some commonplace apology for the unseasonable hour of his visit, condoled with Mademoiselle Colomba, touched on the danger connected with strong emotions, blamed the custom of composing funeral dirges, which the very talent of the *voceratrice* rendered the more harrowing to her auditors, skillfully slipped in a mild reproof concerning the tendency of the improvisation just concluded, and then, changing his tone —

"M. della Rebbia," he said, "I have many messages for you from your English friends. Miss Nevil sends her affectionate regards to your sister. I have a letter for you from her."

"A letter from Miss Nevil!" cried Orso.

"Unluckily I have not got it with me. But you shall have it within five minutes. Her father has not been well. For a little while we were afraid he had caught one of our terrible fevers. Luckily he is all right again, as you will observe for yourself, for I fancy you will see him very soon."

"Miss Nevil must have been very much alarmed!"

"Fortunately she did not become aware of the danger till it was quite gone by. M. della Rebbia, Miss Nevil has talked to me a great deal about you and about your sister."

Orso bowed.

"She has a great affection for you both. Under her charming appearance, and her apparent frivolity, a fund of good sense lies hidden."

"She is a very fascinating person," said Orso.

"I have come here, monsieur, almost at her prayer. Nobody is better acquainted than I with a fatal story which I would fain not have to recall to you. As M. Barricini is still the mayor of Pietranera, and as I am prefect of the department, I need hardly tell you what weight I attach to certain suspicions which, if I am rightly informed, some incautious individuals have communicated to you, and which you, I know, have spurned with the indignation your position and your character would have led me to expect."

"Colomba," said Orso, moving uneasily to his chair. "You are very tired. You had better go to bed."

Colomba shook her head. She had recovered all her usual composure, and her burning eyes were fixed on the prefect.

"M. Barricini," the prefect continued, "is exceedingly anxious to put an end to the sort of enmity . . . or rather, the condition of uncertainty, existing between yourself and him. . . . On my part, I should be delighted to see you both in those relations of friendly intercourse appropriate to people who certainly ought to esteem each other."

"Monsieur," replied Orso in a shaking voice, "I have never charged Barricini with my father's murder. But he committed an act which must always prevent me from having anything to do with him. He forged a threatening letter, in the name of a certain bandit, or at least he hinted in an underhand sort of way that it was forged by my father. That letter, monsieur, was probably the indirect cause of my father's death."

The prefect sat thinking for a moment.

"That your father should have believed that, when his own hasty nature led him into a lawsuit with Signor Barricini, is excusable. But such blindness on your part really can not be admitted. Pray consider that Barricini could have served no interest of his own by forging the letter. I will not talk to you about his character, for you are not acquainted with it, and are prejudiced against it; but you can not suppose that a man conversant with the law — — "

"But, monsieur," said Orso, rising to his feet, "be good enough to recollect that when you tell me the letter was not Barricini's work, you ascribe it to my father. And my father's honour, monsieur, is mine!"

"No man on earth, sir, is more convinced of Colonel della Rebbia's honour than myself! But the writer of the letter is now known."

"Who wrote it?" exclaimed Colomba, making a step toward the prefect.

"A villain, guilty of several crimes — such crimes as you Corsicans never pardon — a thief, one Tomaso Bianchi, at present confined in the prison at Bastia, has acknowledged that he wrote the fatal letter."

"I know nothing of the man," said Orso. "What can have been his object?"

"He belongs to this neighbourhood," said Colomba. "He is brother to a man who was our miller — a scamp and a liar, unworthy of belief."

"You will soon see what his interest in the matter was," continued the prefect. "The miller of whom your sister speaks — I think his name was Teodoro — was the tenant of a mill belonging to the colonel, standing on the very stream the ownership of which M. Barricini was disputing with your father. The colonel, always a generous man, made very little profit out of the mill. Now Tomaso thought that if Barricini got possession of the stream there would be a heavy rent to pay, for it is well known that Barricini is rather fond of money. In short, to oblige his brother, Tomaso forged the letter from the bandit — and there's the whole story. You know that in Corsica the strength of the family tie is so great that it does sometimes lead to crime. Please read over this letter to me from the attorney-general. It confirms what I have just told you."

Orso looked through the letter, which gave a detailed relation of Tomaso's confession, and Colomba read it over his shoulder.

When she had come to the end of it she exclaimed:

"Orlanduccio Barricini went down to Bastia a month ago, when it became known that my brother was coming home. He must have seen Tomaso, and bought this lie of him!"

"Signorina," said the prefect, out of patience, "you explain everything by odious imputations! Is that the way to find out the truth? You, sir, can judge more coolly. Tell me what you think of the business now? Do you believe, like this young lady, that a man who has only a slight sentence to fear would deliberately charge himself with forgery, just to oblige a person he doesn't know?"

Orso read the attorney-general's letter again, weighing every word with the greatest care — for now that he had seen the old lawyer, he felt it more difficult to convince himself than it would have been a few days previously. At last he found himself obliged to admit that the explanation seemed to him to be satisfactory. But Colomba cried out vehemently:

"Tomaso Bianchi is a knave! He'll not be convicted, or he'll escape from prison! I am certain of it!"

The prefect shrugged his shoulders.

"I have laid the information I have received before you, monsieur. I will now depart, and leave you to your own reflections. I shall wait till your own reason has enlightened you, and I trust it may prove stronger than your sister's suppositions."

Orso, after saying a few words of excuse for Colomba, repeated that he now believed Tomaso to be the sole culprit.

The prefect had risen to take his leave.

"If it were not so late," said he, "I would suggest your coming over with me to fetch Miss Nevil's letter. At the same time you might repeat to M. Barricini what you have just said to me, and the whole thing would be settled."

"Orso della Rebbia will never set his foot inside the house of a Barricini!" exclaimed Colomba impetuously.

"This young lady appears to be the *tintinajo* of the family!" remarked the prefect, with a touch of irony.

"Monsieur," replied Colomba resolutely, "you are deceived. You do not know the lawyer. He is the most cunning and knavish of men. I beseech you not to make Orso do a thing that would overwhelm him with dishonour!"

"Colomba!" exclaimed Orso, "your passion has driven you out of your senses!"

"Orso! Orso! By the casket I gave you, I beseech you to listen to me! There is blood between you and the Barricini. You shall not go into their house!"

"Sister!"

"No, brother, you shall not go! Or I will leave this house, and you will never see me again! Have pity on me, Orso!" and she fell on her knees.

"I am grieved," said the prefect, "to find Mademoiselle Colomba so unreasonable. You will convince her, I am sure."

He opened the door and paused, seeming to expect Orso to follow him.

"I can not leave her now," said Orso. "To-morrow, if —— ——
"

"I shall be starting very early," said the prefect.

"Brother," cried Colomba, clasping her hands, "wait till to-morrow morning, in any case. Let me look over my father's papers. You can not refuse me that!"

"Well, you shall look them over to-night. But at all events you shall not torment me afterward with your violent hatreds. A thousand pardons, monsieur! I am so upset myself to-night — it had better be to-morrow."

"The night brings counsel," said the prefect, as he went out. "I hope all your uncertainty will have disappeared by to-morrow."

"Saveria," Colomba called, "take the lantern and attend the Signor Prefetto. He will give you a letter to bring back to my brother."

She added a few words which reached Saveria's ear alone.

"Colomba," said Orso, when the prefect was gone, "you have distressed me very much. Will no evidence convince you?"

"You have given me till to-morrow," she replied. "I have very little time; but I still have some hope."

Then she took a bunch of keys and ran up to a room on the upper story. There he could hear her pulling open drawers, and rummaging in the writing-desk in which Colonel della Rebbia had kept his business papers.

# CHAPTER XIV

Saveria was a long time away, and when she at last reappeared, carrying a letter, and followed by little Chilina, rubbing her eyes, and evidently just waked out of her beauty sleep, Orso was wound up to the highest possible pitch of impatience.

"Chili," said Orso, "what are you doing here at this hour?"

"The signorina sent for me," replied Chilina.

"What the devil does she want with her?" thought Orso to himself. But he was in a hurry to open Miss Lydia's letter, and while he was reading it Chilina went upstairs to his sister's room.

"My father, dear sir, has not been well," Miss Nevil wrote, "and he is so indolent, besides, that I am obliged to act as his secretary. You remember that, instead of admiring the landscape with you and me the other day, he got his feet wet on the seashore — and in your delightful island, that is quite enough to give one a fever! I can see the face you are making! No doubt you are feeling for your dagger. But I will hope you have none now. Well, my father had a little fever, and I had a great fright. The prefect, whom I persist in thinking very pleasant, sent us a doctor, also a very pleasant man, who got us over our trouble in two days. There has been no return of the attack, and my father would like to begin to shoot again. But I have forbidden that. How did you find matters in your mountain home? Is your North Tower still in its old place? Are there any ghosts about it? I ask all these questions because my father remembers you have promised him buck and boar and moufflon — is that the right name for those strange creatures? We intend to crave your hospitality on our way to Bastia, where we are to embark, and I trust the della Rebbia Castle, which you declare is so old and tumble-down, will not fall in upon our heads! Though the prefect is so pleasant that subjects of conversation are never lacking to us — I flatter myself, by the way, that I have turned his head — we have been talking about your worshipful self. The legal people at Bastia have sent him certain confessions, made by a rascal they have under lock and key, which are calculated to destroy your last remaining

224

suspicions. The enmity which sometimes alarmed me for you must therefore end at once. You have no idea what a pleasure this has been to me! When you started hence with the fair *voceratrice*, with your gun in hand, and your brow lowering, you struck me as being more Corsican than ever — too Corsican indeed! *Basta!* I write you this long letter because I am dull. The prefect, alas! is going away. We will send you a message when we start for your mountains, and I shall take the liberty of writing to Signorina Colomba to ask her to give me a *bruccio, ma solenne!* Meanwhile, give her my love. I use her dagger a great deal to cut the leaves of a novel I brought with me. But the doughty steel revolts against such usage, and tears my book for me, after a most pitiful fashion. Farewell, sir! My father sends you 'his best love.' Listen to what the prefect says. He is a sensible man, and is turning out of his way, I believe, on your account. He is going to lay a foundation-stone at Corte. I should fancy the ceremony will be very imposing, and I am very sorry not to see it. A gentleman in an embroidered coat and silk stockings and a white scarf, wielding a trowel — and a speech! And at the end of the performance manifold and reiterated shouts of 'God save the King.' I say again, sir, it will make you very vain to think I have written you four whole pages, and on that account I give you leave to write me a very long letter. By the way, I think it very odd of you not to have let me hear of your safe arrival at the Castle of Pietranera!

"LYDIA.

"P.S. — I beg you will listen to the prefect, and do as he bids you. We have agreed that this is the course you should pursue, and I shall be very glad if you do it."

Orso read the letter three or four times over, making endless mental comments each time as he read. Then he wrote a long answer, which he sent by Saveria's hand to a man in the village, who was to go down to Ajaccio the very next day. Already he had almost dismissed the idea of discussing his grievance, true or false, against the Barricini, with his sister. Miss Lydia's letter had cast a rose-coloured tint over everything about him. He felt neither hatred nor suspicion now. He waited some time for his sister to come down, and finding she did not reappear, he went to bed, with a lighter heart than he had carried for many a day. Colomba, having dismissed Chilina with some secret instructions, spent the greater part of the night in reading old papers. A little before daybreak a few tiny pebbles rattled against the window-pane. At the signal, she went down to the garden, opened a back door, and conducted two very rough men into her house. Her first care was to bring them into the kitchen and give them food. My readers will shortly learn who these men were.

# CHAPTER XV

Toward six o'clock next morning one of the prefect's servants came and knocked at the door of Orso's house. He was received by Colomba, and informed her the prefect was about to start, and was expecting her brother. Without a moment's hesitation Colomba replied that her brother had just had a fall on the stairs, and sprained his foot; and he was unable to walk a single step, that he begged the prefect to excuse him, and would be very grateful if he would condescend to take the trouble of coming over to him. A few minutes after this message had been dispatched, Orso came downstairs, and asked his sister whether the prefect had not sent for him.

With the most perfect assurance she rejoined:

"He begs you'll wait for him here."

Half an hour went by without the slightest perceptible stir in the Barricini dwelling. Meanwhile Orso asked Colomba whether she had discovered anything. She replied that she proposed to make her statement when the prefect came. She affected an extreme composure. But her colour and her eyes betrayed her state of feverish excitement.

At last the door of the Barricini mansion was seen to open. The prefect came out first, in traveling garb; he was followed by the mayor and his two sons. What was the stupefaction of the inhabitants of the village of Pietranera, who had been on the watch since sunrise for the departure of the chief magistrate of their department, when they saw him go straight across the square and enter the della Rebbia dwelling, accompanied by the three Barricini. "They are going to make peace!" exclaimed the village politicians.

"Just as I told you," one old man went on. "Ors' Anton' has lived too much on the mainland to carry things through like a man of mettle."

"Yet," responded a Rebbianite, "you may notice it is the Barricini who have gone across to him. They are suing for mercy."

"It's the prefect who had wheedled them all round," answered the old fellow. "There is no such thing as courage nowadays, and the young chaps make no more fuss about their father's blood than if they were all bastards."

The prefect was not a little astounded to find Orso up and walking about with perfect ease. In the briefest fashion Colomba avowed her own lie, and begged him to forgive it.

"If you had been staying anywhere else, monsieur, my brother would have gone to pay his respects to you yesterday."

Orso made endless apologies, vowing he had nothing to do with his sister's absurd stratagem, by which he appeared deeply mortified. The prefect and the elder Barricini appeared to believe in the sincerity of his regret, and indeed this belief was justified by his evident confusion and the reproaches he addressed to his sister. But the mayor's two sons did not seem satisfied.

"We are being made to look like fools," said Orlanduccio audibly.

"If my sister were to play me such tricks," said Vincentello, "I'd soon cure her fancy for beginning them again."

The words, and the tone in which they were uttered, offended Orso, and diminished his good-will. Glances that were anything but friendly were exchanged between him and the two young men.

Meanwhile, everybody being seated save Colomba, who remained standing close to the kitchen door, the prefect took up his parable, and after a few common-places as to local prejudices, he recalled the fact that the most inveterate enmities generally have their root in some mere misunderstanding. Next, turning to the mayor, he told him that Signor della Rebbia had never believed the Barricini family had played any part, direct or indirect, in the deplorable event which had bereft him of his father; that he had, indeed, nursed some doubts as to one detail in the lawsuit between the two families; that Signor Orso's long absence, and the nature of the information sent him, excused the doubt in question; that in the light of recent revelations he felt completely satisfied, and desired to re-open friendly and neighbourly relations with Signor Barricini and his sons.

Orso bowed stiffly. Signor Barricini stammered a few words that nobody could hear, and his sons stared steadily at the ceiling rafters. The prefect was about to continue his speech, and address the counterpart of the remarks he had made to Signor Barricini, to Orso, when Colomba stepped gravely forward between the contracting parties, at the same time drawing some papers from beneath her neckerchief.

"I should be happy indeed," she said, "to see the quarrel between our two families brought to an end. But if the reconciliation is to be sincere, there must be a full explanation, and nothing must be left in doubt. Signor Prefetto, Tomaso Bianchi's declaration, coming from a man of such vile report, seemed to me justly open to doubt. I said your sons had possibly seen this man in the prison at Bastia."

"It's false!" interrupted Orlanduccio; "I didn't see him!"

Colomba cast a scornful glance at him, and proceeded with great apparent composure.

"You explained Tomaso's probable interest in threatening Signor Barricini, in the name of a dreaded bandit, by his desire to keep his brother Teodoro in possession of the mill which my father allowed him to hire at a very low rent."

"That's quite clear," assented the prefect.

"Where was Tomaso Bianchi's interest?" exclaimed Colomba triumphantly. "His brother's lease had run out. My father had given him notice on the 1st of July. Here is my father's account-book; here is his note of warning given to Teodoro, and the letter from a business man at Ajaccio suggesting a new tenant."

As she spoke she gave the prefect the papers she had been holding in her hand.

There was an astonished pause. The mayor turned visibly pale. Orso, knitting his brows, leaned forward to look at the papers, which the prefect was perusing most attentively.

"We are being made to look like fools!" cried Orlanduccio again, springing angrily to his feet. "Let us be off, father! We ought never to have come here!"

One instant's delay gave Signor Barricini time to recover his composure. He asked leave to see the papers. Without a word the prefect handed them over to him. Pushing his green spectacles up to his forehead, he looked through them with a somewhat indifferent air, while Colomba watched him with the eyes of a tigress who sees a buck drawing near to the lair where she had hidden her cubs.

"Well," said Signor Barricini, as he pulled down his spectacles and returned the documents, "knowing the late colonel's kind heart, Tomaso thought — most likely he thought — that the colonel would change his mind about the notice. As a matter of fact, Bianchi is still at the mill, so — "

"It was I," said Colomba, and there was scorn in her voice, "who left him there. My father was dead, and situated as I was, I was obliged to treat my brother's dependents with consideration."

"Yet," quoth the prefect, "this man Tomaso acknowledges that he wrote the letter. That much is clear."

"The thing that is clear to me," broke in Orso, "is that there is some vile infamy underneath this whole business."

"I have to contradict another assertion made by these gentlemen," said Colomba.

She threw open the door into the kitchen and instantly Brandolaccio, the licentiate in theology, and Brusco, the dog, marched into the room. The two bandits were unarmed — apparently, at all events; they wore their cartridge belts, but the pistols, which are their necessary complement, were absent. As they entered the room they doffed their caps respectfully.

The effect produced by their sudden appearance may be conceived. The mayor almost fell backward. His sons threw themselves boldly in front of him, each one feeling for his dagger in his coat pocket. The prefect made a step toward the door, and Orso, seizing Brandolaccio by the collar, shouted:

"What have you come here for, you villain?"

"This is a trap!" cried the mayor, trying to get the door open. But, by the bandits' orders, as was afterward discovered, Saveria had locked it on the outside.

"Good people," said Brandolaccio, "don't be afraid of me. I'm not such a devil as I look. We mean no harm at all. Signor Prefetto, I'm your very humble servant. Gently, lieutenant! You're strangling me! We're here as witnesses! Now then, Padre, speak up! Your tongue's glib enough!"

"Signor Prefetto," quoth the licentiate, "I have not the honour of being known to you. My name is Giocanto Castriconi, better known as the Padre. Aha, it's coming back to you! The signorina here, whom I have not the pleasure of knowing either, has sent to ask me to supply some information about a fellow of the name of Tomaso Bianchi, with whom I chanced to be shut up, about three weeks ago, in the prison at Bastia. This is what I have to tell you."

"Spare yourself the trouble," said the prefect. "I can not listen to anything from such a man as you. Signor della Rebbia, I am willing to believe you have had nothing to do with this detestable plot. But are you master in your own house? Will you have the door opened? Your sister may have to give an account of the strange relations in which she lives with a set of bandits."

"Signor Prefetto!" cried Colomba, "I beseech you to listen to what this man has to say! You are here to do justice to everybody, and it is your duty to search out the truth. Speak, Giocanto Castriconi!"

"Don't listen to him," chorused the three Barricini.

"If everybody talks at once," remarked the bandit, with a smile, "nobody can contrive to hear what anybody says. Well, in the prison at Bastia I had as my companion — not as my friend — this very man, Tomaso. He received frequent visits from Signor Orlanduccio."

"You lie!" shouted the two brothers together.

"Two negatives make an affirmative," pursued Castriconi coolly. "Tomaso had money, he ate and drank of the best. I have always been fond of good cheer (that's the least of my failings), and in spite of my repugnance to rubbing shoulders with such a wretch, I let myself be tempted, several times over, into dining with him. Out of gratitude, I proposed he should escape with me. A young person — to whom I had shown some kindness — had provided me with the necessary means. I don't intend to compromise anybody. Tomaso refused my offer, telling me he was certain to be all right, as lawyer Barricini had spoken to all the judges for him, and he was sure to get out of prison with a character as white as snow, and with money in his pocket, too. As for me, I thought it better to get into the fresh air. *Dixi.*"

"Everything that fellow has said is a heap of lies," reiterated Orlanduccio stoutly. "If we were in the open country, and each of us had his gun, he wouldn't talk in that way."

"Here's a pretty folly!" cried Brandolaccio. "Don't you quarrel with the Padre, Orlanduccio!"

"Will you be good enough to allow me to leave this room, Signor della Rebbia," said the prefect, and he stamped his foot in his impatience.

"Saveria! Saveria!" shouted Orso, "open the door, in the devil's name!"

"One moment," said Brandolaccio. "We have to slip away first, on our side. Signor Prefetto, the custom, when people meet in the house of a mutual friend, is to allow each other half an hour's law, after departure."

The prefect cast a scornful glance at him.

"Your servant, signorina, and gentlemen all!" said Brandolaccio. Then stretching out his arm, "Hi, Brusco," he cried to his dog, "jump for the Signor Prefetto!"

The dog jumped; the bandits swiftly snatched up their arms in the kitchen, fled across the garden, and at a shrill whistle the door of the room flew open as though by magic.

"Signor Barricini," said Orso, and suppressed fury vibrated in his voice, "I hold you to be a forger! This very day I shall charge you before the public prosecutor with forgery and complicity with Bianchi. I may perhaps have a still more terrible accusation to bring against you!"

"And I, Signor della Rebbia," replied the mayor, "shall lay my charge against you for conspiracy and complicity with bandits. Meanwhile the prefect will desire the gendarmes to keep an eye upon you."

"The prefect will do his duty," said that gentleman sternly. "He will see the public order is not disturbed at Pietranera; he will take care justice is done. I say this to you all, gentlemen!"

The mayor and Vincentello were outside the room already, and Orlanduccio was following them, stepping backward, when Orso said to him in an undertone:

"Your father is an old man. One cuff from me would kill him. It is with you and with your brother that I intend to deal."

Orlanduccio's only response was to draw his dagger and fly like a madman at Orso. But before he could use his weapon Colomba caught hold of his arm and twisted it violently, while Orso gave him a blow in the face with his fist, which made him stagger several paces back, and come into violent collision with the door frame. Orlanduccio's dagger dropped from his hand. But Vincentello had his ready, and was rushing back into the room, when Colomba, snatching up a gun convinced him that the struggle must be unequal. At the same time the prefect threw himself between the combatants.

"We shall soon meet, Ors' Anton'!" shouted Orlanduccio, and slamming the door of the room violently, he turned the key in the lock, so as to insure himself time to retreat.

For a full quarter of an hour Orso and the prefect kept their places in dead silence, at opposite ends of the room. Colomba, the pride of triumph shining on her brow, gazed first at one and then at the other, as she leaned on the gun that had turned the scale of victory.

"What a country! Oh, what a country!" cried the prefect at last, rising hastily from his chair. "Signor della Rebbia, you did wrong! You must give me your word of honour to abstain from all violence, and to wait till the law settles this cursed business."

"Yes, Signor Prefetto, I was wrong to strike that villain. But I did strike him, after all, and I can't refuse him the satisfaction he has demanded of me."

"Pooh! no! He doesn't want to fight you! But supposing he murders you? You've done everything you could to insure it."

"We'll protect ourselves," said Colomba.

"Orlanduccio," said Orso, "strikes me as being a plucky fellow, and I think better of him than that, monsieur. He was very quick about drawing his dagger. But perhaps I should have done the same thing in his place, and I'm glad my sister has not an ordinary fine lady's wrist."

"You are not to fight," exclaimed the prefect. "I forbid it!"

"Allow me to say, monsieur, that in matters that affect my honour the only authority I acknowledge is that of my own conscience."

"You sha'n't fight, I tell you!"

"You can put me under arrest, monsieur — that is, if I let you catch me. But if you were to do that, you would only delay a thing that has now become inevitable. You are a man of honour yourself, monsieur; you know there can be no other course."

"If you were to have my brother arrested," added Colomba, "half the village would take his part, and we should have a fine fusillade."

"I give you fair notice, monsieur, and I entreat you not to think I am talking mere bravado. I warn you that if Signor Barricini abuses his authority as mayor, to have me arrested, I shall defend myself."

"From this very day," said the prefect, "Signor Barricini is suspended. I trust he will exculpate himself. Listen to me, my young gentleman, I have a liking for you. What I ask of you is nothing to speak of. Just to stay quietly at home till I get back from Corte. I shall only be three days away. I'll bring back the public prosecutor with me, and then we'll sift this wretched business to the bottom. Will you promise me you will abstain from all hostilities till then?"

"I can not promise that, monsieur, if, as I expect, Orlanduccio asks me to meet him."

"What, Signor della Rebbia! Would you — a French officer — think of going out with a man you suspect of being a forger?"

"I struck him, monsieur!"

"But supposing you struck a convict, and he demanded satisfaction of you, would you fight him? Come, come, Signor Orso! But I'll ask you to do even less, do nothing to seek out Orlanduccio. I'll consent to your fighting him if he asks you for a meeting."

"He will ask for it, I haven't a doubt of that. But I'll promise I won't give him fresh cuffs to induce him to do it."

"What a country!" cried the prefect once more, as he strode to and fro. "Shall I never get back to France?"

"Signor Prefetto," said Colomba in her most dulcet tones, "it is growing very late. Would you do us the honour of breakfasting here?"

The prefect could not help laughing.

"I've been here too long already — it may look like partiality. And there is that cursed foundation-stone. I must be off. Signorina della Rebbia! what calamities you may have prepared this day!"

"At all events, Signor Prefetto, you will do my sister the justice of believing her convictions are deeply rooted — and I am sure, now, that you yourself believe them to be well-founded."

"Farewell, sir!" said the prefect, waving his hand. "I warn you that the sergeant of gendarmes will have orders to watch everything you do."

When the prefect had departed —

"Orso," said Colomba, "this isn't the Continent. Orlanduccio knows nothing about your duels, and besides, that wretch must not die the death of a brave man."

"Colomba, my dear, you are a clever woman. I owe you a great deal from having saved me from a hearty knife-thrust. Give me your little hand to kiss! But, hark ye, let me have my way. There are certain matters that you don't understand. Give me my breakfast. And as soon as the prefect had started off send for little Chilina, who seems to perform all the commissions she is given in the most wonderful fashion. I shall want her to take a letter for me."

While Colomba was superintending the preparation of his breakfast, Orso went up to his own room and wrote the following note:

"You must be in a hurry to meet me, and I am no less eager. We can meet at six o'clock to-morrow morning in the valley of Acquaviva. I am a skilful pistol-shot, so I do not suggest that weapon to you. I hear you are a good shot with a gun. Let us each take a double-barreled gun. I shall be accompanied by a man from this village. If your brother wishes to go with you, take a second witness, and let me know. In that case only, I should bring two with me.

"ORSO ANTONIO DELLA REBBIA."

After spending an hour with the deputy-mayor, and going into the Barricini house for a few minutes, the prefect, attended by a single gendarme, started for Corte. A quarter of an hour later, Chilina carried over the letter my readers have just perused, and delivered it into Orlanduccio's own hands.

The answer was not prompt, and did not arrive till evening. It bore the signature of the elder Barricini, and informed Orso that he was laying the threatening letter sent to his son before the public prosecutor. His missive concluded thus: "Strong in the sense of a clear conscience, I patiently wait till the law has pronounced on your calumnies."

Meanwhile five or six herdsmen, summoned by Colomba, arrived to garrison the della Rebbia Tower. In spite of Orso's protests, *archere* were arranged in the windows looking onto the square, and all through the evening offers of service kept coming in from various persons belonging to the village. There was even a letter from the bandit-theologian, undertaking, for himself and Brandolaccio, that in the event of the mayor's calling on the gendarmes, they themselves would straightway intervene. The following postscript closed the letter:

"Dare I ask you what the Signor Prefetto thinks of the excellent education bestowed by my friend on Brusco, the dog? Next to Chilina, he is the most docile and promising pupil I have ever come across."

# CHAPTER XVI

The following day went by without any hostile demonstration. Both sides kept on the defensive. Orso did not leave his house, and the door of the Barricini dwelling remained closely shut. The five gendarmes who had been left to garrison Pietranera were to be seen walking about the square and the outskirts of the village, in company with the village constable, the sole representative of the urban police force. The deputy-mayor never put off his sash. But there was no actual symptom of war, except the loopholes in the two opponents' houses. Nobody but a Corsican would have noticed that the group round the evergreen oak in the middle of the square consisted solely of women.

At supper-time Colomba gleefully showed her brother a letter she had just received from Miss Nevil.

"My dear Signorina Colomba," it ran, "I learn with great pleasure, through a letter from your brother, that your enmities are all at an end. I congratulate you heartily. My father can not endure Ajaccio now your brother is not there to talk about war and go out shooting with him. We are starting to-day, and shall sleep at the house of your kinswoman, to whom we have a letter. The day after to-morrow, somewhere about eleven o'clock, I shall come and ask you to let me taste that mountain *bruccio* of yours, which you say is so vastly superior to what we get in the town.

"Farewell, dear Signorina Colomba.

"Your affectionate
"LYDIA NEVIL."

"Then she hasn't received my second letter!" exclaimed Orso.

"You see by the date of this one that Miss Lydia must have already started when your letter reached Ajaccio. But did you tell her not to come?"

"I told her we were in a state of siege. That does not seem to me a condition that permits of our receiving company."

"Bah! These English people are so odd. The very last night I slept in her room she told me she would be sorry to leave Corsica without having seen a good *vendetta*. If you choose, Orso, you might let her see an assault on our enemies' house."

"Do you know, Colomba," said Orso, "Nature blundered when she made you a woman. You'd have made a first-rate soldier."

"Maybe. Anyhow, I'm going to make my *bruccio*."

"Don't waste your time. We must send somebody down to warn them and stop them before they start."

"Do you mean to say you would send a messenger out in such weather, to have him and your letter both swept away by a torrent? How I pity those poor bandits in this storm! Luckily they have good *piloni* (thick cloth cloaks with hoods). Do you know what you ought to do, Orso. If the storm clears you should start off very early to-morrow morning, and get to our kinswoman's house before they leave it. That will be easy enough, for Miss Lydia always gets up so late. You can tell them everything that has happened here, and if they still persist in coming, why! we shall be very glad to welcome them."

Orso lost no time in assenting to this plan, and after a few moments' silence, Colomba continued:

"Perhaps, Orso, you think I was joking when I talked of an assault on the Barricini's house. Do you know we are in force — two to one at the very least? Now that the prefect has suspended the mayor, every man in the place is on our side. We might cut them to pieces. It would be quite easy to bring it about. If you liked, I could go over to the fountain and begin to jeer at their women folk. They would come out. Perhaps — they are such cowards! — they would fire at me through their loopholes. They wouldn't hit me. Then the thing would be done. They would have begun the attack, and the beaten party must take its chance. How is anybody to know which person's aim has been true, in a scuffle? Listen to your own sister, Orso! These lawyers who are coming will blacken lots of paper, and talk a great deal of useless stuff. Nothing will come of it all. That old fox will contrive to make them think they see stars in broad midday. Ah! if the prefect hadn't thrown himself in front of Vincentello, we should have had one less to deal with."

All this was said with the same calm air as that with which she had spoken, an instant previously, of her preparations for making the *bruccio*.

Orso, quite dumfounded, gazed at his sister with an admiration not unmixed with alarm.

"My sweet Colomba," he said, as he rose from the table, "I really am afraid you are the very devil. But make your mind easy. If I don't succeed in getting the Barricini hanged, I'll contrive to get the better of them in some other fashion. 'Hot bullet or cold steel' — you see I haven't forgotten my Corsican."

"The sooner the better," said Colomba, with a sigh. "What horse will you ride to-morrow, Ors' Anton'?"

"The black. Why do you ask?"

"So as to make sure he has some barley."

When Orso went up to his room, Colomba sent Saveria and the herdsmen to their beds, and sat on alone in the kitchen, where the *bruccio* was simmering. Now and then she seemed to listen, and was apparently waiting very anxiously for her brother to go to bed. At last, when she thought he was asleep, she took a knife, made sure it was sharp, slipped her little feet into thick shoes, and passed noiselessly out into the garden.

This garden, which was enclosed by walls, lay next to a good-sized piece of hedged ground, into which the horses were turned — for Corsican horses do not know what a stable means. They are generally turned loose into a field, and left to themselves, to find pasture and shelter from cold winds, as best they may.

Colomba opened the garden gate with the same precaution, entered the enclosure, and whistling gently, soon attracted the horses, to whom she had often brought bread and salt. As soon as the black horse came within reach, she caught him firmly by the mane, and split his ear open with her knife. The horse gave a violent leap, and tore off with that shrill cry which sharp pain occasionally extorts from his kind. Quite satisfied, Colomba was

240

making her way back into the garden, when Orso threw open his window and shouted, "Who goes there?" At the same time she heard him cock his gun. Luckily for her the garden-door lay in the blackest shadow, and was partly screened by a large fig-tree. She very soon gathered, from the light she saw glancing up and down in her brother's room, that he was trying to light his lamp. She lost no time about closing the garden-door, and slipping along the wall, so that the outline of her black garments was lost against the dark foliage of the fruit-trees, and succeeded in getting back into the kitchen a few moments before Orso entered it.

"What's the matter?" she inquired.

"I fancied I heard somebody opening the garden-door," said Orso.

"Impossible! The dog would have barked. But let us go and see!"

Orso went round the garden, and having made sure that the outer door was safely secured, he was going back to his room, rather ashamed of his false alarm.

"I am glad, brother," remarked Colomba, "that you are learning to be prudent, as a man in your position ought to be."

"You are training me well," said Orso. "Good-night!"

By dawn the next morning Orso was up and ready to start. His style of dress betrayed the desire for smartness felt by every man bound for the presence of the lady he would fain please, combined with the caution of a Corsican *in vendetta*. Over a blue coat, that sat closely to his figure, he wore a small tin case full of cartridges, slung across his shoulder by a green silk cord. His dagger lay in his side pocket, and in his hand he carried his handsome Manton, ready loaded. While he was hastily swallowing the cup of coffee Colomba had poured out for him, one of the herdsmen went out to put the bridle and saddle on the black horse. Orso and his sister followed close on his heels and entered the field. The man had caught the horse, but he had dropped both saddle and bridle, and seemed quite paralyzed with horror, while the horse, remembering the wound it had received during the night, and trembling for its other ear, was rearing, kicking, and neighing like twenty fiends.

"Now then! Make haste!" shouted Orso.

"Ho, Ors' Anton'! Ho, Ors' Anton'!" yelled the herdsman. "Holy Madonna!" and he poured out a string of imprecations, numberless, endless, and most of them quite untranslatable.

"What can be the matter?" inquired Colomba. They all drew near to the horse, and at the sight of the creature's bleeding head and split ear there was a general outcry of surprise and indignation. My readers must know that among the Corsicans to mutilate an enemy's horse is at once a vengeance, a challenge, and a mortal threat. "Nothing but a bullet-wound can expiate such a crime."

Though Orso, having lived so long on the mainland, was not so sensitive as other Corsicans to the enormity of the insult, still, if any supporter of the Barricini had appeared in his sight at that moment, he would probably have taken vengeance on him for the outrage he ascribed to his enemies.

"The cowardly wretches!" he cried. "To avenge themselves on a poor brute, when they dare not meet me face to face!"

"What are we waiting for?" exclaimed Colomba vehemently. "They come here and brave us! They mutilate our horses! and we are not to make any response? Are you men?"

"Vengeance!" shouted the herdsmen. "Let us lead the horse through the village, and attack their house!"

"There's a thatched barn that touches their Tower," said old Polo Griffo; "I'd set fire to it in a trice."

Another man wanted to fetch the ladders out of the church steeple. A third proposed they should break in the doors of the house with a heavy beam intended for some house in course of building, which had been left lying in the square. Amid all the angry voices Colomba was heard telling her satellites that before they went to work she would give each man of them a large glass of anisette.

Unluckily, or rather luckily, the impression she had expected to produce by her own cruel treatment of the poor horse was

242

largely lost on Orso. He felt no doubt that the savage mutilation was due to one of his foes, and he specially suspected Orlanduccio; but he did not believe that the young man, whom he himself had provoked and struck, had wiped out his shame by slitting a horse's ear. On the contrary, this mean and ridiculous piece of vengeance had increased Orso's scorn for his opponents, and he now felt, with the prefect, that such people were not worthy to try conclusions with himself. As soon as he was able to make himself heard, he informed his astonished partisans that they would have to relinquish all their bellicose intentions, and that the power of the law, which would shortly be on the spot, would amply suffice to avenge the hurt done to a horse's ear.

"I'm master here!" he added sternly; "and I insist on being obeyed. The first man who dares to say anything more about killing or burning, will quite possibly get a scorching at my hands! Be off! Saddle me the gray horse!"

"What's this, Orso?" said Colomba, drawing him apart. "You allow these people to insult us? No Barricini would have dared to mutilate any beast of ours in my father's time."

"I promise you they shall have reason to repent it. But it is gendarme's and jailer's work to punish wretches who only venture to raise their hands against brute beasts. I've told you already, the law will punish them; and if not, you will not need to remind me whose son I am."

"Patience!" answered Colomba, with a sigh.

"Remember this, sister," continued Orso; "if I find, when I come back, that any demonstration whatever has been made against the Barricini I shall never forgive you." Then, in a gentler tone, he added, "Very possibly — very probably — I shall bring the colonel and his daughter back with me. See that their rooms are well prepared, and that the breakfast is good. In fact, let us make our guests as comfortable as we can. It's a very good thing to be brave, Colomba, but a woman must know how to manage her household, as well. Come, kiss me, and be good! Here's the gray, ready saddled."

"Orso," said Colomba, "you mustn't go alone."

"I don't need anybody," replied Orso; "and I'll promise you nobody shall slit my ear."

"Oh, I'll never consent to your going alone, while there is a feud. Here! Polo Griffo! Gian' Franco! Memmo! Take your guns; you must go with my brother."

After a somewhat lively argument, Orso had to give in, and accept an escort. From the most excited of the herdsmen he chose out those who had been loudest in their desire to commence hostilities; then, after laying fresh injunctions on his sister and the men he was leaving behind, he started, making a detour, this time, so as to avoid the Barricinis' dwelling.

They were a long way from Pietranera, and were traveling along at a great pace, when, as they crossed a streamlet that ran into a marsh, Polo Griffo noticed several porkers wallowing comfortably in the mud, in full enjoyment at once of the warmth of the sun and the coolness of the water. Instantly he took aim at the biggest, fired at its head, and shot it dead. The dead creature's comrades rose and fled with astonishing swiftness, and though another herdsman fired at them they reached a thicket and disappeared into it, safe and sound.

"Idiots!" cried Orso. "You've been taking pigs for wild boars!"

"Not a bit, Ors' Anton'," replied Polo Griffo. "But that herd belongs to the lawyer, and I've taught him, now, to mutilate our horses."

"What! you rascal!" shouted Orso, in a perfect fury. "You ape the vile behaviour of our enemies! Be off, villains! I don't want you! You're only fit to fight with pigs. I swear to God that if you dare follow me I'll blow your brains out!"

The herdsmen stared at each other, struck quite dumb. Orso spurred his horse, galloped off, and was soon out of sight.

"Well, well!" said Polo Griffo. "Here's a pretty thing. You devote yourself to people, and then this is how they treat you. His father, the colonel, was angry with you long ago, because you leveled your gun at the lawyer. Great idiot you were, not to shoot. And now here is his son. You saw what I did for him. And he talks about cracking my skull, just as he would crack a gourd that lets the wine leak out. That's what people learn on the mainland, Memmo!"

"Yes, and if any one finds out it was you who killed that pig there'll be a suit against you, and Ors' Anton' won't speak to the judges, nor buy off the lawyer for you. Luckily nobody saw, and you have Saint Nega to help you out."

After a hasty conclave, the two herdsmen concluded their wisest plan was to throw the dead pig into a bog, and this project they carefully executed, after each had duly carved himself several slices out of the body of this innocent victim of the feud between the Barricini and the della Rebbia.

# CHAPTER XVII

Once rid of his unruly escort, Orso proceeded calmly on his way, far more absorbed by the prospective pleasure of seeing Miss Nevil than stirred by any fear of coming across his enemies.

"The lawsuit I must bring against these Barricini villains," he mused, "will necessitate my going down to Bastia. Why should I not go there with Miss Nevil? And once at Bastia, why shouldn't we all go together to the springs of Orezza?"

Suddenly his childish recollections of that picturesque spot rose up before him. He fancied himself on the verdant lawn that spreads beneath the ancient chestnut-trees. On the lustrous green sward, studded with blue flowers like eyes that smiled upon him, he saw Miss Lydia seated at his side. She had taken off her hat, and her fair hair, softer and finer than any silk, shone like gold in the sunlight that glinted through the foliage. Her clear blue eyes looked to him bluer than the sky itself. With her cheek resting on one hand, she was listening thoughtfully to the words of love he poured tremblingly into her ear. She wore the muslin gown in which she had been dressed that last day at Ajaccio. From beneath its folds peeped out a tiny foot, shod with black satin. Orso told himself that he would be happy indeed if he might dare to kiss that little foot — but one of Miss Lydia's hands was bare and held a daisy. He took the daisy from her, and Lydia's hand pressed his, and then he kissed the daisy, and then he kissed her hand, and yet she did not chide him . . . and all these thoughts prevented him from paying any attention to the road he was traveling, and meanwhile he trotted steadily onward. For the second time, in his fancy, he was about to kiss Miss Nevil's snow-white hand, when, as his horse stopped short, he very nearly kissed its head, in stern reality. Little Chilina had barred his way, and seized his bridle.

"Where are you going to, Ors' Anton'?" she said. "Don't you know your enemy is close by?"

"My enemy!" cried Orso, furious at being interrupted at such a delightful moment. "Where is he?"

"Orlanduccio is close by, he's waiting for you! Go back, go back!"

"Ho! Ho! So he's waiting for me! Did you see him?"

"Yes, Ors' Anton'! I was lying down in the heather when he passed by. He was looking round everywhere through his glass."

"And which way did he go?"

"He went down there. Just where you were going!"

"Thank you!"

"Ors' Anton', hadn't you better wait for my uncle? He must be here soon — and with him you would be safe."

"Don't be frightened, Chili. I don't need your uncle."

"If you would let me, I would go in front of you."

"No, thanks! No, thanks!"

And Orso, spurring his horse, rode rapidly in the direction to which the little girl had pointed.

His first impulse had been one of blind fury, and he had told himself that fortune was offering him an excellent opportunity of punishing the coward who had avenged the blow he had received by mutilating a horse. But as he moved onward the thought of his promise to the prefect, and, above all, his fear of missing Miss Nevil's visit, altered his feelings, and made him almost wish he might not come upon Orlanduccio. Soon, however, the memory of his father, the indignity offered to his own horse, and the threats of the Barricini, stirred his rage afresh, and incited him to seek his foe, and to provoke and force him to a fight. Thus tossed by conflicting feelings, he continued his progress, though now he carefully scrutinized every thicket and hedge, and sometimes even pulled up his horse to listen to the vague sounds to be heard in any open country. Ten minutes after he had left little Chilina (it was then about nine o'clock in the morning) he found himself on the edge of an exceedingly steep declivity. The road, or rather the very slight path, which he was following, ran through a *maquis* that had been lately burned. The ground was covered with whitish ashes, and here and there some shrubs, and a few big trees, blackened by the flames, and entirely stripped of their leaves, still stood erect — though life had long since departed out of them.

The sight of a burned *maquis* is enough to make a man fancy he has been transported into midwinter in some northern clime, and the contrast between the barrenness of the ground over which the flames have passed, with the luxuriant vegetation round about it, heightens this appearance of sadness and desolation. But at that moment the only thing that struck Orso in this particular landscape was one point — an important one, it is true, in his present circumstances. The bareness of the ground rendered any kind of ambush impossible, and the man who has reason to fear that at any moment he may see a gun-barrel thrust out of a thicket straight at his own chest, looks on a stretch of smooth ground, with nothing on it to intercept his view, as a kind of oasis. After this burned *maquis* came a number of cultivated fields, enclosed, according to the fashion of that country, with breast-high walls, built of dry stones. The path ran between these fields, producing, from a distance, the effect of a thick wood.

The steepness of the declivity made it necessary for Orso to dismount. He was walking quickly down the hill, which was slippery with ashes (he had thrown the bridle on his horse's neck), and was hardly five-and-twenty paces from one of these stone fences, when, just in front of him, on the right-hand side of the road, he perceived first of all the barrel of a gun, and then a head, rising over the top of the wall. The gun was leveled, and he recognized Orlanduccio, just ready to fire. Orso swiftly prepared for self-defence, and the two men, taking deliberate aim, stared at each other for several seconds, with that thrill of emotion which the bravest must feel when he knows he must either deal death or endure it.

"Vile coward!" shouted Orso.

The words were hardly out of his mouth when he saw the flash of Orlanduccio's gun, and almost at the same instant a second shot rang out on his left from the other side of the path, fired by a man whom he had not noticed, and who was aiming at him from behind another wall. Both bullets struck him. The first, Orlanduccio's, passed through his left arm, which Orso had turned toward him as he aimed. The second shot struck him in the chest, and tore his coat, but coming in contact with the blade of his dagger, it luckily flattened against it, and only inflicted a trifling bruise. Orso's left arm fell helpless at his side, and the barrel of his gun dropped for a moment, but he raised it at once, and aiming his weapon with his right hand only, he fired at Orlanduccio. His enemy's head, which was only exposed to the level of the eyes, disappeared behind the wall. Then Orso, swinging round to the left, fired the second barrel at a man in a cloud of smoke whom he could hardly see. This face likewise disappeared. The four shots had followed each other with incredible swiftness; no trained soldiers ever fired their volleys in quicker succession. After Orso's last shot a great silence fell. The smoke from his weapon rose slowly up into the sky. There was not a movement, not the slightest sound from behind the wall. But for the pain in his arm, he could have fancied the men on whom he had just fired had been phantoms of his own imagination.

Fully expecting a second volley, Orso moved a few steps, to place himself behind one of the burned trees that still stood upright in the *maquis*. Thus sheltered, he put his gun between his knees, and hurriedly reloaded it. Meanwhile his left arm began to hurt him horribly, and felt as if it were being dragged down by a huge weight.

What had become of his adversaries? He could not understand. If they had taken to flight, if they had been wounded, he would certainly have heard some noise, some stir among the leaves. Were they dead, then? Or, what was far more likely, were they not waiting behind their wall for a chance of shooting at him again. In his uncertainty, and feeling his strength fast failing him, he knelt down on his right knee, rested his wounded arm upon the other, and took advantage of a branch that protruded from the trunk of the burned tree to support his gun. With his finger on the trigger, his eye fixed on the wall, and his ear strained to catch the slightest sound, he knelt there, motionless, for several minutes, which seemed to him a century. At last, behind him, in the far distance, he heard a faint shout, and very soon a dog flew like an arrow down the slope, and stopped short, close to him, wagging its tail. It was Brusco, the comrade and follower of the bandits — the herald, doubtless, of his master's approach. Never was any honest man more impatiently awaited. With his muzzle in the air, and turned toward the nearest fence, the dog sniffed anxiously. Suddenly he gave vent to a low growl, sprang at a bound over the wall, and almost instantly reappeared upon its crest, whence he gazed steadily at Orso with eyes that spoke surprise as clearly as a dog's may do it. Then he sniffed again, this time toward the other enclosure, the wall of which he also crossed. Within a second he was back on the top of that, with the same air of astonishment and alarm, and straightway he bounded into the thicket with his tail between his legs, still gazing at Orso, and retiring from him slowly, and sideways, until he had put some distance between them. Then off he started again, tearing up the slope almost as fast as he had come down it, to meet a man, who, in spite of its steepness, was rapidly descending.

"Help, Brando!" shouted Orso, as soon as he thought he was within hearing.

"Hallo! Ors' Anton'! are you wounded?" inquired Brandolaccio, as he ran up panting. "Is it in your body or your limbs?"

"In the arm."

"The arm — oh, that's nothing! And the other fellow?"

"I think I hit him."

Brandolaccio ran after the dog to the nearest field and leaned over to look at the other side of the wall, then pulling off his cap —

"Signor Orlanduccio, I salute you!" said he, then turning toward Orso, he bowed to him, also, gravely.

"That," he remarked, "is what I call a man who has been properly done for."

"Is he still alive?" asked Orso, who could hardly breathe.

"Oh! he wouldn't wish it! he'd be too much vexed about the bullet you put into his eye! Holy Madonna! What a hole! That's a good gun, upon my soul! what a weight! That spatters a man's brains for you! Hark ye, Ors' Anton'! when I heard the first *piff, piff,* says I to myself: 'Dash it, they're murdering my lieutenant!' Then I heard *boum, boum.* 'Ha, ha!' says I, 'that's the English gun beginning to talk — he's firing back.' But what on earth do you want with me, Brusco?"

The dog guided him to the other field.

"Upon my word," cried Brandolaccio, utterly astonished, "a right and left, that's what it is! Deuce take it! Clear enough, powder must be dear, for you don't waste it!"

"What do you mean, for God's sake?" asked Orso.

"Come, sir, don't try to humbug me; you bring down the dame, and then you want somebody to pick it up for you. Well! there's one man who'll have a queer dessert to-day, and that's Lawyer Barricini! — you want butcher's meat, do you? Well, here you have it. Now, who the devil will be the heir?"

"What! is Vincentello dead too?"

"Dead as mutton. *Salute a noi!* The good point about you is that you don't let them suffer. Just come over and look at Vincentello; he's kneeling here with his head against the wall, as if he were asleep. You may say he sleeps like lead, this time, poor devil."

Orso turned his head in horror.

"Are you certain he's dead?"

"You're like Sampiero Corso, who never had to fire more than once. Look at it there, in his chest, on the left — just where Vincileone was hit at Waterloo. I'll wager that bullet isn't far from his heart — a right and left! Ah! I'll never talk about shooting again. Two with two shots, and bullets at that! The two brothers! If he'd had a third shot he'd have killed their papa. Better luck next time. What a shot! Ors' Anton'! And to think that an honest poor chap like me will never get the chance of a right and a left two gendarmes!"

As he talked the bandit was scanning Orso's arm, and splitting up his sleeve with his dagger.

"This is nothing," said he. "But this coat of yours will give Signorina Colomba work to do. Ha! what's this I see? this gash

251

upon your chest? Nothing went in there, surely? No! you wouldn't be so brisk as you are! Come, try to move your finger. Do you feel my teeth when I bite your little finger? Not very well? Never mind! It won't be much. Let me take your handkerchief and your neckcloth. Well, your coat's spoilt, anyhow! What the devil did you make yourself so smart for? Were you going to a wedding? There! drink a drop of wine. Why on earth don't you carry a flask? Does any Corsican ever go out without a flask?"

Then again he broke off the dressing of the wound to exclaim:

"A right and left! Both of them stone dead! How the Padre will laugh! A right and left! Oh, here's that little dawdle Chilina at last!"

Orso made no reply — he was as pale as death and shaking in every limb.

"Chili!" shouted Brandolaccio, "go and look behind that wall!"

The child, using both hands and feet, scrambled onto the wall, and the moment she caught sight of Orlanduccio's corpse she crossed herself.

"That's nothing," proceeded the bandit; "go and look farther on, over there!"

The child crossed herself again.

"Was it you, uncle?" she asked timidly.

"Me! Don't you know I've turned into a useless old fellow! This, Chili, is the signor's work; offer him your compliments."

"The signorina will be greatly rejoiced," said Chilina, "and she will be very much grieved to know you are wounded, Ors' Anton'."

"Now then, Ors' Anton'," said the bandit, when he had finished binding up the wound. "Chilina, here, has caught your horse. You must get on his back, and come with me to the Stazzona *maquis*. It would be a sly fellow who'd lay his hand on you there. When we get to the Cross of Santa Christina, you'll have to dismount. You'll give over your horse to Chilina, who'll go off and warn the signorina. You can say anything to the child,

Ors' Anton'. She would let herself be cut in pieces rather than betray her friends," and then, fondly, he turned to the little girl, "That's it, you little hussy; a ban on you, a curse on you — you jade!" For Brandolaccio, who was superstitious, like most bandits, feared he might cast a spell on a child if he blessed it or praised it, seeing it is a well-known fact that the mysterious powers that rule the *Annocchiatura* have a vile habit of fulfilling our wishes in the very opposite sense to that we give them.

"Where am I to go, Brando?" queried Orso in a faint voice.

"Faith! you must choose; either to jail or to the *maquis*. But no della Rebbia knows the path that leads him to the jail. To the *maquis*, Ors' Anton'."

"Farewell, then, to all my hopes!" exclaimed the wounded man, sadly.

"Your hopes? Deuce take it! Did you hope to do any better with a double-barreled gun? How on earth did the fellows contrive to hit you? The rascals must have been as hard to kill as cats."

"They fired first," said Orso.

"True, true; I'd forgotten that! — *piff, piff* — *boum, boum!* A right and left, and only one hand! If any man can do better, I'll go hang myself. Come! now you're safely mounted! Before we start, just give a glance at your work. It isn't civil to leave one's company without saying good-bye."

Orso spurred his horse. He would not have looked at the two poor wretches he had just destroyed, for anything on earth.

"Hark ye, Ors' Anton'," quoth the bandit, as he caught hold of the horse's bridle, "shall I tell you the truth? Well, no offence to you! I'm sorry for those poor young fellows! You'll pardon me, I hope; so good-looking, so strong, so young. Orlanduccio, I've shot with him so often! Only four days ago he gave me a bundle of cigars, and Vincentello — he was always so cheery. Of course you've only done what you had to do, and indeed the shot was such a splendid one, nobody could regret it. But I, you see, had nothing to do with your vengeance. I know you're perfectly in the right. When one has an enemy one must get rid of him. But the

253

Barricini were an old family. Here's another of them wiped out, and by a right and left too! It's striking."

As he thus spoke his funeral oration over the Barricini, Brandolaccio hastily guided Orso, Chilina, and Brusco, the dog, toward the Stazzona *maquis*.

# CHAPTER XVIII

Meanwhile, very shortly after Orso's departure, Colomba's spies had warned her that the Barricini were out on the warpath, and from that moment she was racked by the most intense anxiety. She was to be seen moving hither and thither all over the house, between the kitchen and the rooms that were being made ready for her guests, doing nothing, yet always busy, and constantly stopping to look out of a window for any unusual stir in the village. Toward eleven o'clock, a somewhat numerous cavalcade rode into Pietranera. This was the colonel, with his daughter, their servants, and their guide. Colomba's first word, as she welcomed them, was "Have you seen my brother?" Then she questioned the guide as to the road they had taken, and the hour of their departure, and having heard his answers, she could not understand why they had not met him.

"Perhaps," said the guide, "your brother took the higher path; we came by the lower one."

But Colomba only shook her head and asked more questions. In spite of her natural firmness of character, increased as it was by her proud desire to conceal any sign of weakness before strangers, she could not hide her anxiety, and as soon as she had informed them of the attempted reconciliation, and of its unfortunate issue, this was shared by the colonel and Miss Lydia. Miss Nevil became very uneasy, and wanted to have messengers sent off in every direction, and her father offered to remount at once and set out with the guide in search of Orso. Her guests' alarm recalled Colomba to a sense of her duties as a hostess. She strove to force a smile as she pressed the colonel to come to table, and suggested twenty plausible reasons, which she herself demolished within an instant, to account for her brother's delay. The colonel, feeling it to be his duty, as a man, to reassure the ladies, put forward his own explanation.

"I'll wager," he said, "that della Rebbia has come across some game or other. He has not been able to stand out against that temptation, and we shall soon see him come in with a heavy bag. 'Pon my soul," he went on, "we did hear four shots fired on the road. Two of them were louder than the others, and I said to my girl, 'I'll bet anything that's della Rebbia out shooting! My gun is the only one that would make that noise.'"

Colomba turned pale, and Lydia, who was watching her closely, had no difficulty in guessing the suspicions with which the colonel's conjecture had inspired her. After a few minutes' silence, Colomba eagerly inquired whether the two louder reports had been heard before or after the others. But neither the colonel, his daughter, nor the guide had paid much attention to this all-important detail.

Toward one o'clock, as none of Colomba's messengers had yet returned, she gathered all her courage, and insisted that her guests should sit down to table with her. But, except the colonel, none of them could eat. At the slightest sound in the square, Colomba ran to the window. Then drearily she returned to her place, and struggled yet more drearily to carry on a trivial conversation, to which nobody paid the slightest attention, and which was broken by long intervals of silence. All at once they heard a horse's gallop.

"Ah! That must be my brother at last!" said Colomba, rising from her chair. But when she saw Chilina astride on Orso's horse — "My brother is dead!" she cried, in a heart-rending voice.

The colonel dropped his glass. Miss Lydia screamed. They all rushed to the door of the house. Before Chilina could jump off her steed, she was snatched up like a feather by Colomba, who held her so tight that she almost choked her. The child understood her agonized look, and her first words were those of the chorus in Othello: "He lives!" Colomba's grasp relaxed, and nimbly as a kitten Chilina dropped upon the ground.

"The others?" queried Colomba hoarsely. Chilina crossed herself with her first and middle finger. A deep flush instantly replaced the deadly pallor of Colomba's face. She cast one fierce look at the Barricini dwelling, and then, with a smile, she turned to her guests.

"Let us go in and drink our coffee," she said.

The story the bandit's Iris had to tell was a long one. Her narrative, translated literally into Italian by Colomba, and then into English by Miss Nevil, wrung more than one oath from the colonel, more than one sigh from the fair Lydia. But Colomba heard it all unmoved. Only she twisted her damask napkin till it seemed as if she must tear it in pieces. She interrupted the child, five or six times over, to make her repeat again that Brandolaccio had said the wound was not dangerous, and that he had seen many worse. When she had finished her tale, Chilina announced that Orso earnestly begged he might be sent writing materials, and that he desired his sister would beseech a lady who might be staying in his house not to depart from it, until she had received a letter from him.

"That is what was worrying him most," the child added; "and even after I had started he called me back, to bid me not forget the message. It was the third time he had given it to me." When Colomba heard of her brother's injunction she smiled faintly, and squeezed the fair Englishwoman's hand. That young lady burst into tears, and did not seem to think it advisable to translate that particular part of the story to her father.

"Yes, my dear," cried Colomba, kissing Miss Nevil. "You shall stay with me, and you shall help us."

Then, taking a pile of old linen out of a cupboard, she began to cut it up, to make lint and bandages. Any one who saw her flashing eyes, her heightened colour, her alternate fits of anxiety and composure, would have found it hard to say whether distress at her brother's wound, or delight at the extinction of her foes, were most affecting her. One moment she was pouring out the colonel's coffee, and telling him how well she made it, the next she was setting Miss Lydia and Chilina to work, exhorting them to sew bandages, and roll them up. Then, for the twentieth time, she would ask whether Orso's wound was very painful. She constantly broke off her own work to exclaim to the colonel:

"Two such cunning men, such dangerous fellows! And he alone, wounded, with only one arm! He killed the two of them! What courage, colonel! Isn't he a hero? Ah, Miss Nevil! How good it is to live in a peaceful country like yours! I'm sure you did not really know my brother till now! I said it — 'The falcon will spread his wings!' You were deceived by his gentle look! That's because with you, Miss Nevil — Ah! if he could see you working for him now! My poor Orso!"

Miss Lydia was doing hardly any work, and could not find a single word to say. Her father kept asking why nobody went to lay a complaint before a magistrate. He talked about a coroner's inquest, and all sorts of other proceedings quite unknown to Corsican economy. And then he begged to be told whether the country house owned by that worthy Signor Brandolaccio, who had brought succour to the wounded man, was very far away from Pietranera, and whether he could not go there himself, to see his friend.

And Colomba replied, with her usual composure, that Orso was in the *maquis*; that he was being taken care of by a bandit; that it would be a great risk for him to show himself until he was sure of the line the prefect and the judges were likely to take; and, finally, that she would manage to have him secretly attended by a skilful surgeon.

"Above all things, colonel," she added, "remember that you heard the four shots, and that you told me Orso fired last."

The colonel could make neither head nor tail of the business, and his daughter did nothing but heave sighs and dry her eyes.

The day was far advanced, when a gloomy procession wended its way into the village. The bodies of his two sons were brought home to Lawyer Barricini, each corpse thrown across a mule, which was led by a peasant. A crowd of dependents and idlers followed the dreary *cortege*. With it appeared the gendarmes, who always came in too late, and the deputy-mayor, throwing up his hands, and incessantly repeating, "What will Signor Prefetto say!" Some of the women, among them Orlanduccio's foster-mother, were tearing their hair and shrieking wildly. But their clamorous grief was less impressive than the dumb despair of one man, on whom all eyes were fixed. This was the wretched father, who passed from one corpse to the other, lifting up the earth-soiled heads, kissing the blackened lips, supporting the limbs that were stiff already, as if he would save them from the jolting of the road. Now and then he opened his mouth as though about to speak, but not a cry came, not a word. His eyes never left the dead bodies, and as he walked, he knocked himself against the stones, against the trees, against every obstacle that chanced to lie in his path.

The women's lamentations grew louder, and the men's curses deeper, when Orso's house appeared in sight. When some shepherds of the della Rebbia party ventured on a triumphant shout, their enemy's indignation became ungovernable. "Vengeance! Vengeance!" exclaimed several voices. Stones were thrown, and two shots, fired at the windows of the room in which Colomba and her guests were sitting, pierced the outside shutters, and carried splinters of wood on to the table at which the two ladies were working. Miss Lydia screamed violently, the colonel snatched up a gun, and Colomba, before he could stop her, rushed to the door of the house and threw it violently open. There, standing high on the threshold, with her two hands outstretched to curse her enemies:

"Cowards!" she cried. "You fire on women and on foreigners! Are you Corsicans? Are you men? Wretches, who can only murder a man from behind. Come on! I defy you! I am alone! My brother is far away! Come! kill me, kill my guests! It would be worthy of you! . . . But you dare not, cowards that you are! You know we avenge our wrongs! Away with you! Go, weep like women, and be thankful we do not ask you for more blood!"

There was something terrible and imposing in Colomba's voice and mien. At the sight of her the crowd recoiled as though it beheld one of those evil fairies of which so many tales are told on long winter evenings, in Corsica. The deputy-mayor, the gendarmes, and a few women seized the opportunity, and threw themselves between the two factions; for the della Rebbia herdsmen were already loading their guns, and for a moment a general fight in the middle of the square had appeared imminent. But the two parties were both leaderless, and Corsicans, whose rage is always subject to discipline, seldom come to blows unless the chief authors of their internecine quarrels are present. Besides, Colomba, who had learned prudence from victory, restrained her little garrison.

"Let the poor folks weep in peace," she said. "Let the old man carry his own flesh home. What is the good of killing an old fox who has no teeth left to bite with, . . . Giudice Barricini! Remember the 2d of August! Remember the blood-stained pocket-book in which you wrote with your forger's hand! My father had written down your debt! Your sons have paid it. You may go free, old Barricini!"

With folded arms and a scornful smile upon her lips, Colomba watched the bearers carry the corpses of her enemies into their home, and the crowd without it melt gradually away. Then she closed her own door, and, going back into the dining-room, she said to the colonel:

"I beg, sir, you will forgive my fellow-countrymen! I never could have believed that any Corsican would have fired on a house that sheltered strangers, and I am ashamed of my country."

That night, when Miss Lydia had gone up to her room, the colonel followed her, and inquired whether they had not better get out of a village where they ran incessant risk of having a bullet through their heads, the very next morning, and leave this country, seething with treachery and murder, as soon as possible.

Miss Nevil did not answer for some time, and her father's suggestion evidently caused her considerable perplexity. At last she said:

"How can we leave this poor young creature, just when she is so much in need of consolation? Don't you think that would be cruel, father?"

"I only spoke on your account, child," said the colonel. "And I assure you that if I once felt you were safe in the hotel at Ajaccio, I should be very sorry to leave this cursed island myself, without shaking that plucky fellow della Rebbia's hand again."

"Well then, father, let us wait a while, and before we start let us make quite sure we can not be of any use to them."

"Kind soul!" said the colonel, as he kissed his daughter's forehead. "It is a pleasure to see you sacrifice yourself for the sake of softening other people's suffering. Let us stay on. We shall never have to repent having done right."

Miss Lydia tossed sleeplessly to and fro in her bed. Sometimes she took the vague night sounds for preparations for an attack on the house. Sometimes, less alarmed on her own account, she thought of poor wounded Orso, who was probably lying on the cold earth, with no help beyond what she might expect from a bandit's charity. She fancied him covered with blood, and writhing in hideous suffering; and the extraordinary thing was that whenever Orso's image rose up before her mind's eye, she always beheld him as she had seen him when he rode away, pressing the talisman she had bestowed upon him to his lips. Then she mused over his courage. She told herself he had exposed himself to the frightful danger he had just escaped on her account, just for the sake of seeing her a little sooner. A very little more, and she would have persuaded herself that Orso had earned his broken arm in her defence! She reproached herself with being the cause of his wound. But she admired him for it all the more, and if that celebrated right and left was not so splendid a feat in her sight as in Brandolaccio's or Colomba's, still she was convinced few heroes of romance could ever had behaved with such intrepidity and coolness, in so dangerous a pinch.

Her room was that usually occupied by Colomba. Above a kind of oaken *prie-dieu*, and beside a sprig of blessed palm, a little miniature of Orso, in his sub-lieutenant's uniform, hung on the wall. Miss Nevil took the portrait down, looked at it for a long time, and laid it at last on the table by her bed, instead of hanging it up again in its place. She did not fall asleep till daybreak, and when she woke the sun had traveled high above the horizon. In front of her bed she beheld Colomba, waiting, motionless, till she should open her eyes.

"Well, dear lady, are you not very uncomfortable in this poor house of ours?" said Colomba to her. "I fear you have hardly slept at all."

"Have you any news, dear friend?" cried Miss Nevil, sitting up in bed.

Her eye fell on Orso's picture, and she hastily tossed her handkerchief upon it.

"Yes, I have news," said Colomba, with a smile.

Then she took up the picture.

"Do you think it like him? He is better looking than that!"

"Really," stammered Miss Nevil, quite confused, "I took down that picture in a fit of absence! I have a horrid habit of touching everything and never putting anything back! How is your brother?"

"Fairly well. Giocanto came here before four o'clock this morning. He brought me a letter for you, Miss Lydia. Orso hasn't written anything to me! It is addressed to Colomba, indeed, but underneath that he has written 'For Miss N.' But sisters are never jealous! Giocanto says it hurt him dreadfully to write. Giocanto, who writes a splendid hand, offered to do it at his dictation. But he would not let him. He wrote it with a pencil, lying on his back. Brandolaccio held the paper for him. My brother kept trying to raise himself, and then the very slightest movement gave him the most dreadful agony in his arm. Giocanto says it was pitiful. Here is his letter."

Miss Nevil read the letter, which, as an extra precaution, no doubt, was written in English. Its contents were as follows:

"MADEMOISELLE: An unhappy fate has driven me on. I know not what my enemies will say, what slanders they will invent. I care little, so long as you, mademoiselle, give them no credence! Ever since I first saw you I have been nursing wild dreams. I needed this catastrophe to show me my own folly.

"I have come back to my senses now. I know the future that lies before me, and I shall face it with resignation. I dare not keep this ring you gave me, and which I believed to be a lucky talisman. I fear, Miss Nevil, you may regret your gift has been so ill-bestowed. Or rather, I fear it may remind me of the days of my own madness. Colomba will give it to you. Farewell, mademoiselle! You are about to leave Corsica, and I shall never

262

see you again. But tell my sister, at least, that I still possess your esteem — and I tell you, confidently, that I am still worthy of it.

"O.D.R."

Miss Lydia had turned away while she read the letter, and Colomba, who was watching her closely, gave her the Egyptian ring, with an inquiring glance as to what it all meant. But Miss Lydia dared not raise her head, and looked dejectedly at the ring, alternately putting it on her finger and pulling it off again.

"Dear Miss Nevil," said Colomba, "may I not know what my brother says to you? Does he say anything about his health?"

"Indeed," said Miss Lydia, colouring, "he doesn't mention it. His letter is in English. He desires me to tell my father — He hopes the prefect will be able to arrange — — "

With a mischievous smile, Colomba sat down on the bed, took hold of both Miss Nevil's hands, and, looking at her with her piercing eyes —

"Will you be kind?" she said. "Won't you answer my brother's letter? You would do him so much good! For a moment I thought of waking you when his letter came, and then I didn't dare!"

"You did very wrong," replied Miss Nevil. "If a word from me could — "

"I can't send him any letter now. The prefect has arrived, and Pietranera is full of his policemen. Later on, we'll see what we can do. Oh, Miss Nevil, if you only knew my brother, you would love him as dearly as I do. He's so good! He's so brave! Just think of what he has done! One man against two, and wounded as well!"

The prefect had returned. Warned by an express messenger sent by the deputy-mayor, he had brought over the public prosecutor, the registrar, and all their myrmidons, to investigate the fresh and terrible catastrophe which had just complicated, or it may be ended, the warfare between the chief families of Pietranera. Shortly after his arrival, he saw the colonel and his daughter, and did not conceal his fear that the business might take on an ugly aspect.

"You know," he said, "that the fight took place without witnesses, and the reputation of these two unhappy men stood so high, both for bravery and cunning, that nobody will believe Signor della Rebbia can have killed them without the help of the bandits with whom he is now supposed to have taken refuge."

"It's not possible," said the colonel. "Orso della Rebbia is a most honourable fellow. I'll stake my life on that."

"I believe you," said the prefect. "But the public prosecutor (those gentry always are suspicious) does not strike me as being particularly well disposed toward him. He holds one bit of evidence which goes rather against our friend — a threatening letter to Orlanduccio, in which he suggests a meeting, and is inclined to think that meeting was a trap."

"That fellow Orlanduccio refused to fight it out like a gentleman."

"That is not the custom here. In this country, people lie in ambush, and kill each other from behind. There is one deposition in his favour — that of a child, who declares she heard four reports, two of which were louder than the others, and produced by a heavy weapon, such as Signor della Rebbia's gun. Unluckily, the child is the niece of one of the bandits suspected of being his accomplices, and has probably been taught her lesson."

"Sir," broke in Miss Lydia, reddening to the roots of her hair, "we were on the road when those shots were fired, and we heard the same thing."

"Really? That's most important! And you, colonel, no doubt you remarked the very same thing?"

"Yes," responded Miss Lydia quickly. "It was my father, who is so accustomed to firearms, who said to me, 'There's Signor della Rebbia shooting with my gun!'"

"And you are sure those shots you recognized were the last?"

"The two last, weren't they, papa?"

Memory was not the colonel's strong point, but as a standing rule, he knew better than to contradict his daughter.

"I must mention this to the public prosecutor at once, colonel. And besides, we expect a surgeon this evening, who will

264

make an examination of the two bodies, and find out whether the wounds were caused by that particular weapon."

"I gave it to Orso," said the colonel, "and I wish I knew it was at the bottom of the sea. At least — — Plucky boy! I'm heartily glad he had it with him, for I don't quite know how he would have got off if it hadn't been for my Manton."

# CHAPTER XIX

It was rather late when the surgeon put in an appearance. On his road up he had met with an adventure of his own. He had been stopped by Giocanto Castriconi, who, with the most scrupulous politeness, called on him to come and attend a wounded man. He had been conducted to Orso's retreat, and had applied the first dressings to his wound. The bandit had then accompanied the doctor some distance on his way, and had greatly edified him by his talk concerning the most celebrated professors at Pisa, whom he described as his intimate friends.

"Doctor," said the theologian, as they parted, "you have inspired me with such a feeling of respect that I think it hardly necessary to remind you that a physician should be as discreet as a confessor." And as he said the words he clicked the trigger of his gun. "You have quite forgotten the spot at which we have had the honour of meeting. Fare you well! I'm delighted to have made your acquaintance."

Colomba besought the colonel to be present at the post-mortem examination.

"You know my brother's gun better than anybody," she said, "and your presence will be most valuable. Besides there are so many wicked people here that we should run a great risk if there were nobody present to protect our interests."

When she was left alone with Miss Lydia, she complained that her head ached terribly, and proposed that they should take a walk just outside the village.

"The fresh air will do me good," she said. "It is so long since I've been out of doors."

As they walked along she talked about her brother, and Miss Lydia, who found the subject tolerably interesting, did not notice that they had traveled a long way from Pietranera. The sun was setting when she became aware of this fact, and she begged Colomba to return. Colomba said she knew a cross-cut which would greatly shorten the walk back, and turning out of the path, she took another, which seemed much less frequented. Soon she

266

began to climb a hill, so steep that to keep her balance she was continually obliged to catch hold of branches with one hand, while she pulled her companion up after her with the other. After about twenty minutes of this trying ascent, they found themselves on a small plateau, clothed with arbutus and myrtle, growing round great granite boulders that jutted above the soil in every direction. Miss Lydia was very tired, there was no sign of the village, and it was almost quite dark.

"Do you know, Colomba, my dear," she said, "I'm afraid we've lost our way!"

"No fear!" answered Colomba. "Let us get on. You follow me."

"But I assure you we're going wrong. The village can't be over there. I'm certain we're turning our backs on it. Why, look at those lights, far away. Pietranera must be in that direction."

"My dear soul," said Colomba, and she looked very much agitated, "you're perfectly right. But in the *maquis* — less than a hundred yards from here — "

"Well?"

"My brother is lying. If you choose, I might see him, and give him one kiss."

Miss Nevil made a gesture of astonishment.

"I got out of Pietranera without being noticed," continued Colomba, "because I was with you, otherwise I should have been followed. To be so close to him, and not to see him! Why shouldn't you come with me to see my poor brother? You would make him so happy!"

"But, Colomba — That wouldn't be at all proper on my part — — "

"I see. With you women who live in towns, your great anxiety is to be proper. We village women only think of what is kind."

"But it's so late! And then what will your brother think of me?"

"He'll think his friends have not forsaken him, and that will give him courage to bear his sufferings."

267

"And my father? He'll be so anxious!"

"He knows you are with me. Come! Make up your mind. You were looking at his picture this morning," she added, with a sly smile.

"No! Really and truly, I don't dare, Colomba! Think of the bandits who are there."

"Well, what matter? The bandits don't know you. And you were longing to see some."

"Oh, dear!"

"Come, signorina, settle something. I can't leave you alone here. I don't know what might happen to you. Let us go on to see Orso, or else let us go back to the village together. I shall see my brother again. God knows when — never, perhaps!"

"What's that you are saying, Colomba? Well, well, let us go! But only for a minute, and then we'll get home at once."

Colomba squeezed her hand, and without making any reply walked on so quickly that Miss Lydia could hardly keep up with her. She soon halted, luckily, and said to her companion:

"We won't go any farther without warning them. We might have a bullet flying at our heads."

She began to whistle through her fingers. Soon they heard a dog bark, and the bandits' advanced sentry shortly came in sight. This was our old acquaintance Brusco, who recognized Colomba at once and undertook to be her guide. After many windings through the narrow paths in the *maquis* they were met by two men, armed to the teeth.

"Is that you, Brandolaccio?" inquired Colomba. "Where is my brother?"

"Just over there," replied the bandit. "But go quietly. He's asleep, and for the first time since his accident. Zounds, it's clear that where the devil gets through, a woman will get through too!"

The two girls moved forward cautiously, and beside a fire, the blaze of which was carefully concealed by a little wall of stones built round it, they beheld Orso, lying on a pile of heather, and covered with a *pilone*. He was very pale, and they could hear his laboured breathing. Colomba sat down near him, and gazed at him silently, with her hands clasped, as though she were praying in her heart. Miss Lydia hid her face in her handkerchief, and nestled close against her friend, but every now and then she lifted her head to take a look at the wounded man over Colomba's shoulder. Thus a quarter of an hour passed by without a word being said by anybody. At a sign from the theologian, Brandolaccio had plunged with him into the *maquis*, to the great relief of Miss Lydia, who for the first time fancied the local colour of the bandits' wild beards and warlike equipment was a trifle too strong.

At last Orso stirred. Instantly, Colomba bent over him, and kissed him again and again, pouring out questions anent his wound, his suffering, and his needs. After having answered that he was doing as well as possible, Orso inquired, in his turn, whether Miss Nevil was still at Pietranera, and whether she had written to him. Colomba, bending over her brother, completely hid her companion from his sight, and indeed the darkness would have made any recognition difficult. She was holding one of Miss Nevil's hands. With the other she slightly raised her wounded brother's head.

"No, brother," she replied. "She did not give me any letter for you. But are you still thinking about Miss Nevil? You must love her very much!"

"Love her, Colomba! — But — but now she may despise me!"

At this point Miss Nevil made a struggle to withdraw her fingers. But it was no easy matter to get Colomba to slacken her grasp. Small and well-shaped though her hand was, it possessed a strength of which we have already noticed certain proofs.

"Despise you!" cried Colomba. "After what you've done? No, indeed! She praises you! Oh, Orso, I could tell you so many things about her!"

Lydia's hand was still struggling for its freedom, but Colomba kept drawing it closer to Orso.

"But after all," said the wounded man, "why didn't she answer me? If she had sent me a single line, I should have been happy."

By dint of pulling at Miss Nevil's hand, Colomba contrived at last to put it into her brother's. Then, moving suddenly aside, she burst out laughing.

"Orso," she cried, "mind you don't speak evil of Miss Lydia — she understands Corsican quite well."

Miss Lydia took back her hand at once and stammered some unintelligible words. Orso thought he must be dreaming.

"You here, Miss Nevil? Good heavens! how did you dare? Oh, how happy you have made me!"

And raising himself painfully, he strove to get closer to her.

"I came with your sister," said Miss Lydia, "so that nobody might suspect where she was going. And then I — I wanted to make sure for myself. Alas! how uncomfortable you are here!"

Colomba had seated herself behind Orso. She raised him carefully so that his head might rest on her lap. She put her arms round his neck and signed to Miss Lydia to come near him.

"Closer! closer!" she said. "A sick man mustn't talk too loud." And when Miss Lydia hesitated, she caught her hand and forced her to sit down so close to Orso that her dress touched him, and her hand, still in Colomba's grasp, lay on the wounded man's shoulder.

"Now he's very comfortable!" said Colomba cheerily. "Isn't it good to lie out in the *maquis* on such a lovely night? Eh, Orso?"

"How you must be suffering!" exclaimed Miss Lydia.

"My suffering is all gone now," said Orso, "and I should like to die here!" And his right hand crept up toward Miss Lydia's, which Colomba still held captive.

"You really must be taken to some place where you can be properly cared for, Signor della Rebbia," said Miss Nevil. "I shall never be able to sleep in my bed, now that I have seen you lying here, so uncomfortable, in the open air."

"If I had not been afraid of meeting you, Miss Nevil, I should have tried to get back to Pietranera, and I should have given myself up to the authorities."

"And why were you afraid of meeting her, Orso?" inquired Colomba.

"I had disobeyed you, Miss Nevil, and I should not have dared to look at you just then."

"Do you know you make my brother do everything you choose, Miss Lydia?" said Colomba, laughing. "I won't let you see him any more."

"I hope this unlucky business will soon be cleared up, and that you will have nothing more to fear," said Miss Nevil. "I shall be so happy, when we go away, to know justice has been done you, and that both your loyalty and your bravery have been acknowledged."

"Going away, Miss Nevil! Don't say that word yet!"

"What are we to do? My father can not spend his whole life shooting. He wants to go."

Orso's hand, which had been touching Miss Lydia's, dropped away, and there was silence for a moment.

"Nonsense!" said Colomba. "We won't let you go yet. We have plenty of things to show you still at Pietranera. Besides, you have promised to paint my picture, and you haven't even begun it so far. And then I've promised to compose you a *serenata*, with seventy-five verses. And then — but what can Brusco be growling about? And here's Brandolaccio running after him. I must go and see what's amiss."

She rose at once, and laying Orso's head, without further ceremony, on Miss Lydia's lap, she ran after the bandits.

Miss Nevil, somewhat startled at finding herself thus left in sole charge of a handsome young Corsican gentleman in the middle of a *maquis*, was rather puzzled what to do next.

For she was afraid that any sudden movement on her part might hurt the wounded man. But Orso himself resigned the exquisite pillow on which his sister had just laid his head, and raising himself on his right arm, he said:

"So you will soon be gone, Miss Lydia? I never expected your stay in this unhappy country would have been a long one. And yet since you have come to me here, the thought that I must bid you farewell has grown a hundred times more bitter to me. I am only a poor lieutenant. I had no future — and now I am an outlaw. What a moment in which to tell you that I love you, Miss Lydia! But no doubt this is my only chance of saying it. And I think I feel less wretched now I have unburdened my heart to you."

Miss Lydia turned away her head, as if the darkness were not dark enough to hide her blushes.

"Signor della Rebbia," she said, and her voice shook, "should I have come here at all if — — " and as she spoke she laid the Egyptian talisman in Orso's hand. Then, with a mighty effort to recover her usual bantering tone — "It's very wrong of you, Signor Orso, to say such things! You know very well that here, in the middle of the *maquis*, and with your bandits all about me, I should never dare to be angry with you."

Orso made an attempt to kiss the hand that held out the talisman. Miss Lydia drew it quickly back; he lost his balance, and fell on his wounded arm. He could not stifle a moan of pain.

"Oh, dear, you've hurt yourself, and it was my fault!" she cried, as she raised him up. "Forgive me!" They talked for some time longer, very low, and very close together.

Colomba, running hastily up, found them in the very same position in which she had left them.

"The soldiers!" she cried. "Orso! try to get up and walk! I'll help you!"

"Leave me!" said Orso. "Tell the bandits to escape. What do I care if I am taken? But take away Miss Lydia. For God's sake, don't let anybody see her here!"

"I won't leave you," said Brandolaccio, who had come up on Colomba's heels.

"The sergeant in charge is the lawyer's godson. He'll shoot you instead of arresting you, and then he'll say he didn't do it on purpose."

Orso tried to rise; he even took a few steps. But he soon halted. "I can't walk," he said. "Fly, all of you! Good-bye, Miss Nevil! Give me your hand! Farewell!"

"We won't leave you!" cried the two girls.

"If you can't walk," said Brandolaccio, "I must carry you. Come, sir, a little courage! We shall have time to slip away by the ravine. The Signor Padre will keep them busy."

"No, leave me!" said Orso, lying down on the ground. "Colomba, take Miss Nevil away! — for God's sake!"

"You're strong, Signorina Colomba," said Brandolaccio. "Catch hold of his shoulders; I'll take his feet. That's it! Now, then march!"

In spite of his protests, they began to carry him rapidly along. Miss Lydia was following them, in a terrible fright, when a gun was fired, and five or six other reports instantly responded. Miss Lydia screamed and Brandolaccio swore an oath, but he doubled his pace, and Colomba, imitating him, tore through the thicket without paying the slightest heed to the branches that slashed her face and tore her dress.

"Bend down, bend down, dear!" she called out to her companion. "You may be hit by some stray bullet!"

They had walked, or rather run, some five hundred paces in this fashion when Brandolaccio vowed he could go no further, and dropped on the ground, regardless of all Colomba's exhortations and reproaches.

"Where is Miss Nevil?" was Orso's one inquiry.

Terrified by the firing, checked at every step by the thick growth of the *maquis*, Miss Nevil had soon lost sight of the fugitives, and been left all alone in a state of the most cruel alarm.

"She has been left behind," said Brandolaccio, "but she'll not be lost — women always turn up again. Do listen to the row the Padre is making with your gun, Ors' Anton'! Unluckily, it's as black as pitch, and nobody takes much harm from being shot at in the dark."

"Hush!" cried Colomba. "I hear a horse. We're saved!"

Startled by the firing, a horse which had been wandering through the *maquis*, was really coming close up to them.

"Saved, indeed!" repeated Brandolaccio. It did not take the bandit more than an instant to rush up to the creature, catch hold of his mane, and with Colomba's assistance, bridle him with a bit of knotted rope.

"Now we must warn the Padre," he said. He whistled twice; another distant whistle answered the signal, and the loud voice of the Manton gun was hushed. Then Brandolaccio sprang on the horse's back. Colomba lifted her brother up in front of the bandit, who held him close with one hand and managed his bridle with the other.

In spite of the double load, the animal, urged by a brace of hearty kicks, started off nimbly, and galloped headlong down a steep declivity on which anything but a Corsican steed would have broken its neck a dozen times.

Then Colomba retraced her steps, calling Miss Nevil at the top of her voice; but no answering cry was heard.

After walking hither and thither for some time, trying to recover the path, she stumbled on two riflemen, who shouted, "Who goes there?"

"Well, gentlemen," cried Colomba jeeringly, "here's a pretty racket! How many of you are killed?"

"You were with the bandits!" said one of the soldiers. "You must come with us."

"With pleasure!" she replied. "But there's a friend of mine somewhere close by, and we must find her first."

"You friend is caught already, and both of you will sleep in jail to-night!"

"In jail, you say? Well, that remains to be seen. But take me to her, meanwhile."

The soldiers led her to the bandits' camp, where they had collected the trophies of their raid — to wit, the cloak which had covered Orso, an old cooking-pot, and a pitcher of cold water. On the same spot she found Miss Nevil, who had fallen among the soldiers, and, being half dead with terror, did nothing but sob in answer to their questions as to the number of the bandits, and the direction in which they had gone.

Colomba threw herself into her arms and whispered in her ear, "They are safe!" Then, turning to the sergeant, she said: "Sir, you can see this young lady knows none of the things you are trying to find out from her. Give us leave to go back to the village, where we are anxiously expected."

"You'll be taken there, and faster than you like, my beauty," rejoined the sergeant. "And you'll have to explain what you were after at this time of night with the ruffians who have just got away. I don't know what witchcraft those villains practice, but they certainly do bewitch the women — for wherever there are bandits about, you are dead certain to find pretty girls."

"You're very flattering, sergeant!" said Colomba, "but you'll do well to be careful what you say. This young lady is related to the prefect, and you'd better be careful of your language before her."

"A relation of the prefect's," whispered one of the soldiers to his chief. "Why, she does wear a hat!"

"Hats have nothing to do with it," said the sergeant. "They were both of them with the Padre — the greatest woman-wheedler in the whole country, so it's my business to march them off. And, indeed, there's nothing more for us to do here. But for that d — — d Corporal Taupin — the drunken Frenchman showed himself before I'd surrounded the *maquis* — we should have had them all like fish in a net."

"Are there only seven of you here?" inquired Colomba. "It strikes me, gentlemen, that if the three Poli brothers — Gambini, Sarocchi, and Teodoro — should happen to be at the Cross of Santa Christina, with Brandolaccio and the Padre, they might give you a good deal of corn to grind. If you mean to have a talk with the Commandante della Campagna, I'd just as soon not be there. In the dark, bullets don't show any respect for persons."

The idea of coming face to face with the dreaded bandits mentioned by Colomba made an evident impression on the soldiers. The sergeant, still cursing Corporal Taupin — "that dog of a Frenchman" — gave the order to retire, and his little party moved toward Pietranera, carrying the *pilone* and the cooking-pot; as for the pitcher, its fate was settled with a kick.

One of the men would have laid hold of Miss Lydia's arm, but Colomba instantly pushed him away.

"Let none of you dare to lay a finger on her!" she said. "Do you fancy we want to run away? Come, Lydia, my dear, lean on me, and don't cry like a baby. We've had an adventure, but it will end all right. In half an hour we shall be at our supper, and for my part I'm dying to get to it."

"What will they think of me!" Miss Nevil whispered.

"They'll think you lost your way in the *maquis*, that's all."

"What will the prefect say? Above all, what will my father say?"

"The prefect? You can tell him to mind his own business! Your father? I should have thought, from the way you and Orso were talking, that you had something to say to your father."

Miss Nevil squeezed her arm, and answered nothing.

"Doesn't my brother deserve to be loved?" whispered Colomba in her ear. "Don't you love him a little?"

"Oh, Colomba!" answered Miss Nevil, smiling in spite of her blushes, "you've betrayed me! And I trusted you so!"

Colomba slipped her arm round her, and kissed her forehead.

"Little sister," she whispered very low, "will you forgive me?"

"Why, I suppose I must, my masterful sister," answered Lydia, as she kissed her back.

The prefect and the public prosecutor were staying with the deputy-mayor, and the colonel, who was very uneasy about his daughter, was paying them his twentieth call, to ask if they had heard of her, when a rifleman, whom the sergeant had sent on in advance, arrived with the full story of the great fight with the brigands — a fight in which nobody had been either killed or wounded, but which had resulted in the capture of a cooking-pot, a *pilone*, and two girls, whom the man described as the mistresses, or the spies, of the two bandits.

Thus heralded, the two prisoners appeared, surrounded by their armed escort.

My readers will imagine Colomba's radiant face, her companion's confusion, the prefect's surprise, the colonel's astonishment and joy. The public prosecutor permitted himself the mischievous entertainment of obliging poor Lydia to undergo a kind of cross-examination, which did not conclude until he had quite put her out of countenance.

"It seems to me," said the prefect, "that we may release everybody. These young ladies went out for a walk — nothing is more natural in fine weather. They happened to meet a charming young man, who has been lately wounded — nothing could be more natural, again." Then, taking Colomba aside —

"Signorina," he said, "you can send word to your brother that this business promises to turn out better than I had expected. The post-mortem examination and the colonel's deposition both prove that he only defended himself, and that he was alone when the fight took place. Everything will be settled — only he must leave the *maquis* and give himself up to the authorities."

It was almost eleven o'clock when the colonel, his daughter, and Colomba sat down at last to their supper, which had grown cold. Colomba ate heartily, and made great fun of the prefect, the public prosecutor, and the soldiers. The colonel ate too, but never said a word, and gazed steadily at his daughter, who would not lift her eyes from her plate. At last, gently but seriously, he said in English:

"Lydia, I suppose you are engaged to della Rebbia?"

"Yes, father, to-day," she answered, steadily, though she blushed. Then she raised her eyes, and reading no sign of anger in her father's face, she threw herself into his arms and kissed him, as all well-brought-up young ladies do on such occasions.

"With all my heart!" said the colonel. "He's a fine fellow. But, by G — d, we won't live in this d — -d country of his, or I'll refuse my consent."

"I don't know English," said Colomba, who was watching them with an air of the greatest curiosity, "but I'll wager I've guessed what you are saying!"

"We are saying," quoth the colonel, "that we are going to take you for a trip to Ireland."

"Yes, with pleasure; and I'll be the Surella Colomba. Is it settled, colonel? Shall we shake hands on it?"

"In such a case," remarked the colonel, "people exchanges kisses!"

# CHAPTER XX

One afternoon, a few months after the double shot which, as the newspapers said, "plunged the village of Pietranera into a state of consternation," a young man with his left arm in a sling, rode out of Bastia, toward the village of Cardo, celebrated for its spring, which in summer supplies the more fastidious inhabitants of the town with delicious water. He was accompanied by a young lady, tall and remarkably handsome, mounted on a small black horse, the strength and shape of which would have attracted the admiration of a connoisseur, although, by some strange accident, one of its ears had been lacerated. On reaching the village, the girl sprang nimbly to the ground, and, having helped her comrade to dismount, she unfastened the somewhat heavy wallets strapped to his saddle-bow. The horses were left in charge of a peasant. The girl, laden with the wallets, which she had concealed under her *mezzaro*, and the young man, carrying a double-barreled gun, took their way toward the mountain, along a very steep path that did not appear to lead to any dwelling. When they had climbed to one of the lower ridges of the Monte Querico, they halted, and sat down on the grass. They were evidently expecting somebody, for they kept perpetually looking toward the mountain, and the young lady often consulted a pretty gold watch — as much, it may be, for the pleasure of admiring what appeared a somewhat newly acquired trinket, as in order to know whether the hour appointed for some meeting or other had come. They had not long to wait. A dog ran out of the *maquis*, and when the girl called out "Brusco!" it approached at once, and fawned upon them. Presently two bearded men appeared, with guns under their arms, cartridge-belts round their waists, and pistols hanging at their sides. Their torn and patched garments contrasted oddly with their weapons, which were brilliantly polished, and came from a famous Continental factory. In spite of the apparent inequality of their positions, the four actors in this scene greeted one another in terms of old and familiar friendship.

"Well, Ors' Anton'," said the elder bandit to the young man, "so your business is settled — the indictment against you has fallen through? I congratulate you. I'm sorry the lawyer has left the island. I'd like to see his rage. And how's your arm?"

"They tell me I shall get rid of my sling in a fortnight," said the young man. "Brando, my good friend, I'm going to Italy to-morrow — I wanted to say good-bye to you and to the cure. That's why I asked you to come here."

"You're in a fine hurry," said Brandolaccio. "Only acquitted yesterday, and you're off to-morrow."

"Business must be attended to," said the young lady merrily. "Gentlemen, I've brought some supper. Fall to, if you please, and don't you forget my friend Brusco."

"You spoil Brusco, Mademoiselle Colomba. But he's a grateful dog. You shall see. Here, Brusco," and he held out his gun horizontally, "jump for the Barricini!"

The dog stood motionless, licking his chops, and staring at his master.

"Jump for the della Rebbia!" And he leaped two feet higher than he need have done.

"Look here, my friends," said Orso, "you're plying a bad trade; and even if you don't end your career on that square below us, the best you can look for is to die in the *maquis* by some gendarme's bullet."

"Well, well," said Castriconi, "that's no more than death, anyhow; and it's better than being killed in your bed by a fever, with your heirs sniveling more or less honestly all round you. To men who are accustomed to the open air like us, there's nothing so good as to die 'in your shoes,' as the village folk say."

"I should like to see you get out of this country," said Orso, "and lead a quieter life. For instance, why shouldn't you settle in Sardinia, as several of your comrades have done? I could make the matter easy for you."

"In Sardinia!" cried Brandolaccio. "*Istos Sardos!* Devil take them and their lingo! We couldn't live in such bad company."

"Sardinia's a country without resources," added the theologian. "For my part, I despise the Sardinians. They keep mounted men to hunt their bandits. That's a stigma on both the bandits and the country.[41] Out upon Sardinia, say I! The thing that astounds me, Signor della Rebbia, is that you, who are a man of taste and understanding, should not have taken to our life in the *maquis*, after having once tried it, as you did."

"Well," said Orso, with a smile, "when I was lucky enough to be your guest, I wasn't in very good case for enjoying the charms of your position, and my ribs still ache when I think of the ride I took one lovely night, thrown like a bundle across an unsaddled horse that my good friend Brandolaccio guided."

"And the delight of escaping from your pursuers," rejoined Castriconi; "is that nothing to you? How can you fail to realize the charm of absolute freedom in such a beautiful climate as ours? With this to insure respect," and he held up his gun, "we are kings of everything within its range. We can give orders, we can redress wrongs. That's a highly moral entertainment, monsieur, and a very pleasant one, which we don't deny ourselves. What can be more beautiful than a knight-errant's life, when he has good weapons, and more common sense than Don Quixote had? Listen! The other day I was told that little Lilla Luigi's uncle — old miser that he is — wouldn't give her a dowry. So I wrote to him. I didn't use threats — that's not my way. Well, well, in one moment the man was convinced. He married his niece, and I made two people happy. Believe me, Orso, there's no life like the bandit's life! Pshaw! You'd have joined us, perhaps, if it hadn't been for a certain young Englishwoman whom I have scarcely seen myself, but about whose beauty every one in Bastia is talking."

"My future sister-in-law doesn't like the *maquis*," laughed Colomba. "She got too great a fright in one of them."

---

[41] I owe this criticism of Sardinia to an ex-bandit of my acquaintance, and he alone must bear the responsibility of it. He means that bandits who let themselves be caught by horse soldiers are idiots, and that soldiers who try to catch bandits on horseback have very little chance of getting at them.

"Well," said Orso, "you are resolved to stay here? So be it! But tell me whether there is anything I can do for you?"

"Nothing," said Brandolaccio. "You've heaped kindnesses upon us. Here's little Chilina with her dowry ready, so that there'll be no necessity for my friend the cure to write one of his persuasive letters to insure her marrying well. We know the man on your farm will give us bread and powder whenever we need them. So fare you well! I hope we shall see you back in Corsica one of these days."

"In case of pressing need," said Orso, "a few gold coins are very useful. Now we are such old friends, you won't refuse this little *cartouche*. It will help you to provide cartridges of another kind."

"No money between you and me, sir," said Brandolaccio resolutely.

"In the world money is everything," remarked Castriconi, "but in the *maquis*, all a man need care for is a brave heart, and a gun that carries true."

"I don't want to leave you without giving you something to remember me by," persisted Orso. "Come, Brandolaccio, what can I leave with you?"

The bandit scratched his head and cast a sidelong glance at Orso's gun.

"By my faith, if I dared — but no! you're too fond of it."

"What would you like?"

"Nothing! 'Tisn't anything at all. It's knowing how to use it as well. I keep thinking of that devil of a double-shot of yours — and with only one hand, too! Oh! that never could happen twice over!"

"Is it the gun you fancy? I bought it for you. But see you don't use it more than you are obliged."

"Oh, I won't promise to make as good use of it as you. But make your mind easy. When any other man has it, you may be certain it's all over with Brando Savelli."

"And you, Castriconi — what am I to give you?"

282

"Since you really insist on giving me some tangible keepsake, I'll simply ask you to send me the smallest Horace you can get. It will amuse me, and prevent me from forgetting all my Latin. There's a little woman who sells cigars on the jetty at Bastia. If you give it to her, she'll see I get it."

"You shall have an Elzevir, my erudite friend. There just happens to be one among some books I was going to take away with me. Well, good friends, we must part! Give me your hands. If you should ever think of Sardinia write to me. Signor N., the notary, will give you my address on the mainland."

"To-morrow, lieutenant," said Brando, "when you get out in the harbour, look up to this spot on the mountain-side. We shall be here, and we'll wave our handkerchiefs to you."

And so they parted. Orso and his sister took their way back to Cardo, and the bandits departed up the mountain.

# CHAPTER XXI

One lovely April morning, Sir Thomas Nevil, his daughter, a newly made bride — Orso, and Colomba, drove out of Pisa to see a lately discovered Etruscan vault to which all strangers who came to that part of the country paid a visit.

Orso and his wife went down into the ancient building, pulled out their pencils, and began to sketch the mural paintings. But the colonel and Colomba, who neither of them cared much for archaeology, left them to themselves, and walked about in the neighbourhood.

"My dear Colomba," said the colonel, "we shall never get back to Pisa in time for lunch. Aren't you hungry? There are Orso and his wife buried in their antiquities; when once they begin sketching together, it lasts forever!"

"Yes," remarked Colomba. "And yet they never bring the smallest sketch home with them."

"I think," proceeded the colonel, "our best plan would be to make our way to that little farm-house yonder. We should find bread there, and perhaps some *aleatico*. Who knows, we might even find strawberries and cream! And then we should be able to wait patiently for our artists."

"You are quite right, colonel. You and I are the reasonable members of this family. We should be very foolish if we let ourselves by martyrized by that pair of lovers, who live on poetry! Give me your arm! Don't you think I'm improving? I lean on people's arms, wear fashionable hats and gowns and trinkets — I'm learning I don't know how many fine things — I'm not at all a young savage any more. Just observe the grace with which I wear this shawl. That fair-haired spark — that officer belonging to your regiment who came to the wedding — oh, dear! I can't recollect his name! — a tall, curly-headed man, whom I could knock over with one hand — — "

"Chatsworth?" suggested the colonel.

"That's it! — but I never shall be able to say it! — Well, you know he's over head and ears in love with me!"

"O Colomba, you're growing a terrible flirt! We shall have another wedding before long."

"I! Marry! And then who will there be to bring up my nephew — when Orso provides me with a nephew? And who'll teach him to talk Corsican? Yes, he shall talk Corsican, and I'll make him a peaked cap, just to vex you."

"Well, well, wait till you have your nephew, and then you shall teach him to use a dagger, if you choose."

"Farewell to daggers!" said Colomba merrily. "I have a fan now, to rap your fingers with when you speak ill of my country."

Chatting thus, they reached the farm-house, where they found wine, strawberries, and cream. Colomba helped the farmer's wife to gather the strawberries, while the colonel drank his *aleatico*. At the turning of a path she caught sight of an old man, sitting in the sun, on a straw chair. He seemed ill, his cheeks were fallen in, his eyes were hollow, he was frightfully thin; as he sat there, motionless, pallid, staring fixedly in front of him, he looked more like a corpse than like a living creature. Colomba watched him for some minutes, and with a curiosity so great that it attracted the woman's attention.

"That poor old fellow is a countryman of yours," she said. "For I know you are from Corsica by the way you talk, signorina! He has had great trouble in his own country. His children met with some terrible death. They say — you'll excuse me, signorina — that when they quarrel, your compatriots don't show each other very much mercy. Then the poor old gentleman, being left all alone, came over to Pisa, to a distant relation of his, who owns this farm. Between his misfortunes and his sorrow, the good man is a little cracked. . . . The lady found him troublesome — for she sees a great deal of company. So she sent him out here. He's very gentle — no worry at all. He doesn't speak three words the whole day long. In fact, his brain's quite gone. The doctor comes to see him every week. He says he won't live long."

"There's no hope for him, then!" said Colomba. "In such a case, death will be a mercy."

"You might say a word to him in Corsican, signorina. Perhaps it would cheer him up to hear the speech of his own country."

"I'll see!" said Colomba, and her smile was mysterious.

She drew nearer to the old man, till her shadow fell across his chair. Then the poor idiot lifted his head and stared at Colomba, while she looked at him, smiling still. After a moment, the old man passed his hand across his forehead, and closed his eyes, as though he would have shut out the sight of Colomba. He opened them again, desperately wide this time. His lips began to work, he tried to stretch out his hands, but, fascinated by Colomba's glance, he sat, nailed, as it were, to his chair, unable to move or utter a word. At last great tears dropped from his eyes, and a few sobs escaped from his heaving chest.

"'Tis the first time I've seen him like this," said the good woman. "This signorina belongs to your own country; she has come to see you," said she to the old man.

"Mercy!" he cried in a hoarse voice. "Mercy! Are you not content? The leaf I burned. How did you read it? But why did you take them both? Orlanduccio! You can't have read anything against him! You should have left me one, only one! Orlanduccio — you didn't read *his* name!"

"I had to have them both!" answered Colomba, speaking low and in the Corsican dialect. "The branches are topped off! If the stem had not been rotten, I would have torn it up! Come! make no moan. You will not suffer long! *I* suffered for two years!"

The old man cried out, and then his head dropped on his breast. Colomba turned her back on him, and went slowly into the house, humming some meaningless lines out of a *ballata*:

"I must have the hand that fired, the eye that aimed, the heart that planned."

While the farmer's wife ran to attend on the old man, Colomba, with blazing eyes and brilliant cheeks, sat down to luncheon opposite the colonel.

"What's the matter with you?" he said. "You look just as you did that day at Pietranera, when they fired at us while we were at dinner."

"Old Corsican memories had come back to me. But all that's done with. I shall be godmother, sha'n't I? Oh! what fine names I'll give him! Ghilfuccio — Tomaso — Orso — Leone!"

The farmer's wife came back into the room.

"Well?" inquired Colomba, with the most perfect composure. "Is he dead, or had he only fainted?"

"It was nothing, signorina. But it's curious what an effect the sight of you had on him."

"And the doctor says he won't last long?"

"Not two months, very likely."

"He'll be no great loss!" remarked Colomba.

"What the devil are you talking about?" inquired the colonel.

"About an idiot from my own country, who is boarded out here. I'll send from time to time to find out how he is. Why, Colonel Nevil, aren't you going to leave any strawberries for Lydia and my brother?"

When Colomba left the farm-house and got into the carriage, the farmer's wife looked after her for a while. Then, turning to her daughter:

"Dost see that pretty young lady yonder?" she said. "Well, I'm certain she has the evil eye!"

CROISILLES
BY ALFRED DE MUSSET

I

At the beginning of the reign of Louis XV., a young man named Croisilles, son of a goldsmith, was returning from Paris to Havre, his native town. He had been entrusted by his father with the transaction of some business, and his trip to the great city having turned out satisfactorily, the joy of bringing good news caused him to walk the sixty leagues more gaily and briskly than was his wont; for, though he had a rather large sum of money in his pocket, he traveled on foot for pleasure. He was a good-tempered fellow, and not without wit, but so very thoughtless and flighty that people looked upon him as being rather weak-minded. His doublet buttoned awry, his periwig flying to the wind, his hat under his arm, he followed the banks of the Seine, at times finding enjoyment in his own thoughts and again indulging in snatches of song; up at daybreak, supping at wayside inns, and always charmed with this stroll of his through one of the most beautiful regions of France. Plundering the apple-trees of Normandy on his way, he puzzled his brain to find rhymes (for all these rattlepates are more or less poets), and tried hard to turn out a madrigal for a certain fair damsel of his native place. She was no less than a daughter of a fermier-général, Mademoiselle Godeau, the pearl of Havre, a rich heiress, and much courted. Croisilles was not received at M. Godeau's otherwise than in a casual sort of way, that is to say, he had sometimes himself taken there articles of jewelry purchased at his father's. M. Godeau, whose somewhat vulgar surname ill-fitted his immense fortune, avenged himself by his arrogance for the stigma of his birth, and showed himself on all occasions enormously and pitilessly rich. He certainly was not the man to allow the son of a goldsmith to enter his drawing-room; but, as Mademoiselle Godeau had the most beautiful eyes in the world, and Croisilles was not ill-favored, and as nothing can prevent a fine fellow from falling in love with a pretty girl, Croisilles adored Mademoiselle Godeau, who did not seem vexed thereat. Thus was he thinking of her as he turned his steps toward Havre; and, as he had never reflected seriously upon anything, instead of thinking of the invincible obstacles which separated him from his lady-love, he busied himself only with finding a rhyme for the Christian name she bore. Mademoiselle Godeau was called Julie, and the rhyme was found easily enough. So Croisilles, having reached Honfleur, embarked with a satisfied heart, his money and his madrigal in his pocket, and as soon as he jumped ashore ran to the paternal house.

He found the shop closed, and knocked again and again, not without astonishment and apprehension, for it was not a holiday; but nobody came. He called his father, but in vain. He went to a neighbor's to ask what had happened; instead of replying, the neighbor turned away, as though not wishing to recognize him. Croisilles repeated his questions; he learned that his father, his affairs having long been in an embarrassed condition, had just become bankrupt, and had fled to America, abandoning to his creditors all that he possessed.

Not realizing as yet the extent of his misfortune, Croisilles felt overwhelmed by the thought that he might never again see his father. It seemed to him incredible that he should be thus suddenly abandoned; he tried to force an entrance into the store; but was given to understand that the official seals had been affixed; so he sat down on a stone, and giving way to his grief, began to weep piteously, deaf to the consolations of those around him, never ceasing to call his father's name, though he knew him to be already far away. At last he rose, ashamed at seeing a crowd about him, and, in the most profound despair, turned his steps towards the harbor.

On reaching the pier, he walked straight before him like a man in a trance, who knows neither where he is going nor what is to become of him. He saw himself irretrievably lost, possessing no longer a shelter, no means of rescue and, of course, no longer any friends. Alone, wandering on the sea-shore, he felt tempted to drown himself, then and there. Just at the moment when, yielding to this thought, he was advancing to the edge of a high cliff, an old servant named Jean, who had served his family for a number of years, arrived on the scene.

"Ah! my poor Jean!" he exclaimed, "you know all that has happened since I went away. Is it possible that my father could leave us without warning, without farewell?"

"He is gone," answered Jean, "but indeed not without saying good-bye to you."

At the same time he drew from his pocket a letter, which he gave to his young master. Croisilles recognized the handwriting of his father, and, before opening the letter, kissed it rapturously; but it contained only a few words. Instead of feeling his trouble softened, it seemed to the young man still harder to bear. Honorable until then, and known as such, the old gentleman, ruined by an unforeseen disaster (the bankruptcy of a partner), had left for his son nothing but a few commonplace words of consolation, and no hope, except, perhaps, that vague hope without aim or reason which constitutes, it is said, the last possession one loses.

"Jean, my friend, you carried me in your arms," said Croisilles, when he had read the letter, "and you certainly are to-day the only being who loves me at all; it is a very sweet thing to me, but a very sad one for you; for, as sure as my father embarked there, I will throw myself into the same sea which is bearing him away; not before you nor at once, but some day I will do it, for I am lost."

"What can you do?" replied Jean, not seeming to have understood, but holding fast to the skirt of Croisilles' coat; "What can you do, my dear master? Your father was deceived; he was expecting money which did not come, and it was no small amount either. Could he stay here? I have seen him, sir, as he made his fortune, during the thirty years that I served him. I have seen him working, attending to his business, the crown-pieces coming in one by one. He was an honorable man, and skilful; they took a cruel advantage of him. Within the last few days, I was still there, and as fast as the crowns came in, I saw them go out of the shop again. Your father paid all he could, for a whole day, and, when his desk was empty, he could not help telling me, pointing to a drawer where but six francs remained: 'There were a hundred thousand francs there this morning!' That does not look like a rascally failure, sir? There is nothing in it that can dishonor you."

"I have no more doubt of my father's integrity," answered Croisilles, "than I have of his misfortune. Neither do I doubt his affection. But I wish I could have kissed him, for what is to become of me? I am not accustomed to poverty, I have not the necessary cleverness to build up my fortune. And, if I had it, my father is gone. It took him thirty years, how long would it take me to repair this disaster? Much longer. And will he be living then? Certainly not; he will die over there, and I cannot even go and find him; I can join him only by dying."

Utterly distressed as Croisilles was, he possessed much religious feeling. Although his despondency made him wish for death, he hesitated to take his life. At the first words of this interview, he had taken hold of old Jean's arm, and thus both returned to the town. When they had entered the streets and the sea was no longer so near:

"It seems to me, sir," said Jean, "that a good man has a right to live and that a misfortune proves nothing. Since your father has not killed himself, thank God, how can you think of dying? Since there is no dishonor in his case, and all the town knows it is so, what would they think of you? That you felt unable to endure poverty. It would be neither brave nor Christian; for, at the very worst, what is there to frighten you? There are plenty of people born poor, and who have never had either mother or father to help them on. I know that we are not all alike, but, after all, nothing is impossible to God. What would you do in such a case? Your father was not born rich, far from it, — meaning no offence — and that is perhaps what consoles him now. If you had been here, this last month, it would have given you courage. Yes, sir, a man may be ruined, nobody is secure from bankruptcy; but your

291

father, I make bold to say, has borne himself through it all like a man, though he did leave us so hastily. But what could he do? It is not every day that a vessel starts for America. I accompanied him to the wharf, and if you had seen how sad he was! How he charged me to take care of you; to send him news from you! — Sir, it is a right poor idea you have, that throwing the helve after the hatchet. Every one has his time of trial in this world, and I was a soldier before I was a servant. I suffered severely at the time, but I was young; I was of your age, sir, and it seemed to me that Providence could not have spoken His last word to a young man of twenty-five. Why do you wish to prevent the kind God from repairing the evil that has befallen you? Give Him time, and all will come right. If I might advise you, I would say, just wait two or three years, and I will answer for it, you will come out all right. It is always easy to go out of this world. Why will you seize an unlucky moment?"

While Jean was thus exerting himself to persuade his master, the latter walked in silence, and, as those who suffer often do, was looking this way and that as though seeking for something which might bind him to life. As chance would have it, at this juncture, Mademoiselle Godeau, the daughter of the fermier-général, happened to pass with her governess. The mansion in which she lived was not far distant; Croisilles saw her enter it. This meeting produced on him more effect than all the reasonings in the world. I have said that he was rather erratic, and nearly always yielded to the first impulse. Without hesitating an instant, and without explanation, he suddenly left the arm of his old servant, and crossing the street, knocked at Monsieur Godeau's door.

# II

When we try to picture to ourselves, nowadays, what was called a "financier" in times gone by, we invariably imagine enormous corpulence, short legs, a gigantic wig, and a broad face with a triple chin, — and it is not without reason that we have become accustomed to form such a picture of such a personage. Everyone knows to what great abuses the royal tax-farming led, and it seems as though there were a law of nature which renders fatter than the rest of mankind those who fatten, not only upon their own laziness, but also upon the work of others.

Monsieur Godeau, among financiers, was one of the most classical to be found, — that is to say, one of the fattest. At the present time he had the gout, which was nearly as fashionable in his day as the nervous headache is in ours. Stretched upon a lounge, his eyes half-closed, he was coddling himself in the coziest corner of a dainty boudoir. The panel-mirrors which surrounded him, majestically duplicated on every side his enormous person; bags filled with gold covered the table; around him, the furniture, the wainscot, the doors, the locks, the mantel-piece, the ceiling were gilded; so was his coat. I do not know but that his brain was gilded too. He was calculating the issue of a little business affair which could not fail to bring him a few thousand louis; and was even deigning to smile over it to himself when Croisilles was announced. The young man entered with an humble, but resolute air, and with every outward manifestation of that inward tumult with which we find no difficulty in crediting a man who is longing to drown himself. Monsieur Godeau was a little surprised at this unexpected visit; then he thought his daughter had been buying some trifle, and was confirmed in that thought by seeing her appear almost at the same time with the young man. He made a sign to Croisilles not to sit down but to speak. The young lady seated herself on a sofa, and Croisilles, remaining standing, expressed himself in these terms:

"Sir, my father has failed. The bankruptcy of a partner has forced him to suspend his payments and unable to witness his own shame he has fled to America, after having paid his last sou to his creditors. I was absent when all this happened; I have just come back and have known of these events only two hours. I am absolutely without resources, and determined to die. It is very probable that, on leaving your house, I shall throw myself into the water. In all probability, I would already have done so, if I had not chanced to meet, at the very moment, this young lady, your daughter. I love her, from the very depths of my heart; for two years I have been in love with her, and my silence, until now, proves better than anything else the respect I feel for her; but to-day, in declaring my passion to you, I fulfill an imperative duty, and I would think I was offending God, if, before giving myself over to death, I did not come to ask you Mademoiselle Julie in marriage. I have not the slightest hope that you will grant this request; but I have to make it, nevertheless, for I am a good Christian, sir, and when a good Christian sees himself come to such a point of misery that he can no longer suffer life, he must at least, to extenuate his crime, exhaust all the chances which remain to him before taking the final and fatal step."

At the beginning of this speech, Monsieur Godeau had supposed that the young man came to borrow money, and so he prudently threw his handkerchief over the bags that were lying around him, preparing in advance a refusal, and a polite one, for he always felt some good-will toward the father of Croisilles. But when he had heard the young man to the end, and understood the purport of his visit, he never doubted one moment that the poor fellow had gone completely mad. He was at first tempted to ring the bell and have him put out; but, noticing his firm demeanor, his determined look, the fermier-général took pity on so inoffensive a case of insanity. He merely told his daughter to retire, so that she might be no longer exposed to hearing such improprieties.

While Croisilles was speaking, Mademoiselle Godeau had blushed as a peach in the month of August. At her father's bidding, she retired, the young man making her a profound bow, which she did not seem to notice. Left alone with Croisilles,

294

Monsieur Godeau coughed, rose, then dropped again upon the cushions, and, trying to assume a paternal air, delivered himself to the following effect:

"My boy," said he, "I am willing to believe that you are not poking fun at me, but you have really lost your head. I not only excuse this proceeding, but I consent not to punish you for it. I am sorry that your poor devil of a father has become bankrupt and has skipped. It is indeed very sad, and I quite understand that such a misfortune should affect your brain. Besides, I wish to do something for you; so take this stool and sit down there."

"It is useless, sir," answered Croisilles. "If you refuse me, as I see you do, I have nothing left but to take my leave. I wish you every good fortune."

"And where are you going?"

"To write to my father and say good-bye to him."

"Eh! the devil! Any one would swear you were speaking the truth. I'll be damned if I don't think you are going to drown yourself."

"Yes, sir; at least I think so, if my courage does not forsake me."

"That's a bright idea! Fie on you! How can you be such a fool? Sit down, sir, I tell you, and listen to me."

Monsieur Godeau had just made a very wise reflection, which was that it is never agreeable to have it said that a man, whoever he may be, threw himself into the water on leaving your house. He therefore coughed once more, took his snuff-box, cast a careless glance upon his shirt-frill, and continued:

"It is evident that you are nothing but a simpleton, a fool, a regular baby. You do not know what you are saying. You are ruined, that's what has happened to you. But, my dear friend, all that is not enough; one must reflect upon the things of this world. If you came to ask me — well, good advice, for instance, — I might give it to you; but what is it you are after? You are in love with my daughter?"

"Yes, sir, and I repeat to you, that I am far from supposing that you can give her to me in marriage; but as there is nothing in the world but that, which could prevent me from dying, if you believe in God, as I do not doubt you do, you will understand the reason that brings me here."

"Whether I believe in God or not, is no business of yours. I do not intend to be questioned. Answer me first: where have you seen my daughter?"

"In my father's shop, and in this house, when I brought jewelry for Mademoiselle Julie."

"Who told you her name was Julie? What are we coming to, great heavens! But be her name Julie or Javotte, do you know what is wanted in any one who aspires to the hand of the daughter of a fermier-général?"

"No, I am completely ignorant of it, unless it is to be as rich as she."

"Something more is necessary, my boy; you must have a name."

"Well! my name is Croisilles."

"Your name is Croisilles, poor wretch! Do you call that a name?"

"Upon my soul and conscience, sir, it seems to me to be as good a name as Godeau."

"You are very impertinent, sir, and you shall rue it."

"Indeed, sir, do not be angry; I had not the least idea of offending you. If you see in what I said anything to wound you, and wish to punish me for it, there is no need to get angry. Have I not told you that on leaving here I am going straight to drown myself?"

Although M. Godeau had promised himself to send Croisilles away as gently as possible, in order to avoid all scandal, his prudence could not resist the vexation of his wounded pride. The interview to which he had to resign himself was monstrous enough in itself; it may be imagined, then, what he felt at hearing himself spoken to in such terms.

"Listen," he said, almost beside himself, and determined to close the matter at any cost. "You are not such a fool that you cannot understand a word of common sense. Are you rich? No.

Are you noble? Still less so. What is this frenzy that brings you here? You come to worry me; you think you are doing something clever; you know perfectly well that it is useless; you wish to make me responsible for your death. Have you any right to complain of me? Do I owe a son to your father? Is it my fault that you have come to this? Mon Dieu! When a man is going to drown himself, he keeps quiet about it — "

"That is what I am going to do now. I am your very humble servant."

"One moment! It shall not be said that you had recourse to me in vain. There, my boy, here are three louis d'or: go and have dinner in the kitchen, and let me hear no more about you."

"Much obliged; I am not hungry, and I have no use for your money."

So Croisilles left the room, and the financier, having set his conscience at rest by the offer he had just made, settled himself more comfortably in his chair, and resumed his meditations.

Mademoiselle Godeau, during this time, was not so far away as one might suppose; she had, it is true, withdrawn in obedience to her father; but, instead of going to her room, she had remained listening behind the door. If the extravagance of Croisilles seemed incredible to her, still she found nothing to offend her in it; for love, since the world has existed, has never passed as an insult. On the other hand, as it was not possible to doubt the despair of the young man, Mademoiselle Godeau found herself a victim, at one and the same time, to the two sentiments most dangerous to women — compassion and curiosity. When she saw the interview at an end, and Croisilles ready to come out, she rapidly crossed the drawing-room where she stood, not wishing to be surprised eavesdropping, and hurried towards her apartment; but she almost immediately retraced her steps. The idea that perhaps Croisilles was really going to put an end to his life troubled her in spite of herself. Scarcely aware of what she was doing, she walked to meet him; the drawing-room was large, and the two young people came slowly towards each other. Croisilles was as pale as death, and Mademoiselle Godeau vainly sought words to express her feelings.

In passing beside him, she let fall on the floor a bunch of violets which she held in her hand. He at once bent down and picked up the bouquet in order to give it back to her, but instead of taking it, she passed on without uttering a word, and entered her father's room. Croisilles, alone again, put the flowers in his breast, and left the house with a troubled heart, not knowing what to think of his adventure.

# III

Scarcely had he taken a few steps in the street, when he saw his faithful friend Jean running towards him with a joyful face.

"What has happened?" he asked; "have you news to tell me?"

"Yes," replied Jean; "I have to tell you that the seals have been officially broken and that you can enter your home. All your father's debts being paid, you remain the owner of the house. It is true that all the money and all the jewels have been taken away; but at least the house belongs to you, and you have not lost everything. I have been running about for an hour, not knowing what had become of you, and I hope, my dear master, that you will now be wise enough to take a reasonable course."

"What course do you wish me to take?"

"Sell this house, sir, it is all your fortune. It will bring you about thirty thousand francs. With that at any rate you will not die of hunger; and what is to prevent you from buying a little stock in trade, and starting business for yourself? You would surely prosper."

"We shall see about this," answered Croisilles, as he hurried to the street where his home was. He was eager to see the paternal roof again. But when he arrived there so sad a spectacle met his gaze, that he had scarcely the courage to enter. The shop was in utter disorder, the rooms deserted, his father's alcove empty. Everything presented to his eyes the wretchedness of utter ruin. Not a chair remained; all the drawers had been ransacked, the till broken open, the chest taken away; nothing had escaped the greedy search of creditors and lawyers; who, after having pillaged the house, had gone, leaving the doors open, as though to testify to all passers-by how neatly their work was done.

"This, then," exclaimed Croisilles, "is all that remains after thirty years of work and a respectable life, — and all through the failure to have ready, on a given day, money enough to honor a signature imprudently given!"

While the young man walked up and down given over to the saddest thoughts, Jean seemed very much embarrassed. He supposed that his master was without ready money, and that he might perhaps not even have dined. He was therefore trying to think of some way to question him on the subject, and to offer him, in case of need, some part of his savings. After having tortured his mind for a quarter of an hour to try and hit upon some way of leading up to the subject, he could find nothing better than to come up to Croisilles, and ask him, in a kindly voice:

"Sir, do you still like roast partridges?"

The poor man uttered this question in a tone at once so comical and so touching, that Croisilles, in spite of his sadness, could not refrain from laughing.

"And why do you ask me that?" said he.

"My wife," replied Jean, "is cooking me some for dinner, sir, and if by chance you still liked them — "

Croisilles had completely forgotten till now the money which he was bringing back to his father. Jean's proposal reminded him that his pockets were full of gold.

"I thank you with all my heart," said he to the old man, "and I accept your dinner with pleasure; but, if you are anxious about my fortune, be reassured. I have more money than I need to have a good supper this evening, which you, in your turn, will share with me."

Saying this, he laid upon the mantel four well-filled purses, which he emptied, each containing fifty louis.

"Although this sum does not belong to me," he added, "I can use it for a day or two. To whom must I go to have it forwarded to my father?"

"Sir," replied Jean, eagerly, "your father especially charged me to tell you that this money belongs to you, and, if I did not speak of it before, it was because I did not know how your affairs in Paris had turned out. Where he has gone your father will want for nothing; he will lodge with one of your correspondents, who will receive him most gladly; he has moreover taken with him enough for his immediate needs, for he was quite sure of still leaving behind more than was necessary to pay all his just debts.

300

All that he has left, sir, is yours; he says so himself in his letter, and I am especially charged to repeat it to you. That gold is, therefore, legitimately your property, as this house in which we are now. I can repeat to you the very words your father said to me on embarking: 'May my son forgive me for leaving him; may he remember that I am still in the world only to love me, and let him use what remains after my debts are paid as though it were his inheritance.' Those, sir, are his own expressions; so put this back in your pocket, and, since you accept my dinner, pray let us go home."

The honest joy which shone in Jean's eyes, left no doubt in the mind of Croisilles. The words of his father had moved him to such a point that he could not restrain his tears; on the other hand, at such a moment, four thousand francs were no bagatelle. As to the house, it was not an available resource, for one could realize on it only by selling it, and that was both difficult and slow. All this, however, could not but make a considerable change in the situation the young man found himself in; so he felt suddenly moved — shaken in his dismal resolution, and, so to speak, both sad and, at the same time, relieved of much of his distress. After having closed the shutters of the shop, he left the house with Jean, and as he once more crossed the town, could not help thinking how small a thing our affections are, since they sometimes serve to make us find an unforeseen joy in the faintest ray of hope. It was with this thought that he sat down to dinner beside his old servant, who did not fail, during the repast, to make every effort to cheer him.

Heedless people have a happy fault. They are easily cast down, but they have not even the trouble to console themselves, so changeable is their mind. It would be a mistake to think them, on that account, insensible or selfish; on the contrary they perhaps feel more keenly than others and are but too prone to blow their brains out in a moment of despair; but, this moment once passed, if they are still alive, they must dine, they must eat, they must drink, as usual; only to melt into tears again at bed-time. Joy and pain do not glide over them but pierce them through like arrows. Kind, hot-headed natures which know how to suffer, but not how to lie, through which one can clearly read, — not fragile and empty like glass, but solid and transparent like rock crystal.

After having clinked glasses with Jean, Croisilles, instead of drowning himself, went to the play. Standing at the back of the pit, he drew from his bosom Mademoiselle Godeau's bouquet, and, as he breathed the perfume in deep meditation, he began to think in a calmer spirit about his adventure of the morning. As soon as he had pondered over it for awhile, he saw clearly the truth; that is to say, that the young lady, in leaving the bouquet in his hands, and in refusing to take it back, had wished to give him a mark of interest; for otherwise this refusal and this silence could only have been marks of contempt, and such a supposition was not possible. Croisilles, therefore, judged that Mademoiselle Godeau's heart was of a softer grain than her father's and he remembered distinctly that the young lady's face, when she crossed the drawing-room, had expressed an emotion the more true that it seemed involuntary. But was this emotion one of love, or only of sympathy? Or was it perhaps something of still less importance, — mere commonplace pity? Had Mademoiselle Godeau feared to see him die — him, Croisilles — or merely to be the cause of the death of a man, no matter what man? Although withered and almost leafless, the bouquet still retained so exquisite an odor and so brave a look, that in breathing it and looking at it, Croisilles could not help hoping. It was a thin garland of roses round a bunch of violets. What mysterious depths of sentiment an Oriental might have read in these flowers, by interpreting their language! But after all, he need not be an Oriental in this case. The flowers which fall from the breast of a pretty woman, in Europe, as in the East, are never mute; were they but to tell what they have seen while reposing in that lovely bosom, it would be enough for a lover, and this, in fact, they do. Perfumes have more than one resemblance to love, and there are even people who think love to be but a sort of perfume; it is true the flowers which exhale it are the most beautiful in creation.

While Croisilles mused thus, paying very little attention to the tragedy that was being acted at the time, Mademoiselle Godeau herself appeared in a box opposite.

The idea did not occur to the young man that, if she should notice him, she might think it very strange to find the would-be suicide there after what had transpired in the morning. He, on the contrary, bent all his efforts towards getting nearer to her; but he could not succeed. A fifth-rate actress from Paris had come to play Mérope, and the crowd was so dense that one could not move. For lack of anything better, Croisilles had to content himself with fixing his gaze upon his lady-love, not lifting his eyes from her for a moment. He noticed that she seemed pre-occupied and moody, and that she spoke to every one with a sort of repugnance. Her box was surrounded, as may be imagined, by all the fops of the neighborhood, each of whom passed several times before her in the gallery, totally unable to enter the box, of which her father filled more than three-fourths. Croisilles noticed further that she was not using her opera-glasses, nor was she listening to the play. Her elbows resting on the balustrade, her chin in her hand, with her far-away look, she seemed, in all her sumptuous apparel, like some statue of Venus disguised en marquise. The display of her dress and her hair, her rouge, beneath which one could guess her paleness, all the splendor of her toilet, did but the more distinctly bring out the immobility of her countenance. Never had Croisilles seen her so beautiful. Having found means, between the acts, to escape from the crush, he hurried off to look at her from the passage leading to her box, and, strange to say, scarcely had he reached it, when Mademoiselle Godeau, who had not stirred for the last hour, turned round. She started slightly as she noticed him and only cast a glance at him; then she resumed her former attitude. Whether that glance expressed surprise, anxiety, pleasure or love; whether it meant "What, not dead!" or "God be praised! There you are, living!" — I do not pretend to explain. Be that as it may; at that glance, Croisilles inwardly swore to himself to die or gain her love.

# IV

Of all the obstacles which hinder the smooth course of love, the greatest is, without doubt, what is called false shame, which is indeed a very potent obstacle.

Croisilles was not troubled with this unhappy failing, which both pride and timidity combine to produce; he was not one of those who, for whole months, hover round the woman they love, like a cat round a caged bird. As soon as he had given up the idea of drowning himself, he thought only of letting his dear Julie know that he lived solely for her. But how could he tell her so? Should he present himself a second time at the mansion of the fermier-général, it was but too certain that M. Godeau would have him ejected.

Julie, when she happened to take a walk, never went without her maid; it was therefore useless to undertake to follow her. To pass the nights under the windows of one's beloved is a folly dear to lovers, but, in the present case, it would certainly prove vain. I said before that Croisilles was very religious; it therefore never entered his mind to seek to meet his lady-love at church. As the best way, though the most dangerous, is to write to people when one cannot speak to them in person, he decided on the very next day to write to the young lady.

His letter possessed, naturally, neither order nor reason. It read somewhat as follows:

"Mademoiselle, — Tell me exactly, I beg of you, what fortune one must possess to be able to pretend to your hand. I am asking you a strange question; but I love you so desperately, that it is impossible for me not to ask it, and you are the only person in the world to whom I can address it. It seemed to me, last evening, that you looked at me at the play. I had wished to die; would to God I were indeed dead, if I am mistaken, and if that look was not meant for me. Tell me if Fate can be so cruel as to let a man deceive himself in a manner at once so sad and so sweet. I believe that you commanded me to live. You are rich, beautiful. I know it. Your father is arrogant and miserly, and you have a right to be proud; but I love you, and the rest is a dream. Fix your charming eyes on me; think of what love can do, when I who suffer so cruelly, who must stand in fear of every thing, feel, nevertheless, an inexpressible joy in writing you this mad letter, which will perhaps bring down your anger upon me. But think also, mademoiselle that you are a little to blame for this, my folly. Why did you drop that bouquet? Put yourself for an instant, if possible, in my place; I dare think that you love me, and I dare ask you to tell me so. Forgive me, I beseech you. I would give my life's blood to be sure of not offending you, and to see you listening to my love with that angel smile which belongs only to you.

"Whatever you may do, your image remains mine; you can remove it only by tearing out my heart. As long as your look lives in my remembrance, as long as the bouquet keeps a trace of its perfume, as long as a word will tell of love, I will cherish hope."

Having sealed his letter, Croisilles went out and walked up and down the street opposite the Godeau mansion, waiting for a servant to come out. Chance, which always serves mysterious loves, when it can do so without compromising itself, willed it that Mademoiselle Julie's maid should have arranged to purchase a cap on that day. She was going to the milliner's when Croisilles accosted her, slipped a louis into her hand, and asked her to take charge of his letter.

The bargain was soon struck; the servant took the money to pay for her cap and promised to do the errand out of gratitude. Croisilles, full of joy, went home and sat at his door awaiting an answer.

Before speaking of this answer, a word must be said about Mademoiselle Godeau. She was not quite free from the vanity of her father, but her good nature was ever uppermost. She was, in the full meaning of the term, a spoilt child. She habitually spoke very little, and never was she seen with a needle in her hand; she spent her days at her toilet, and her evenings on the sofa, not seeming to hear the conversation going on around her. As regards her dress, she was prodigiously coquettish, and her own face was surely what she thought most of on earth. A wrinkle in her collaret, an ink-spot on her finger, would have distressed her; and, when her dress pleased her, nothing can describe the last look which she cast at her mirror before leaving the room. She showed neither taste nor aversion for the pleasures in which young ladies usually delight. She went to balls willingly enough, and renounced going to them without a show of temper, sometimes without motive.

The play wearied her, and she was in the constant habit of falling asleep there. When her father, who worshipped her, proposed to make her some present of her own choice, she took an hour to decide, not being able to think of anything she cared for. When M. Godeau gave a reception or a dinner, it often happened that Julie would not appear in the drawing-room, and at such times she passed the evening alone in her own room, in full dress, walking up and down, her fan in her hand. If a compliment was addressed to her, she turned away her head, and if any one attempted to pay court to her, she responded only by a look at once so dazzling and so serious as to disconcert even the boldest. Never had a sally made her laugh; never had an air in an opera, a flight of tragedy, moved her; indeed, never had her heart given a sign of life; and, on seeing her pass in all the splendor of her nonchalant loveliness one might have taken her for a beautiful somnambulist, walking through the world as in a trance.

So much indifference and coquetry did not seem easy to understand. Some said she loved nothing, others that she loved nothing but herself. A single word, however, suffices to explain her character, — she was waiting. From the age of fourteen she had heard it ceaselessly repeated that nothing was so charming as she. She was convinced of this, and that was why she paid so much attention to dress. In failing to do honor to her own person, she would have thought herself guilty of sacrilege. She walked, in her beauty, so to speak, like a child in its holiday dress; but she was very far from thinking that her beauty was to remain useless.

Beneath her apparent unconcern she had a will, secret, inflexible, and the more potent the better it was concealed. The coquetry of ordinary women, which spends itself in ogling, in simpering, and in smiling, seemed to her a childish, vain, almost contemptible way of fighting with shadows. She felt herself in possession of a treasure, and she disdained to stake it piece by piece; she needed an adversary worthy of herself; but, too accustomed to see her wishes anticipated, she did not seek that adversary; it may even be said that she felt astonished at his failing to present himself.

For the four or five years that she had been out in society and had conscientiously displayed her flowers, her furbelows, and her beautiful shoulders, it seemed to her inconceivable that she had not yet inspired some great passion.

Had she said what was really behind her thoughts, she certainly would have replied to her many flatterers: "Well! if it is true that I am so beautiful, why do you not blow your brains out for me?" An answer which many other young girls might make, and which more than one who says nothing hides away in a corner of her heart, not far perhaps from the tip of her tongue.

What is there, indeed, in the world, more tantalizing for a woman than to be young, rich, beautiful, to look at herself in her mirror and see herself charmingly dressed, worthy in every way to please, fully disposed to allow herself to be loved, and to have to say to herself: "I am admired, I am praised, all the world thinks me charming, but nobody loves me. My gown is by the best maker, my laces are superb, my coiffure is irreproachable, my face the most beautiful on earth, my figure slender, my foot prettily turned, and all this helps me to nothing but to go and yawn in the corner of some drawing-room! If a young man speaks to me he treats me as a child; if I am asked in marriage, it is for my dowry; if somebody presses my hand in a dance, it is sure to be some provincial fop; as soon as I appear anywhere, I excite a murmur of admiration; but nobody speaks low, in my ear, a word that makes my heart beat. I hear impertinent men praising me in loud tones, a couple of feet away, and never a look of humbly sincere adoration

307

meets mine. Still I have an ardent soul full of life, and I am not, by any means, only a pretty doll to be shown about, to be made to dance at a ball, to be dressed by a maid in the morning and undressed at night — beginning the whole thing over again the next day."

That is what Mademoiselle Godeau had many times said to herself; and there were hours when that thought inspired her with so gloomy a feeling that she remained mute and almost motionless for a whole day. When Croisilles wrote her, she was in just such a fit of ill-humor. She had just been taking her chocolate and was deep in meditation, stretched upon a lounge, when her maid entered and handed her the letter with a mysterious air. She looked at the address, and not recognizing the handwriting, fell again to musing.

The maid then saw herself forced to explain what it was, which she did with a rather disconcerted air, not being at all sure how the young lady would take the matter. Mademoiselle Godeau listened without moving, then opened the letter, and cast only a glance at it; she at once asked for a sheet of paper, and nonchalantly wrote these few words:

"No, sir, I assure you I am not proud. If you had only a hundred thousand crowns, I would willingly marry you."

Such was the reply which the maid at once took to Croisilles, who gave her another louis for her trouble.

# V

A hundred thousand crowns are not found "in a donkey's hoof-print," and if Croisilles had been suspicious he might have thought in reading Mademoiselle Godeau's letter that she was either crazy or laughing at him. He thought neither, for he only saw in it that his darling Julie loved him, and that he must have a hundred thousand crowns, and he dreamed from that moment of nothing but trying to secure them.

He possessed two hundred louis in cash, plus a house which, as I have said, might be worth about thirty thousand francs. What was to be done? How was he to go about transfiguring these thirty-four thousand francs, at a jump, into three hundred thousand. The first idea which came into the mind of the young man was to find some way of staking his whole fortune on the toss-up of a coin, but for that he must sell the house. Croisilles therefore began by putting a notice upon the door, stating that his house was for sale; then, while dreaming what he would do with the money that he would get for it, he awaited a purchaser.

A week went by, then another; not a single purchaser applied. More and more distressed, Croisilles spent these days with Jean, and despair was taking possession of him once more, when a Jewish broker rang at the door.

"This house is for sale, sir, is it not? Are you the owner of it?"

"Yes, sir."

"And how much is it worth?"

"Thirty thousand francs, I believe; at least I have heard my father say so."

The Jew visited all the rooms, went upstairs and down into the cellar, knocking on the walls, counting the steps of the staircase, turning the doors on their hinges and the keys in their locks, opening and closing the windows; then, at last, after having thoroughly examined everything, without saying a word and without making the slightest proposal, he bowed to Croisilles and retired.

Croisilles, who for a whole hour had followed him with a palpitating heart, as may be imagined, was not a little disappointed at this silent retreat. He thought that perhaps the Jew had wished to give himself time to reflect and that he would return presently. He waited a week for him, not daring to go out for fear of missing his visit, and looking out of the windows from morning till night. But it was in vain; the Jew did not reappear. Jean, true to his unpleasant role of adviser, brought moral pressure to bear to dissuade his master from selling his house in so hasty a manner and for so extravagant a purpose. Dying of impatience, ennui, and love, Croisilles one morning took his two hundred louis and went out, determined to tempt fortune with this sum, since he could not have more.

The gaming-houses at that time were not public, and that refinement of civilization which enables the first comer to ruin himself at all hours, as soon as the wish enters his mind, had not yet been invented.

Scarcely was Croisilles in the street before he stopped, not knowing where to go to stake his money. He looked at the houses of the neighborhood, and eyed them, one after the other, striving to discover suspicious appearances that might point out to him the object of his search. A good-looking young man, splendidly dressed, happened to pass. Judging from his mien, he was certainly a young man of gentle blood and ample leisure, so Croisilles politely accosted him.

"Sir," he said, "I beg your pardon for the liberty I take. I have two hundred louis in my pocket and I am dying either to lose them or win more. Could you not point out to me some respectable place where such things are done?"

At this rather strange speech the young man burst out laughing.

"Upon my word, sir!" answered he, "if you are seeking any such wicked place you have but to follow me, for that is just where I am going."

Croisilles followed him, and a few steps farther they both entered a house of very attractive appearance, where they were received hospitably by an old gentleman of the highest breeding.

Several young men were already seated round a green cloth. Croisilles modestly took a place there, and in less than an hour his two hundred louis were gone.

He came out as sad as a lover can be who thinks himself beloved. He had not enough to dine with, but that did not cause him any anxiety.

"What can I do now," he asked himself, "to get money? To whom shall I address myself in this town? Who will lend me even a hundred louis on this house that I can not sell?"

While he was in this quandary, he met his Jewish broker. He did not hesitate to address him, and, featherhead as he was, did not fail to tell him the plight he was in.

The Jew did not much want to buy the house; he had come to see it only through curiosity, or, to speak more exactly, for the satisfaction of his own conscience, as a passing dog goes into a kitchen, the door of which stands open, to see if there is anything to steal. But when he saw Croisilles so despondent, so sad, so bereft of all resources, he could not resist the temptation to put himself to some inconvenience, even, in order to pay for the house. He therefore offered him about one-fourth of its value. Croisilles fell upon his neck, called him his friend and saviour, blindly signed a bargain that would have made one's hair stand on end, and, on the very next day, the possessor of four hundred new louis, he once more turned his steps toward the gambling-house where he had been so politely and speedily ruined the night before.

On his way, he passed by the wharf. A vessel was about leaving; the wind was gentle, the ocean tranquil. On all sides, merchants, sailors, officers in uniform were coming and going. Porters were carrying enormous bales of merchandise. Passengers and their friends were exchanging farewells, small boats were rowing about in all directions; on every face could be read fear, impatience, or hope; and, amidst all the agitation which surrounded it, the majestic vessel swayed gently to and fro under the wind that swelled her proud sails.

"What a grand thing it is," thought Croisilles, "to risk all one possesses and go beyond the sea, in perilous search of fortune! How it fills me with emotion to look at this vessel setting out on her voyage, loaded with so much wealth, with the welfare of so many families! What joy to see her come back again, bringing twice as much as was entrusted to her, returning so much prouder and richer than she went away! Why am I not one of those merchants? Why could I not stake my four hundred louis in this way? This immense sea! What a green cloth, on which to boldly tempt fortune! Why should I not myself buy a few bales of cloth or silk? What is to prevent my doing so, since I have gold? Why should this captain refuse to take charge of my merchandise? And who knows? Instead of going and throwing away this — my little all — in a gambling-house, I might double it, I might triple it, perhaps, by honest industry. If Julie truly loves me, she will wait a few years, she will remain true to me until I am able to marry her. Commerce sometimes yields greater profits than one thinks; examples are wanting in this world of wealth gained with astonishing rapidity in this way on the changing waves — why should Providence not bless an endeavor made for a purpose so laudable, so worthy of His assistance? Among these merchants who have accumulated so much and who send their vessels to the ends of the world, more than one has begun with a smaller sum than I have now. They have prospered with the help of God; why should I not prosper in my turn? It seems to me as though a good wind were filling these sails, and this vessel inspires confidence. Come! the die is cast; I will speak to the captain, who seems to be a good fellow; I will then write to Julie, and set out to become a clever and successful trader."

The greatest danger incurred by those who are habitually but half crazy, is that of becoming, at times, altogether so.

The poor fellow, without further deliberation, put his whim into execution. To find goods to buy, when one has money and knows nothing about the goods, is the easiest thing in the world.

The captain, to oblige Croisilles, took him to one of his friends, a manufacturer, who sold him as much cloth and silk as he could pay for. The whole of it, loaded upon a cart, was promptly taken on board. Croisilles, delighted and full of hope, had himself written in large letters his name upon the bales. He watched them being put on board with inexpressible joy; the hour of departure soon came, and the vessel weighed anchor.

I need not say that in this transaction, Croisilles had kept no money in hand. His house was sold; and there remained to him, for his sole fortune, the clothes he had on his back; — no home, and not a son. With the best will possible, Jean could not suppose that his master was reduced to such an extremity; Croisilles was not too proud, but too thoughtless to tell him of it. So he determined to sleep under the starry vault, and as for his meals, he made the following calculation; he presumed that the vessel which bore his fortune would be six months before coming back to Havre; Croisilles, therefore, not without regret, sold a gold watch his father had given him, and which he had fortunately kept; he got thirty-six livres for it. That was sufficient to live on for about six months, at the rate of four sous a day. He did not doubt that it would be enough, and, reassured for the present, he wrote to Mademoiselle Godeau to inform her of what he had done. He was very careful in his letter not to speak of his distress; he announced to her, on the contrary, that he had undertaken a magnificent commercial enterprise, of the speedy and fortunate issue of which there could be no doubt; he explained to her that La Fleurette, a merchant-vessel of one hundred and fifty tons, was carrying to the Baltic his cloths and his silks, and implored her to remain faithful to him for a year, reserving to himself the right of asking, later on, for a further delay, while, for his part, he swore eternal love to her.

When Mademoiselle Godeau received this letter she was sitting before the fire, and had in her hand, using it as a screen, one of those bulletins which are printed in seaports, announcing the arrival and departure of vessels, and which also report disasters at sea. It had never occurred to her, as one can well imagine, to take an interest in this sort of thing; she had in fact never glanced at any of these sheets.

The perusal of Croisilles' letter prompted her to read the bulletin she had been holding in her hand; the first word that caught her eye was no other than the name of La Fleurette.

The vessel had been wrecked on the coast of France, on the very night following its departure. The crew had barely escaped, but all the cargo was lost.

Mademoiselle Godeau, at this news, no longer remembered that Croisilles had made to her an avowal of his poverty; she was as heartbroken as though a million had been at stake.

In an instant, the horrors of the tempest, the fury of the winds, the cries of the drowning, the ruin of the man who loved her, presented themselves to her mind like a scene in a romance. The bulletin and the letter fell from her hands. She rose in great agitation, and, with heaving breast and eyes brimming with tears, paced up and down, determined to act, and asking herself how she should act.

There is one thing that must be said in justice to love; it is that the stronger, the clearer, the simpler the considerations opposed to it, in a word, the less common sense there is in the matter, the wilder does the passion become and the more does the lover love. It is one of the most beautiful things under heaven, this irrationality of the heart. We should not be worth much without it. After having walked about the room (without forgetting either her dear fan or the passing glance at the mirror), Julie allowed herself to sink once more upon her lounge. Whoever had seen her at this moment would have looked upon a lovely sight; her eyes sparkled, her cheeks were on fire; she sighed deeply, and murmured in a delicious transport of joy and pain:

"Poor fellow! He has ruined himself for me!"

Independently of the fortune which she could expect from her father, Mademoiselle Godeau had in her own right the property her mother had left her. She had never thought of it.

At this moment, for the first time in her life, she remembered that she could dispose of five hundred thousand francs. This thought brought a smile to her lips; a project, strange, bold, wholly feminine, almost as mad as Croisilles himself, entered her head; — she weighed the idea in her mind for some time, then decided to act upon it at once.

She began by inquiring whether Croisilles had any relatives or friends; the maid was sent out in all directions to find out.

Having made minute inquiries in all quarters, she discovered, on the fourth floor of an old rickety house, a half-crippled aunt, who never stirred from her arm-chair, and had not been out for four or five years. This poor woman, very old, seemed to have been left in the world expressly as a specimen of hungry misery. Blind, gouty, almost deaf, she lived alone in a garret; but a gayety, stronger than misfortune and illness, sustained her at eighty years of age, and made her still love life. Her neighbors never passed her door without going in to see her, and the antiquated tunes she hummed enlivened all the girls of the neighborhood. She possessed a little annuity which sufficed to maintain her; as long as day lasted, she knitted. She did not know what had happened since the death of Louis XIV.

It was to this worthy person that Julie had herself privately conducted. She donned for the occasion all her finery; feathers, laces, ribbons, diamonds, nothing was spared. She wanted to be fascinating; but the real secret of her beauty, in this case, was the whim that was carrying her away. She went up the steep, dark staircase which led to the good lady's chamber, and, after the most graceful bow, spoke somewhat as follows:

"You have, madame, a nephew, called Croisilles, who loves me and has asked for my hand; I love him too and wish to marry him; but my father, Monsieur Godeau, fermier-général of this town, refuses his consent, because your nephew is not rich. I would not, for the world, give occasion to scandal, nor cause trouble to anybody; I would therefore never think of disposing of myself without the consent of my family. I come to ask you a favor, which I beseech you to grant me. You must come yourself and propose this marriage to my father. I have, thank God, a little fortune which is quite at your disposal; you may take possession, whenever you see fit, of five hundred thousand francs at my notary's. You will say that this sum belongs to your nephew, which in fact it does. It is not a present that I am making him, it is a debt which I am paying, for I am the cause of the ruin of

Croisilles, and it is but just that I should repair it. My father will not easily give in; you will be obliged to insist and you must have a little courage; I, for my part, will not fail. As nobody on earth excepting myself has any right to the sum of which I am speaking to you, nobody will ever know in what way this amount will have passed into your hands. You are not very rich yourself, I know, and you may fear that people will be astonished to see you thus endowing your nephew; but remember that my father does not know you, that you show yourself very little in town, and that, consequently it will be easy for you to pretend that you have just arrived from some journey. This step will doubtless be some exertion to you; you will have to leave your arm-chair and take a little trouble; but you will make two people happy, madame, and if you have ever known love, I hope you will not refuse me."

The old lady, during this discourse, had been in turn surprised, anxious, touched, and delighted. The last words persuaded her.

"Yes, my child," she repeated several times, "I know what it is, — I know what it is."

As she said this she made an effort to rise; her feeble limbs could barely support her; Julie quickly advanced and put out her hand to help her; by an almost involuntary movement they found themselves, in an instant, in each other's arms.

A treaty was at once concluded; a warm kiss sealed it in advance, and the necessary and confidential consultation followed without further trouble.

All the explanations having been made, the good lady drew from her wardrobe a venerable gown of taffeta, which had been her wedding-dress. This antique piece of property was not less than fifty years old; but not a spot, not a grain of dust had disfigured it; Julie was in ecstasies over it. A coach was sent for, the handsomest in the town. The good lady prepared the speech she was going to make to Monsieur Godeau; Julie tried to teach her how she was to touch the heart of her father, and did not hesitate to confess that love of rank was his vulnerable point.

"If you could imagine," said she, "a means of flattering this weakness, you will have won our cause."

The good lady pondered deeply, finished her toilet without Another word, clasped the hands of her future niece, and entered the carriage.

She soon arrived at the Godeau mansion; there, she braced herself up so gallantly for her entrance that she seemed ten years younger. She majestically crossed the drawing-room where Julie's bouquet had fallen, and when the door of the boudoir opened, said in a firm voice to the lackey who preceded her:

"Announce the dowager Baroness de Croisilles."

These words settled the happiness of the two lovers. Monsieur Godeau was bewildered by them. Although five hundred thousand francs seemed little to him, he consented to everything, in order to make his daughter a baroness, and such she became; — who would dare contest her title? For my part, I think she had thoroughly earned it.

A SIMPLE SOUL
BY GUSTAVE FLAUBERT

CHAPTER I
FELICITÉ

For half a century the housewives of Pont-l'Eveque had envied Madame Aubain her servant Felicité.

For a hundred francs a year, she cooked and did the housework, washed, ironed, mended, harnessed the horse, fattened the poultry, made the butter and remained faithful to her mistress — although the latter was by no means an agreeable person.

Madame Aubain had married a comely youth without any money, who died in the beginning of 1809, leaving her with two young children and a number of debts. She sold all her property excepting the farm of Toucques and the farm of Geffosses, the income of which barely amounted to 5,000 francs; then she left her house in Saint-Melaine, and moved into a less pretentious one which had belonged to her ancestors and stood back of the market-place. This house, with its slate-covered roof, was built between a passage-way and a narrow street that led to the river. The interior was so unevenly graded that it caused people to stumble. A narrow hall separated the kitchen from the parlour, where Madame Aubain sat all day in a straw armchair near the window. Eight mahogany chairs stood in a row against the white wainscoting. An old piano, standing beneath a barometer, was covered with a pyramid of old books and boxes. On either side of the yellow marble mantelpiece, in Louis XV style, stood a tapestry armchair. The clock represented a temple of Vesta; and the whole room smelled musty, as it was on a lower level than the garden.

On the first floor was Madame's bedchamber, a large room papered in a flowered design and containing the portrait of Monsieur dressed in the costume of a dandy. It communicated with a smaller room, in which there were two little cribs, without any mattresses. Next, came the parlour (always closed), filled with furniture covered with sheets. Then a hall, which led to the study, where books and papers were piled on the shelves of a book-case that enclosed three quarters of the big black desk. Two panels were entirely hidden under pen-and-ink sketches, Gouache landscapes and Audran engravings, relics of better times and vanished luxury. On the second floor, a garret-window lighted Felicité's room, which looked out upon the meadows.

She arose at daybreak, in order to attend mass, and she worked without interruption until night; then, when dinner was over, the dishes cleared away and the door securely locked, she would bury the log under the ashes and fall asleep in front of the hearth with a rosary in her hand. Nobody could bargain with greater obstinacy, and as for cleanliness, the lustre on her brass saucepans was the envy and despair of other servants. She was most economical, and when she ate she would gather up crumbs with the tip of her finger, so that nothing should be wasted of the loaf of bread weighing twelve pounds which was baked especially for her and lasted three weeks.

Summer and winter she wore a dimity kerchief fastened in the back with a pin, a cap which concealed her hair, a red skirt, grey stockings, and an apron with a bib like those worn by hospital nurses.

Her face was thin and her voice shrill. When she was twenty-five, she looked forty. After she had passed fifty, nobody could tell her age; erect and silent always, she resembled a wooden figure working automatically.

# CHAPTER II
## THE HEROINE

Like every other woman, she had had an affair of the heart. Her father, who was a mason, was killed by falling from a scaffolding. Then her mother died and her sisters went their different ways; a farmer took her in, and while she was quite small, let her keep cows in the fields. She was clad in miserable rags, beaten for the slightest offence and finally dismissed for a theft of thirty sous which she did not commit. She took service on another farm where she tended the poultry; and as she was well thought of by her master, her fellow-workers soon grew jealous.

One evening in August (she was then eighteen years old), they persuaded her to accompany them to the fair at Colleville. She was immediately dazzled by the noise, the lights in the trees, the brightness of the dresses, the laces and gold crosses, and the crowd of people all hopping at the same time. She was standing modestly at a distance, when presently a young man of well-to-do appearance, who had been leaning on the pole of a wagon and smoking his pipe, approached her, and asked her for a dance. He treated her to cider and cake, bought her a silk shawl, and then, thinking she had guessed his purpose, offered to see her home. When they came to the end of a field he threw her down brutally. But she grew frightened and screamed, and he walked off.

One evening, on the road leading to Beaumont, she came upon a wagon loaded with hay, and when she overtook it, she recognized Theodore. He greeted her calmly, and asked her to forget what had happened between them, as it "was all the fault of the drink."

She did not know what to reply and wished to run away.

Presently he began to speak of the harvest and of the notables of the village; his father had left Colleville and bought the farm of Les Ecots, so that now they would be neighbors. "Ah!" she exclaimed. He then added that his parents were looking around for a wife for him, but that he, himself, was not so anxious and preferred to wait for a girl who suited him. She hung her head. He then asked her whether she had ever thought of marrying. She replied, smilingly, that it was wrong of him to make fun of her. "Oh! no, I am in earnest," he said, and put his left arm around her waist while they sauntered along. The air was soft, the stars were bright, and the huge load of hay oscillated in front of them, drawn by four horses whose ponderous hoofs raised clouds of dust. Without a word from their driver they turned to the right. He kissed her again and she went home. The following week, Theodore obtained meetings.

They met in yards, behind walls or under isolated trees. She was not ignorant, as girls of well-to-do families are — for the animals had instructed her; — but her reason and her instinct of honour kept her from falling. Her resistance exasperated Theodore's love and so in order to satisfy it (or perchance ingenuously), he offered to marry her. She would not believe him at first, so he made solemn promises. But, in a short time he mentioned a difficulty; the previous year, his parents had purchased a substitute for him; but any day he might be drafted and the prospect of serving in the army alarmed him greatly. To Felicité his cowardice appeared a proof of his love for her, and her devotion to him grew stronger. When she met him, he would torture her with his fears and his entreaties. At last, he announced that he was going to the prefect himself for information, and would let her know everything on the following Sunday, between eleven o'clock and midnight.

When the time drew near, she ran to meet her lover.

But instead of Theodore, one of his friends was at the meeting-place.

He informed her that she would never see her sweetheart again; for, in order to escape the conscription, he had married a rich old woman, Madame Lehoussais, of Toucques.

The poor girl's sorrow was frightful. She threw herself on the ground, she cried and called on the Lord, and wandered around desolately until sunrise. Then she went back to the farm, declared her intention of leaving, and at the end of the month, after she had received her wages, she packed all her belongings in a handkerchief and started for Pont-l'Eveque.

In front of the inn, she met a woman wearing widow's weeds, and upon questioning her, learned that she was looking for a cook. The girl did not know very much, but appeared so willing and so modest in her requirements, that Madame Aubain finally said:

"Very well, I will give you a trial."

And half an hour later Felicité was installed in her house.

At first she lived in a constant anxiety that was caused by "the style of the household" and the memory of "Monsieur," that hovered over everything. Paul and Virginia, the one aged seven, and the other barely four, seemed made of some precious material; she carried them pig-a-back, and was greatly mortified when Madame Aubain forbade her to kiss them every other minute.

But in spite of all this, she was happy. The comfort of her new surroundings had obliterated her sadness.

Every Thursday, friends of Madame Aubain dropped in for a game of cards, and it was Felicité's duty to prepare the table and heat the foot-warmers. They arrived at exactly eight o'clock and departed before eleven.

Every Monday morning, the dealer in second-hand goods, who lived under the alley-way, spread out his wares on the sidewalk. Then the city would be filled with a buzzing of voices in which the neighing of horses, the bleating of lambs, the grunting of pigs, could be distinguished, mingled with the sharp sound of wheels on the cobble-stones. About twelve o'clock, when the market was in full swing, there appeared at the front door a tall, middle-aged peasant, with a hooked nose and a cap on the back of his head; it was Robelin, the farmer of Geffosses. Shortly afterwards came Liebard, the farmer of Toucques, short, rotund and ruddy, wearing a grey jacket and spurred boots.

Both men brought their landlady either chickens or cheese. Felicité would invariably thwart their ruses and they held her in great respect.

At various times, Madame Aubain received a visit from the Marquis de Gremanville, one of her uncles, who was ruined and lived at Falaise on the remainder of his estates. He always came at dinner-time and brought an ugly poodle with him, whose paws soiled the furniture. In spite of his efforts to appear a man of breeding (he even went so far as to raise his hat every time he said "My deceased father"), his habits got the better of him, and he would fill his glass a little too often and relate broad stories. Felicité would show him out very politely and say: "You have had enough for this time, Monsieur de Gremanville! Hoping to see you again!" and would close the door.

She opened it gladly for Monsieur Bourais, a retired lawyer. His bald head and white cravat, the ruffling of his shirt, his flowing brown coat, the manner in which he took his snuff, his whole person, in fact, produced in her the kind of awe which we feel when we see extraordinary persons. As he managed Madame's estates, he spent hours with her in Monsieur's study; he was in constant fear of being compromised, had a great regard for the magistracy and some pretensions to learning.

In order to facilitate the children's studies, he presented them with an engraved geography which represented various scenes of the world: cannibals with feather head-dresses, a gorilla kidnapping a young girl, Arabs in the desert, a whale being harpooned, etc.

Paul explained the pictures to Felicité. And, in fact, this was her only literary education.

The children's studies were under the direction of a poor devil employed at the town-hall, who sharpened his pocketknife on his boots and was famous for his penmanship.

When the weather was fine, they went to Geffosses. The house was built in the centre of the sloping yard; and the sea looked like a grey spot in the distance. Felicité would take slices of cold meat from the lunch basket and they would sit down and eat in a room next to the dairy. This room was all that remained of a cottage that had been torn down. The dilapidated wall-paper trembled in the drafts. Madame Aubain, overwhelmed by recollections, would hang her head, while the children were afraid to open their mouths. Then, "Why don't you go and play?" their mother would say; and they would scamper off.

Paul would go to the old barn, catch birds, throw stones into the pond, or pound the trunks of the trees with a stick till they resounded like drums. Virginia would feed the rabbits and run to pick the wild flowers in the fields, and her flying legs would disclose her little embroidered pantalettes. One autumn evening, they struck out for home through the meadows. The new moon illumined part of the sky and a mist hovered like a veil over the sinuosities of the river. Oxen, lying in the pastures, gazed mildly at the passing persons. In the third field, however, several of them got up and surrounded them. "Don't be afraid," cried Felicité; and murmuring a sort of lament she passed her hand over the back of the nearest ox; he turned away and the others followed. But when they came to the next pasture, they heard frightful bellowing.

It was a bull which was hidden from them by the fog. He advanced towards the two women, and Madame Aubain prepared to flee for her life. "No, no! not so fast," warned Felicité. Still they hurried on, for they could hear the noisy breathing of the bull close behind them. His hoofs pounded the grass like hammers, and presently he began to gallop! Felicité turned around and threw patches of grass in his eyes. He hung his head, shook his horns and bellowed with fury. Madame Aubain and the children, huddled at the end of the field, were trying to jump over the ditch. Felicité continued to back before the bull, blinding him with dirt, while she shouted to them to make haste.

Madame Aubain finally slid into the ditch, after shoving first Virginia and then Paul into it, and though she stumbled several times she managed, by dint of courage, to climb the other side of it.

The bull had driven Felicité up against a fence; the foam from his muzzle flew in her face and in another minute he would have disemboweled her. She had just time to slip between two bars and the huge animal, thwarted, paused.

325

For years, this occurrence was a topic of conversation in Pont-l'Eveque. But Felicité took no credit to herself, and probably never knew that she had been heroic.

Virginia occupied her thoughts solely, for the shock she had sustained gave her a nervous affection, and the physician, M. Poupart, prescribed the saltwater bathing at Trouville. In those days, Trouville was not greatly patronized. Madame Aubain gathered information, consulted Bourais, and made preparations as if they were going on an extended trip.

The baggage was sent the day before on Liebard's cart. On the following morning, he brought around two horses, one of which had a woman's saddle with a velveteen back to it, while on the crupper of the other was a rolled shawl that was to be used for a seat. Madame Aubain mounted the second horse, behind Liebard. Felicité took charge of the little girl, and Paul rode M. Lechaptois' donkey, which had been lent for the occasion on the condition that they should be careful of it.

The road was so bad that it took two hours to cover the eight miles. The two horses sank knee-deep into the mud and stumbled into ditches; sometimes they had to jump over them. In certain places, Liebard's mare stopped abruptly. He waited patiently till she started again, and talked of the people whose estates bordered the road, adding his own moral reflections to the outline of their histories. Thus, when they were passing through Toucques, and came to some windows draped with nasturtiums, he shrugged his shoulders and said: "There's a woman, Madame Lehoussais, who, instead of taking a young man — " Felicité could not catch what followed; the horses began to trot, the donkey to gallop, and they turned into a lane; then a gate swung open, two farm-hands appeared and they all dismounted at the very threshold of the farm-house.

Mother Liebard, when she caught sight of her mistress, was lavish with joyful demonstrations. She got up a lunch which comprised a leg of mutton, tripe, sausages, a chicken fricassee, sweet cider, a fruit tart and some preserved prunes; then to all this the good woman added polite remarks about Madame, who

326

appeared to be in better health, Mademoiselle, who had grown to be "superb," and Paul, who had become singularly sturdy; she spoke also of their deceased grandparents, whom the Liebards had known, for they had been in the service of the family for several generations.

Like its owners, the farm had an ancient appearance. The beams of the ceiling were mouldy, the walls black with smoke and the windows grey with dust. The oak sideboard was filled with all sorts of utensils, plates, pitchers, tin bowls, wolf-traps. The children laughed when they saw a huge syringe. There was not a tree in the yard that did not have mushrooms growing around its foot, or a bunch of mistletoe hanging in its branches. Several of the trees had been blown down, but they had started to grow in the middle and all were laden with quantities of apples. The thatched roofs, which were of unequal thickness, looked like brown velvet and could resist the fiercest gales. But the wagon-shed was fast crumbling to ruins. Madame Aubain said that she would attend to it, and then gave orders to have the horses saddled.

It took another thirty minutes to reach Trouville. The little caravan dismounted in order to pass Les Ecores, a cliff that overhangs the bay, and a few minutes later, at the end of the dock, they entered the yard of the Golden Lamb, an inn kept by Mother David.

During the first few days, Virginia felt stronger, owing to the change of air and the action of the sea-baths. She took them in her little chemise, as she had no bathing suit, and afterwards her nurse dressed her in the cabin of a customs officer, which was used for that purpose by other bathers.

In the afternoon, they would take the donkey and go to the Roches-Noires, near Hennequeville. The path led at first through undulating grounds, and thence to a plateau, where pastures and tilled fields alternated. At the edge of the road, mingling with the brambles, grew holly bushes, and here and there stood large dead trees whose branches traced zigzags upon the blue sky.

Ordinarily, they rested in a field facing the ocean, with Deauville on their left, and Havre on their right. The sea glittered brightly in the sun and was as smooth as a mirror, and so calm that they could scarcely distinguish its murmur; sparrows chirped joyfully and the immense canopy of heaven spread over it all. Madame Aubain brought out her sewing, and Virginia amused herself by braiding reeds; Felicité wove lavender blossoms, while Paul was bored and wished to go home.

Sometimes they crossed the Toucques in a boat, and started to hunt for seashells. The outgoing tide exposed starfish and sea-urchins, and the children tried to catch the flakes of foam which the wind blew away. The sleepy waves lapping the sand unfurled themselves along the shore that extended as far as the eye could see, but where land began, it was limited by the downs which separated it from the "Swamp," a large meadow shaped like a hippodrome. When they went home that way, Trouville, on the slope of a hill below, grew larger and larger as they advanced, and, with all its houses of unequal height, seemed to spread out before them in a sort of giddy confusion.

When the heat was too oppressive, they remained in their rooms. The dazzling sunlight cast bars of light between the shutters. Not a sound in the village, not a soul on the sidewalk. This silence intensified the tranquillity of everything. In the distance, the hammers of some caulkers pounded the hull of a ship, and the sultry breeze brought them an odour of tar.

The principal diversion consisted in watching the return of the fishing-smacks. As soon as they passed the beacons, they began to ply to windward. The sails were lowered to one third of the masts, and with their foresails swelled up like balloons they glided over the waves and anchored in the middle of the harbour. Then they crept up alongside of the dock and the sailors threw the quivering fish over the side of the boat; a line of carts was waiting for them, and women with white caps sprang forward to receive the baskets and embrace their men-folk.

One day, one of them spoke to Felicité, who, after a little while, returned to the house gleefully. She had found one of her sisters, and presently Nastasie Barette, wife of Leroux, made her appearance, holding an infant in her arms, another child by the hand, while on her left was a little cabin-boy with his hands in his pockets and his cap on his ear.

At the end of fifteen minutes, Madame Aubain bade her go.

They always hung around the kitchen, or approached Felicité when she and the children were out walking. The husband, however, did not show himself.

Felicité developed a great fondness for them; she bought them a stove, some shirts and a blanket; it was evident that they exploited her. Her foolishness annoyed Madame Aubain, who, moreover did not like the nephew's familiarity, for he called her son "thou"; — and, as Virginia began to cough and the season was over, she decided to return to Pont-l'Eveque.

Monsieur Bourais assisted her in the choice of a college. The one at Caen was considered the best. So Paul was sent away and bravely said good-bye to them all, for he was glad to go to live in a house where he would have boy companions.

Madame Aubain resigned herself to the separation from her son because it was unavoidable. Virginia brooded less and less over it. Felicité regretted the noise he made, but soon a new occupation diverted her mind; beginning from Christmas, she accompanied the little girl to her catechism lesson every day.

# CHAPTER III
## DEATH

After she had made a curtsey at the threshold, she would walk up the aisle between the double lines of chairs, open Madame Aubain's pew, sit down and look around.

Girls and boys, the former on the right, the latter on the left-hand side of the church, filled the stalls of the choir; the priest stood beside the reading-desk; on one stained window of the side-aisle the Holy Ghost hovered over the Virgin; on another one, Mary knelt before the Child Jesus, and behind the altar, a wooden group represented Saint Michael felling the dragon.

The priest first read a condensed lesson of sacred history. Félicité evoked Paradise, the Flood, the Tower of Babel, the blazing cities, the dying nations, the shattered idols; and out of this she developed a great respect for the Almighty and a great fear of His wrath. Then, when she listened to the Passion, she wept. Why had they crucified Him who loved little children, nourished the people, made the blind see, and who, out of humility, had wished to be born among the poor, in a stable? The sowings, the harvests, the wine-presses, all those familiar things which the Scriptures mention, formed a part of her life; the word of God sanctified them; and she loved the lambs with increased tenderness for the sake of the Lamb, and the doves because of the Holy Ghost.

She found it hard, however, to think of the latter as a person, for was it not a bird, a flame, and sometimes only a breath? Perhaps it is its light that at night hovers over swamps, its breath that propels the clouds, its voice that renders church-bells harmonious. And Félicité worshipped devoutly, while enjoying the coolness and the stillness of the church.

As for the dogma, she could not understand it and did not even try. The priest discoursed, the children recited, and she went to sleep, only to awaken with a start when they were leaving the church and their wooden shoes clattered on the stone pavement.

In this way, she learned her catechism, her religious education having been neglected in her youth; and thenceforth she imitated all Virginia's religious practices, fasted when she did, and went to confession with her. At the Corpus-Christi Day they both decorated an altar.

She worried in advance over Virginia's first communion. She fussed about the shoes, the rosary, the book and the gloves. With what nervousness she helped the mother dress the child!

During the entire ceremony, she felt anguished. Monsieur Bourais hid part of the choir from view, but directly in front of her, the flock of maidens, wearing white wreaths over their lowered veils, formed a snow-white field, and she recognized her darling by the slenderness of her neck and her devout attitude. The bell tinkled. All the heads bent and there was a silence. Then, at the peals of the organ the singers and the worshippers struck up the Agnus Dei; the boys' procession began; behind them came the girls. With clasped hands, they advanced step by step to the lighted altar, knelt at the first step, received one by one the Host, and returned to their seats in the same order. When Virginia's turn came, Felicité leaned forward to watch her, and through that imagination which springs from true affection, she at once became the child, whose face and dress became hers, whose heart beat in her bosom, and when Virginia opened her mouth and closed her lids, she did likewise and came very near fainting.

The following day, she presented herself early at the church so as to receive communion from the cure. She took it with the proper feeling, but did not experience the same delight as on the previous day.

Madame Aubain wished to make an accomplished girl of her daughter; and as Guyot could not teach English nor music, she decided to send her to the Ursulines at Honfleur.

The child made no objection, but Felicité sighed and thought Madame was heartless. Then, she thought that perhaps her mistress was right, as these things were beyond her sphere. Finally, one day, an old *fiacre* stopped in front of the door and a nun stepped out. Felicité put Virginia's luggage on top of the carriage, gave the coachman some instructions, and smuggled six jars of jam, a dozen pears and a bunch of violets under the seat.

At the last minute, Virginia had a fit of sobbing; she embraced her mother again and again, while the latter kissed her on her forehead, and said: "Now, be brave, be brave!" The step was pulled up and the *fiacre* rumbled off.

Then Madame Aubain had a fainting spell, and that evening all her friends, including the two Lormeaus, Madame Lechaptois, the ladies Rochefeuille, Messieurs de Houppeville and Bourais, called on her and tendered their sympathy.

At first the separation proved very painful to her. But her daughter wrote her three times a week and the other days she, herself, wrote to Virginia. Then she walked in the garden, read a little, and in this way managed to fill out the emptiness of the hours.

Each morning, out of habit, Felicité entered Virginia's room and gazed at the walls. She missed combing her hair, lacing her shoes, tucking her in her bed, and the bright face and little hand when they used to go out for a walk. In order to occupy herself she tried to make lace. But her clumsy fingers broke the threads; she had no heart for anything, lost her sleep and "wasted away," as she put it.

In order to have some distraction, she asked leave to receive the visits of her nephew Victor.

He would come on Sunday, after church, with ruddy cheeks and bared chest, bringing with him the scent of the country. She would set the table and they would sit down opposite each other, and eat their dinner; she ate as little as possible, herself, to avoid any extra expense, but would stuff him so with food that he would finally go to sleep. At the first stroke of vespers, she would wake him up, brush his trousers, tie his cravat and walk to church with him, leaning on his arm with maternal pride.

His parents always told him to get something out of her, either a package of brown sugar, or soap, or brandy, and sometimes even money. He brought her his clothes to mend, and she accepted the task gladly, because it meant another visit from him.

In August, his father took him on a coasting-vessel.

It was vacation time and the arrival of the children consoled Felicité. But Paul was capricious, and Virginia was growing too old to be thee-and-thou'd, a fact which seemed to produce a sort of embarrassment in their relations.

Victor went successively to Morlaix, to Dunkirk, and to Brighton; whenever he returned from a trip he would bring her a present. The first time it was a box of shells; the second, a coffee-cup; the third, a big doll of ginger-bread. He was growing handsome, had a good figure, a tiny moustache, kind eyes, and a little leather cap that sat jauntily on the back of his head. He amused his aunt by telling her stones mingled with nautical expressions.

One Monday, the 14th of July, 1819 (she never forgot the date), Victor announced that he had been engaged on merchant-vessel and that in two days he would take the steamer at Honfleur and join his sailer, which was going to start from Havre very soon. Perhaps he might be away two years.

The prospect of his departure filled Felicité with despair, and in order to bid him farewell, on Wednesday night, after Madame's dinner, she put on her patens and trudged the four miles that separated Pont-l'Eveque from Honfleur.

When she reached the Calvary, instead of turning to the right, she turned to the left and lost herself in coal-yards; she had to retrace her steps; some people she spoke to advised her to hasten. She walked helplessly around the harbour filled with vessels, and knocked against hawsers. Presently the ground sloped abruptly, lights flittered to and fro, and she thought all at once that she had gone mad when she saw some horses in the sky.

Others, on the edge of the dock, neighed at the sight of the ocean. A derrick pulled them up in the air and dumped them into a boat, where passengers were bustling about among barrels of cider, baskets of cheese and bags of meal; chickens cackled, the captain swore and a cabin-boy rested on the railing, apparently indifferent to his surroundings. Felicité, who did not recognize him, kept shouting: "Victor!" He suddenly raised his eyes, but while she was preparing to rush up to him, they withdrew the gangplank.

The packet, towed by singing women, glided out of the harbour. Her hull squeaked and the heavy waves beat up against her sides. The sail had turned and nobody was visible; — and on the ocean, silvered by the light of the moon, the vessel formed a black spot that grew dimmer and dimmer, and finally disappeared.

When Felicité passed the Calvary again, she felt as if she must entrust that which was dearest to her to the Lord; and for a long while she prayed, with uplifted eyes and a face wet with tears. The city was sleeping; some customs officials were taking the air; and the water kept pouring through the holes of the dam with a deafening roar. The town clock struck two.

The parlour of the convent would not open until morning, and surely a delay would annoy Madame; so, in spite of her desire to see the other child, she went home. The maids of the inn were just arising when she reached Pont-l'Eveque.

So the poor boy would be on the ocean for months! His previous trips had not alarmed her. One can come back from England and Brittany; but America, the colonies, the islands, were all lost in an uncertain region at the very end of the world.

From that time on, Felicité thought solely of her nephew. On warm days she feared he would suffer from thirst, and when it stormed, she was afraid he would be struck by lightning. When she harkened to the wind that rattled in the chimney and dislodged the tiles on the roof, she imagined that he was being buffeted by the same storm, perched on top of a shattered mast, with his whole body bent backward and covered with sea-foam; or, — these were recollections of the engraved geography — he was being devoured by savages, or captured in a forest by apes, or dying on some lonely coast. She never mentioned her anxieties, however.

Madame Aubain worried about her daughter.

The sisters thought that Virginia was affectionate but delicate. The slightest emotion enervated her. She had to give up her piano lessons. Her mother insisted upon regular letters from the convent. One morning, when the postman failed to come, she grew impatient and began to pace to and fro, from her chair to the window. It was really extraordinary! No news since four days!

In order to console her mistress by her own example, Felicité said:

"Why, Madame, I haven't had any news since six months!" —

"From whom?" —

The servant replied gently:

"Why — from my nephew."

"Oh, yes, your nephew!" And shrugging her shoulders, Madame Aubain continued to pace the floor as if to say: "I did not think of it. — Besides, I do not care, a cabin-boy, a pauper! — but my daughter — what a difference! just think of it! — "

Felicité, although she had been reared roughly, was very indignant. Then she forgot about it.

It appeared quite natural to her that one should lose one's head about Virginia.

The two children were of equal importance; they were united in her heart and their fate was to be the same.

The chemist informed her that Victor's vessel had reached Havana. He had read the information in a newspaper.

Felicité imagined that Havana was a place where people did nothing but smoke, and that Victor walked around among negroes in a cloud of tobacco. Could a person, in case of need, return by land? How far was it from Pont-l'Eveque? In order to learn these things she questioned Monsieur Bourais. He reached for his map and began some explanations concerning longitudes, and smiled with superiority at Felicité's bewilderment. At last, he took his pencil and pointed out an imperceptible black point in the scallops of an oval blotch, adding: "There it is." She bent over the map; the maze of coloured lines hurt her eyes without enlightening her; and when Bourais asked her what puzzled her, she requested him to show her the house Victor lived in. Bourais threw up his hands, sneezed, and then laughed uproariously; such ignorance delighted his soul; but Felicité failed to understand the cause of his mirth, she whose intelligence was so limited that she perhaps expected to see even the picture of her nephew!

It was two weeks later that Liebard came into the kitchen at market-time, and handed her a letter from her brother-in-law. As neither of them could read, she called upon her mistress.

Madame Aubain, who was counting the stitches of her knitting, laid her work down beside her, opened the letter, started, and in a low tone and with a searching look said: "They tell you of a — misfortune. Your nephew — ."

He had died. The letter told nothing more.

Felicité dropped on a chair, leaned her head against the back and closed her lids; presently they grew pink. Then, with drooping head, inert hands and staring eyes she repeated at intervals:

"Poor little chap! poor little chap!"

Liebard watched her and sighed. Madame Aubain was trembling.

She proposed to the girl to go see her sister in Trouville.

With a single motion, Felicité replied that it was not necessary.

There was a silence. Old Liebard thought it about time for him to take leave.

Then Felicité uttered:

"They have no sympathy, they do not care!"

Her head fell forward again, and from time to time, mechanically, she toyed with the long knitting-needles on the work-table.

Some women passed through the yard with a basket of wet clothes.

When she saw them through the window, she suddenly remembered her own wash; as she had soaked it the day before, she must go and rinse it now. So she arose and left the room.

Her tub and her board were on the bank of the Toucques. She threw a heap of clothes on the ground, rolled up her sleeves and grasped her bat; and her loud pounding could be heard in the neighbouring gardens. The meadows were empty, the breeze wrinkled the stream, at the bottom of which were long grasses that looked like the hair of corpses floating in the water. She restrained her sorrow and was very brave until night; but, when she had gone to her own room, she gave way to it, burying her face in the pillow and pressing her two fists against her temples.

A long while afterward, she learned through Victor's captain, the circumstances which surrounded his death. At the hospital they had bled him too much, treating him for yellow fever. Four doctors held him at one time. He died almost instantly, and the chief surgeon had said:

"Here goes another one!"

His parents had always treated him barbarously; she preferred not to see them again, and they made no advances, either from forgetfulness or out of innate hardness.

Virginia was growing weaker.

A cough, continual fever, oppressive breathing and spots on her cheeks indicated some serious trouble. Monsieur Poupart had advised a sojourn in Provence. Madame Aubain decided that they would go, and she would have had her daughter come home at once, had it not been for the climate of Pont-l'Eveque.

She made an arrangement with a livery-stable man who drove her over to the convent every Tuesday. In the garden there was a terrace, from which the view extends to the Seine. Virginia walked in it, leaning on her mother's arm and treading the dead vine leaves. Sometimes the sun, shining through the clouds, made her blink her lids, when she gazed at the sails in the distance, and let her eyes roam over the horizon from the chateau of Tancarville to the lighthouses of Havre. Then they rested in the arbour. Her mother had bought a little cask of fine Malaga wine, and Virginia, laughing at the idea of becoming intoxicated, would drink a few drops of it, but never more.

Her strength returned. Autumn passed. Felicité began to reassure Madame Aubain. But, one evening, when she returned home after an errand, she met M. Boupart's coach in front of the door; M. Boupart himself was standing in the vestibule and Madame Aubain was tying the strings of her bonnet. "Give me my foot-warmer, my purse and my gloves; and be quick about it," she said.

Virginia had congestion of the lungs; perhaps it was desperate.

"Not yet," said the physician, and both got into the carriage, while the snow fell in thick flakes. It was almost night and very cold.

Felicité rushed to the church to light a candle. Then she ran after the coach which she overtook after an hour's chase, sprang up behind and held on to the straps. But suddenly a thought crossed her mind: "The yard had been left open; supposing that burglars got in!" And down she jumped.

The next morning, at daybreak, she called at the doctor's. He had been home, but had left again. Then she waited at the inn, thinking that strangers might bring her a letter. At last, at daylight she took the diligence for Lisieux.

The convent was at the end of a steep and narrow street. When she arrived about at the middle of it, she heard strange noises, a funeral knell. "It must be for some one else," thought she; and she pulled the knocker violently.

After several minutes had elapsed, she heard footsteps, the door was half opened and a nun appeared. The good sister, with an air of compunction, told her that "she had just passed away." And at the same time the tolling of Saint-Leonard's increased.

Felicité reached the second floor. Already at the threshold, she caught sight of Virginia lying on her back, with clasped hands, her mouth open and her head thrown back, beneath a black crucifix inclined toward her, and stiff curtains which were less white than her face. Madame Aubain lay at the foot of the couch, clasping it with her arms and uttering groans of agony. The Mother Superior was standing on the right side of the bed.

The three candles on the bureau made red blurs, and the windows were dimmed by the fog outside. The nuns carried Madame Aubain from the room.

For two nights, Felicité never left the corpse. She would repeat the same prayers, sprinkle holy water over the sheets, get up, come back to the bed and contemplate the body. At the end of the first vigil, she noticed that the face had taken on a yellow tinge, the lips grew blue, the nose grew pinched, the eyes were sunken. She kissed them several times and would not have been greatly astonished had Virginia opened them; to souls like these the supernatural is always quite simple. She washed her, wrapped her in a shroud, put her into the casket, laid a wreath of flowers on her head and arranged her curls. They were blond and of an extraordinary length for her age. Felicité cut off a big lock and put half of it into her bosom, resolving never to part with it.

The body was taken to Pont-l'Eveque, according to Madame Aubain's wishes; she followed the hearse in a closed carriage.

After the ceremony it took three quarters of an hour to reach the cemetery. Paul, sobbing, headed the procession; Monsieur Bourais followed, and then came the principal inhabitants of the town, the women covered with black capes, and Felicité. The memory of her nephew, and the thought that she had not been able to render him these honours, made her doubly unhappy, and she felt as if he were being buried with Virginia.

Madame Aubain's grief was uncontrollable. At first she rebelled against God, thinking that he was unjust to have taken away her child — she who had never done anything wrong, and whose conscience was so pure! But no! she ought to have taken her South. Other doctors would have saved her. She accused herself, prayed to be able to join her child, and cried in the midst of her dreams. Of the latter, one more especially haunted her. Her husband, dressed like a sailor, had come back from a long voyage, and with tears in his eyes told her that he had received the order to take Virginia away. Then they both consulted about a hiding-place.

Once she came in from the garden, all upset. A moment before (and she showed the place), the father and daughter had appeared to her, one after the other; they did nothing but look at her.

During several months she remained inert in her room. Felicité scolded her gently; she must keep up for her son and also for the other one, for "her memory."

"Her memory!" replied Madame Aubain, as if she were just awakening, "Oh! yes, yes, you do not forget her!" This was an allusion to the cemetery where she had been expressly forbidden to go.

But Felicité went there every day. At four o'clock exactly, she would go through the town, climb the hill, open the gate and arrive at Virginia's tomb. It was a small column of pink marble with a flat stone at its base, and it was surrounded by a little plot enclosed by chains. The flower-beds were bright with blossoms. Felicité watered their leaves, renewed the gravel, and knelt on the ground in order to till the earth properly. When Madame Aubain was able to visit the cemetery she felt very much relieved and consoled.

Years passed, all alike and marked by no other events than the return of the great church holidays: Easter, Assumption, All Saints' Day. Household happenings constituted the only data to which in later years they often referred. Thus, in 1825, workmen painted the vestibule; in 1827, a portion of the roof almost killed a man by falling into the yard. In the summer of 1828, it was Madame's turn to offer the hallowed bread; at that time, Bourais disappeared mysteriously; and the old acquaintances, Guyot, Liebard, Madame Lechaptois, Robelin, old Gremanville, paralyzed since a long time, passed away one by one. One night, the driver of the mail in Pont-l'Eveque announced the Revolution of July. A few days afterward a new sub-prefect was nominated, the Baron de Larsonniere, ex-consul in America, who, besides his wife, had his sister-in-law and her three grown daughters with him. They were often seen on their lawn, dressed in loose blouses, and they had a parrot and a negro servant. Madame Aubain received a call, which she returned promptly. As soon as she caught sight of them, Felicité would run and notify her mistress. But only one thing was capable of arousing her: a letter from her son.

He could not follow any profession as he was absorbed in drinking. His mother paid his debts and he made fresh ones; and the sighs that she heaved while she knitted at the window reached the ears of Felicité who was spinning in the kitchen.

They walked in the garden together, always speaking of Virginia, and asking each other if such and such a thing would have pleased her, and what she would probably have said on this or that occasion.

All her little belongings were put away in a closet of the room which held the two little beds. But Madame Aubain looked them over as little as possible. One summer day, however, she resigned herself to the task and when she opened the closet the moths flew out.

Virginia's frocks were hung under a shelf where there were three dolls, some hoops, a doll-house, and a basin which she had used. Felicité and Madame Aubain also took out the skirts, the handkerchiefs, and the stockings and spread them on the beds, before putting them away again. The sun fell on the piteous things, disclosing their spots and the creases formed by the motions of the body. The atmosphere was warm and blue, and a blackbird trilled in the garden; everything seemed to live in happiness. They found a little hat of soft brown plush, but it was entirely moth-eaten. Felicité asked for it. Their eyes met and filled with tears; at last the mistress opened her arms and the servant threw herself against her breast and they hugged each other and giving vent to their grief in a kiss which equalized them for a moment.

It was the first time that this had ever happened, for Madame Aubain was not of an expansive nature. Felicité was as grateful for it as if it had been some favour, and thenceforth loved her with animal-like devotion and a religious veneration.

Her kind-heartedness developed. When she heard the drums of a marching regiment passing through the street, she would stand in the doorway with a jug of cider and give the soldiers a drink. She nursed cholera victims. She protected Polish refugees, and one of them even declared that he wished to marry her. But they quarreled, for one morning when she returned from the Angelus she found him in the kitchen coolly eating a dish which he had prepared for himself during her absence.

After the Polish refugees, came Colmiche, an old man who was credited with having committed frightful misdeeds in '93. He lived near the river in the ruins of a pig-sty. The urchins peeped at him through the cracks in the walls and threw stones that fell on his miserable bed, where he lay gasping with catarrh, with long hair, inflamed eyelids, and a tumour as big as his head on one arm.

She got him some linen, tried to clean his hovel and dreamed of installing him in the bake-house without his being in Madame's way. When the cancer broke, she dressed it every day; sometimes she brought him some cake and placed him in the sun on a bundle of hay; and the poor old creature, trembling and drooling, would thank her in his broken voice, and put out his hands whenever she left him. Finally he died; and she had a mass said for the repose of his soul.

That day a great joy came to her: at dinner-time, Madame de Larsonniere's servant called with the parrot, the cage, and the perch and chain and lock. A note from the baroness told Madame Aubain that as her husband had been promoted to a prefecture, they were leaving that night, and she begged her to accept the bird as a remembrance and a token of her esteem.

Since a long time the parrot had been on Felicité's mind, because he came from America, which reminded her of Victor, and she had approached the negro on the subject.

Once even, she had said:

"How glad Madame would be to have him!"

The man had repeated this remark to his mistress who, not being able to keep the bird, took this means of getting rid of it.

# CHAPTER IV
## THE BIRD

He was called Loulou. His body was green, his head blue, the tips of his wings were pink and his breast was golden.

But he had the tiresome tricks of biting his perch, pulling his feathers out, scattering refuse and spilling the water of his bath. Madame Aubain grew tired of him and gave him to Felicité for good.

She undertook his education, and soon he was able to repeat: "Pretty boy! Your servant, sir! I salute you, Marie!" His perch was placed near the door and several persons were astonished that he did not answer to the name of "Jacquot," for every parrot is called Jacquot. They called him a goose and a log, and these taunts were like so many dagger thrusts to Felicité. Strange stubbornness of the bird which would not talk when people watched him!

Nevertheless, he sought society; for on Sunday, when the ladies Rochefeuille, Monsieur de Houppeville and the new habitués, Onfroy, the chemist, Monsieur Varin and Captain Mathieu, dropped in for their game of cards, he struck the window-panes with his wings and made such a racket that it was impossible to talk.

Bourais' face must have appeared very funny to Loulou. As soon as he saw him he would begin to roar. His voice re-echoed in the yard, and the neighbours would come to the windows and begin to laugh, too; and in order that the parrot might not see him, Monsieur Bourais edged along the wall, pushed his hat over his eyes to hide his profile, and entered by the garden door, and the looks he gave the bird lacked affection. Loulou, having thrust his head into the butcher-boy's basket, received a slap, and from that time he always tried to nip his enemy. Fabu threatened to wring his neck, although he was not cruelly inclined, notwithstanding his big whiskers and tattooings. On the contrary, he rather liked the bird and, out of deviltry, tried to teach him oaths. Felicité, whom his manner alarmed, put Loulou in the kitchen, took off his chain and let him walk all over the house.

When he went downstairs, he rested his beak on the steps, lifted his right foot and then his left one; but his mistress feared that such feats would give him vertigo. He became ill and was unable to eat. There was a small growth under his tongue like those chickens are sometimes afflicted with. Felicité pulled it off with her nails and cured him. One day, Paul was imprudent enough to blow the smoke of his cigar in his face; another time, Madame Lormeau was teasing him with the tip of her umbrella and he swallowed the tip. Finally he got lost.

She had put him on the grass to cool him and went away only for a second; when she returned, she found no parrot! She hunted among the bushes, on the bank of the river, and on the roofs, without paying any attention to Madame Aubain who screamed at her: "Take care! you must be insane!" Then she searched every garden in Pont-l'Eveque and stopped the passers-by to inquire of them: "Haven't you perhaps seen my parrot?" To those who had never seen the parrot, she described him minutely. Suddenly she thought she saw something green fluttering behind the mills at the foot of the hill. But when she was at the top of the hill she could not see it. A hod-carrier told her that he had just seen the bird in Saint-Melaine, in Mother Simon's store. She rushed to the place. The people did not know what she was talking about. At last she came home, exhausted, with her slippers worn to shreds, and despair in her heart. She sat down on the bench near Madame and was telling of her search when presently a light weight dropped on her shoulder — Loulou! What the deuce had he been doing? Perhaps he had just taken a little walk around the town!

She did not easily forget her scare, in fact, she never got over it. In consequence of a cold, she caught a sore throat; and some time afterward she had an earache. Three years later she was stone deaf, and spoke in a very loud voice even in church. Although her sins might have been proclaimed throughout the diocese without any shame to herself, or ill effects to the community, the cure thought it advisable to receive her confession in the vestry-room.

344

Imaginary buzzings also added to her bewilderment. Her mistress often said to her: "My goodness, how stupid you are!" and she would answer: "Yes, Madame," and look for something.

The narrow circle of her ideas grew more restricted than it already was; the bellowing of the oxen, the chime of the bells no longer reached her intelligence. All things moved silently, like ghosts. Only one noise penetrated her ears: the parrot's voice.

As if to divert her mind, he reproduced for her the tick-tack of the spit in the kitchen, the shrill cry of the fish-vendors, the saw of the carpenter who had a shop opposite, and when the door-bell rang, he would imitate Madame Aubain: "Felicité! go to the front door."

They held conversations together, Loulou repeating the three phrases of his repertory over and over, Felicité replying by words that had no greater meaning, but in which she poured out her feelings. In her isolation, the parrot was almost a son, a lover. He climbed upon her fingers, pecked at her lips, clung to her shawl, and when she rocked her head to and fro like a nurse, the big wings of her cap and the wings of the bird flapped in unison. When clouds gathered on the horizon and the thunder rumbled, Loulou would scream, perhaps because he remembered the storms in his native forests. The dripping of the rain would excite him to frenzy; he flapped around, struck the ceiling with his wings, upset everything, and would finally fly into the garden to play. Then he would come back into the room, light on one of the andirons, and hop around in order to get dry.

One morning during the terrible winter of 1837, when she had put him in front of the fire-place on account of the cold, she found him dead in his cage, hanging to the wire bars with his head down. He had probably died of congestion. But she believed that he had been poisoned, and although she had no proofs whatever, her suspicion rested on Fabu.

She wept so sorely that her mistress said: "Why don't you have him stuffed?"

She asked the advice of the chemist, who had always been kind to the bird.

He wrote to Havre for her. A certain man named Fellacher consented to do the work. But, as the diligence driver often lost parcels entrusted to him, Felicité resolved to take her pet to Honfleur herself.

Leafless apple-trees lined the edges of the road. The ditches were covered with ice. The dogs on the neighbouring farms barked; and Felicité, with her hands beneath her cape, her little black sabots and her basket, trotted along nimbly in the middle of the sidewalk. She crossed the forest, passed by the Haut-Chene and reached Saint-Gatien.

Behind her, in a cloud of dust and impelled by the steep incline, a mail-coach drawn by galloping horses advanced like a whirlwind. When he saw a woman in the middle of the road, who did not get out of the way, the driver stood up in his seat and shouted to her and so did the postilion, while the four horses, which he could not hold back, accelerated their pace; the two leaders were almost upon her; with a jerk of the reins he threw them to one side, but, furious at the incident, he lifted his big whip and lashed her from her head to her feet with such violence that she fell to the ground unconscious.

Her first thought, when she recovered her senses, was to open the basket. Loulou was unharmed. She felt a sting on her right cheek; when she took her hand away it was red, for the blood was flowing.

She sat down on a pile of stones, and sopped her cheek with her handkerchief; then she ate a crust of bread she had put in her basket, and consoled herself by looking at the bird.

Arriving at the top of Ecquemanville, she saw the lights of Honfleur shining in the distance like so many stars; further on, the ocean spread out in a confused mass. Then a weakness came over her; the misery of her childhood, the disappointment of her first love, the departure of her nephew, the death of Virginia; all these things came back to her at once, and, rising like a swelling tide in her throat, almost choked her.

Then she wished to speak to the captain of the vessel, and without stating what she was sending, she gave him some instructions.

Fellacher kept the parrot a long time. He always promised that it would be ready for the following week; after six months he announced the shipment of a case, and that was the end of it. Really, it seemed as if Loulou would never come back to his home. "They have stolen him," thought Felicité.

Finally he arrived, sitting bolt upright on a branch which could be screwed into a mahogany pedestal, with his foot in the air, his head on one side, and in his beak a nut which the naturalist, from love of the sumptuous, had gilded. She put him in her room.

This place, to which only a chosen few were admitted, looked like a chapel and a second-hand shop, so filled was it with devotional and heterogeneous things. The door could not be opened easily on account of the presence of a large wardrobe. Opposite the window that looked out into the garden, a bull's-eye opened on the yard; a table was placed by the cot and held a washbasin, two combs, and a piece of blue soap in a broken saucer. On the walls were rosaries, medals, a number of Holy Virgins, and a holy-water basin made out of a cocoanut; on the bureau, which was covered with a napkin like an altar, stood the box of shells that Victor had given her; also a watering-can and a balloon, writing-books, the engraved geography and a pair of shoes; on the nail which held the mirror, hung Virginia's little plush hat! Felicité carried this sort of respect so far that she even kept one of Monsieur's old coats. All the things which Madame Aubain discarded, Felicité begged for her own room. Thus, she had artificial flowers on the edge of the bureau, and the picture of the Comte d'Artois in the recess of the window. By means of a board, Loulou was set on a portion of the chimney which advanced into the room. Every morning when she awoke, she saw him in the dim light of dawn and recalled bygone days and the smallest details of insignificant actions, without any sense of bitterness or grief.

As she was unable to communicate with people, she lived in a sort of somnambulistic torpor. The processions of Corpus-Christi Day seemed to wake her up. She visited the neighbours to beg for candlesticks and mats so as to adorn the temporary altars in the street.

In church, she always gazed at the Holy Ghost, and noticed that there was something about it that resembled a parrot. The likeness appeared even more striking on a coloured picture by Espinal, representing the baptism of our Saviour. With his scarlet wings and emerald body, it was really the image of Loulou. Having bought the picture, she hung it near the one of the Comte d'Artois so that she could take them in at one glance.

They associated in her mind, the parrot becoming sanctified through the neighbourhood of the Holy Ghost, and the latter becoming more lifelike in her eyes, and more comprehensible. In all probability the Father had never chosen as messenger a dove, as the latter has no voice, but rather one of Loulou's ancestors. And Felicité said her prayers in front of the coloured picture, though from time to time she turned slightly toward the bird.

She desired very much to enter in the ranks of the "Daughters of the Virgin." But Madame Aubain dissuaded her from it.

A most important event occurred: Paul's marriage.

After being first a notary's clerk, then in business, then in the customs, and a tax collector, and having even applied for a position in the administration of woods and forests, he had at last, when he was thirty-six years old, by a divine inspiration, found his vocation: registrature! and he displayed such a high ability that an inspector had offered him his daughter and his influence.

Paul, who had become quite settled, brought his bride to visit his mother.

But she looked down upon the customs of Pont-l'Eveque, put on airs, and hurt Felicité's feelings. Madame Aubain felt relieved when she left.

The following week they learned of Monsieur Bourais' death in an inn. There were rumours of suicide, which were confirmed; doubts concerning his integrity arose. Madame Aubain looked over her accounts and soon discovered his numerous embezzlements; sales of wood which had been concealed from her, false receipts, etc. Furthermore, he had an illegitimate child, and entertained a friendship for "a person in Dozule."

These base actions affected her very much. In March, 1853, she developed a pain in her chest; her tongue looked as if it were coated with smoke, and the leeches they applied did not relieve her oppression; and on the ninth evening she died, being just seventy-two years old.

People thought that she was younger, because her hair, which she wore in bands framing her pale face, was brown. Few friends regretted her loss, for her manner was so haughty that she did not attract them. Felicité mourned for her as servants seldom mourn for their masters. The fact that Madame should die before herself perplexed her mind and seemed contrary to the order of things, and absolutely monstrous and inadmissible. Ten days later (the time to journey from Besancon), the heirs arrived. Her daughter-in-law ransacked the drawers, kept some of the furniture, and sold the rest; then they went back to their own home.

Madame's armchair, foot-warmer, work-table, the eight chairs, everything was gone! The places occupied by the pictures formed yellow squares on the walls. They had taken the two little beds, and the wardrobe had been emptied of Virginia's belongings! Felicité went upstairs, overcome with grief.

The following day a sign was posted on the door; the chemist screamed in her ear that the house was for sale.

For a moment she tottered, and had to sit down.

What hurt her most was to give up her room, — so nice for poor Loulou! She looked at him in despair and implored the Holy Ghost, and it was this way that she contracted the idolatrous habit of saying her prayers kneeling in front of the bird. Sometimes the sun fell through the window on his glass eye, and lighted a great spark in it which sent Felicité into ecstasy.

349

Her mistress had left her an income of three hundred and eighty francs. The garden supplied her with vegetables. As for clothes, she had enough to last her till the end of her days, and she economized on the light by going to bed at dusk.

She rarely went out, in order to avoid passing in front of the second-hand dealer's shop where there was some of the old furniture. Since her fainting spell, she dragged her leg, and as her strength was failing rapidly, old Mother Simon, who had lost her money in the grocery business, came every morning to chop the wood and pump the water.

Her eyesight grew dim. She did not open the shutters after that. Many years passed. But the house did not sell or rent. Fearing that she would be put out, Felicité did not ask for repairs. The laths of the roof were rotting away, and during one whole winter her bolster was wet. After Easter she spit blood.

Then Mother Simon went for a doctor. Felicité wished to know what her complaint was. But, being too deaf to hear, she caught only one word: "Pneumonia." She was familiar with it and gently answered: — "Ah! like Madame," thinking it quite natural that she should follow her mistress.

The time for the altars in the street drew near.

The first one was always erected at the foot of the hill, the second in front of the post-office, and the third in the middle of the street. This position occasioned some rivalry among the women and they finally decided upon Madame Aubain's yard.

Felicité's fever grew worse. She was sorry that she could not do anything for the altar. If she could, at least, have contributed something toward it! Then she thought of the parrot. Her neighbours objected that it would not be proper. But the cure gave his consent and she was so grateful for it that she begged him to accept after her death, her only treasure, Loulou. From Tuesday until Saturday, the day before the event, she coughed more frequently. In the evening her face was contracted, her lips stuck to her gums and she began to vomit; and on the following day, she felt so low that she called for a priest.

Three neighbours surrounded her when the dominie administered the Extreme Unction. Afterwards she said that she wished to speak to Fabu.

He arrived in his Sunday clothes, very ill at ease among the funereal surroundings.

"Forgive me," she said, making an effort to extend her arm, "I believed it was you who killed him!"

What did such accusations mean? Suspect a man like him of murder! And Fabu became excited and was about to make trouble.

"Don't you see she is not in her right mind?"

From time to time Felicité spoke to shadows. The women left her and Mother Simon sat down to breakfast.

A little later, she took Loulou and holding him up to Felicité:

"Say good-bye to him, now!" she commanded.

Although he was not a corpse, he was eaten up by worms; one of his wings was broken and the wadding was coming out of his body. But Felicité was blind now, and she took him and laid him against her cheek. Then Mother Simon removed him in order to set him on the altar.

# CHAPTER V
## THE VISION

The grass exhaled an odour of summer; flies buzzed in the air, the sun shone on the river and warmed the slated roof. Old Mother Simon had returned to Felicité and was peacefully falling asleep.

The ringing of bells woke her; the people were coming out of church. Felicité's delirium subsided. By thinking of the procession, she was able to see it as if she had taken part in it. All the school-children, the singers and the firemen walked on the sidewalks, while in the middle of the street came first the custodian of the church with his halberd, then the beadle with a large cross, the teacher in charge of the boys and a sister escorting the little girls; three of the smallest ones, with curly heads, threw rose leaves into the air; the deacon with outstretched arms conducted the music; and two incense-bearers turned with each step they took toward the Holy Sacrament, which was carried by M. le Cure, attired in his handsome chasuble and walking under a canopy of red velvet supported by four men. A crowd of people followed, jammed between the walls of the houses hung with white sheets; at last the procession arrived at the foot of the hill.

A cold sweat broke out on Felicité's forehead. Mother Simon wiped it away with a cloth, saying inwardly that some day she would have to go through the same thing herself.

The murmur of the crowd grew louder, was very distinct for a moment and then died away. A volley of musketry shook the window-panes. It was the postilions saluting the Sacrament.

Felicité rolled her eyes and said as loudly as she could:

"Is he all right?" meaning the parrot.

Her death agony began. A rattle that grew more and more rapid shook her body. Froth appeared at the corners of her mouth, and her whole frame trembled. In a little while could be heard the music of the bass horns, the clear voices of the children and the men's deeper notes. At intervals all was still, and their shoes sounded like a herd of cattle passing over the grass.

The clergy appeared in the yard. Mother Simon climbed on a chair to reach the bull's-eye, and in this manner could see the altar. It was covered with a lace cloth and draped with green wreaths. In the middle stood a little frame containing relics; at the corners were two little orange-trees, and all along the edge were silver candlesticks, porcelain vases containing sun-flowers, lilies, peonies, and tufts of hydrangeas. This mound of bright colours descended diagonally from the first floor to the carpet that covered the sidewalk. Rare objects arrested one's eye. A golden sugar-bowl was crowned with violets, earrings set with Alencon stones were displayed on green moss, and two Chinese screens with their bright landscapes were near by. Loulou, hidden beneath roses, showed nothing but his blue head which looked like a piece of lapis-lazuli.

The singers, the canopy-bearers and the children lined up against the sides of the yard. Slowly the priest ascended the steps and placed his shining sun on the lace cloth. Everybody knelt. There was deep silence; and the censers slipping on their chains were swung high in the air. A blue vapour rose in Felicité's room. She opened her nostrils and inhaled it with a mystic sensuousness; then she closed her lids. Her lips smiled. The beats of her heart grew fainter and fainter, and vaguer, like a fountain giving out, like an echo dying away; — and when she exhaled her last breath, she thought she saw in the half-opened heavens a gigantic parrot hovering above her head.

# JEAN GOURDON'S FOUR DAYS
## BY EMILE ZOLA

## SPRING

On that particular day, at about five o'clock in the morning, the sun entered with delightful abruptness into the little room I occupied at the house of my uncle Lazare, parish priest of the hamlet of Dourgues. A broad yellow ray fell upon ray closed eyelids, and I awoke in light.

My room, which was whitewashed, and had deal furniture, was full of attractive gaiety. I went to the window and gazed at the Durance, which traced its broad course amidst the dark green verdure of the valley. Fresh puffs of wind caressed my face, and the murmur of the trees and river seemed to call me to them.

I gently opened my door. To get out I had to pass through my uncle's room. I proceeded on tip-toe, fearing the creaking of my thick boots might awaken the worthy man, who was still slumbering with a smiling countenance. And I trembled at the sound of the church bell tolling the Angelus. For some days past my uncle Lazare had been following me about everywhere, looking sad and annoyed. He would perhaps have prevented me going over there to the edge of the river, and hiding myself among the willows on the bank, so as to watch for Babet passing, that tall dark girl who had come with the spring.

But my uncle was sleeping soundly. I felt something like remorse in deceiving him and running away in this manner. I stayed for an instant and gazed on his calm countenance, with its gentle expression enhanced by rest, and I recalled to mind with feeling the day when he had come to fetch me in the chilly and deserted home which my mother's funeral was leaving. Since that day, what tenderness, what devotedness, what good advice he had bestowed on me! He had given me his knowledge and his kindness, all his intelligence and all his heart.

I was tempted for a moment to cry out to him:

"Get up, uncle Lazare! let us go for a walk together along that path you are so fond of beside the Durance. You will enjoy the fresh air and morning sun. You will see what an appetite you will have on your return!"

And Babet, who was going down to the river in her light morning gown, and whom I should not be able to see! My uncle would be there, and I would have to lower my eyes. It must be so nice under the willows, lying flat on one's stomach, in the fine grass! I felt a languid feeling creeping over me, and, slowly, taking short steps, holding my breath, I reached the door. I went downstairs, and began running like a madcap in the delightful, warm May morning air.

The sky was quite white on the horizon, with exquisitely delicate blue and pink tints. The pale sun seemed like a great silver lamp, casting a shower of bright rays into the Durance. And the broad, sluggish river, expanding lazily over the red sand, extended from one end of the valley to the other, like a stream of liquid metal. To the west, a line of low rugged hills threw slight violet streaks on the pale sky.

I had been living in this out-of-the-way corner for ten years. How often had I kept my uncle Lazare waiting to give me my Latin lesson! The worthy man wanted to make me learned. But I was on the other side of the Durance, ferreting out magpies, discovering a hill which I had not yet climbed. Then, on my return, there were remonstrances: the Latin was forgotten, my poor uncle scolded me for having torn my trousers, and he shuddered when he noticed sometimes that the skin underneath was cut. The valley was mine, really mine; I had conquered it with my legs, and I was the real landlord by right of friendship. And that bit of river, those two leagues of the Durance, how I loved them, how well we understood one another when together! I knew all the whims of my dear stream, its anger, its charming ways, its different features at each hour of the day.

When I reached the water's edge on that particular morning, I felt something like giddiness at seeing it so gentle and so white. It had never looked so gay. I slipped rapidly beneath the willows, to an open space where a broad patch of sunlight fell on the dark grass. There I laid me down on my stomach, listening, watching the pathway by which Babet would come, through the branches.

"Oh! how sound uncle Lazare must be sleeping!" I thought.

And I extended myself at full length on the moss. The sun struck gentle heat into my back, whilst my breast, buried in the grass, was quite cool.

Have you never examined the turf, at close quarters, with your eyes on the blades of grass? Whilst I was waiting for Babet, I pried indiscreetly into a tuft which was really a whole world. In my bunch of grass there were streets, cross roads, public squares, entire cities. At the bottom of it, I distinguished a great dark patch where the shoots of the previous spring were decaying sadly, then slender stalks were growing up, stretching out, bending into a multitude of elegant forms, and producing frail colonnades, churches, virgin forests. I saw two lean insects wandering in the midst of this immensity; the poor children were certainly lost, for they went from colonnade to colonnade, from street to street, in an affrighted, anxious way.

It was just at this moment that, on raising my eyes, I saw Babet's white skirts standing out against the dark ground at the top of the pathway. I recognized her printed calico gown, which was grey, with small blue flowers. I sunk down deeper in the grass, I heard my heart thumping against the earth and almost raising me with slight jerks. My breast was burning now, I no longer felt the freshness of the dew.

The young girl came nimbly down the pathway, her skirts skimming the ground with a swinging motion that charmed me, I saw her at full length, quite erect, in her proud and happy gracefulness. She had no idea I was there behind the willows; she walked with a light step, she ran without giving a thought to the wind, which slightly raised her gown. I could distinguish her feet, trotting along quickly, quickly, and a piece of her white stockings, which was perhaps as large as one's hand, and which made me blush in a manner that was alike sweet and painful.

Oh! then, I saw nothing else, neither the Durance, nor the willows, nor the whiteness of the sky. What cared I for the valley! It was no longer my sweetheart; I was quite indifferent to its joy and its sadness. What cared I for my friends, the stories, and the trees on the hills! The river could run away all at once if it liked; I would not have regretted it.

And the spring, I did not care a bit about the spring! Had it borne away the sun that warmed my back, its leaves, its rays, all its May morning, I should have remained there, in ecstasy, gazing at Babet, running along the pathway, and swinging her skirts deliciously. For Babet had taken the valley's place in my heart, Babet was the spring, I had never spoken to her. Both of us blushed when we met one another in my uncle Lazare's church. I could have vowed she detested me.

She talked on that particular day for a few minutes with the women who were washing. The sound of her pearly laughter reached as far as me, mingled with the loud voice of the Durance. Then she stooped down to take a little water in the hollow of her hand; but the bank was high, and Babet, who was on the point of slipping, saved herself by clutching the grass. I gave a frightful shudder, which made my blood run cold. I rose hastily, and, without feeling ashamed, without reddening, ran to the young girl. She cast a startled look at me; then she began to smile. I bent down, at the risk of falling. I succeeded in filling my right hand with water by keeping my fingers close together. And I presented this new sort of cup to Babet' asking her to drink.

The women who were washing laughed. Babet, confused, did not dare accept; she hesitated, and half turned her head away. At last she made up her mind, and delicately pressed her lips to the tips of my fingers; but she had waited too long, all the water had run away. Then she burst out laughing, she became a child again, and I saw very well that she was making fun of me.

I was very silly. I bent forward again. This time I took the water in both hands and hastened to put them to Babet's lips. She drank, and I felt the warm kiss from her mouth run up my arms to my breast, which it filled with heat.

357

"Oh! how my uncle must sleep!" I murmured to myself.

Just as I said that, I perceived a dark shadow beside me, and, having turned round, I saw my uncle Lazare, in person, a few paces away, watching Babet and me as if offended. His cassock appeared quite white in the sun; in his look I saw reproaches which made me feel inclined to cry.

Babet was very much afraid. She turned quite red, and hurried off stammering:

"Thanks, Monsieur Jean, I thank you very much."

As for me, wiping my wet hands, I stood motionless and confused before my uncle Lazare.

The worthy man, with folded arms, and bringing back a corner of his cassock, watched Babet, who was running up the pathway without turning her head. Then, when she had disappeared behind the hedges, he lowered his eyes to me, and I saw his pleasant countenance smile sadly.

"Jean," he said to me, "come into the broad walk. Breakfast is not ready. We have half an hour to spare."

He set out with his rather heavy tread, avoiding the tufts of grass wet with dew. A part of the bottom of his cassock that was dragging along the ground, made a dull crackling sound. He held his breviary under his arm; but he had forgotten his morning lecture, and he advanced dreamily, with bowed head, and without uttering a word.

His silence tormented me. He was generally so talkative. My anxiety increased at each step. He had certainly seen me giving Babet water to drink. What a sight, O Lord! The young girl, laughing and blushing, kissed the tips of my fingers, whilst I, standing on tip-toe, stretching out my arms, was leaning forward as if to kiss her. My action now seemed to me frightfully audacious. And all my timidity returned. I inquired of myself how I could have dared to have my fingers kissed so sweetly.

And my uncle Lazare, who said nothing, who continued walking with short steps in front of me, without giving a single glance at the old trees he loved! He was assuredly preparing a sermon. He was only taking me into the broad walk to scold me at his ease. It would occupy at least an hour: breakfast would get cold, and I would be unable to return to the water's edge and dream of the warm burns that Babet's lips had left on my hands.

We were in the broad walk. This walk, which was wide and short, ran beside the river; it was shaded by enormous oak trees, with trunks lacerated by seams, stretching out their great, tall branches. The fine grass spread like a carpet beneath the trees, and the sun, riddling the foliage, embroidered this carpet with a rosaceous pattern in gold. In the distance, all around, extended raw green meadows.

My uncle went to the bottom of the walk, without altering his step and without turning round. Once there, he stopped, and I kept beside him, understanding that the terrible moment had arrived.

The river made a sharp curve; a low parapet at the end of the walk formed a sort of terrace. This vault of shade opened on a valley of light. The country expanded wide before us, for several leagues. The sun was rising in the heavens, where the silvery rays of morning had become transformed into a stream of gold; blinding floods of light ran from the horizon, along the hills, and spread out into the plain with the glare of fire.

After a moment's silence, my uncle Lazare turned towards me.

"Good heavens, the sermon!" I thought, and I bowed my head. My uncle pointed out the valley to me, with an expansive gesture; then, drawing himself up, he said, slowly:

"Look, Jean, there is the spring. The earth is full of joy, my boy, and I have brought you here, opposite this plain of light, to show you the first smiles of the young season. Observe what brilliancy and sweetness! Warm perfumes rise from the country and pass across our faces like puffs of life."

He was silent and seemed dreaming. I had raised my head, astonished, breathing at ease. My uncle was not preaching.

"It is a beautiful morning," he continued, "a morning of youth. Your eighteen summers find full enjoyment amidst this verdure which is at most eighteen days old. All is great brightness and perfume, is it not? The broad valley seems to you a delightful place: the river is there to give you its freshness, the trees to lend you their shade, the whole country to speak to you of tenderness, the heavens themselves to kiss those horizons that you are searching with hope and desire. The spring belongs to fellows of your age. It is it that teaches the boys how to give young girls to drink — "

I hung my head again. My uncle Lazare had certainly seen me.

"An old fellow like me," he continued, "unfortunately knows what trust to place in the charms of spring. I, my poor Jean, I love the Durance because it waters these meadows and gives life to all the valley; I love this young foliage because it proclaims to me the coming of the fruits of summer and autumn; I love this sky because it is good to us, because its warmth hastens the fecundity of the earth. I should have had to tell you this one day or other; I prefer telling it you now, at this early hour. It is spring itself that is giving you the lesson. The earth is a vast workshop wherein there is never a slack season. Observe this flower at our feet; to you it is perfume; to me it is labour, it accomplishes its task by producing its share of life, a little black seed which will work in its turn, next spring. And, now, search the vast horizon. All this joy is but the act of generation. If the country be smiling, it is because it is beginning the everlasting task again. Do you hear it now, breathing hard, full of activity and haste? The leaves sigh, the flowers are in a hurry, the corn grows without pausing; all the plants, all the herbs are quarrelling as to which shall spring up the quickest; and the running water, the river comes to assist in the common labour, and the young sun which rises in the heavens is entrusted with the duty of enlivening the everlasting task of the labourers."

At this point my uncle made me look him straight in the face. He concluded in these terms:

"Jean, you hear what your friend the spring says to you. He is youth, but he is preparing ripe age; his bright smile is but the gaiety of labour. Summer will be powerful, autumn bountiful, for

360

the spring is singing at this moment, while courageously performing its work."

I looked very stupid. I understood my uncle Lazare. He was positively preaching me a sermon, in which he told me I was an idle fellow and that the time had come to work.

My uncle appeared as much embarrassed as myself. After having hesitated for some instants he said, slightly stammering:

"Jean, you were wrong not to have come and told me all — as you love Babet and Babet loves you — "

"Babet loves me!" I exclaimed.

My uncle made me an ill-humoured gesture.

"Eh! allow me to speak. I don't want another avowal. She owned it to me herself."

"She owned that to you, she owned that to you!"

And I suddenly threw my arms round my uncle Lazare's neck.

"Oh! how nice that is!" I added. "I had never spoken to her, truly. She told you that at the confessional, didn't she? I would never have dared ask her if she loved me, and I would never have known anything. Oh! how I thank you!"

My uncle Lazare was quite red. He felt that he had just committed a blunder. He had imagined that this was not my first meeting with the young girl, and here he gave me a certainty, when as yet I only dared dream of a hope. He held his tongue now; it was I who spoke with volubility.

"I understand all," I continued. "You are right, I must work to win Babet. But you will see how courageous I shall be. Ah! how good you are, my uncle Lazare, and how well you speak! I understand what the spring says: I, also, will have a powerful summer and an autumn of abundance. One is well placed here, one sees all the valley; I am young like it, I feel youth within me demanding to accomplish its task — "

My uncle calmed me.

"Very good, Jean," he said to me. "I had long hoped to make a priest of you, and I imparted to you my knowledge with that sole aim. But what I saw this morning at the waterside compels me to definitely give up my fondest hope. It is Heaven that disposes of us. You will love the Almighty in another way. You cannot now remain in this village, and I only wish you to return when ripened by age and work. I have chosen the trade of printer for you; your education will serve you. One of my friends, who is a printer at Grenoble, is expecting you next Monday."

I felt anxious.

"And I shall come back and marry Babet?" I inquired.

My uncle smiled imperceptibly; and, without answering in a direct manner, said:

"The remainder is the will of Heaven."

"You are heaven, and I have faith in your kindness. Oh! uncle, see that Babet does not forget me. I will work for her."

Then my uncle Lazare again pointed out to me the valley which the warm golden light was overspreading more and more.

"There is hope," he said to me. "Do not be as old as I am, Jean. Forget my sermon, be as ignorant as this land. It does not trouble about the autumn; it is all engrossed with the joy of its smile; it labours, courageously and without a care. It hopes."

And we returned to the parsonage, strolling along slowly in the grass, which was scorched by the sun, and chatting with concern of our approaching separation.

Breakfast was cold, as I had foreseen; but that did not trouble me much. I had tears in my eyes each time I looked at my uncle Lazare. And, at the thought of Babet, my heart beat fit to choke me.

I do not remember what I did during the remainder of the day. I think I went and lay down under the willows at the riverside. My uncle was right, the earth was at work. On placing my ear to the grass I seemed to hear continual sounds. Then I dreamed of what my life would be. Buried in the grass until nightfall, I arranged an existence full of labour divided between Babet and my uncle Lazare. The energetic youthfulness of the soil had penetrated my breast, which I pressed with force against the common mother, and at times I imagined myself to be one of the strong willows that lived around me. In the evening I could not dine. My uncle, no doubt, understood the thoughts that were choking me, for he feigned not to notice my want of appetite. As soon as I was able to rise from table, I hastened to return and breathe the open air outside.

A fresh breeze rose from the river, the dull splashing of which I heard in the distance. A soft light fell from the sky. The valley expanded, peaceful and transparent, like a dark shoreless ocean. There were vague sounds in the air, a sort of impassioned tremor, like a great flapping of wings passing above my head. Penetrating perfumes rose with the cool air from the grass.

I had gone out to see Babet; I knew she came to the parsonage every night, and I went and placed myself in ambush behind a hedge. I had got rid of my timidness of the morning; I considered it quite natural to be waiting for her there, because she loved me and I had to tell her of my departure.

"When I perceived her skirts in the limpid night, I advanced noiselessly. Then I murmured in a low voice:

"Babet, Babet, I am here."

She did not recognize me, at first, and started with fright. When she discovered who it was, she seemed still more frightened, which very much surprised me.

"It's you, Monsieur Jean," she said to me. "What are you doing there? What do you want?"

I was beside her and took her hand.

"You love me fondly, do you not?"

"I! who told you that?"

"My uncle Lazare."

She stood there in confusion. Her hand began to tremble in mine. As she was on the point of running away, I took her other hand. We were face to face, in a sort of hollow in the hedge, and I felt Babet's panting breath running all warm over my face. The freshness of the air, the rustling silence of the night, hung around us.

"I don't know," stammered the young girl, "I never said that — his reverence the curé misunderstood — For mercy's sake, let me be, I am in a hurry."

363

"No, no," I continued, "I want you to know that I am going away to-morrow, and to promise to love me always."

"You are leaving to-morrow!"

Oh! that sweet cry, and how tenderly Babet uttered it! I seem still to hear her apprehensive voice full of affliction and love.

"You see," I exclaimed in my turn, "that my uncle Lazare said the truth. Besides, he never tells fibs. You love me, you love me, Babet! Your lips this morning confided the secret very softly to my fingers."

And I made her sit down at the foot of the hedge. My memory has retained my first chat of love in its absolute innocence. Babet listened to me like a little sister. She was no longer afraid, she told me the story of her love. And there were solemn sermons, ingenious avowals, projects without end. She vowed she would marry no one but me, I vowed to deserve her hand by labour and tenderness. There was a cricket behind the hedge, who accompanied our chat with his chaunt of hope, and all the valley, whispering in the dark, took pleasure in hearing us talk so softly.

On separating we forgot to kiss each other.

When I returned to my little room, it appeared to me that I had left it for at least a year. That day which was so short, seemed an eternity of happiness. It was the warmest and most sweetly-scented spring-day of my life, and the remembrance of it is now like the distant, faltering voice of my youth.

# II
## SUMMER

When I awoke at about three o'clock in the morning on that particular day, I was lying on the hard ground tired out, and with my face bathed in perspiration. The hot heavy atmosphere of a July night weighed me down.

My companions were sleeping around me, wrapped in their hooded cloaks; they speckled the grey ground with black, and the obscure plain panted; I fancied I heard the heavy breathing of a slumbering multitude. Indistinct sounds, the neighing of horses, the clash of arms rang out amidst the rustling silence.

The army had halted at about midnight, and we had received orders to lie down and sleep. We had been marching for three days, scorched by the sun and blinded by dust. The enemy were at length in front of us, over there, on those hills on the horizon. At daybreak a decisive battle would be fought.

I had been a victim to despondency. For three days I had been as if trampled on, without energy and without thought for the future. It was the excessive fatigue, indeed, that had just awakened me. Now, lying on my back, with my eyes wide open, I was thinking whilst gazing into the night, I thought of this battle, this butchery, which the sun was about to light up. For more than six years, at the first shot in each fight, I had been saying good-bye to those I loved the most fondly, Babet and uncle Lazare. And now, barely a month before my discharge, I had to say good-bye again, and this time perhaps for ever.

Then my thoughts softened. With closed eyelids I saw Babet and my uncle Lazare. How long it was since I had kissed them! I remembered the day of our separation; my uncle weeping because he was poor, and allowing me to leave like that, and Babet, in the evening, had vowed she would wait for me, and that she would never love another. I had had to quit all, my master at Grenoble, my friends at Dourgues. A few letters had come from time to time to tell me they always loved me, and that happiness was awaiting me in my well-beloved valley. And I, I was going to fight, I was going to get killed.

I began dreaming of my return. I saw my poor old uncle on the threshold of the parsonage extending his trembling arms; and behind him was Babet, quite red, smiling through her tears. I fell into their arms and kissed them, seeking for expressions —

Suddenly the beating of drums recalled me to stern reality. Daybreak had come, the grey plain expanded in the morning mist. The ground became full of life, indistinct forms appeared on all sides; a sound that became louder and louder filled the air; it was the call of bugles, the galloping of horses, the rumble of artillery, the shouting out of orders. War came threatening, amidst my dream of tenderness. I rose with difficulty; it seemed to me that my bones were broken, and that my head was about to split. I hastily got my men together; for I must tell you that I had won the rank of sergeant. We soon received orders to bear to the left and occupy a hillock above the plain.

As we were about to move, the sergeant-major came running along and shouting:

"A letter for Sergeant Gourdon!"

And he handed me a dirty crumpled letter, which had been lying perhaps for a week in the leather bags of the post-office. I had only just time to recognize the writing of my uncle Lazare.

"Forward, march!" shouted the major.

I had to march. For a few seconds I held the poor letter in my hand, devouring it with my eyes; it burnt my fingers; I would have given everything in the world to have sat down and wept at ease whilst reading it. I had to content myself with slipping it under my tunic against my heart.

I have never experienced such agony. By way of consolation I said to myself what my uncle had so often repeated to me: I was in the summer of my life, at the moment of the fierce struggle, and it was essential that I should perform my duty bravely, if I would have a peaceful and bountiful autumn. But these reasons exasperated me the more: this letter, which had come to speak to me of happiness, burnt my heart, which had revolted against the folly of war. And I could not even read it! I was perhaps going to die without knowing what it contained, without perusing my uncle Lazare's affectionate remarks for the last time.

We had reached the top of the hill. We were to await orders there to advance. The battle-field had been marvelously chosen to slaughter one another at ease. The immense plain expanded for several leagues, and was quite bare, without a house or tree. Hedges and bushes made slight spots on the whiteness of the ground. I have never since seen such a country, an ocean of dust, a chalky soil, bursting open here and there, and displaying its tawny bowels. And never either have I since witnessed a sky of such intense purity, a July day so lovely and so warm; at eight o'clock the sultry heat was already scorching our faces. O the splendid morning, and what a sterile plain to kill and die in!

Firing had broken out with irregular crackling sounds, a long time since, supported by the solemn growl of the cannon. The enemy, Austrians dressed in white, had quitted the heights, and the plain was studded with long files of men, who looked to me about as big as insects. One might have thought it was an ant-hill in insurrection. Clouds of smoke hung over the battle-field. At times, when these clouds broke asunder, I perceived soldiers in flight, smitten with terrified panic. Thus there were currents of fright which bore men away, and outbursts of shame and courage which brought them back under fire.

I could neither hear the cries of the wounded, nor see the blood flow. I could only distinguish the dead which the battalions left behind them, and which resembled black patches. I began to watch the movements of the troops with curiosity, irritated at the smoke which hid a good half of the show, experiencing a sort of egotistic pleasure at the knowledge that I was in security, whilst others were dying.

At about nine o'clock we were ordered to advance. We went down the hill at the double and proceeded towards the centre which was giving way. The regular beat of our footsteps appeared to me funeral-like. The bravest among us panting, pale and with haggard features.

I have made up my mind to tell the truth. At the first whistle of the bullets, the battalion suddenly came to a halt, tempted to fly.

"Forward, forward!" shouted the chiefs.

But we were riveted to the ground, bowing our heads when a bullet whistled by our ears. This movement is instinctive; if shame had not restrained me, I would have thrown myself flat on my stomach in the dust.

"Before us was a huge veil of smoke which we dared not penetrate. Red flashes passed through this smoke. And, shuddering, we still stood still. But the bullets reached us; soldiers fell with yells. The chiefs shouted louder:

"Forward, forward!"

The rear ranks, which they pushed on, compelled us to march. Then, closing our eyes, we made a fresh dash and entered the smoke.

We were seized with furious rage. When the cry of "Halt!" resounded, we experienced difficulty in coming to a standstill. As soon as one is motionless, fear returns and one feels a wish to run away. Firing commenced. We shot in front of us, without aiming, finding some relief in discharging bullets into the smoke. I remember I pulled my trigger mechanically, with lips firmly set together and eyes wide open; I was no longer afraid, for, to tell the truth, I no longer knew if I existed. The only idea I had in my head, was that I would continue firing until all was over. My companion on the left received a bullet full in the face and fell on me; I brutally pushed him away, wiping my cheek which he had drenched with blood. And I resumed firing.

I still remember having seen our colonel, M. de Montrevert, firm and erect upon his horse, gazing quietly towards the enemy. That man appeared to me immense. He had no rifle to amuse himself with, and his breast was expanded to its full breadth above us. From time to time, he looked down, and exclaimed in a dry voice:

"Close the ranks, close the ranks!"

We closed our ranks like sheep, treading on the dead, stupefied, and continuing firing. Until then, the enemy had only sent us bullets; a dull explosion was heard and a shell carried off five of our men. A battery which must have been opposite us and which we could not see, had just opened fire. The shells struck into the middle of us, almost at one spot, making a sanguinary gap which we closed unceasingly with the obstinacy of ferocious brutes.

"Close the ranks, close the ranks!" the colonel coldly repeated.

We were giving the cannon human flesh. Each time a soldier was struck down, I was taking a step nearer death, I was approaching the spot where the shells were falling heavily, crushing the men whose turn had come to die. The corpses were forming heaps in that place, and soon the shells would strike into nothing more than a mound of mangled flesh; shreds of limbs flew about at each fresh discharge. We could no longer close the ranks.

The soldiers yelled, the chiefs themselves were moved.

"With the bayonet, with the bayonet!"

And amidst a shower of bullets the battalion rushed in fury towards the shells. The veil of smoke was torn asunder; we perceived the enemy's battery flaming red, which was firing at us from the mouths of all its pieces, on the summit of a hillock. But the dash forward had commenced, the shells stopped the dead only.

I ran beside Colonel Montrevert, whose horse had just been killed, and who was fighting like a simple soldier. Suddenly I was struck down; it seemed to me as if my breast opened and my shoulder was taken away. A frightful wind passed over my face.

And I fell. The colonel fell beside me. I felt myself dying. I thought of those I loved, and fainted whilst searching with a withering hand for my uncle Lazare's letter.

When I came to myself again I was lying on my side in the dust. I was annihilated by profound stupor. I gazed before me with my eyes wide open without seeing anything; it seemed to me that I had lost my limbs, and that my brain was empty. I did not suffer, for life seemed to have departed from my flesh.

The rays of a hot implacable sun fell upon my face like molten lead. I did not feel it. Life returned to me little by little; my limbs became lighter, my shoulder alone remained crushed beneath an enormous weight. Then, with the instinct of a wounded animal, I wanted to sit up. I uttered a cry of pain, and fell back upon the ground.

But I lived now, I saw, I understood. The plain spread out naked and deserted, all white in the broad sunlight. It exhibited its desolation beneath the intense serenity of heaven; heaps of corpses were sleeping in the warmth, and the trees that had been brought down, seemed to be other dead who were dying. There was not a breath of air. A frightful silence came from those piles of inanimate bodies; then, at times, there were dismal groans which broke this silence, and conveyed a long tremor to it. Slender clouds of grey smoke hanging over the low hills on the horizon, was all that broke the bright blue of the sky. The butchery was continuing on the heights.

I imagined we were conquerors, and I experienced selfish pleasure in thinking I could die in peace on this deserted plain. Around me the earth was black. On raising my head I saw the enemy's battery on which we had charged, a few feet away from me. The struggle must have been horrible: the mound was covered with hacked and disfigured bodies; blood had flowed so abundantly that the dust seemed like a large red carpet. The cannon stretched out their dark muzzles above the corpses. I shuddered when I observed the silence of those guns.

Then gently, with a multitude of precautions, I succeeded in turning on my stomach. I rested my head on a large stone all splashed with gore, and drew my uncle Lazare's letter from my breast. I placed it before my eyes; but my tears prevented my reading it.

And whilst the sun was roasting me in the back, the acrid smell of blood was choking me. I could form an idea of the woeful plain around me, and was as if stiffened with the rigidness of the dead. My poor heart was weeping in the warm and loathsome silence of murder.

Uncle Lazare wrote to me:

"My Dear Boy, — I hear war has been declared; but I still hope you will get your discharge before the campaign opens. Every morning I beseech the Almighty to spare you new dangers; He will grant my prayer; He will, one of these days, let you close my eyes.

"Ah! my poor Jean, I am becoming old, I have great need of your arm. Since your departure I no more feel your youthfulness beside me, which gave me back my twenty summers. Do you remember our strolls in the morning along the oak-tree walk? Now I no longer dare to go beneath those trees; I am alone, I am afraid. The Durance weeps. Come quickly and console me, assuage my anxiety — — "

The tears were choking me, I could not continue. At that moment a heartrending cry was uttered a few steps away from me; I saw a soldier suddenly rise, with the muscles of his face contracted; he extended his arms in agony, and fell to the ground, where he writhed in frightful convulsions; then he ceased moving.

"I have placed my hope in the Almighty," continued my uncle, "He will bring you back safe and sound to Dourgues, and we will resume our peaceful existence. Let me dream out loud and tell you my plans for the future.

"You will go no more to Grenoble, you will remain with me; I will make my child a son of the soil, a peasant who shall live gaily whilst tilling the fields.

"And I will retire to your farm. In a short time my trembling hands will no longer be able to hold the Host. I only ask Heaven for two years of such an existence. That will be my reward for the few good deeds I may have done. Then you will sometimes lead me along the paths of our dear valley, where every rock, every hedge will remind me of your youth which I so greatly loved — — "

I had to stop again. I felt such a sharp pain In my shoulder, that I almost fainted a second time. A terrible anxiety had just taken possession of me; it, seemed as if the sound of the fusillade was approaching, and I thought with terror that our army was perhaps retreating, and that in its flight it would descend to the plain and pass over my body. But I still saw nothing but the slight cloud, of smoke hanging over the low hills.

My uncle Lazare added:

"And we shall be three to love one another. Ah! my well-beloved Jean, how right you were to give her to drink that morning beside the Durance. I was afraid of Babet, I was ill-humoured, and now I am jealous, for I can see very well that I shall never be able to love you as much as she does, 'Tell him,' she repeated to me yesterday, blushing, 'that if he gets killed, I shall go and throw myself into the river at the spot where he gave me to drink.'

"For the love of God! be careful of your life. There are things that I cannot understand, but I feel that happiness awaits you here. I already call Babet my daughter; I can see her on your arm, in the church, when I shall bless your union. I wish that to be my last mass.

"Babet is a fine, tall girl now. She will, assist you in your work — — "

The sound of the fusillade had gone farther away. I was weeping sweet tears. There were dismal moans among soldiers who were in their last agonies between the cannon wheels. I perceived one who was endeavoring to get rid of a comrade, wounded as he was, whose body was crushing his chest; and, as this wounded man struggled and complained, the soldier pushed him brutally away, and made him roll down the slope of the mound, whilst the wretched creature yelled with pain. At that cry a murmur came from the heap of corpses. The sun, which was sinking, shed rays of a light fallow colour. The blue of the sky was softer.

I finished reading my uncle Lazare's letter.

"I simply wished," he continued, "to give you news of ourselves, and to beg you to come as soon as possible and make us happy. And here I am weeping and gossiping like an old child. Hope, my poor Jean, I pray, and God is good.

"Answer me quickly, and give me, if possible, the date of your return. Babet and I are counting the weeks. We trust to see you soon; be hopeful."

The date of my return! — I kissed the letter, sobbing, and fancied for a moment that I was kissing Babet and my uncle. No doubt I should never see them again. I would die like a dog in the dust, beneath the leaden sun. And it was on that desolated plain, amidst the death-rattle of the dying, that those whom I loved dearly were saying good-bye. A buzzing silence filled my ears; I gazed at the pale earth spotted with blood, which extended, deserted, to the grey lines of the horizon. I repeated: "I must die." Then, I closed my eyes, and thought of Babet and my uncle Lazare.

I know not how long I remained in a sort of painful drowsiness. My heart suffered as much as my flesh. Warm tears ran slowly down my cheeks. Amidst the nightmare that accompanied the fever, I heard a moan similar to the continuous plaintive cry of a child in suffering. At times, I awoke and stared at the sky in astonishment.

At last I understood that it was M. de Montrevert, lying a few paces off, who was moaning in this manner. I had thought him dead. He was stretched out with his face to the ground and his arms extended. This man had been good to me; I said to myself that I could not allow him to die thus, with his face to the ground, and I began crawling slowly towards him.

Two corpses separated us. For a moment I thought of passing over the stomachs of these dead men to shorten the distance; for, my shoulder made me suffer frightfully at every movement. But I did not dare. I proceeded on my knees, assisting myself with one hand. When I reached the colonel, I gave a sigh of relief; it seemed to me that I was less alone; we would die together, and this death shared by both of us no longer terrified me.

I wanted him to see the sun, and I turned him over as gently as possible. When the rays fell upon his face, he breathed hard; he opened his eyes. Leaning over his body, I tried to smile at him. He closed his eyelids again; I understood by his trembling lips that he was conscious of his sufferings.

"It's you, Gourdon," he said to me at last, in a feeble voice; "is the battle won?"

"I think so, colonel," I answered him.

There was a moment of silence. Then, opening his eyes and looking at me, he inquired —

"Where are you wounded?"

"In the shoulder — and you, colonel?"

"My elbow must be smashed. I remember; it was the same bullet that arranged us both like this, my boy."

He made an effort to sit up.

"But come," he said with sudden gaiety, "we are not going to sleep here?"

You cannot believe how much this courageous display of joviality contributed towards giving me strength and hope. I felt quite different since we were two to struggle against death.

"Wait," I exclaimed, "I will bandage up your arm with my handkerchief, and we will try and support one another as far as the nearest ambulance."

"That's it, my boy. Don't make it too tight. Now, let us take each other by the good hand and try to get up."

We rose staggering. We had lost a great deal of blood; our heads were swimming and our legs failed us. Any one would have mistaken us for drunkards, stumbling, supporting, pushing one another, and making zigzags to avoid the dead. The sun was setting with a rosy blush, and our gigantic shadows danced in a strange way over the field of battle. It was the end of a fine day.

The colonel joked; his lips were crisped by shudders, his laughter resembled sobs. I could see that we were going to fall down in some corner never to rise again. At times we were seized with giddiness, and were obliged to stop and close our eyes. The ambulances formed small grey patches on the dark ground at the extremity of the plain.

We knocked up against a large stone, and were thrown down one on the other. The colonel swore like a pagan. We tried to walk on all-fours, catching hold of the briars. In this way we did a hundred yards on our knees. But our knees were bleeding.

"I have had enough of it," said the colonel, lying down; "they may come and fetch me if they will. Let us sleep."

I still had the strength to sit half up, and shout with all the breath that remained within me. Men were passing along in the distance picking up the wounded; they ran to us and placed us side by side on a stretcher.

"Comrade," the colonel said to me during the journey, "Death will not have us. I owe you my life; I will pay my debt, whenever you have need of me. Give me your hand."

I placed my hand in his, and it was thus that we reached the ambulances. They had lighted torches; the surgeons were cutting and sawing, amidst frightful yells; a sickly smell came from the blood-stained linen, whilst the torches cast dark rosy flakes into the basins.

The colonel bore the amputation of his arm with courage; I only saw his lips turn pale and a film come over his eyes. When it was my turn, a surgeon examined my shoulder.

"A shell did that for you," he said; "an inch lower and your shoulder would have been carried away. The flesh, only, has suffered."

And when I asked the assistant, who was dressing my wound, whether it was serious, he answered me with a laugh:

"Serious! you will have to keep to your bed for three weeks, and make new blood."

I turned my face to the wall, not wishing to show my tears. And with my heart's eyes I perceived Babet and my uncle Lazare stretching out their arms towards me. I had finished with the sanguinary struggles of my summer day.

# III
# AUTUMN

It was nearly fifteen years since I had married Babet In my uncle Lazare's little church. We had sought happiness in our dear valley. I had made myself a farmer; the Durance, my first sweetheart, was now a good mother to me, who seemed to take pleasure in making my fields rich and fertile. Little by little, by following the new methods of agriculture, I became one of the wealthiest landowners in the neighbourhood.

We had purchased the oak-tree walk and the meadows bordering on the river, at the death of my wife's parents. I had had a modest house built on this land, but we were soon obliged to enlarge it; each year I found a means of rounding off our property by the addition of some neighbouring field, and our granaries were too small for our harvests.

Those first fifteen years were uneventful and happy. They passed away in serene joy, and all they have left within me is the remembrance of calm and continued happiness. My uncle Lazare, on retiring to our home, had realized his dream; his advanced age did not permit of his reading his breviary of a morning; he sometimes regretted his dear church, but consoled himself by visiting the young vicar who had succeeded him. He came down from the little room he occupied at sunrise, and often accompanied me to the fields, enjoying himself in the open air, and finding a second youth amidst the healthy atmosphere of the country.

One sadness alone made us sometimes sigh. Amidst the fruitfulness by which we were surrounded, Babet remained childless. Although we were three to love one another we sometimes found ourselves too much alone; we would have liked to have had a little fair head running about amongst us, who would have tormented and caressed us.

Uncle Lazare had a frightful dread of dying before he was a great-uncle. He had become a child again, and felt sorrowful that Babet did not give him a comrade who would have played with him. On the day when my wife confided to us with hesitation, that we would no doubt soon be four, I saw my uncle turn quite pale, and make efforts not to cry. He kissed us, thinking already of the christening, and speaking of the child as if it were already three or four years old.

And the months passed in concentrated tenderness. We talked together in subdued voices, awaiting some one. I no longer loved Babet: I worshipped her with joined hands; I worshipped her for two, for herself and the little one.

The great day was drawing nigh. I had brought a midwife from Grenoble who never moved from the farm. My uncle was in a dreadful fright; he understood nothing about such things; he went so far as to tell me that he had done wrong in taking holy orders, and that he was very sorry he was not a doctor.

One morning in September, at about six o'clock, I went into the room of my dear Babet, who was still asleep. Her smiling face was peacefully reposing on the white linen pillow-case. I bent over her, holding my breath. Heaven had blessed me with the good things of this world. I all at once thought of that summer day when I was moaning in the dust, and at the same time I felt around me the comfort due to labour and the quietude that comes from happiness. My good wife was asleep, all rosy, in the middle of her great bed; whilst the whole room recalled to me our fifteen years of tender affection.

I kissed Babet softly on the lips. She opened her eyes and smiled at me without speaking. I felt an almost uncontrollable desire to take her in my arms, and clasp her to my heart; but, latterly, I had hardly dared press her hand, she seemed so fragile and sacred to me.

I seated myself at the edge of the bed, and asked her in a low voice:

"Is it for to-day?"

"No, I don't think so," she replied. "I dreamt I had a boy: he was already very tall and wore adorable little black mustachios. Uncle Lazare told me yesterday that he also had seen him in a dream."

I acted very stupidly.

"I know the child better than you do," I said. "I see it every night. It's a girl — — "

And as Babet turned her face to the wall, ready to cry, I realized how foolish I had been, and hastened to add:

"When I say a girl — I am not quite sure. I see a very small child with a long white gown. — it's certainly a boy."

Babet kissed me for that pleasing remark.

"Go and look after the vintage," she continued, "I feel calm this morning."

"You will send for me if anything happens?"

"Yes, yes, I am very tired: I shall go to sleep again. You'll not be angry with me for my laziness?"

And Babet closed her eyes, looking languid and affected. I remained leaning over her, receiving the warm breath from her lips in my face. She gradually went off to sleep, without ceasing to smile. Then I disengaged my hand from hers with a multitude of precautions. I had to maneuver for five minutes to bring this delicate task to a happy issue. After that I gave her a kiss on her forehead, which she did not feel, and withdrew with a palpitating heart, overflowing with love.

In the courtyard below, I found my uncle Lazare, who was gazing anxiously at the window of Babet's room. So soon as he perceived me he inquired:

"Well, is it for to-day?"

He had been putting this question to me regularly every morning for the past month.

"It appears not," I answered him. "Will you come with me and see them picking the grapes?"

He fetched his stick, and we went down the oak-tree walk. When we were at the end of it, on that terrace which overlooks the Durance, both of us stopped, gazing at the valley.

Small white clouds floated in the pale sky. The sun was shedding soft rays, which cast a sort of gold dust over the country, the yellow expanse of which spread out all ripe. One saw neither the brilliant light nor the dark shadows of summer. The

378

foliage gilded the black earth in large patches. The river ran more slowly, weary at the task of having rendered the fields fruitful for a season. And the valley remained calm and strong. It already wore the first furrows of winter, but it preserved within it the warmth of its last labour, displaying its robust charms, free from the weeds of spring, more majestically beautiful, like that second youth, of woman who has given birth to life.

My uncle Lazare remained silent; then, turning towards me, said:

"Do you remember, Jean? It is more than twenty years ago since I brought you here early one May morning. On that particular day I showed you the valley full of feverish activity, labouring for the fruits of autumn. Look; the valley has just performed its task again."

"I remember, dear uncle," I replied. "I was quaking with fear on that day; but you were good, and your lesson was convincing. I owe you all my happiness."

"Yes, you have reached the autumn. You have laboured and are gathering in the harvest. Man, my boy, was created after the way of the earth. And we, like the common mother, are eternal: the green leaves are born again each year from dry leaves; I am born again in you, and you will be born again in your children. I am telling you this so that old age may not alarm you, so that you may know how to die in peace, as dies this verdure, which will shoot out again from its own germs next spring."

I listened to my uncle and thought of Babet, who was sleeping in her great bed spread with white linen. The dear creature was about to give birth to a child after the manner of this fertile soil which had given us fortune. She also had reached the autumn: she had the beaming smile and serene robustness of the valley. I seemed to see her beneath the yellow sun, tired and happy, experiencing noble delight at being a mother. And I no longer knew whether my uncle Lazare was talking to me of my dear valley, or of my dear Babet.

We slowly ascended the hills. Below, along the Durance, were the meadows, broad, raw green swards; next came the yellow fields, intersected here and there by grayish olive and slender almond trees, planted wide apart in rows; then, right up above, were the vines, great stumps with shoots trailing along the ground.

The vine is treated in the south of France like a hardy housewife, and not like a delicate young lady, as in the north. It grows somewhat as it likes, according to the good will of rain and sun. The stumps, which are planted in double rows, and form long lines, throw sprays of dark verdure around them. Wheat or oats are sown between. A vineyard resembles an immense piece of striped material, made of the green bands formed by the vine leaves, and of yellow ribbon represented by the stubble.

Men and women stooping down among the vines, were cutting the bunches of grapes, which they then threw to the bottom of large baskets. My uncle and I walked slowly through the stubble. As we passed along, the vintagers turned their heads and greeted us. My uncle sometimes stopped to speak to some of the oldest of the labourers.

"Heh! Father André," he said, "are the grapes thoroughly ripe? Will the wine be good this year?"

And the country folk, raising their bare arms, displayed the long bunches, which were as black as ink, in the sun; and when the grapes were pressed they seemed to burst with abundance and strength.

"Look, Mr. Curé," they exclaimed, "these are small ones. There are some weighing several pounds. We have not had such a task these ten years."

Then they returned among the leaves. Their brown jackets formed patches in the verdure. And the women, bareheaded, with small blue handkerchiefs round their necks, were stooping down singing. There were children rolling in the sun, in the stubble, giving utterance to shrill laughter and enlivening this open-air workshop with their turbulence. Large carts remained motionless at the edge of the field waiting for the grapes; they stood out prominently against the clear sky, whilst men went and came unceasingly, carrying away full baskets, and bringing back empty ones.

I confess that in the centre of this field, I had feelings of pride. I heard the ground producing beneath my feet; ripe age ran all powerful in the veins of the vine, and loaded the air with great puffs of it. Hot blood coursed in my flesh, I was as if elevated by the fecundity overflowing from the soil and ascending within me. The labour of this swarm of work-people was my doing, these vines were my children; this entire farm became my large and obedient family. I experienced pleasure in feeling my feet sink into the heavy land.

Then, at a glance, I took in the fields that sloped down to the Durance, and I was the possessor of those vines, those meadows, that stubble, those olive-trees. The house stood all white beside the oak-tree walk; the river seemed like a fringe of silver placed at the edge of the great green mantle of my pasture-land. I fancied, for a moment, that my frame was increasing in size, that by stretching out my arms, I would be able to embrace the entire property, and press it to my breast, trees, meadows, house, and ploughed land.

And as I looked, I saw one of our servant-girls racing, out of breath, up the narrow pathway that ascended the hill. Confused by the speed at which she was traveling, she stumbled over the stones, agitating both her arms, and hailing us with gestures of bewilderment. I felt choking with inexpressible emotion.

"Uncle, uncle," I shouted, "look how Marguerite's running. I think it must be for to-day."

My uncle Lazare turned quite pale. The servant had at length reached the plateau; she came towards us jumping over the vines. When she reached me, she was out of breath; she was stifling and pressing her hands to her bosom.

"Speak!" I said to her. "What has happened?"

She heaved a heavy sigh, agitated her hands, and finally was able to pronounce this single word:

"Madame — — "

I waited for no more.

"Come! come quick, uncle Lazare! Ah! my poor dear Babet!"

And I bounded down the pathway at a pace fit to break my bones. The vintagers, who had stood up, smiled as they saw me running. Uncle Lazare, who could not overtake me, shook his walking stick in despair.

"Heh! Jean, the deuce!" he shouted, "wait for me. I don't want to be the last."

But I no longer heard Uncle Lazare, and continued running.

I reached the farm panting for breath, full of hope and terror. I rushed upstairs and knocked with my fist at Babet's door, laughing, crying, and half crazy. The midwife set the door ajar, to tell me in an angry voice not to make so much noise. I stood there abashed and in despair.

"You can't come in," she added. "Go and wait in the courtyard."

And as I did not move, she continued: "All is going on very well. I will call you."

The door was closed. I remained standing before it, unable to make up my mind to go away. I heard Babet complaining in a broken voice. And, while I was there, she gave utterance to a heartrending scream that struck me right in the breast like a bullet. I felt an almost irresistible desire to break the door open with my shoulder. So as not to give way to it, I placed my hands to my ears, and dashed downstairs.

In the courtyard I found my uncle Lazare, who had just arrived out of breath. The worthy man was obliged to seat himself on the brink of the well.

"Hallo! where is the child?" he inquired of me.

"I don't know," I answered; "they shut the door in my face — Babet is in pain and in tears." We gazed at one another, not daring to utter a word. We listened in agony, without taking our eyes off Babet's window, endeavouring to see through the little white curtains. My uncle, who was trembling, stood still, with both his hands resting heavily on his walking-stick; I, feeling very feverish, walked up and down before him, taking long strides. At times we exchanged anxious smiles.

The carts of the vintagers arrived one by one. The baskets of grapes were placed against a wall of the courtyard, and bare-legged men trampled the bunches under foot in wooden troughs. The mules neighed, the carters swore, whilst the wine fell with a dull sound to the bottom of the vat. Acrid smells pervaded the warm air.

And I continued pacing up and down, as if made tipsy by those perfumes. My poor head was breaking, and as I watched the red juice run from the grapes I thought of Babet. I said to myself with manly joy, that my child was born at the prolific time of vintage, amidst the perfume of new wine.

I was tormented by impatience, I went upstairs again. But I did not dare knock, I pressed my ear against the door, and heard Babet's low moans and sobs. Then my heart failed me, and I cursed suffering. Uncle Lazare, who had crept up behind me, had to lead me back into the courtyard. He wished to divert me, and told me the wine would be excellent; but he spoke without attending to what he said. And at times we were both silent, listening anxiously to one of Babet's more prolonged moans.

Little by little the cries subsided, and became nothing more than a painful murmur, like the voice of a child falling off to sleep in tears. Then there was absolute silence. This soon caused me unutterable terror. The house seemed empty, now that Babet had ceased sobbing. I was just going upstairs, when the midwife opened the window noiselessly. She leant out and beckoned me with her hand:

"Come," she said to me.

I went slowly upstairs, feeling additional delight at each step I took. My uncle Lazare was already knocking at the door, whilst I was only half way up to the landing, experiencing a sort of strange delight in delaying the moment when I would kiss my wife.

I stopped on the threshold, my heart was beating double. My uncle had leant over the cradle. Babet, quite pale, with closed eyelids, seemed asleep. I forgot all about the child, and going straight to Babet, took her dear hand between mine. The tears had not dried on her cheeks, and her quivering lips were dripping with them. She raised her eyelids wearily. She did not speak to me, but I understood her to say: "I have suffered a great deal, my dear Jean, but I was so happy to suffer! I felt you within me."

Then I bent down, I kissed Babet's eyes and drank her tears. She laughed with much sweetness; she resigned herself with caressing languidness. The fatigue had made her all aches and pains. She slowly moved her hands from the sheet, and taking me by the neck placed her lips to my ear:

"It's a boy," she murmured in a weak voice, but with an air of triumph.

Those were the first words she uttered after the terrible shock she had undergone.

"I knew it would be a boy," she continued, "I saw the child every night. Give him me, put him beside me."

I turned round and saw the midwife and my uncle quarrelling.

The midwife had all the trouble in the world to prevent uncle Lazare taking the little one in his arms. He wanted to nurse it.

I looked at the child whom the mother had made me forget. He was all rosy. Babet said with conviction that he was like me; the midwife discovered that he had his mother's eyes; I, for my part, could not say, I was almost crying, I smothered the dear little thing with kisses, imagining I was still kissing Babet.

I placed the child on the bed. He kept on crying, but this sounded to us like celestial music. I sat on the edge of the bed, my uncle took a large arm-chair, and Babet, weary and serene, covered up to her chin, remained with open eyelids and smiling eyes.

The window was wide open. The smell of grapes came in along with the warmth of the mild autumn afternoon. One heard the trampling of the vintagers, the shocks of the carts, the cracking of whips; at times the shrill song of a servant working in the courtyard reached us. All this noise was softened in the serenity of that room, which still resounded with Babet's sobs. And the window-frame enclosed a large strip of landscape, carved out of the heavens and open country. We could see the oak-tree walk in its entire length; then the Durance, looking like a white satin ribbon, passed amidst the gold and purple leaves; whilst above this square of ground were the limpid depths of a pale sky with blue and rosy tints.

It was amidst the calm of this horizon, amidst the exhalations of the vat and the joys attendant upon labour and reproduction, that we three talked together, Babet, uncle Lazare, and myself, whilst gazing at the dear little new-born babe.

"Uncle Lazare," said Babet, "what name will you give the child?"

"Jean's mother was named Jacqueline," answered my uncle. "I shall call the child Jacques."

"Jacques, Jacques," repeated Babet. "Yes, it's a pretty name. And, tell me, what shall we make the little man: parson or soldier, gentleman or peasant?"

I began to laugh.

"We shall have time to think of that," I said.

"But no," continued Babet almost angry, "he will grow rapidly. See how strong he is. He already speaks with his eyes."

My uncle Lazare was exactly of my wife's opinion. He answered in a very grave tone:

"Make him neither priest nor soldier, unless he have an irresistible inclination for one of those callings — to make him a gentleman would be a serious — — "

Babet looked at me anxiously. The dear creature had not a bit of pride for herself; but, like all mothers, she would have liked to be humble and proud before her son. I could have sworn that she already saw him a notary or a doctor. I kissed her and gently said to her:

"I wish our son to live in our dear valley. One day, he will find a Babet of sixteen, on the banks of the Durance, to whom he will give some water. Do you remember, my dear — — ? The country has brought us peace: our son shall be a peasant as we are, and happy as we are."

Babet, who was quite touched, kissed me in her turn. She gazed at the foliage and the river, the meadows and the sky, through the window; then she said to me, smiling:

"You are right, Jean. This place has been good to us, it will be the same to our little Jacques. Uncle Lazare, you will be the godfather of a farmer."

Uncle Lazare made a languid, affectionate sign of approval with the head. I had been examining him for a moment, and saw his eyes becoming filmy, and his lips turning pale. Leaning back in the arm-chair, opposite the window, he had placed his white hands on his knees, and was watching the heavens fixedly with an expression of thoughtful ecstasy.

I felt very anxious.

"Are you in pain, uncle Lazare?" I inquired of him, "What is the matter with you? Answer, for mercy's sake."

He gently raised one of his hands, as if to beg me to speak lower; then he let it fall again, and said in a weak voice:

"I am broken down," he said. "Happiness, at my age, is mortal. Don't make a noise. It seems as if my flesh were becoming quite light: I can no longer feel my legs or arms."

Babet raised herself in alarm, with her eyes on uncle Lazare. I knelt down before him, watching him anxiously. He smiled.

"Don't be frightened," he resumed. "I am in no pain; a feeling of calmness is gaining possession of me; I believe I am going off into a good and just sleep. It came over me all at once, and I thank the Almighty. Ah! my poor Jean, I ran too fast down, the pathway on the hillside; the child caused me too great joy."

And as we understood, we burst out into tears. Uncle Lazare continued, without ceasing to watch the sky:

"Do not spoil my joy, I beg of you. If you only knew how happy it makes me, to fall asleep for ever in this armchair! I have never dared expect such a consoling death. All I love is here, beside me — and see what a blue sky! The Almighty has sent a lovely evening."

The sun was sinking behind the oak-tree walk. Its slanting rays cast sheets of gold beneath the trees, which took the tones of

386

old copper. The verdant fields melted into vague serenity in the distance. Uncle Lazare became weaker and weaker amidst the touching silence of this peaceful sunset, entering by the open window. He slowly passed away, like those slight gleams that were dying out on the lofty branches.

"Ah! my good valley," he murmured, "you are sending me a tender farewell. I was afraid of coming to my end in the winter, when you would be all black."

We restrained our tears, not wishing to trouble this saintly death. Babet prayed in an undertone. The child continued uttering smothered cries.

My uncle Lazare heard its wail in the dreaminess of his agony. He endeavoured to turn towards Babet, and, still smiling, said:

"I have seen the child and die very happy."

Then he gazed at the pale sky and yellow fields, and, throwing back his head, heaved a gentle sigh.

No tremor agitated uncle Lazare's body; he died as one falls asleep.

We had become so calm that we remained silent and with dry eyes. In the presence of such great simplicity in death, all we experienced was a feeling of serene sadness. Twilight had set in, uncle Lazare's farewell had left us confident, like the farewell of the sun which dies at night to be born again in the morning.

Such was my autumn day, which gave me a son, and carried off my uncle Lazare in the peacefulness of the twilight.

# IV
## WINTER

There are dreadful mornings in January that chill one's heart. I awoke on this particular day with a vague feeling of anxiety. It had thawed during the night, and when I cast my eyes over the country from the threshold, it looked to me like an immense dirty grey rag, soiled with mud and rent to tatters.

The horizon was shrouded in a curtain of fog, in which the oak-trees along the walk lugubriously extended their dark arms, like a row of spectres guarding the vast mass of vapour spreading out behind them. The fields had sunk, and were covered with great sheets of water, at the edge of which hung the remnants of dirty snow. The loud roar of the Durance was increasing in the distance.

Winter imparts health and strength to one's frame when the sun is clear and the ground dry. The air makes the tips of your ears tingle, you walk merrily along the frozen pathways, which ring with a silvery sound beneath your tread. But I know of nothing more saddening than dull, thawing weather: I hate the damp fogs which weigh one's shoulders down.

I shivered in the presence of that copper-like sky, and hastened to retire indoors, making up my mind that I would not go out into the fields that day. There was plenty of work in and around the farm-buildings.

Jacques had been up a long time. I heard him whistling in a shed, where he was helping some men remove sacks of corn. The boy was already eighteen years old; he was a tall fellow, with strong arms. He had not had an uncle Lazare to spoil him and teach him Latin, and he did not go and dream beneath the willows at the riverside. Jacques had become a real peasant, an untiring worker, who got angry when I touched anything, telling me I was getting old and ought to rest.

And as I was watching him from a distance, a sweet lithe creature, leaping on my shoulders, clapped her little hands to my eyes, inquiring:

"Who is it?"

I laughed and answered:

"It's little Marie, who has just been dressed by her mamma."

The dear little girl was completing her tenth year, and for ten years she had been the delight of the farm. Having come the last, at a time when we could no longer hope to have any more children, she was doubly loved. Her precarious health made her particularly dear to us. She was treated as a young lady; her mother absolutely wanted to make a lady of her, and I had not the heart to oppose her wish, so little Marie was a pet, in lovely silk skirts trimmed with ribbons.

Marie was still seated on my shoulders.

"Mamma, mamma," she cried, "come and look; I'm playing at horses."

Babet, who was entering, smiled. Ah! my poor Babet, how old we were! I remember we were shivering with weariness, on that day, gazing sadly at one another when alone.

Our children brought back our youth.

Lunch was eaten in silence. We had been compelled to light the lamp. The reddish glimmer that hung round the room was sad enough to drive one crazy.

"Bah!" said Jacques, "this tepid rainy weather is better than intense cold that would freeze our vines and olives."

And he tried to joke. But he was as anxious as we were, without knowing why. Babet had had bad dreams. We listened to the account of her nightmare, laughing with our lips but sad at heart.

"This weather quite upsets one," I said to cheer us all up.

"Yes, yes, it's the weather," Jacques hastened to add. "I'll put some vine branches on the fire."

There was a bright flame which cast large sheets of light upon the walls. The branches burnt with a cracking sound, leaving rosy ashes. We had seated ourselves in front of the chimney; the air, outside, was tepid; but great drops of icy cold damp fell from the ceilings inside the farmhouse. Babet had taken little Marie on her knees; she was talking to her in an undertone, amused at her childish chatter.

"Are you coming, father?" Jacques inquired of me. "We are going to look at the cellars and lofts."

I went out with him. The harvests had been getting bad for some years past. We were suffering great losses: our vines and trees were caught by frost, whilst hail had chopped up our wheat and oats. And I sometimes said that I was growing old, and that fortune, who is a woman, does not care for old men. Jacques laughed, answering that he was young, and was going to court fortune.

I had reached the winter, the cold season. I felt distinctly that all was withering around me. At each pleasure that departed, I thought of uncle Lazare, who had died so calmly; and with fond remembrances of him, asked for strength.

Daylight had completely disappeared at three o'clock. We went down into the common room. Babet was sewing in the chimney corner, with her head bent over her work; and little Marie was seated on the ground, in front of the fire, gravely dressing a doll. Jacques and I had placed ourselves at a mahogany writing-table, which had come to us from uncle Lazare, and were engaged in checking our accounts.

The window was as if blocked up; the fog, sticking to the panes of glass, formed a perfect wall of gloom. Behind this wall stretched emptiness, the unknown. A great noise, a loud roar, alone arose in the silence and spread through the obscurity.

We had dismissed the workpeople, keeping only our old woman-servant, Marguerite, with us. When I raised my head and listened, it seemed to me that the farmhouse hung suspended in the middle of a chasm. No human sound came from the outside. I heard naught but the riot of the abyss. Then I gazed at my wife and children, and experienced the cowardice of those old people who feel themselves too weak to protect those surrounding them against unknown peril.

The noise became harsher, and it seemed to us that there was a knocking at the door. At the same instant, the horses in the stable began to neigh furiously, whilst the cattle lowed as if choking. We had all risen, pale with anxiety, Jacques dashed to the door and threw it wide open.

A wave of muddy water burst into the room.

The Durance was overflowing. It was it that had been making the noise, that had been increasing in the distance since morning. The snow melting on the mountains had transformed each hillside into a torrent which had swelled the river. The curtain of fog had hidden from us this sudden rise of water.

It had often advanced thus to the gates of the farm, when the thaw came after severe winters. But the flood had never increased so rapidly. We could see through the open door that the courtyard was transformed into a lake. The water already reached our ankles.

Babet had caught up little Marie, who was crying and clasping her doll to her. Jacques wanted to run and open the doors of the stables and cowhouses; but his mother held him back by his clothes, begging him not to go out. The water continued rising. I pushed Babet towards the staircase.

"Quick, quick, let us go up into the bedrooms," I cried.

And I obliged Jacques to pass before me. I left the ground-floor the last.

Marguerite came down in terror from the loft where she happened to find herself. I made her sit down at the end of the room beside Babet, who remained silent, pale, and with beseeching eyes. We put little Marie into bed; she had insisted on keeping her doll, and went quietly to sleep pressing it in her arms. This child's sleep relieved me; when I turned round and saw Babet, listening to the little girl's regular breathing, I forgot the danger, all I heard was the water beating against the walls.

But Jacques and I could not help looking the peril in the face. Anxiety made us endeavour to discover the progress of the inundation. We had thrown the window wide open, we leant out at the risk of falling, searching into the darkness. The fog, which was thicker, hung above the flood, throwing out fine rain which gave us the shivers. Vague steel-like flashes were all that showed the moving sheet of water, amidst the profound obscurity. Below, it was splashing in the courtyard, rising along the walls in gentle undulations. And we still heard naught but the anger of the Durance, and the affrighted cattle and horses.

The neighing and lowing of these poor beasts pierced me to the heart. Jacques questioned me with his eyes; he would have liked to try and deliver them. Their agonizing moans soon became lamentable, and a great cracking sound was heard. The oxen had just broken down the stable doors. We saw them pass before us, borne away by the flood, rolled over and over in the current. And they disappeared amid the roar of the river.

Then I felt choking with anger. I became as one possessed, I shook my fist at the Durance. Erect, facing the window, I insulted it.

"Wicked thing!" I shouted amidst the tumult of the waters, "I loved you fondly, you were my first sweetheart, and now you are plundering me. You come and disturb my farm, and carry off my cattle. Ah! cursed, cursed thing. — — Then you gave me Babet, you ran gently at the edge of my meadows. I took you for a good mother. I remembered uncle Lazare felt affection for your limpid stream, and I thought I owed you gratitude. You are a barbarous mother, I only owe you my hatred — — "

But the Durance stifled my cries with its thundering voice; and, broad and indifferent, expanded and drove its flood onward with tranquil obstinacy.

I turned back to the room and went and kissed Babet, who was weeping. Little Marie was smiling in her sleep.

"Don't be afraid," I said to my wife. "The water cannot always rise. It will certainly go down. There is no danger."

"No, there is no danger," Jacques repeated feverishly. "The house is solid."

At that moment Marguerite, who had approached the window, tormented by that feeling of curiosity which is the outcome of fear, leant forward like a mad thing and fell, uttering a cry. I threw myself before the window, but could not prevent Jacques plunging into the water. Marguerite had nursed him, and he felt the tenderness of a son for the poor old woman. Babet had risen in terror, with joined hands, at the sound of the two splashes. She remained there, erect, with open mouth and distended eyes, watching the window.

I had seated myself on the wooden handrail, and my ears were ringing with the roar of the flood. I do not know how long it was that Babet and I were in this painful state of stupor, when a voice called to me. It was Jacques who was holding on to the wall beneath the window. I stretched out my hand to him, and he clambered up.

Babet clasped him in her arms. She could sob now; and she relieved herself.

No reference was made to Marguerite. Jacques did not dare say he had been unable to find her, and we did not dare question him anent his search.

He took me apart and brought me back to the window.

"Father," he said to me in an undertone, "there are more than seven feet of water in the courtyard, and the river is still rising. We cannot remain here any longer."

Jacques was right. The house was falling to pieces, the planks of the outbuildings were going away one by one. Then this death of Marguerite weighed upon us. Babet, bewildered, was beseeching us. Marie alone remained peaceful in the big bed? with her doll between her arms, and slumbering with the happy smile of an angel.

The peril increased at every minute. The water was on the point of reaching the handrail of the window and pouring into the room. Any one would have said that it was an engine of war making the farmhouse totter with regular, dull, hard blows. The current must be running right against the facade, and we could not hope for any human assistance.

"Every minute is precious," said Jacques in agony. "We shall be crushed beneath the ruins. Let us look for boards, let us make a raft."

He said that in his excitement. I would naturally have preferred a thousand times to be in the middle of the river, on a few beams lashed together, than beneath the roof of this house which was about to fall in. But where could we lay hands on the beams we required? In a rage I tore the planks from the cupboards, Jacques broke the furniture, we took away the shutters, every piece of wood we could reach. And feeling it was impossible to utilize these fragments, we cast them into the middle of the room in a fury, and continued searching.

Our last hope was departing, we understood our misery and want of power. The water was rising; the harsh voice of the Durance was calling to us in anger. Then, I burst out sobbing, I took Babet in my trembling arms, I begged Jacques to come near us. I wished us all to die in the same embrace.

Jacques had returned to the window. And, suddenly, he exclaimed:

"Father, we are saved! — Come and see."

The sky was clear. The roof of a shed, torn away by the current, had come to a standstill beneath our window. This roof, which was several yards broad, was formed of light beams and thatch; it floated, and would make a capital raft, I joined my hands together and would have worshipped this wood and straw.

Jacques jumped on the roof, after having firmly secured it. He walked on the thatch, making sure it was everywhere strong. The thatch resisted; therefore we could adventure on it without fear.

"Oh! it will carry us all very well," said Jacques joyfully. "See how little it sinks into the water! The difficulty will be to steer it."

He looked around him and seized two poles drifting along in the current, as they passed by.

"Ah! here are oars," he continued. "You will go to the stern, father, and I forward, and we will maneuver the raft easily. There are not twelve feet of water. Quick, quick! get on board, we must not lose a minute."

My poor Babet tried to smile. She wrapped little Marie carefully up in her shawl; the child had just woke up, and, quite alarmed, maintained a silence which was broken by deep sobs. I placed a chair before the window and made Babet get on the raft. As I held her in my arms I kissed her with poignant emotion, feeling this kiss was the last.

The water was beginning to pour into the room. Our feet were soaking. I was the last to embark; then I undid the cord. The current hurled us against the wall; it required precautions and many efforts to quit the farmhouse.

The fog had little by little dispersed. It was about midnight when we left. The stars were still buried in mist; the moon which was almost at the edge of the horizon, lit up the night with a sort of wan daylight.

The inundation then appeared to us in all its grandiose horror. The valley had become a river. The Durance, swollen to enormous proportions and washing the two hillsides, passed between dark masses of cultivated land, and was the sole thing displaying life in the inanimate space bounded by the horizon. It thundered with a sovereign voice, maintaining in its anger the majesty of its colossal wave. Clumps of trees emerged in places, staining the sheet of pale water with black streaks. Opposite us I recognized the tops of the oaks along the walk; the current carried us towards these branches, which for us were so many reefs. Around the raft floated various kinds of remains, pieces of wood, empty barrels, bundles of grass; the river was bearing along the ruins it had made in its anger.

To the left we perceived the lights of Dourgues — flashes of lanterns moving about in the darkness. The water could not have risen as high as the village; only the low land had been submerged. No doubt assistance would come. We searched the patches of light hanging over the water; it seemed to us at every instant that we heard the sound of oars.

We had started at random. As soon as the raft was in the middle of the current, lost amidst the whirlpools of the river, anguish of mind overtook us again; we almost regretted having left the farm. I sometimes turned round and gazed at the house, which still remained standing, presenting a grey aspect on the white water. Babet, crouching down in the centre of the raft, in the thatch of the roof, was holding little Marie on her knees, the child's head against her breast, to hide the horror of the river from her. Both were bent double, leaning forward in an embrace, as if reduced in stature by fear. Jacques, standing upright in the front, was leaning on his pole with all his weight; from time to time he cast a rapid glance towards us, and then silently resumed his task. I seconded him as well as I could, but our efforts to reach the bank remained fruitless. Little by little, notwithstanding our poles, which we buried into the mud until we nearly broke them, we drifted into the open; a force that seemed to come from the depths of the water drove us away. The Durance was slowly taking possession of us.

Struggling, bathed in perspiration, we had worked ourselves into a passion; we were fighting with the river as with a living being, seeking to vanquish, wound, kill it. It strained us in its giant-like arms, and our poles in our hands became weapons which we thrust into its breast. It roared, flung its slaver into our faces, wriggled beneath our strokes. We resisted its victory with clenched teeth. We would not be conquered. And we had mad impulses to fell the monster, to calm it with blows from our fists.

We went slowly towards the offing. We were already at the entrance to the oak-tree walk. The dark branches pierced through the water, which they tore with a lamentable sound. Death, perhaps, awaited us there in a collision. I cried out to Jacques to follow the walk by clinging close to the branches. And it was thus that I passed for the last time in the middle of this oak-tree alley, where I had walked in my youth and ripe age. In the terrible darkness, above the howling depth, I thought of uncle Lazare, and saw the happy days of my youth smiling at me sadly.

The Durance triumphed at the end of the alley. Our poles no longer touched the bottom. The water bore us along in its impetuous bound of victory. And now it could do what it pleased with us. We gave ourselves up. We went downstream with frightful rapidity. Great clouds, dirty tattered rags hung about the sky; when the moon was hidden there came lugubrious obscurity. Then we rolled in chaos. Enormous billows as black as ink, resembling the backs of fish, bore us along, spinning us round. I could no longer see either Babet or the children. I already felt myself dying.

I know not how long this last run lasted. The moon was suddenly unveiled, and the horizon became clear. And in that light I perceived an immense black mass in front of us which blocked the way, and towards which we were being carried with all the violence of the current. We were lost, we would be broken there.

Babet had stood upright. She held out little Marie to me:

"Take the child," she exclaimed. "Leave me alone, leave me alone!"

Jacques had already caught Babet in his arms. In a loud voice he said:

"Father, save the little one — I will save mother."

We had come close to the black mass. I thought I recognized a tree. The shock was terrible, and the raft, split in two, scattered its straw and beams in the whirlpool of water.

I fell, clasping little Marie tightly to me. The icy cold water brought back all my courage. On rising to the surface of the river, I supported the child, I half laid her on my neck and began to swim laboriously. If the little creature had not lost consciousness but had struggled, we should both have remained at the bottom of the deep.

And, whilst I swam, I felt choking with anxiety. I called Jacques, I tried to see in the distance; but I heard nothing save the roar of the waters, I saw naught but the pale sheet of the Durance. Jacques and Babet were at the bottom. She must have clung to him, dragged him down in a deadly strain of her arms. What frightful agony! I wanted to die; I sunk slowly, I was going to find them beneath the black water. And as soon as the flood touched little Marie's face, I struggled again with impetuous anguish to get near the waterside.

It was thus that I abandoned Babet and Jacques, in despair at having been unable to die with them, still calling out to them in a husky voice. The river cast me on the stones, like one of those

397

bundles of grass it leaves on its way. When I came to myself again, I took my daughter, who was opening her eyes, in my arms. Day was breaking. My winter night was at an end, that terrible night which had been an accomplice in the murder of my wife and son.

At this moment, after years of regret, one last consolation remains to me. I am the icy winter, but I feel the approaching spring stirring within me. As my uncle Lazare said, we never die. I have had four seasons, and here I am returning to the spring, there is my dear Marie commencing the everlasting joys and sorrows over again.

# THE LAST LESSON
## BY ALPHONSE DAUDET

I started for school very late that morning and was in great dread of a scolding, especially because M. Hamel had said that he would question us on participles, and I did not know the first word about them. For a moment I thought of running away and spending the day out of doors. It was so warm, so bright! The birds were chirping at the edge of the woods; and in the open field back of the saw-mill the Prussian soldiers were drilling. It was all much more tempting than the rule for participles, but I had the strength to resist, and hurried off to school.

When I passed the town hall there was a crowd in front of the bulletin-board. For the last two years all our bad news had come from there — the lost battles, the draft, the orders of the commanding officer — and I thought to myself, without stopping:

"What can be the matter now?"

Then, as I hurried by as fast as I could go, the blacksmith, Wachter, who was there, with his apprentice, reading the bulletin, called after me:

"Don't go so fast, bub; you'll get to your school in plenty of time!"

I thought he was making fun of me, and reached M. Hamel's little garden all out of breath.

Usually, when school began, there was a great bustle, which could be heard out in the street, the opening and closing of desks, lessons repeated in unison, very loud, with our hands over our ears to understand better, and the teacher's great ruler rapping on the table. But now it was all so still! I had counted on the commotion to get to my desk without being seen; but, of course, that day everything had to be as quiet as Sunday morning. Through the window I saw my classmates, already in their places, and M. Hamel walking up and down with his terrible iron ruler under his arm. I had to open the door and go in before everybody. You can imagine how I blushed and how frightened I was.

But nothing happened, M. Hamel saw me and said very kindly:

"Go to your place quickly, little Franz. We were beginning without you."

I jumped over the bench and sat down at my desk. Not till then, when I had got a little over my fright, did I see that our teacher had on his beautiful green coat, his frilled shirt, and the little black silk cap, all embroidered, that he never wore except on inspection and prize days. Besides, the whole school seemed so strange and solemn. But the thing that surprised me most was to see, on the back benches that were always empty, the village people sitting quietly like ourselves; old Hauser, with his three-cornered hat, the former mayor, the former postmaster, and several others besides. Everybody looked sad; and Hauser had brought an old primer, thumbed at the edges, and he held it open on his knees with his great spectacles lying across the pages.

While I was wondering about it all, M. Hamel mounted his chair, and, in the same grave and gentle tone which he had used to me, said:

"My children, this is the last lesson I shall give you. The order has come from Berlin to teach only German in the schools of Alsace and Lorraine. The new master comes to-morrow. This is your last French lesson. I want you to be very attentive."

What a thunder-clap these words were to me!

Oh, the wretches; that was what they had put up at the town-hall!

My last French lesson! Why, I hardly knew how to write! I should never learn any more! I must stop there, then! Oh, how sorry I was for not learning my lessons, for seeking birds' eggs, or going sliding on the Saar! My books, that had seemed such a nuisance a while ago, so heavy to carry, my grammar, and my history of the saints, were old friends now that I couldn't give up. And M. Hamel, too; the idea that he was going away, that I should never see him again, made me forget all about his ruler and how cranky he was.

Poor man! It was in honor of this last lesson that he had put on his fine Sunday-clothes, and now I understood why the old men of the village were sitting there in the back of the room. It was because they were sorry, too, that they had not gone to school more. It was their way of thanking our master for his forty years of faithful service and of showing their respect for the country that was theirs no more.

While I was thinking of all this, I heard my name called. It was my turn to recite. What would I not have given to be able to say that dreadful rule for the participle all through, very loud and clear, and without one mistake? But I got mixed up on the first words and stood there, holding on to my desk, my heart beating, and not daring to look up. I heard M. Hamel say to me:

"I won't scold you, little Franz; you must feel bad enough. See how it is! Every day we have said to ourselves: 'Bah! I've plenty of time. I'll learn it to-morrow.' And now you see where we've come out. Ah, that's the great trouble with Alsace; she puts off learning till to-morrow. Now those fellows out there will have the right to say to you: 'How is it; you pretend to be Frenchmen, and yet you can neither speak nor write your own language?' But you are not the worst, poor little Franz. We've all a great deal to reproach ourselves with.

"Your parents were not anxious enough to have you learn. They preferred to put you to work on a farm or at the mills, so as to have a little more money. And I? I've been to blame also. Have I not often sent you to water my flowers instead of learning your lessons? And when I wanted to go fishing, did I not just give you a holiday?"

Then, from one thing to another, M. Hamel went on to talk of the French language, saying that it was the most beautiful language in the world — the clearest, the most logical; that we must guard it among us and never forget it, because when a people are enslaved, as long as they hold fast to their language it is as if they had the key to their prison. Then he opened a grammar and read us our lesson. I was amazed to see how well I understood it. All he said seemed so easy, so easy! I think, too, that I had never listened so carefully, and that he had never explained everything with so much patience. It seemed almost as if the poor man wanted to give us all he knew before going away, and to put it all into our heads at one stroke.

After the grammar, we had a lesson in writing. That day M. Hamel had new copies for us, written in a beautiful round hand: France, Alsace, France, Alsace. They looked like little flags floating everywhere in the school-room, hung from the rod at the top of our desks. You ought to have seen how every one set to work, and how quiet it was! The only sound was the scratching of the pens over the paper. Once some beetles flew in; but nobody paid any attention to them, not even the littlest ones, who worked right on tracing their fish-hooks, as if that was French, too. On the roof the pigeons cooed very low, and I thought to myself:

"Will they make them sing in German, even the pigeons?"

Whenever I looked up from my writing I saw M. Hamel sitting motionless in his chair and gazing first at one thing, then at another, as if he wanted to fix in his mind just how everything looked in that little school-room. Fancy! For forty years he had been there in the same place, with his garden outside the window and his class in front of him, just like that. Only the desks and benches had been worn smooth; the walnut-trees in the garden were taller, and the hop-vine, that he had planted himself twined about the windows to the roof. How it must have broken his heart to leave it all, poor man; to hear his sister moving about in the room above, packing their trunks! For they must leave the country next day.

But he had the courage to hear every lesson to the very last. After the writing, we had a lesson in history, and then the babies chanted their ba, be, bi, bo, bu. Down there at the back of the room old Hauser had put on his spectacles and, holding his primer in both hands, spelled the letters with them. You could see that he, too, was crying; his voice trembled with emotion, and it was so funny to hear him that we all wanted to laugh and cry. Ah, how well I remember it, that last lesson!

All at once the church-clock struck twelve. Then the Angelus. At the same moment the trumpets of the Prussians, returning from drill, sounded under our windows. M. Hamel stood up, very pale, in his chair. I never saw him look so tall.

"My friends," said he, "I — I — " But something choked him. He could not go on.

Then he turned to the blackboard, took a piece of chalk, and, bearing on with all his might, he wrote as large as he could:

"Vive La France!"

Then he stopped and leaned his head against the wall, and, without a word, he made a gesture to us with his hand; "School is dismissed — you may go."

# A PIECE OF BREAD
## BY FRANCOIS COPPEE

The young Due de Hardimont happened to be at Aix in Savoy, whose waters he hoped would benefit his famous mare, Perichole, who had become wind-broken since the cold she had caught at the last Derby, — and was finishing his breakfast while glancing over the morning paper, when he read the news of the disastrous engagement at Reichshoffen.

He emptied his glass of chartreuse, laid his napkin upon the restaurant table, ordered his valet to pack his trunks, and two hours later took the express to Paris; arriving there, he hastened to the recruiting office and enlisted in a regiment of the line.

In vain had he led the enervating life of a fashionable swell — that was the word of the time — and had knocked about race-course stables from the age of nineteen to twenty-five. In circumstances like these, he could not forget that Enguerrand de Hardimont died of the plague at Tunis the same day as Saint Louis, that Jean de Hardimont commanded the Free Companies under Du Guesclin, and that Francois-Henri de Hardimont was killed at Fontenoy with "Red" Maison. Upon learning that France had lost a battle on French soil, the young duke felt the blood mount to his face, giving him a horrible feeling of suffocation.

And so, early in November, 1870, Henri de Hardimont returned to Paris with his regiment, forming part of Vinoy's corps, and his company being the advance guard before the redoubt of Hautes Bruyères, a position fortified in haste, and which protected the cannon of Fort Bicêtre.

It was a gloomy place; a road planted with clusters of broom, and broken up into muddy ruts, traversing the leprous fields of the neighborhood; on the border stood an abandoned tavern, a tavern with arbors, where the soldiers had established their post. They had fallen back here a few days before; the grape-shot had broken down some of the young trees, and all of them bore upon their bark the white scars of bullet wounds. As for the house, its appearance made one shudder; the roof had been torn by a shell, and the walls seemed whitewashed with blood. The torn and shattered arbors under their network of twigs, the rolling of an upset cask, the high swing whose wet rope groaned in the damp wind, and the inscriptions over the door, furrowed by bullets; "Cabinets de societé — Absinthe — Vermouth — Vin à 60 cent. le litre" — encircling a dead rabbit painted over two billiard cues tied in a cross by a ribbon, — all this recalled with cruel irony the popular entertainment of former days. And over all, a wretched winter sky, across which rolled heavy leaden clouds, an odious sky, angry and hateful.

At the door of the tavern stood the young duke, motionless, with his gun in his shoulder-belt, his cap over his eyes, his benumbed hands in the pockets of his red trousers, and shivering in his sheepskin coat. He gave himself up to his sombre thoughts, this defeated soldier, and looked with sorrowful eyes toward a line of hills, lost in the fog, where could be seen each moment, the flash and smoke of a Krupp gun, followed by a report.

Suddenly he felt hungry.

Stooping, he drew from his knapsack, which stood near him leaning against the wall, a piece of ammunition bread, and as he had lost his knife, he bit off a morsel and slowly ate it.

But after a few mouthfuls, he had enough of it; the bread was hard and had a bitter taste. No fresh would be given until the next morning's distribution, so the commissary officer had willed it. This was certainly a very hard life sometimes. The remembrance of former breakfasts came to him, such as he had called "hygienic," when, the day after too over-heating a supper, he would seat himself by a window on the ground floor of the Café-Anglais, and be served with a cutlet, or buttered eggs with asparagus tips, and the butler, knowing his tastes, would bring him a fine bottle of old Léoville, lying in its basket, and which he would pour out with the greatest care. The deuce take it! That was a good time, all the same, and he would never become accustomed to this life of wretchedness.

And, in a moment of impatience, the young man threw the rest of his bread into the mud.

At the same moment a soldier of the line came from the tavern, stooped and picked up the bread, drew back a few steps, wiped it with his sleeve and began to devour it eagerly.

Henri de Hardimont was already ashamed of his action, and now with a feeling of pity, watched the poor devil who gave proof of such a good appetite. He was a tall, large young fellow, but badly made; with feverish eyes and a hospital beard, and so thin that his shoulder-blades stood out beneath his well-worn cape.

"You are very hungry?" he said, approaching the soldier.

"As you see," replied the other with his mouth full.

"Excuse me then. For if I had known that you would like the bread, I would not have thrown it away."

"It does not harm it," replied the soldier, "I am not dainty."

"No matter," said the gentleman, "it was wrong to do so, and I reproach myself. But I do not wish you to have a bad opinion of me, and as I have some old cognac in my can, let us drink a drop together."

The man had finished eating. The duke and he drank a mouthful of brandy; the acquaintance was made.

"What is your name?" asked the soldier of the line.

"Hardimont," replied the duke, omitting his title. "And yours?"

"Jean-Victor — I have just entered this company — I am just out of the ambulance — I was wounded at Châtillon — oh! but it was good in the ambulance, and in the infirmary they gave me horse bouillon. But I had only a scratch, and the major signed my dismissal. So much the worse for me! Now I am going to commence to be devoured by hunger again — for, believe me, if you will, comrade, but, such as you see me, I have been hungry all my life."

The words were startling, especially to a Sybarite who had just been longing for the kitchen of the Café-Anglais, and the Duc de Hardimont looked at his companion in almost terrified amazement. The soldier smiled sadly, showing his hungry, wolf-like teeth, as white as his sickly face, and, as if understanding that the other expected something further in the way of explanation or confidence:

"Come," said he, suddenly ceasing his familiar way of speaking, doubtless divining that his companion belonged to the rich and happy; "let us walk along the road to warm our feet, and I will tell you things, which probably you have never heard of — I am called Jean-Victor, that is all, for I am a foundling, and my only happy remembrance is of my earliest childhood, at the Asylum. The sheets were white on our little beds in the dormitory; we played in a garden under large trees, and a kind Sister took care of us, quite young and as pale as a wax-taper — she died afterwards of lung trouble — I was her favorite, and would rather walk by her than play with the other children, because she used to draw me to her side and lay her warm thin hand on my forehead. But when I was twelve years old, after my first communion, there was nothing but poverty. The managers put me as apprentice with a chair mender in Faubourg Saint-Jacques. That is not a trade, you know, it is impossible to earn one's living at it, and as proof of it, the greater part of the time the master was only able to engage the poor little blind boys from the Blind Asylum. It was there that I began to suffer with hunger. The master and mistress, two old Limousins — afterwards murdered, were terrible misers, and the bread, cut in tiny pieces for each meal, was kept under lock and key the rest of the time. You should have seen the mistress at supper time serving the soup, sighing at each ladleful she dished out. The other apprentices, two blind boys, were less unhappy; they were not given more than I, but they could not see the reproachful look the wicked woman used to give me as she handed me my plate. And then, unfortunately, I was always so terribly hungry. Was it my fault, do you think? I served there for three years, in a continual fit of hunger. Three years! And one can learn the work in one month. But the managers could not know everything, and had no suspicion that the children were abused. Ah! you were astonished just now when you saw me take the bread out of the mud? I am

407

used to that for I have picked up enough of it; and crusts from the dust, and when they were too hard and dry, I would soak them all night in my basin. I had windfalls sometimes, such as pieces of bread nibbled at the ends, which the children would take out of their baskets and throw on the sidewalks as they came from school. I used to try to prowl around there when I went on errands. At last my time was ended at this trade by which no man can support himself. Well, I did many other things, for I was willing enough to work. I served the masons; I have been shop-boy, floor-polisher, I don't know what all! But, pshaw; to-day, work is lacking, another time I lose my place: Briefly, I never have had enough to eat. Heavens! how often have I been crazy with hunger as I have passed the bakeries! Fortunately for me; at these times I have always remembered the good Sister at the Asylum, who so often told me to be honest, and I seemed to feel her warm little hand upon my forehead. At last, when I was eighteen I enlisted; you know as well as I do, that the trooper has only just enough. Now, — I could almost laugh — here is the siege and famine! You see, I did not lie, when I told you, just now that I have always, always, been hungry!"

The young duke had a kind heart and was profoundly moved by this terrible story, told him by a man like himself, by a soldier whose uniform made him his equal. It was even fortunate for the phlegm of this dandy, that the night wind dried the tears which dimmed his eyes.

"Jean-Victor," said he, ceasing in his turn, by a delicate tact, to speak familiarly to the foundling, "if we survive this dreadful war, we will meet again, and I hope that I may be useful to you. But, in the meantime, as there is no bakery but the commissary, and as my ration of bread is twice too large for my delicate appetite, — it is understood, is it not? — we will share it like good comrades."

It was strong and hearty, the hand-clasp which followed: then, harassed and worn by their frequent watches and alarms, as night fell, they returned to the tavern, where twelve soldiers were sleeping on the straw; and throwing themselves down side by side, they were soon sleeping soundly.

Toward midnight Jean-Victor awoke, being hungry probably. The wind had scattered the clouds, and a ray of moonlight made its way into the room through a hole in the roof, lighting up the handsome blonde head of the young duke, who was sleeping like an Endymion.

Still touched by the kindness of his comrade, Jean-Victor was gazing at him with admiration, when the sergeant of the platoon opened the door and called the five men who were to relieve the sentinels of the out-posts. The duke was of the number, but he did not waken when his name was called.

"Hardimont, stand up!" repeated the non-commissioned officer.

"If you are willing, sergeant," said Jean-Victor rising, "I will take his duty, he is sleeping so soundly — and he is my comrade."

"As you please."

The five men left, and the snoring recommenced.

But half an hour later the noise of near and rapid firing burst upon the night. In an instant every man was on his feet, and each with his hand on the chamber of his gun, stepped cautiously out, looking earnestly along the road, lying white in the moonlight.

"What time is it?" asked the duke. "I was to go on duty to-night."

"Jean-Victor went in your place."

At that moment a soldier was seen running toward them along the road.

"What is it?" they cried as he stopped, out of breath.

"The Prussians have attacked us, let us fall back to the redoubt."

"And your comrades?"

"They are coming — all but poor Jean-Victor."

"Where is he?" cried the duke.

"Shot through the head with a bullet — died without a word! — ough!"

\* \* \* \* \*

One night last winter, the Due de Hardimont left his club about two o'clock in the morning, with his neighbor, Count de Saulnes; the duke had lost some hundred louis, and had a slight headache.

"If you are willing, André," he said to his companion, "we will go home on foot — I need the air."

"Just as you please, I am willing, although the walking may he bad."

They dismissed their coupés, turned up the collars of their overcoats, and set off toward the Madeleine. Suddenly an object rolled before the duke which he had struck with the toe of his boot; it was a large piece of bread spattered with mud.

Then to his amazement, Monsieur de Saulnes saw the Due de Hardimont pick up the piece of bread, wipe it carefully with his handkerchief embroidered with his armorial bearings, and place it on a bench, in full view under the gaslight.

"What did you do that for?" asked the count, laughing heartily, "are you crazy?"

"It is in memory of a poor fellow who died for me," replied the duke in a voice which trembled slightly, "do not laugh, my friend, it offends me."

# THE MIRROR
## BY CATULLE MENDES

There was once a kingdom where mirrors were unknown. They had all been broken and reduced to fragments by order of the queen, and if the tiniest bit of looking-glass had been found in any house, she would not have hesitated to put all the inmates to death with the most frightful tortures.

Now for the secret of this extraordinary caprice. The queen was dreadfully ugly, and she did not wish to be exposed to the risk of meeting her own image; and, knowing herself to be hideous, it was a consolation to know that other women at least could not see that they were pretty.

You may imagine that the young girls of the country were not at all satisfied. What was the use of being beautiful if you could not admire yourself?

They might have used the brooks and lakes for mirrors; but the queen had foreseen that, and had hidden all of them under closely joined flagstones. Water was drawn from wells so deep that it was impossible to see the liquid surface, and shallow basins must be used instead of buckets, because in the latter there might be reflections.

Such a dismal state of affairs, especially for the pretty coquettes, who were no more rare in this country than in others.

The queen had no compassion, being well content that her subjects should suffer as much annoyance from the lack of a mirror as she felt at the sight of one.

However, in a suburb of the city there lived a young girl called Jacinta, who was a little better off than the rest, thanks to her sweetheart, Valentin. For if someone thinks you are beautiful, and loses no chance to tell you so, he is almost as good as a mirror.

"Tell me the truth," she would say; "what is the color of my eyes?"

"They are like dewy forget-me-nots."

"And my skin is not quite black?"

411

"You know that your forehead is whiter than freshly fallen snow, and your cheeks are like blush roses."

"How about my lips?"

"Cherries are pale beside them."

"And my teeth, if you please?"

"Grains of rice are not as white."

"But my ears, should I be ashamed of them?"

"Yes, if you would be ashamed of two little pink shells among your pretty curls."

And so on endlessly; she delighted, he still more charmed, for his words came from the depth of his heart and she had the pleasure of hearing herself praised, he the delight of seeing her. So their love grew more deep and tender every hour, and the day that he asked her to marry him she blushed certainly, but it was not with anger. But, unluckily, the news of their happiness reached the wicked queen, whose only pleasure was to torment others, and Jacinta more than anyone else, on account of her beauty.

A little while before the marriage Jacinta was walking in the orchard one evening, when an old crone approached, asking for alms, but suddenly jumped back with a shriek as if she had stepped on a toad, crying: "Heavens, what do I see?"

"What is the matter, my good woman? What is it you see? Tell me."

"The ugliest creature I ever beheld."

"Then you are not looking at me," said Jacinta, with innocent vanity.

"Alas! yes, my poor child, it is you. I have been a long time on this earth, but never have I met anyone so hideous as you!"

"What! am I ugly?"

"A hundred times uglier than I can tell you."

"But my eyes — "

"They are a sort of dirty gray; but that would be nothing if you had not such an outrageous squint!"

"My complexion — "

"It looks as if you had rubbed coal-dust on your forehead and cheeks."

"My mouth — "

"It is pale and withered, like a faded flower."

"My teeth — "

"If the beauty of teeth is to be large and yellow, I never saw any so beautiful as yours."

"But, at least, my ears — "

"They are so big, so red, and so misshapen, under your coarse elf-locks, that they are revolting. I am not pretty myself, but I should die of shame if mine were like them." After this last blow, the old witch, having repeated what the queen had taught her, hobbled off, with a harsh croak of laughter, leaving poor Jacinta dissolved in tears, prone on the ground beneath the apple-trees.

※ ※ ※ ※

Nothing could divert her mind from her grief. "I am ugly — I am ugly," she repeated constantly. It was in vain that Valentin assured and reassured her with the most solemn oaths. "Let me alone; you are lying out of pity. I understand it all now; you never loved me; you are only sorry for me. The beggar woman had no interest in deceiving me. It is only too true — I am ugly. I do not see how you can endure the sight of me."

To undeceive her, he brought people from far and near; every man declared that Jacinta was created to delight the eyes; even the women said as much, though they were less enthusiastic. But the poor child persisted in her conviction that she was a repulsive object, and when Valentin pressed her to name their wedding-day — "I, your wife!" cried she. "Never! I love you too dearly to burden you with a being so hideous as I am." You can fancy the despair of the poor fellow so sincerely in love. He threw himself on his knees; he prayed; he supplicated; she answered still that she was too ugly to marry him.

What was he to do? The only way to give the lie to the old woman and prove the truth to Jacinta was to put a mirror before her. But there was no such thing in the kingdom, and so great was the terror inspired by the queen that no workman dared make one.

"Well, I shall go to Court," said the lover, in despair. "Harsh as our mistress is, she cannot fail to be moved by the tears and the beauty of Jacinta. She will retract, for a few hours at least, this cruel edict which has caused our trouble."

It was not without difficulty that he persuaded the young girl to let him take her to the palace. She did not like to show herself, and asked of what use would be a mirror, only to impress her more deeply with her misfortune; but when he wept, her heart was moved, and she consented, to please him.

✳ ✳ ✳ ✳ ✳

"What is all this?" said the wicked queen. "Who are these people? and what do they want?"

"Your Majesty, you have before you the most unfortunate lover on the face of the earth."

"Do you consider that a good reason for coming here to annoy me?"

"Have pity on me."

"What have I to do with your love affairs?"

"If you would permit a mirror —— "

The queen rose to her feet, trembling with rage. "Who dares to speak to me of a mirror?" she said, grinding her teeth.

"Do not be angry, your Majesty, I beg of you, and deign to hear me. This young girl whom you see before you, so fresh and pretty, is the victim of a strange delusion. She imagines that she is ugly."

"Well," said the queen, with a malicious grin, "she is right. I never saw a more hideous object."

Jacinta, at these cruel words, thought she would die of mortification. Doubt was no longer possible, she must be ugly. Her eyes closed, she fell on the steps of the throne in a deadly swoon.

But Valentin was affected very differently. He cried out loudly that her Majesty must be mad to tell such a lie. He had no time to say more. The guards seized him, and at a sign from the queen the headsman came forward. He was always beside the throne, for she might need his services at any moment.

"Do your duty," said the queen, pointing out the man who had insulted her. The executioner raised his gleaming axe just as Jacinta came to herself and opened her eyes. Then two shrieks pierced the air. One was a cry of joy, for in the glittering steel Jacinta saw herself, so charmingly pretty — and the other a scream of anguish, as the wicked soul of the queen took flight, unable to bear the sight of her face in the impromptu mirror.

## MY NEPHEW JOSEPH
## BY LUDOVIC HALEVY

(*Scene passes at Versailles; two old gentlemen are conversing, seated on a bench in the King's garden.*)

Journalism, my dear Monsieur, is the evil of the times. I tell you what, if I had a son, I would hesitate a long while before giving him a literary education. I would have him learn chemistry, mathematics, fencing, cosmography, swimming, drawing, but not composition — no, not composition. Then, at least, he would be prevented from becoming a journalist. It is so easy, so tempting. They take pen and paper and write, it doesn't matter what, apropos to it doesn't matter what, and you have a newspaper article. In order to become a watchmaker, a lawyer, an upholsterer, in short, all the liberal arts, study, application, and a special kind of knowledge are necessary; but nothing like that is required for a journalist."

"You are perfectly right, my dear Monsieur, the profession of journalism should be restricted by examinations, the issuing of warrants, the granting of licenses — "

"And they could pay well for their licenses, these gentlemen. Do you know that journalism is become very profitable? There are some young men in it who, all at once, without a fixed salary, and no capital whatever, make from ten, twenty to thirty thousand francs a year."

"Now, that is strange! But how do they become journalists?"

"Ah! It appears they generally commence by being reporters. Reporters slip in everywhere, in official gatherings, and theatres, never missing a first night, nor a fire, nor a great ball, nor a murder."

"How well acquainted you are with all this!"

"Yes, very well acquainted. Ah! Mon Dieu! You are my friend, you will keep my secret, and if you will not repeat this in Versailles — I will tell you how it is — we have one in the family."

"One what?"

"A reporter."

"A reporter in your family, which always seemed so united! How can that be?"

"One can almost say that the devil was at the bottom of it. You know my nephew Joseph — "

"Little Joseph! Is he a reporter?"

"Yes."

"Little Joseph, I can see him in the park now, rolling a hoop, bare-legged, with a broad white collar, not more than six or seven years ago — and now he writes for newspapers!"

"Yes, newspapers! You know my brother keeps a pharmacy in the Rue Montorgueil, an old and reliable firm, and naturally my brother said to himself, 'After me, my son.' Joseph worked hard at chemistry, followed the course of study, and had already passed an examination. The boy was steady and industrious, and had a taste for the business. On Sundays for recreation he made tinctures, prepared prescriptions, pasted the labels and rolled pills. When, as misfortune would have it, a murder was committed about twenty feet from my brother's pharmacy — "

"The murder of the Rue Montorgueil — that clerk who killed his sweetheart, a little brewery maid?"

"The very same. Joseph was attracted by the cries, saw the murderer arrested, and after the police were gone stayed there in the street, talking and jabbering. The Saturday before, Joseph had a game of billiards with the murderer."

"With the murderer!"

"Oh! accidentally — he knew him by sight, went to the same café, that's all, and they had played at pool together, Joseph and the murderer — a man named Nicot. Joseph told this to the crowd, and you may well imagine how important that made him, when suddenly a little blond man seized him. 'You know the murderer?' 'A little, not much; I played pool with him.' 'And do you know the motive of the crime?' 'It was love, Monsieur, love; Nicot had met a girl, named Eugénie — ' 'You knew the victim, too?' 'Only by sight, she was there in the café the night we played.' 'Very well; but don't tell that to anybody; come, come, quick.' He took possession of Joseph and made him get into a cab, which went rolling off at great speed down the Boulevard des Italiens. Ten minutes after, Joseph found himself in a hall where there was a big table, around which five or six young men were writing. 'Here is a fine sensation,' said the little blond on entering. 'The best kind of a murder! a murder for love, in the Rue Montorgueil, and I have here the murderer's most intimate friend.' 'No, not at all,' cried Joseph, 'I scarcely know him.' 'Be still,' whispered the little blond to Joseph; then he continued, 'Yes, his most intimate friend. They were brought up together, and a quarter of an hour before the crime was committed were playing billiards. The murderer won, he was perfectly calm — — ' 'That's not it, it was last Saturday that I played with — — ' 'Be still, will you! A quarter of an hour, it is more to the point. Let's go. Come, come.' He took Joseph into a small room where they were alone, and said to him: 'That affair ought to make about a hundred lines — you talk — I'll write — there will be twenty francs for you.' 'Twenty francs!' 'Yes, and here they are in advance; but be quick, to business!' Joseph told all he knew to the gentleman — how an old and retired Colonel, who lived in the house where the murder was committed, was the first to hear the victim's cries; but he was paralyzed in both limbs, this old Colonel, and could only ring for the servant, an old cuirassier, who arrested the assassin. In short, with all the information concerning the game of billiards, Eugénie and the paralytic old Colonel, the man composed his little article, and sent Joseph away with twenty francs. Do you think it ended there?"

"I don't think anything — I am amazed! Little Joseph a reporter!"

"Hardly had Joseph stepped outside, when another man seized him — a tall, dark fellow. 'I've been watching for you,' he said to Joseph. 'You were present when the murder was committed in the Rue Montorgueil!' 'Why, no, I was not present — — ' 'That will do. I am well informed, come.' 'Where to?' 'To my newspaper office.' 'What for?' 'To tell me about the murder.' 'But I've already told all I know, there, in that house.' 'Come, you will still remember a few more little incidents — and I will give you twenty francs.' 'Twenty francs!' 'Come, come.' Another hall, another table, more young men writing, and again Joseph was interrogated. He recommenced the history of the old Colonel. 'Is that what you told them down there?' inquired the tall, dark man of Joseph. 'Yes, Monsieur.' 'That needs some revision, then.' And the tall, dark man made up a long story. How this old Colonel had been paralyzed for fourteen years, but on hearing the victim's heartrending screams, received such a shock that all at once, as if by a miracle, had recovered the use of his legs; and it was he who had started out in pursuit of the murderer and had him arrested.

"While dashing this off with one stroke of his pen, the man exclaimed: 'Good! this is perfect! a hundred times better than the other account.' 'Yes,' said Joseph, 'but it is not true.' 'Not true for you, because you are acquainted with the affair; but for our hundred thousand readers, who do not know about it, it will be true enough. They were not there, those hundred thousand readers. What do they want? A striking account — well! they shall have it!' And thereupon he discharged Joseph, who went home with his forty francs, and who naturally did not boast of his escapade. It is only of late that he has acknowledged it. However, from that day Joseph has shown less interest in the pharmacy. He bought a number of penny papers, and shut himself up in his room to write — no one knows what. At last he wore a business-like aspect, which was very funny. About six months ago I went to Paris to collect the dividends on my Northern stock."

"The Northern is doing very well; it went up this week — — "

"Oh! it's good stock. Well, I had collected my dividends and had left the Northern Railway Station. It was beautiful weather, so I walked slowly down the Rue Lafayette. (I have a habit of strolling a little in Paris after I have collected my dividends.) When at the corner of the Faubourg Montmartre, whom should I see but my nephew, Joseph, all alone in a victoria, playing the fine gentleman. I saw very well that he turned his head away, the vagabond! But I overtook the carriage and stopped the driver.

'What are you doing there?' 'A little drive, uncle.' 'Wait, I will go with you,' and in I climbed. 'Hurry up,' said the driver, 'or I'll lose the trail.' 'What trail?' 'Why, the two cabs we are following.' The man drove at a furious rate, and I asked Joseph why he was there in that victoria, following two cabs. 'Mon Dieu, uncle,' he replied, 'there was a foreigner, a Spaniard, who came to our place in the Rue Montorgueil and bought a large amount of drugs, and has not paid us, so I am going after him to find out if he has not given us a wrong address.' 'And that Spaniard is in both the cabs?' 'No, uncle, he is only in one, the first.' 'And who is in the second?' 'I don't know, probably another creditor, like myself, in pursuit of the Spaniard.' 'Well, I am going to stay with you; I have two hours to myself before the train leaves at five o'clock and I adore this sort of thing, riding around Paris in an open carriage. Let's follow the Spaniard!' And then the chase commenced, down the boulevards, across the squares, through the streets, the three drivers cracking their whips and urging their horses on. This man-hunt began to get exciting. It recalled to my mind the romances in the Petit Journal. Finally, in a little street, belonging to the Temple Quarter, the first cab stopped."

"The Spaniard?"

"Yes. A man got out of it — he had a large hat drawn down over his eyes and a big muffler wrapped about his neck. Presently three gentlemen, who had jumped from the second cab, rushed upon that man. I wanted to do the same, but Joseph tried to prevent me. 'Don't stir, uncle!' 'Why not? But they are going to deprive us of the Spaniard!' And I dashed forward. 'Take care, uncle, don't be mixed up in that affair.' But I was already gone. When I arrived they were putting the handcuffs on the Spaniard. I broke through the crowd which had collected, and cried, 'Wait, Messieurs, wait; I also demand a settlement with this man.' They made way for me. 'You know this man?' asked one of the gentlemen from the second cab, a short, stout fellow. 'Perfectly; he is a Spaniard.' 'I a Spaniard!' 'Yes, a Spaniard.' 'Good,' said the short, stout man, 'Here's the witness!' and, addressing himself to one of the men, 'Take Monsieur to the Prefecture immediately.'

420

'But I have not the time; I live in Versailles; my wife expects me by the five o'clock train, and we have company to dinner, and I must take home a pie. I will come back to-morrow at any hour you wish.' 'No remarks,' said the short, stout man, 'but be off; I am the Police Commissioner.' 'But, Monsieur the Commissioner, I know nothing about it; it is my nephew Joseph who will tell you,' and I called 'Joseph! Joseph!' but no Joseph came."

"He had decamped?"

"With the victoria. They packed me in one of the two cabs with the detective, a charming man and very distinguished. Arriving at the Prefecture, they deposited me in a small apartment filled with vagabonds, criminals, and low, ignorant people. An hour after they came for me in order to bring me up for examination."

"You were brought up for examination?"

"Yes, my dear Monsieur, I was. A policeman conducted me through the Palais de Justice, before the magistrate, a lean man, who asked me my name and address. I replied that I lived in Versailles, and that I had company to dinner; he interrupted me, 'You know the prisoner?' pointing to the man with the muffler, 'Speak up.' But he questioned me so threateningly that I became disconcerted, for I felt that he was passing judgment upon me. Then in my embarrassment the words did not come quickly. I finished, moreover, by telling him that I knew the man without knowing him; then he became furious: 'What's that you say? You know a man without knowing him! At least explain yourself!' I was all of a tremble, and said that I knew he was a Spaniard, but the man replied that he was not a Spaniard. 'Well, well,' said the Judge. 'Denial, always denial; it is your way.' 'I tell you that my name is Rigaud, and that I was born in Josey, in Josas; they are not Spaniards that are born in Josey, in Josas.' 'Always contradiction; very good, very good!' And the Judge addressed himself to me. 'Then this man is a Spaniard?' 'Yes, Monsieur the Judge, so I have been told.' 'Do you know anything more about him?' 'I know he made purchases at my brother's pharmacy in the Rue Montorgueil.' 'At a pharmacy! and he bought, did he not,

421

some chlorate of potash, azotite of potash, and sulfur powder; in a word, materials to manufacture explosives.' 'I don't know what he bought. I only know that he did not pay, that's all.' 'Parbleu! Anarchists never pay — ' 'I did not need to pay. I never bought chlorate of potash in the Rue Montorgueil,' cried the man; but the Judge exclaimed, louder still, 'Yes, it is your audacious habit of lying, but I will sift this matter to the bottom; sift it, do you understand. And now why is that muffler on in the month of May?' 'I have a cold,' replied the other. 'Haven't I the right to have a cold?' 'That is very suspicious, very suspicious. I am going to send for the druggist in the Rue Montorgueil!'"

"Then they sent for your brother?"

"Yes; I wanted to leave, tried to explain to the Judge that my wife was expecting me in Versailles, that I had already missed the five o'clock train, that I had company to dinner, and must bring home a pie. 'You shall not go,' replied the Judge, 'and cease to annoy me with your dinner and your pie; I will need you for a second examination. The affair is of the gravest sort.' I tried to resist, but they led me away somewhat roughly, and thrust me again into the little apartment with the criminals. After waiting an hour I was brought up for another examination. My brother was there. But we could not exchange two words, for he entered the courtroom by one door and I by another. All this was arranged perfectly. The man with the muffler was again brought out. The Judge addressed my brother. 'Do you recognize the prisoner?' 'No.' 'Ah! you see he does not know me!' 'Be silent!' said the Judge, and he continued talking excitedly: 'You know the man?' 'Certainly not.' 'Think well; you ought to know him.' 'I tell you, no.' 'I tell you, yes, and that he bought some chlorate of potash from you.' 'No!' 'Ah!' cried the Judge, in a passion. 'Take care, weigh well your words; you are treading on dangerous ground.' 'I!' exclaimed my brother. 'Yes, for there is your brother; you recognize him, I think.' 'Yes, I recognize him.' 'That is fortunate. Well, your brother there says that man owes you money for having bought at your establishment — I specify — materials to manufacture explosives.' 'But you did not say that.' 'No, I wish to re-establish the facts.' But that Judge would give no one a chance to speak. 'Don't interrupt me. Who is conducting this examination, you or I?' 'You, Monsieur the Judge?' 'Well, at all events, you said the prisoner owed your brother some money.' 'That I acknowledge.' 'But who told you all this?' asked my brother. 'Your son, Joseph!' 'Joseph!' 'He followed the man for the sake of the money, which he owed you for the drugs.' 'I understand nothing of all this,' said my brother; 'Neither do I,' said the man with the muffler; 'Neither do I,' I repeated in my turn; 'Neither do I any more,' cried the Judge; 'Or rather, yes, there is something that I understand very well; we have captured a gang, all these men understand one another, and side with one another; they are a band of Anarchists!' 'That is putting it too strong,' I protested to the Judge, 'I, a landowner, an Anarchist! Can a man be an Anarchist when he owns a house on the Boulevard de la Reine at Versailles and a cottage at Houlgate, Calvados? These are facts.'"

"That was well answered."

"But this Judge would not listen to anything. He said to my brother, 'Where does your son live?' 'With me in the Rue Montorgueil.' 'Well, he must be sent for; and in the meanwhile, these two brothers are to be placed in separate cells.' Then, losing patience, I cried that this was infamy! But I felt myself seized and dragged through the corridors and locked in a little box four feet square. In there I passed three hours."

"Didn't they find your nephew Joseph?"

"No, it was not that. It was the Judge. He went off to his dinner, and took his time about it! Finally, at midnight, they had another examination. Behold all four of us before the Judge! The man with the muffler, myself, my brother and Joseph. The Judge began, addressing my nephew: 'This man is indeed your father?' 'Yes.' 'This man is indeed your uncle?' 'Yes.' 'And that man is indeed the Spaniard who purchased some chlorate of potash from you?' 'No.' 'What! No?' 'There,' exclaimed the fellow with the muffler. 'You can see now that these men do not know me.' 'Yes, yes,' answered the Judge, not at all disconcerted. 'Denial again!

Let's see, young man, did you not say to your uncle — — ' 'Yes, Monsieur the Judge, that is true.' 'Ah! the truth! Here is the truth!' exclaimed the Judge, triumphantly. 'Yes, I told my uncle that the man purchased drugs from us, but that is not so.' 'Why isn't it?' 'Wait, I will tell you. Unknown to my family I am a journalist.' 'Journalist! My son a journalist! Don't believe that, Monsieur the Judge, my son is an apprentice in a pharmacy.' 'Yes, my nephew is an apprentice in a pharmacy,' I echoed. 'These men contradict themselves; this is a gang, decidedly a gang — are you a journalist, young man, or an apprentice in a pharmacy?' 'I am both.' 'That is a lie!' cried my brother, now thoroughly angry. 'And for what newspaper do you write?' 'For no paper at all,' replied my brother, 'I know that, for he is not capable.' 'I do not exactly write, Monsieur the Judge; I procure information; I am a reporter.' 'Reporter! My son a reporter? What's that he says?' 'Will you be still!' cried the Judge. For what newspaper are you a reporter?' Joseph told the name of the paper. 'Well,' resumed the Judge, 'we must send for the chief editor immediately — immediately, he must be awakened and brought here. I will pass the night at court. I've discovered a great conspiracy. Lead these men away and keep them apart.' The Judge beamed, for he already saw himself Court Counsellor. They brought us back, and I assure you I no longer knew where I was. I came and went up and down the staircases and through the corridors. If anyone had asked me at the time if I were an accomplice of Ravachol, I would have answered, 'Probably.'"

"When did all this take place?"

"One o'clock in the morning; and the fourth examination did not take place until two. But, thank Heaven! in five minutes it was all made clear. The editor of the newspaper arrived, and burst into a hearty laugh when he learned of the condition of affairs; and this is what he told the Judge. My nephew had given them the particulars of a murder, and had been recompensed for it, and then the young man had acquired a taste for that occupation, and had come to apply for the situation. They had found him clear-headed, bold, and intelligent, and had sent him to take notes at the executions, at fires, etc., and the morning after the editor had a good idea. 'The detectives were on the lookout for Anarchists, so I sent my reporters on the heels of each detective, and in this way I would be the first to hear of all the arrests. Now, you see, it all explains itself; the detective followed an Anarchist.'"

"And your nephew Joseph followed the detective?"

"Yes, but he dared not tell the truth, so he told me he was one of papa's debtors.' The man with the muffler was triumphant. 'Am I still a Spaniard?' 'No, well and good,' replied the Judge. 'But an Anarchist is another thing.' And in truth he was; but he only held one, that Judge, and was so vexed because he believed he had caught a whole gang, and was obliged to discharge us at four o'clock in the morning. I had to take a carriage to return to Versailles — got one for thirty francs. But found my poor wife in such a state!"

"And your nephew still clings to journalism?"

"Yes, and makes money for nothing but to ride about Paris that way in a cab, and to the country in the railway trains. The newspaper men are satisfied with him."

"What does your brother say to all this?"

"He began by turning him out of doors. But when he knew that some months he made two and three hundred francs, he softened; and then Joseph is as cute as a monkey. You know my brother invented a cough lozenge, 'Dervishes' lozenges'?"

"Yes, you gave me a box of them."

"Ah! so I did. Well, Joseph found means to introduce into the account of a murderer's arrest an advertisement of his father's lozenges." — "How did he do it?"

"He told how the murderer was hidden in a panel, and that he could not be found. But having the influenza, had sneezed, and that had been the means of his capture. And Joseph added that this would not have happened to him had he taken the Dervishes Lozenges. You see that pleased my brother so much that he forgave him. Ah! there is my wife coming to look for me. Not a word of all this! It is not necessary to repeat that there is a reporter in the family, and there is another reason for not telling it. When I want to sell off to the people of Versailles, I go and find Joseph and tell him of my little plan. He arranges everything for me as it should be, puts it in the paper quietly, and they don't know how it comes there!"

## ABANDONED
## BY GUY DE MAUPASSANT

"I really think you must be mad, my dear, to go for a country walk in such weather as this. You have had some very strange notions for the last two months. You drag me to the seaside in spite of myself, when you have never once had such a whim during all the forty-four years that we have been married. You chose Fécamp, which is a very dull town, without consulting me in the matter, and now you are seized with such a rage for walking, you who hardly ever stir out on foot, that you want to take a country walk on the hottest day of the year. Ask d'Apreval to go with you, as he is ready to gratify all your whims. As for me, I am going back to have a nap."

Madame de Cadour turned to her old friend and said:

"Will you come with me, Monsieur d'Apreval?"

He bowed with a smile, and with all the gallantry of former years:

"I will go wherever you go," he replied.

"Very well, then, go and get a sunstroke," Monsieur de Cadour said; and he went back to the Hôtel des Bains to lie down for an hour or two.

As soon as they were alone, the old lady and her old companion set off, and she said to him in a low voice, squeezing his hand:

"At last! at last!"

"You are mad," he said in a whisper. "I assure you that you are mad. Think of the risk you are running. If that man — "

She started.

"Oh! Henri, do not say that man, when you are speaking of him."

"Very well," he said abruptly, "if our son guesses anything, if he has any suspicions, he will have you, he will have us both in his power. You have got on without seeing him for the last forty years. What is the matter with you to-day?"

427

They had been going up the long street that leads from the sea to the town, and now they turned to the right, to go to Etretat. The white road stretched in front of them under a blaze of brilliant sunshine, so they went on slowly in the burning heat. She had taken her old friend's arm, and was looking straight in front of her, with a fixed and haunted gaze, and at last she said:

"And so you have not seen him again, either?"

"No, never."

"Is it possible?"

"My dear friend, do not let us begin that discussion again. I have a wife and children and you have a husband, so we both of us have much to fear from other people's opinion."

She did not reply; she was thinking of her long past youth and of many sad things that had occurred. How well she recalled all the details of their early friendship, his smiles, the way he used to linger, in order to watch her until she was indoors. What happy days they were, the only really delicious days she had ever enjoyed, and how quickly they were over!

And then — her discovery — of the penalty she paid! What anguish!

Of that journey to the South, that long journey, her sufferings, her constant terror, that secluded life in the small, solitary house on the shores of the Mediterranean, at the bottom of a garden, which she did not venture to leave. How well she remembered those long days which she spent lying under an orange tree, looking up at the round, red fruit, amid the green leaves. How she used to long to go out, as far as the sea, whose fresh breezes came to her over the wall, and whose small waves she could hear lapping on the beach. She dreamed of its immense blue expanse sparkling under the sun, with the white sails of the small vessels, and a mountain on the horizon. But she did not dare to go outside the gate. Suppose anybody had recognized her!

And those days of waiting, those last days of misery and expectation! The impending suffering, and then that terrible night! What misery she had endured, and what a night it was! How she had groaned and screamed! She could still see the pale face of her lover, who kissed her hand every moment, and the clean-shaven face of the doctor and the nurse's white cap.

And what she felt when she heard the child's feeble cries, that wail, that first effort of a human's voice!

And the next day! the next day! the only day of her life on which she had seen and kissed her son; for, from that time, she had never even caught a glimpse of him.

And what a long, void existence hers had been since then, with the thought of that child always, always floating before her. She had never seen her son, that little creature that had been part of herself, even once since then; they had taken him from her, carried him away, and had hidden him. All she knew was that he had been brought up by some peasants in Normandy, that he had become a peasant himself, had married well, and that his father, whose name he did not know, had settled a handsome sum of money on him.

How often during the last forty years had she wished to go and see him and to embrace him! She could not imagine to herself that he had grown! She always thought of that small human atom which she had held in her arms and pressed to her bosom for a day.

How often she had said to M. d'Apreval: "I cannot bear it any longer; I must go and see him."

But he had always stopped her and kept her from going. She would be unable to restrain and to master herself; their son would guess it and take advantage of her, blackmail her; she would be lost.

"What is he like?" she said.

"I do not know. I have not seen him again, either."

"Is it possible? To have a son and not to know him; to be afraid of him and to reject him as if he were a disgrace! It is horrible."

They went along the dusty road, overcome by the scorching sun, and continually ascending that interminable hill.

"One might take it for a punishment," she continued; "I have never had another child, and I could no longer resist the longing to see him, which has possessed me for forty years. You men cannot understand that. You must remember that I shall not live much longer, and suppose I should never see him, never have seen him! ... Is it possible? How could I wait so long? I have thought about him every day since, and what a terrible existence mine has been! I have never awakened, never, do you understand, without my first thoughts being of him, of my child. How is he? Oh, how guilty I feel toward him! Ought one to fear what the world may say in a case like this? I ought to have left everything to go after him, to bring him up and to show my love for him. I should certainly have been much happier, but I did not dare, I was a coward. How I have suffered! Oh, how those poor, abandoned children must hate their mothers!"

She stopped suddenly, for she was choked by her sobs. The whole valley was deserted and silent in the dazzling light and the overwhelming heat, and only the grasshoppers uttered their shrill, continuous chirp among the sparse yellow grass on both sides of the road.

"Sit down a little," he said.

She allowed herself to be led to the side of the ditch and sank down with her face in her hands. Her white hair, which hung in curls on both sides of her face, had become tangled. She wept, overcome by profound grief, while he stood facing her, uneasy and not knowing what to say, and he merely murmured: "Come, take courage."

She got up.

"I will," she said, and wiping her eyes, she began to walk again with the uncertain step of an elderly woman.

A little farther on the road passed beneath a clump of trees, which hid a few houses, and they could distinguish the vibrating and regular blows of a blacksmith's hammer on the anvil; and presently they saw a wagon standing on the right side of the road in front of a low cottage, and two men shoeing a horse under a shed.

Monsieur d'Apreval went up to them.

"Where is Pierre Benedict's farm?" he asked.

"Take the road to the left, close to the inn, and then go straight on; it is the third house past Poret's. There is a small spruce fir close to the gate; you cannot make a mistake."

They turned to the left. She was walking very slowly now, her legs threatened to give way, and her heart was beating so violently that she felt as if she should suffocate, while at every step she murmured, as if in prayer:

"Oh! Heaven! Heaven!"

Monsieur d'Apreval, who was also nervous and rather pale, said to her somewhat gruffly:

"If you cannot manage to control your feelings, you will betray yourself at once. Do try and restrain yourself."

"How can I?" she replied. "My child! When I think that I am going to see my child."

They were going along one of those narrow country lanes between farmyards, that are concealed beneath a double row of beech trees at either side of the ditches, and suddenly they found themselves in front of a gate, beside which there was a young spruce fir.

"This is it," he said.

She stopped suddenly and looked about her. The courtyard, which was planted with apple trees, was large and extended as far as the small thatched dwelling house. On the opposite side were the stable, the barn, the cow house and the poultry house, while the gig, the wagon and the manure cart were under a slated outhouse. Four calves were grazing under the shade of the trees and black hens were wandering all about the enclosure.

All was perfectly still; the house door was open, but nobody was to be seen, and so they went in, when immediately a large black dog came out of a barrel that was standing under a pear tree, and began to bark furiously.

There were four bee-hives on boards against the wall of the house.

Monsieur d'Apreval stood outside and called out:

"Is anybody at home?"

431

Then a child appeared, a little girl of about ten, dressed in a chemise and a linen petticoat, with dirty, bare legs and a timid and cunning look. She remained standing in the doorway, as if to prevent any one going in.

"What do you want?" she asked.

"Is your father in?"

"No."

"Where is he?"

"I don't know."

"And your mother?"

"Gone after the cows."

"Will she be back soon?"

"I don't know."

Then suddenly the lady, as if she feared that her companion might force her to return, said quickly:

"I shall not go without having seen him."

"We will wait for him, my dear friend."

As they turned away, they saw a peasant woman coming toward the house, carrying two tin pails, which appeared to be heavy and which glistened brightly in the sunlight.

She limped with her right leg, and in her brown knitted jacket, that was faded by the sun and washed out by the rain, she looked like a poor, wretched, dirty servant.

"Here is mamma." the child said.

When she got close to the house, she looked at the strangers angrily and suspiciously, and then she went in, as if she had not seen them. She looked old and had a hard, yellow, wrinkled face, one of those wooden faces that country people so often have.

Monsieur d'Apreval called her back.

"I beg your pardon, madame, but we came in to know whether you could sell us two glasses of milk."

She was grumbling when she reappeared in the door, after putting down her pails.

"I don't sell milk," she replied.

"We are very thirsty," he said, "and madame is very tired. Can we not get something to drink?"

The peasant woman gave them an uneasy and cunning glance and then she made up her mind.

"As you are here, I will give you some," she said, going into the house, and almost immediately the child came out and brought two chairs, which she placed under an apple tree, and then the mother, in turn brought out two bowls of foaming milk, which she gave to the visitors. She did not return to the house, however, but remained standing near them, as if to watch them and to find out for what purpose they had come there.

"You have come from Fécamp?" she said.

"Yes," Monsieur d'Apreval replied, "we are staying at Fécamp for the summer."

And then, after a short silence he continued:

"Have you any fowls you could sell us every week?"

The woman hesitated for a moment and then replied:

"Yes, I think I have. I suppose you want young ones?"

"Yes, of course."

"What do you pay for them in the market?"

D'Apreval, who had not the least idea, turned to his companion:

"What are you paying for poultry in Fécamp, my dear lady?"

"Four francs and four francs fifty centimes," she said, her eyes full of tears, while the farmer's wife, who was looking at her askance, asked in much surprise:

"Is the lady ill, as she is crying?"

He did not know what to say, and replied with some hesitation:

"No — no — but she lost her watch as we came along, a very handsome watch, and that troubles her. If anybody should find it, please let us know."

Mother Benedict did not reply, as she thought it a very equivocal sort of answer, but suddenly she exclaimed:

"Oh, here is my husband!"

She was the only one who had seen him, as she was facing the gate. D'Apreval started and Madame de Cadour nearly fell as she turned round suddenly on her chair.

A man bent nearly double, and out of breath, stood there, ten yards from them, dragging a cow at the end of a rope. Without taking any notice of the visitors, he said:

"Confound it! What a brute!"

And he went past them and disappeared in the cow house.

Her tears had dried quickly as she sat there startled, without a word and with the one thought in her mind, that this was her son, and D'Apreval, whom the same thought had struck very unpleasantly, said in an agitated voice:

"Is this Monsieur Benedict?"

"Who told you his name?" the wife asked, still rather suspiciously.

"The blacksmith at the corner of the highroad," he replied, and then they were all silent, with their eyes fixed on the door of the cow house, which formed a sort of black hole in the wall of the building. Nothing could be seen inside, but they heard a vague noise, movements and footsteps and the sound of hoofs, which were deadened by the straw on the floor, and soon the man reappeared in the door, wiping his forehead, and came toward the house with long, slow strides. He passed the strangers without seeming to notice them and said to his wife:

"Go and draw me a jug of cider; I am very thirsty."

Then he went back into the house, while his wife went into the cellar and left the two Parisians alone.

"Let us go, let us go, Henri," Madame de Cadour said, nearly distracted with grief, and so d'Apreval took her by the arm, helped her to rise, and sustaining her with all his strength, for he felt that she was nearly fainting, he led her out, after throwing five francs on one of the chairs.

As soon as they were outside the gate, she began to sob and said, shaking with grief:

"Oh! oh! is that what you have made of him?"

He was very pale and replied coldly:

"I did what I could. His farm is worth eighty thousand francs, and that is more than most of the sons of the middle classes have."

434

They returned slowly, without speaking a word. She was still crying; the tears ran down her cheeks continually for a time, but by degrees they stopped, and they went back to Fécamp, where they found Monsieur de Cadour waiting dinner for them. As soon as he saw them, he began to laugh and exclaimed:

"So my wife has had a sunstroke, and I am very glad of it. I really think she has lost her head for some time past!"

Neither of them replied, and when the husband asked them, rubbing his hands:

"Well, I hope that, at least, you have had a pleasant walk?"

Monsieur d'Apreval replied:

"A delightful walk, I assure you; perfectly delightful."

# SIMON'S PAPA

Noon had just struck. The school door opened and the youngsters darted out, jostling each other in their haste to get out quickly. But instead of promptly dispersing and going home to dinner as usual, they stopped a few paces off, broke up into knots, and began whispering.

The fact was that, that morning, Simon, the son of La Blanchotte, had, for the first time, attended school.

They had all of them in their families heard talk of La Blanchotte; and, although in public she was welcome enough, the mothers among themselves treated her with a somewhat disdainful compassion, which the children had imitated without in the least knowing why.

As for Simon himself, they did not know him, for he never went out, and did not run about with them in the streets of the village, or along the banks of the river. And they did not care for him; so it was with a certain delight, mingled with considerable astonishment, that they met and repeated to each other what had been said by a lad of fourteen or fifteen who appeared to know all about it, so sagaciously did he wink. "You know — Simon — well, he has no papa."

Just then La Blanchotte's son appeared in the doorway of the school.

He was seven or eight years old, rather pale, very neat, with a timid and almost awkward manner.

He was starting home to his mother's house when the groups of his schoolmates, whispering and watching him with the mischievous and heartless eyes of children bent upon playing a nasty trick, gradually closed in around him and ended by surrounding him altogether. There he stood in their midst, surprised and embarrassed, not understanding what they were going to do with him. But the lad who had brought the news, puffed up with the success he had met with already, demanded:

"What is your name, you?"

He answered: "Simon."

"Simon what?" retorted the other.

The child, altogether bewildered, repeated: "Simon."

The lad shouted at him: "One is named Simon something — that is not a name — Simon indeed."

The child, on the brink of tears, replied for the third time: "My name is Simon."

The urchins began to laugh. The triumphant tormentor cried: "You can see plainly that he has no papa."

A deep silence ensued. The children were dumfounded by this extraordinary, impossible, monstrous thing — a boy who had not a papa; they looked upon him as a phenomenon, an unnatural being, and they felt that hitherto inexplicable contempt of their mothers for La Blanchotte growing upon them. As for Simon, he had leaned against a tree to avoid falling, and he remained as if prostrated by an irreparable disaster. He sought to explain, but could think of nothing-to say to refute this horrible charge that he had no papa. At last he shouted at them quite recklessly: "Yes, I have one."

"Where is he?" demanded the boy.

Simon was silent, he did not know. The children roared, tremendously excited; and those country boys, little more than animals, experienced that cruel craving which prompts the fowls of a farmyard to destroy one of their number as soon as it is wounded. Simon suddenly espied a little neighbor, the son of a widow, whom he had seen, as he himself was to be seen, always alone with his mother.

"And no more have you," he said; "no more have you a papa."

"Yes," replied the other, "I have one."

"Where is he?" rejoined Simon.

"He is dead," declared the brat, with superb dignity; "he is in the cemetery, is my papa."

A murmur of approval rose among the little wretches as if this fact of possessing a papa dead in a cemetery had caused their comrade to grow big enough to crush the other one who had no papa at all. And these boys, whose fathers were for the most part bad men, drunkards, thieves, and who beat their wives, jostled each other to press closer and closer, as though they, the legitimate ones, would smother by their pressure one who was illegitimate.

The boy who chanced to be next Simon suddenly put his tongue out at him with a mocking air and shouted at him:

"No papa! No papa!"

Simon seized him by the hair with both hands and set to work to disable his legs with kicks, while he bit his cheek ferociously. A tremendous struggle ensued between the two combatants, and Simon found himself beaten, torn, bruised, rolled on the ground in the midst of the ring of applauding schoolboys. As he arose, mechanically brushing with his hand his little blouse all covered with dust, some one shouted at him:

"Go and tell your papa."

Then he felt a great sinking at his heart. They were stronger than he was, they had beaten him, and he had no answer to give them, for he knew well that it was true that he had no papa. Full of pride, he attempted for some moments to struggle against the tears which were choking him. He had a feeling of suffocation, and then without any sound he commenced to weep, with great shaking sobs. A ferocious joy broke out among his enemies, and, with one accord, just like savages in their fearful festivals, they took each other by the hand and danced round him in a circle, repeating as a refrain:

"No papa! No papa!"

But suddenly Simon ceased sobbing. He became ferocious. There were stones under his feet; he picked them up and with all his strength hurled them at his tormentors. Two or three were struck and rushed off yelling, and so formidable did he appear that the rest became panic-stricken. Cowards, as the mob always is in presence of an exasperated man, they broke up and fled. Left alone, the little fellow without a father set off running toward the fields, for a recollection had been awakened in him which determined his soul to a great resolve. He made up his mind to drown himself in the river.

He remembered, in fact, that eight days before, a poor devil who begged for his livelihood had thrown himself into the water because he had no more money. Simon had been there when they fished him out again; and the wretched man, who usually seemed to him so miserable, and ugly, had then struck him as being so peaceful with his pale cheeks, his long drenched beard, and his open eyes full of calm. The bystanders had said:

"He is dead."

And some one had said:

"He is quite happy now."

And Simon wished to drown himself also, because he had no father, just like the wretched being who had no money.

He reached the water and watched it flowing. Some fish were sporting briskly in the clear stream and occasionally made a little bound and caught the flies flying on the surface. He stopped crying in order to watch them, for their maneuvers interested him greatly. But, at intervals, as in a tempest intervals of calm alternate suddenly with tremendous gusts of wind, which snap off the trees and then lose themselves in the horizon, this thought would return to him with intense pain:

"I am going to drown myself because I have no papa."

It was very warm, fine weather. The pleasant sunshine warmed the grass. The water shone like a mirror. And Simon enjoyed some minutes of happiness, of that languor which follows weeping, and felt inclined to fall asleep there upon the grass in the warm sunshine.

A little green frog leaped from under his feet. He endeavored to catch it. It escaped him. He followed it and lost it three times in succession. At last he caught it by one of its hind legs and began to laugh as he saw the efforts the creature made to escape. It gathered itself up on its hind legs and then with a violent spring suddenly stretched them out as stiff as two bars; while it beat the air with its front legs as though they were hands, its round eyes staring in their circle of yellow. It reminded him of a toy made of straight slips of wood nailed zigzag one on the other; which by a similar movement regulated the movements of the little soldiers fastened thereon. Then he thought of his home, and then of his mother, and, overcome by sorrow, he again began to weep. A shiver passed over him. He knelt down and said his prayers as before going to bed. But he was unable to finish them, for tumultuous, violent sobs shook his whole frame. He no longer thought, he no longer saw anything around him, and was wholly absorbed in crying.

Suddenly a heavy hand was placed upon his shoulder, and a rough voice asked him:

"What is it that causes you so much grief, my little man?"

Simon turned round. A tall workman with a beard and black curly hair was staring at him good-naturedly. He answered with his eyes and throat full of tears:

"They beat me — because — I — I have no — papa — no papa."

"What!" said the man, smiling; "why, everybody has one."

The child answered painfully amid his spasms of grief:

"But I — I — I have none."

Then the workman became serious. He had recognized La Blanchotte's son, and, although himself a new arrival in the neighborhood, he had a vague idea of her history.

"Well," said he, "console yourself, my boy, and come with me home to your mother. They will give you — a papa."

And so they started on the way, the big fellow holding the little fellow by the hand, and the man smiled, for he was not sorry to see this Blanchotte, who was, it was said, one of the prettiest girls of the countryside, and, perhaps, he was saying to himself, at the bottom of his heart, that a lass who had erred might very well err again.

They arrived in front of a very neat little white house.

"There it is," exclaimed the child, and he cried, "Mamma!"

A woman appeared, and the workman instantly left off smiling, for he saw at once that there was no fooling to be done with the tall pale girl who stood austerely at her door as though to defend from one man the threshold of that house where she

440

had already been betrayed by another. Intimidated, his cap in his hand, he stammered out:

"See, madame, I have brought you back your little boy who had lost himself near the river."

But Simon flung his arms about his mother's neck and told her, as he again began to cry:

"No, mamma, I wished to drown myself, because the others had beaten me — had beaten me — because I have no papa."

A burning redness covered the young woman's cheeks; and, hurt to the quick, she embraced her child passionately, while the tears coursed down her face. The man, much moved, stood there, not knowing how to get away.

But Simon suddenly ran to him and said:

"Will you be my papa?"

A deep silence ensued. La Blanchotte, dumb and tortured with shame, leaned herself against the wall, both her hands upon her heart. The child, seeing that no answer was made him, replied:

"If you will not, I shall go back and drown myself."

The workman took the matter as a jest and answered, laughing:

"Why, yes, certainly I will."

"What is your name," went on the child, "so that I may tell the others when they wish to know your name?"

"Philip," answered the man:

Simon was silent a moment so that he might get the name well into his head; then he stretched out his arms, quite consoled, as he said:

"Well, then, Philip, you are my papa."

The workman, lifting him from the ground, kissed him hastily on both cheeks, and then walked away very quickly with great strides. When the child returned to school next day he was received with a spiteful laugh, and at the end of school, when the lads were on the point of recommencing, Simon threw these words at their heads as he would have done a stone: "He is named Philip, my papa."

Yells of delight burst out from all sides.

"Philip who? Philip what? What on earth is Philip? Where did you pick up your Philip?"

Simon answered nothing; and, immovable in his faith, he defied them with his eye, ready to be martyred rather than fly before them. The school master came to his rescue and he returned home to his mother.

During three months, the tall workman, Philip, frequently passed by La Blanchotte's house, and sometimes he made bold to speak to her when he saw her sewing near the window. She answered him civilly, always sedately, never joking with him, nor permitting him to enter her house. Notwithstanding, being, like all men, a bit of a coxcomb, he imagined that she was often rosier than usual when she chatted with him.

But a lost reputation is so difficult to regain and always remains so fragile that, in spite of the shy reserve of La Blanchotte, they already gossiped in the neighborhood.

As for Simon he loved his new papa very much, and walked with him nearly every evening when the day's work was done. He went regularly to school, and mixed with great dignity with his schoolfellows without ever answering them back.

One day, however, the lad who had first attacked him said to him:

"You have lied. You have not a papa named Philip."

"Why do you say that?" demanded Simon, much disturbed.

The youth rubbed his hands. He replied:

"Because if you had one he would be your mamma's husband."

Simon was confused by the truth of this reasoning; nevertheless, he retorted:

"He is my papa, all the same."

"That can very well be," exclaimed the urchin with a sneer, "but that is not being your papa altogether."

La Blanchotte's little one bowed his head and went off dreaming in the direction of the forge belonging to old Loizon, where Philip worked. This forge was as though buried beneath trees. It was very dark there; the red glare of a formidable furnace

442

alone lit up with great flashes five blacksmiths; who hammered upon their anvils with a terrible din. They were standing enveloped in flame, like demons, their eyes fixed on the red-hot iron they were pounding; and their dull ideas rose and fell with their hammers.

Simon entered without being noticed, and went quietly to pluck his friend by the sleeve. The latter turned round. All at once the work came to a standstill, and all the men looked on, very attentive. Then, in the midst of this unaccustomed silence, rose the slender pipe of Simon:

"Say, Philip, the Michaude boy told me just now that you were not altogether my papa."

"Why not?" asked the blacksmith,

The child replied with all innocence:

"Because you are not my mamma's husband."

No one laughed. Philip remained standing, leaning his forehead upon the back of his great hands, which supported the handle of his hammer standing upright upon the anvil. He mused. His four companions watched him, and Simon, a tiny mite among these giants, anxiously waited. Suddenly, one of the smiths, answering to the sentiment of all, said to Philip:

"La Blanchotte is a good, honest girl, and upright and steady in spite of her misfortune, and would make a worthy wife for an honest man."

"That is true," remarked the three others.

The smith continued:

"Is it the girl's fault if she went wrong? She had been promised marriage; and I know more than one who is much respected to-day, and who sinned every bit as much."

"That is true," responded the three men in chorus.

He resumed:

"How hard she has toiled, poor thing, to bring up her child all alone, and how she has wept all these years she has never gone out except to church, God only knows."

"This is also true," said the others.

443

Then nothing was heard but the bellows which fanned the fire of the furnace. Philip hastily bent himself down to Simon:

"Go and tell your mother that I am coming to speak to her this evening." Then he pushed the child out by the shoulders. He returned to his work, and with a single blow the five hammers again fell upon their anvils. Thus they wrought the iron until nightfall, strong, powerful, happy, like contented hammers. But just as the great bell of a cathedral resounds upon feast days above the jingling of the other bells, so Philip's hammer, sounding above the rest, clanged second after second with a deafening uproar. And he stood amid the flying sparks plying his trade vigorously.

The sky was full of stars as he knocked at La Blanchotte's door. He had on his Sunday blouse, a clean shirt, and his beard was trimmed. The young woman showed herself upon the threshold, and said in a grieved tone:

"It is ill to come thus when night has fallen, Mr. Philip."

He wished to answer, but stammered and stood confused before her.

She resumed:

"You understand, do you not, that it will not do for me to be talked about again."

"What does that matter to me, if you will be my wife!"

No voice replied to him, but he believed that he heard in the shadow of the room the sound of a falling body. He entered quickly; and Simon, who had gone to bed, distinguished the sound of a kiss and some words that his mother murmured softly. Then, all at once, he found himself lifted up by the hands of his friend, who, holding him at the length of his Herculean arms, exclaimed:

"You will tell them, your schoolmates, that your papa is Philip Remy, the blacksmith, and that he will pull the ears of all who do you any harm."

On the morrow, when the school was full and lessons were about to begin, little Simon stood up, quite pale with trembling lips:

"My papa," said he in a clear voice, "is Philip Remy, the blacksmith, and he has promised to pull the ears of all who does me any harm."

This time no one laughed, for he was very well known, was Philip Remy, the blacksmith, and was a papa of whom any one in the world would have been proud.

# THE CHILD

Lemonnier had remained a widower with one child. He had loved his wife devotedly, with a tender and exalted love, without a slip, during their entire married life. He was a good, honest man, perfectly simple, sincere, without suspicion or malice.

He fell in love with a poor neighbor, proposed and was accepted. He was making a very comfortable living out of the wholesale cloth business, and he did not for a minute suspect that the young girl might have accepted him for anything else but himself.

She made him happy. She was everything to him; he only thought of her, looked at her continually, with worshiping eyes. During meals he would make any number of blunders, in order not to have to take his eyes from the beloved face; he would pour the wine in his plate and the water in the salt-cellar, then he would laugh like a child, repeating:

"You see, I love you too much; that makes me crazy."

She would smile with a calm and resigned look; then she would look away, as though embarrassed by the adoration of her husband, and try to make him talk about something else; but he would take her hand under the table and he would hold it in his, whispering:

"My little Jeanne, my darling little Jeanne!"

She sometimes lost patience and said:

"Come, come, be reasonable; eat and let me eat."

He would sigh and break off a mouthful of bread, which he would then chew slowly.

For five years they had no children. Then suddenly she announced to him that this state of affairs would soon cease. He was wild with joy. He no longer left her for a minute, until his old nurse, who had brought him up and who often ruled the house, would push him out and close the door behind him, in order to compel him to go out in the fresh air.

He had grown very intimate with a young man who had known his wife since childhood, and who was one of the prefect's

446

secretaries. M. Duretour would dine three times a week with the Lemonniers, bringing flowers to madame, and sometimes a box at the theater; and often, at the end of the dinner, Lemonnier, growing tender, turning towards his wife, would explain: "With a companion like you and a friend like him, a man is completely happy on earth."

She died in childbirth. The shock almost killed him. But the sight of the child, a poor, moaning little creature, gave him courage.

He loved it with a passionate and sorrowful love, with a morbid love in which stuck the memory of death, but in which lived something of his worship for the dead mother. It was the flesh of his wife, her being continued, a sort of quintessence of herself. This child was her very life transferred to another body; she had disappeared that it might exist, and the father would smother it in with kisses. But also, this child had killed her; he had stolen this beloved creature, his life was at the cost of hers. And M. Lemonnier would place his son in the cradle and would sit down and watch him. He would sit this way by the hour, looking at him, dreaming of thousands of things, sweet or sad. Then, when the little one was asleep, he would bend over him and sob.

The child grew. The father could no longer spend an hour away from him; he would stay near him, take him out for walks, and himself dress him, wash him, make him eat. His friend, M. Duretour, also seemed to love the boy; he would kiss him wildly, in those frenzies of tenderness which are characteristic of parents. He would toss him in his arms, he would trot him on his knees, by the hour, and M. Lemonnier, delighted, would mutter:

"Isn't he a darling? Isn't he a darling?"

And M. Duretour would hug the child in his arms and tickle his neck with his mustache.

Celeste, the old nurse, alone, seemed to have no tenderness for the little one. She would grow angry at his pranks, and seemed impatient at the caresses of the two men. She would exclaim:

"How can you expect to bring a child up like that? You'll make a perfect monkey out of him."

Years went by, and Jean was nine years old. He hardly knew how to read; he had been so spoiled, and only did as he saw fit. He was willful, stubborn and quick-tempered. The father always gave in to him and let him have his own way. M. Duretour would always buy him all the toys he wished, and he fed him on cake and candies. Then Celeste would grow angry and exclaim:

"It's a shame, monsieur, a shame. You are spoiling this child. But it will have to stop; yes, sir, I tell you it will have to stop, and before long, too."

M. Lemonnier would answer, smiling:

"What can you expect? I love him too much, I can't resist him; you must get used to it."

Jean was delicate, rather. The doctor said that he was anaemic, prescribed iron, rare meat and broth.

But the little fellow loved only cake and refused all other nourishment; and the father, in despair, stuffed him with cream-puffs and chocolate éclairs.

One evening, as they were sitting down to supper, Celeste brought on the soup with an air of authority and an assurance which she did not usually have. She took off the cover and, dipping the ladle into the dish, she declared:

"Here is some broth such as I have never made; the young one will have to take some this time."

M. Lemonnier, frightened, bent his head. He saw a storm brewing.

Celeste took his plate, filled it herself and placed it in front of him.

He tasted the soup and said:

"It is, indeed, excellent."

The servant took the boy's plate and poured a spoonful of soup in it. Then she retreated a few steps and waited.

Jean smelled the food and pushed his plate away with an expression of disgust. Celeste, suddenly pale, quickly stepped forward and forcibly poured a spoonful down the child's open mouth.

He choked, coughed, sneezed, spat; howling, he seized his glass and threw it at his nurse. She received it full in the stomach. Then, exasperated, she took the young shaver's head under her arm and began pouring spoonful after spoonful of soup down his throat. He grew as red as a beet, and he would cough it up, stamping, twisting, choking, beating the air with his hands.

At first the father was so surprised that he could not move. Then, suddenly, he rushed forward, wild with rage, seized the servant by the throat and threw her up against the wall stammering:

"Out! Out! Out! you brute!"

But she shook him off, and, her hair streaming down her back, her eyes snapping, she cried out:

"What's gettin' hold of you? You're trying to thrash me because I am making this child eat soup when you are filling him with sweet stuff!"

He kept repeating, trembling from head to foot:

"Out! Get out-get out, you brute!"

Then, wild, she turned to him and, pushing her face up against his, her voice trembling:

"Ah! — you think-you think that you can treat me like that? Oh! no. And for whom? — for that brat who is not even yours. No, not yours! No, not yours — not yours! Everybody knows it, except yourself! Ask the grocer, the butcher, the baker, all of them, any one of them!"

She was growling and mumbling, choked with passion; then she stopped and looked at him.

He was motionless livid, his arms hanging by his sides. After a short pause, he murmured in a faint, shaky voice, instinct with deep feeling:

"You say? you say? What do you say?"

She remained silent, frightened by his appearance. Once more he stepped forward, repeating:

"You say — what do you say?"

Then in a calm voice, she answered:

"I say what I know, what everybody knows."

He seized her and, with the fury of a beast, he tried to throw her down. But, although old, she was strong and nimble. She slipped under his arm, and running around the table once more furious, she screamed:

"Look at him, just look at him, fool that you are! Isn't he the living image of M. Durefour? just look at his nose and his eyes! Are yours like that? And his hair! Is it like his mother's? I tell you that everyone knows it, everyone except yourself! It's the joke of the town! Look at him!"

She went to the door, opened it, and disappeared.

Jean, frightened, sat motionless before his plate of soup.

At the end of an hour, she returned gently, to see how matters stood. The child, after doing away with all the cakes and a pitcher full of cream and one of syrup, was now emptying the jam-pot with his soup-spoon.

The father had gone out.

Celeste took the child, kissed him, and gently carried him to his room and put him to bed. She came back to the dining-room, cleared the table, put everything in place, feeling very uneasy all the time.

Not a single sound could be heard throughout the house. She put her ear against her master's door. He seemed to be perfectly still. She put her eye to the keyhole. He was writing, and seemed very calm.

Then she returned to the kitchen and sat down, ready for any emergency. She slept on a chair and awoke at daylight.

She did the rooms as she had been accustomed to every morning; she swept and dusted, and, towards eight o'clock, prepared M. Lemonnier's breakfast.

But she did not dare bring it to her master, knowing too well how she would be received; she waited for him to ring. But he did not ring. Nine o'clock, then ten o'clock went by.

Celeste, not knowing what to think, prepared her tray and started up with it, her heart beating fast.

She stopped before the door and listened. Everything was still. She knocked; no answer. Then, gathering up all her courage, she opened the door and entered. With a wild shriek, she dropped the breakfast tray which she had been holding in her hand.

In the middle of the room, M. Lemonnier was hanging by a rope from a ring in the ceiling. His tongue was sticking out horribly. His right slipper was lying on the ground, his left one still on his foot. An upturned chair had rolled over to the bed.

Celeste, dazed, ran away shrieking. All the neighbors crowded together. The physician declared that he had died at about midnight.

A letter addressed to M. Duretdur was found on the table of the suicide. It contained these words:

"I leave and entrust the child to you!"

# A COUNTRY EXCURSION

For five months they had been talking of going to take luncheon in one of the country suburbs of Paris on Madame Dufour's birthday, and as they were looking forward very impatiently to the outing, they rose very early that morning. Monsieur Dufour had borrowed the milkman's wagon and drove himself. It was a very tidy, two-wheeled conveyance, with a cover supported by four iron rods, with curtains that had been drawn up, except the one at the back, which floated out like a sail. Madame Dufour, resplendent in a wonderful, cherry colored silk dress, sat by the side of her husband.

The old grandmother and a girl sat behind them on two chairs, and a boy with yellow hair was lying at the bottom of the wagon, with nothing to be seen of him except his head.

When they reached the bridge of Neuilly, Monsieur Dufour said: "Here we are in the country at last!" and at that signal his wife grew sentimental about the beauties of nature. When they got to the crossroads at Courbevoie they were seized with admiration for the distant landscape. On the right was Argenteuil with its bell tower, and above it rose the hills of Sannois and the mill of Orgemont, while on the left the aqueduct of Marly stood out against the clear morning sky, and in the distance they could see the terrace of Saint-Germain; and opposite them, at the end of a low chain of hills, the new fort of Cormeilles. Quite in the distance; a very long way off, beyond the plains and village, one could see the sombre green of the forests.

The sun was beginning to burn their faces, the dust got into their eyes, and on either side of the road there stretched an interminable tract of bare, ugly country with an unpleasant odor. One might have thought that it had been ravaged by a pestilence, which had even attacked the buildings, for skeletons of dilapidated and deserted houses, or small cottages, which were left in an unfinished state, because the contractors had not been paid, reared their four roofless walls on each side.

Here and there tall factory chimneys rose up from the barren soil. The only vegetation on that putrid land, where the spring breezes wafted an odor of petroleum and slate, blended with another odor that was even less agreeable. At last, however, they crossed the Seine a second time, and the bridge was a delight. The river sparkled in the sun, and they had a feeling of quiet enjoyment, felt refreshed as they drank in the purer air that was not impregnated by the black smoke of factories nor by the miasma from the deposits of night soil. A man whom they met told them that the name of the place was Bezons. Monsieur Dufour pulled up and read the attractive announcement outside an eating house: Restaurant Poulin, matelottes and fried fish, private rooms, arbors, and swings.

"Well, Madame Dufour, will this suit you? Will you make up your mind at last?"

She read the announcement in her turn and then looked at the house for some time.

It was a white country inn, built by the roadside, and through the open door she could see the bright zinc of the counter, at which sat two workmen in their Sunday clothes. At last she made up her mind and said:

"Yes, this will do; and, besides, there is a view."

They drove into a large field behind the inn, separated from the river by the towing path, and dismounted. The husband sprang out first and then held out his arms for his wife, and as the step was very high Madame Dufour, in order to reach him, had to show the lower part of her limbs, whose former slenderness had disappeared in fat, and Monsieur Dufour, who was already getting excited by the country air, pinched her calf, and then, taking her in his arms, he set her on the ground, as if she had been some enormous bundle. She shook the dust out of the silk dress and then looked round to see in what sort of a place she was.

She was a stout woman, of about thirty-six, full-blown, and delightful to look at. She could hardly breathe, as her corsets were laced too tightly, and their pressure forced her superabundant bosom up to her double chin. Next the girl placed her hand on

453

her father's shoulder and jumped down lightly. The boy with the yellow hair had got down by stepping on the wheel, and he helped Monsieur Dufour to lift his grandmother out. Then they unharnessed the horse, which they had tied to a tree, and the carriage fell back, with both shafts in the air. The men took off their coats and washed their hands in a pail of water and then went and joined the ladies, who had already taken possession of the swings.

Mademoiselle Dufour was trying to swing herself standing up, but she could not succeed in getting a start. She was a pretty girl of about eighteen, one of those women who suddenly excite your desire when you meet them in the street and who leave you with a vague feeling of uneasiness and of excited senses. She was tall, had a small waist and large hips, with a dark skin, very large eyes and very black hair. Her dress clearly marked the outlines of her firm, full figure, which was accentuated by the motion of her hips as she tried to swing herself higher. Her arms were stretched upward to hold the rope, so that her bosom rose at every movement she made. Her hat, which a gust of wind had blown off, was hanging behind her, and as the swing gradually rose higher and higher, she showed her delicate limbs up to the knees each time, and the breeze from her flying skirts, which was more heady than the fumes of wine, blew into the faces of the two men, who were looking at her and smiling.

Sitting in the other swing, Madame Dufour kept saying in a monotonous voice:

"Cyprian, come and swing me; do come and swing me, Cyprian!"

At last he went, and turning up his shirt sleeves, as if undertaking a hard piece of work, with much difficulty he set his wife in motion. She clutched the two ropes and held her legs out straight, so as not to touch the ground. She enjoyed feeling dizzy at the motion of the swing, and her whole figure shook like a jelly on a dish, but as she went higher and higher; she became too giddy and was frightened. Each time the swing came down she uttered a piercing scream, which made all the little urchins in the

454

neighborhood come round, and down below, beneath the garden hedge, she vaguely saw a row of mischievous heads making various grimaces as they laughed.

When a servant girl came out they ordered luncheon.

"Some fried fish, a rabbit saute, salad and dessert," Madame Dufour said, with an important air.

"Bring two quarts of beer and a bottle of claret," her husband said.

"We will have lunch on the grass," the girl added.

The grandmother, who had an affection for cats, had been running after one that belonged to the house, trying to coax it to come to her for the last ten minutes. The animal, who was no doubt secretly flattered by her attentions, kept close to the good woman, but just out of reach of her hand, and quietly walked round the trees, against which she rubbed herself, with her tail up, purring with pleasure.

"Hello!" suddenly exclaimed the young man with the yellow hair, who was wandering about. "Here are two swell boats!" They all went to look at them and saw two beautiful canoes in a wooden shed; they were as beautifully finished as if they had been ornamental furniture. They hung side by side, like two tall, slender girls, in their narrow shining length, and made one wish to float in them on warm summer mornings and evenings along the flower-covered banks of the river, where the trees dip their branches into the water, where the rushes are continually rustling in the breeze and where the swift kingfishers dart about like flashes of blue lightning.

The whole family looked at them with great respect.

"Oh, they are indeed swell boats!" Monsieur Dufour repeated gravely, as he examined them like a connoiseur. He had been in the habit of rowing in his younger days, he said, and when he had spat in his hands — and he went through the action of pulling the oars — he did not care a fig for anybody. He had beaten more than one Englishman formerly at the Joinville regattas. He grew quite excited at last and offered to make a bet that in a boat like that he could row six leagues an hour without exerting himself.

"Luncheon is ready," the waitress said, appearing at the entrance to the boathouse, and they all hurried off. But two young men had taken the very seats that Madame Dufour had selected and were eating their luncheon. No doubt they were the owners of the sculls, for they were in boating costume. They were stretched out, almost lying on the chairs; they were sun-browned and their thin cotton jerseys, with short sleeves, showed their bare arms, which were as strong as a blacksmith's. They were two strong, athletic fellows, who showed in all their movements that elasticity and grace of limb which can only be acquired by exercise and which is so different to the deformity with which monotonous heavy work stamps the mechanic.

They exchanged a rapid smile when they saw the mother and then a glance on seeing the daughter.

"Let us give up our place," one of them said; "it will make us acquainted with them."

The other got up immediately, and holding his black and red boating cap in his hand, he politely offered the ladies the only shady place in the garden. With many excuses they accepted, and that it might be more rural, they sat on the grass, without either tables or chairs.

The two young men took their plates, knives, forks, etc., to a table a little way off and began to eat again, and their bare arms, which they showed continually, rather embarrassed the girl. She even pretended to turn her head aside and not to see them, while Madame Dufour, who was rather bolder, tempted by feminine curiosity, looked at them every moment, and, no doubt, compared them with the secret unsightliness of her husband. She had squatted herself on ground, with her legs tucked under her, after the manner of tailors, and she kept moving about restlessly, saying that ants were crawling about her somewhere. Monsieur Dufour, annoyed at the presence of the polite strangers, was trying to find a comfortable position which he did not, however, succeed in doing, and the young man with the yellow hair was eating as silently as an ogre.

"It is lovely weather, monsieur," the stout lady said to one of the boating men. She wished to be friendly because they had given up their place.

"It is, indeed, madame," he replied. "Do you often go into the country?"

"Oh, only once or twice a year to get a little fresh air. And you, monsieur?"

"I come and sleep here every night."

"Oh, that must be very nice!"

"Certainly it is, madame." And he gave them such a practical account of his daily life that it awakened afresh in the hearts of these shopkeepers who were deprived of the meadows and who longed for country walks, to that foolish love of nature which they all feel so strongly the whole year round behind the counter in their shop.

The girl raised her eyes and looked at the oarsman with emotion and Monsieur Dufour spoke for the first time.

"It is indeed a happy life," he said. And then he added: "A little more rabbit, my dear?"

"No, thank you," she replied, and turning to the young men again, and pointing to their arms, asked: "Do you never feel cold like that?"

They both began to laugh, and they astonished the family with an account of the enormous fatigue they could endure, of their bathing while in a state of tremendous perspiration, of their rowing in the fog at night; and they struck their chests violently to show how hollow they sounded.

"Ah! You look very strong," said the husband, who did not talk any more of the time when he used to beat the English. The girl was looking at them sideways now, and the young fellow with the yellow hair, who had swallowed some wine the wrong way, was coughing violently and bespattering Madame Dufour's cherry-colored silk dress. She got angry and sent for some water to wash the spots.

Meanwhile it had grown unbearably hot, the sparkling river looked like a blaze of fire and the fumes of the wine were getting into their heads. Monsieur Dufour, who had a violent hiccough, had unbuttoned his waistcoat and the top button of his trousers, while his wife, who felt choking, was gradually unfastening her dress. The apprentice was shaking his yellow wig in a happy frame of mind, and kept helping himself to wine, and the old grandmother, feeling the effects of the wine, was very stiff and dignified. As for the girl, one noticed only a peculiar brightness in her eyes, while the brown cheeks became more rosy.

The coffee finished, they suggested singing, and each of them sang or repeated a couplet, which the others applauded frantically. Then they got up with some difficulty, and while the two women, who were rather dizzy, were trying to get a breath of air, the two men, who were altogether drunk, were attempting gymnastics. Heavy, limp and with scarlet faces they hung on, awkwardly to the iron rings, without being able to raise themselves.

Meanwhile the two boating men had got their boats into the water, and they came back and politely asked the ladies whether they would like a row.

"Would you like one, Monsieur Dufour?" his wife exclaimed. "Please come!"

He merely gave her a drunken nod, without understanding what she said. Then one of the rowers came up with two fishing rods in his hands, and the hope of catching a gudgeon, that great vision of the Parisian shopkeeper, made Dufour's dull eyes gleam, and he politely allowed them to do whatever they liked, while he sat in the shade under the bridge, with his feet dangling over the river, by the side of the young man with the yellow hair, who was sleeping soundly.

One of the boating men made a martyr of himself and took the mother.

"Let us go to the little wood on the Ile aux Anglais!" he called out as he rowed off. The other boat went more slowly, for the rower was looking at his companion so intently that by thought of nothing else, and his emotion seemed to paralyze his strength, while the girl, who was sitting in the bow, gave herself up to the enjoyment of being on the water. She felt a disinclination to think, a lassitude in her limbs and a total enervation, as if she were intoxicated, and her face was flushed and her breathing quickened. The effects of the wine, which were increased by the extreme heat, made all the trees on the bank seem to bow as she passed. A vague wish for enjoyment and a fermentation of her blood seemed to pervade her whole body, which was excited by the heat of the day, and she was also disturbed at this tête-à-tête on the water, in a place which seemed depopulated by the heat, with this young man who thought her pretty, whose ardent looks seemed to caress her skin and were as penetrating and pervading as the sun's rays.

Their inability to speak increased their emotion, and they looked about them. At last, however, he made an effort and asked her name.

"Henriette," she said.

"Why, my name is Henri," he replied. The sound of their voices had calmed them, and they looked at the banks. The other boat had passed them and seemed to be waiting for them, and the rower called out:

"We will meet you in the wood; we are going as far as Robinson's, because Madame Dufour is thirsty." Then he bent over his oars again and rowed off so quickly that he was soon out of sight.

Meanwhile a continual roar, which they had heard for some time, came nearer, and the river itself seemed to shiver, as if the dull noise were rising from its depths.

"What is that noise?" she asked. It was the noise of the weir which cut the river in two at the island, and he was explaining it to her, when, above the noise of the waterfall, they heard the song of a bird, which seemed a long way off.

"Listen!" he said; "the nightingales are singing during the day, so the female birds must be sitting."

A nightingale! She had never heard one before, and the idea of listening to one roused visions of poetic tenderness in her heart. A nightingale! That is to say, the invisible witness of her love trysts which Juliet invoked on her balcony; that celestial music which it attuned to human kisses, that eternal inspirer of all those languorous romances which open an ideal sky to all the poor little tender hearts of sensitive girls!

She was going to hear a nightingale.

"We must not make a noise," her companion said, "and then we can go into the wood, and sit down close beside it."

The boat seemed to glide. They saw the trees on the island, the banks of which were so low that they could look into the depths of the thickets. They stopped, he made the boat fast, Henriette took hold of Henri's arm, and they went beneath the trees.

"Stoop," he said, so she stooped down, and they went into an inextricable thicket of creepers, leaves and reed grass, which formed an undiscoverable retreat, and which the young man laughingly called "his private room."

Just above their heads, perched in one of the trees which hid them, the bird was still singing. He uttered trills and roulades, and then loud, vibrating notes that filled the air and seemed to lose themselves on the horizon, across the level country, through that burning silence which weighed upon the whole landscape. They did not speak for fear of frightening it away. They were sitting close together, and, slowly, Henri's arm stole round the girl's waist and squeezed it gently. She took that daring hand without any anger, and kept removing it whenever he put it round her; without, however, feeling at all embarrassed by this caress, just as if it had been something quite natural, which she was resisting just as naturally.

She was listening to the bird in ecstasy. She felt an infinite longing for happiness, for some sudden demonstration of tenderness, for the revelation of superhuman poetry, and she felt such a softening at her heart, and relaxation of her nerves, that she began to cry, without knowing why. The young man was now straining her close to him, yet she did not remove his arm; she did not think of it. Suddenly the nightingale stopped, and a voice called out in the distance:

"Henriette!"

"Do not reply," he said in a low voice; "you will drive the bird away."

But she had no idea of doing so, and they remained in the same position for some time. Madame Dufour had sat down somewhere or other, for from time to time they heard the stout lady break out into little bursts of laughter.

The girl was still crying; she was filled with strange sensations. Henri's head was on her shoulder, and suddenly he kissed her on the lips. She was surprised and angry, and, to avoid him, she stood up.

They were both very pale when they left their grassy retreat. The blue sky appeared to them clouded and the ardent sun darkened; and they felt the solitude and the silence. They walked rapidly, side by side, without speaking or touching each other, for they seemed to have become irreconcilable enemies, as if disgust and hatred had arisen between them, and from time to time Henriette called out: "Mamma!"

By and by they heard a noise behind a bush, and the stout lady appeared, looking rather confused, and her companion's face was wrinkled with smiles which he could not check.

Madame Dufour took his arm, and they returned to the boats, and Henri, who was ahead, walked in silence beside the young girl. At last they got back to Bezons. Monsieur Dufour, who was now sober, was waiting for them very impatiently, while the young man with the yellow hair was having a mouthful of something to eat before leaving the inn. The carriage was waiting in the yard, and the grandmother, who had already got in, was very frightened at the thought of being overtaken by night before they reached Paris, as the outskirts were not safe.

They all shook hands, and the Dufour family drove off.

"Good-by, until we meet again!" the oarsmen cried, and the answer they got was a sigh and a tear.

Two months later, as Henri was going along the Rue des Martyrs, he saw Dufour, Ironmonger, over a door, and so he went in, and saw the stout lady sitting at the counter. They recognized each other immediately, and after an interchange of polite greetings, he asked after them all.

"And how is Mademoiselle Henriette?" he inquired specially.

"Very well, thank you; she is married."

"Ah!" He felt a certain emotion, but said: "Whom did she marry?"

"That young man who accompanied us, you know; he has joined us in business."

"I remember him perfectly."

He was going out, feeling very unhappy, though scarcely knowing why, when madame called him back.

"And how is your friend?" she asked rather shyly.

"He is very well, thank you."

"Please give him our compliments, and beg him to come and call, when he is in the neighborhood."

She then added: "Tell him it will give me great pleasure."

"I will be sure to do so. Adieu!"

"Do not say that; come again very soon."

The next year, one very hot Sunday, all the details of that adventure, which Henri had never forgotten, suddenly came back to him so clearly that he returned alone to their room in the wood, and was overwhelmed with astonishment when he went in. She was sitting on the grass, looking very sad, while by her side, still in his shirt sleeves, the young man with the yellow hair was sleeping soundly, like some animal.

She grew so pale when she saw Henri that at first he thought she was going to faint; then, however, they began to talk quite naturally. But when he told her that he was very fond of that spot, and went there frequently on Sundays to indulge in memories, she looked into his eyes for a long time.

"I too, think of it," she replied.

"Come, my dear," her husband said, with a yawn. "I think it is time for us to be going."

# ROSE

The two young women appear to be buried under a blanket of flowers. They are alone in the immense landau, which is filled with flowers like a giant basket. On the front seat are two small hampers of white satin filled with violets, and on the bearskin by which their knees are covered there is a mass of roses, mimosas, pinks, daisies, tuberoses and orange blossoms, interwoven with silk ribbons; the two frail bodies seem buried under this beautiful perfumed bed, which hides everything but the shoulders and arms and a little of the dainty waists.

The coachman's whip is wound with a garland of anemones, the horses' traces are dotted with carnations, the spokes of the wheels are clothed in mignonette, and where the lanterns ought to be are two enormous round bouquets which look as though they were the eyes of this strange, rolling, flower-bedecked creature.

The landau drives rapidly along the road, through the Rue d'Antibes, preceded, followed, accompanied, by a crowd of other carriages covered with flowers, full of women almost hidden by a sea of violets. It is the flower carnival at Cannes.

The carriage reaches the Boulevard de la Fonciere, where the battle is waged. All along the immense avenue a double row of flower-bedecked vehicles are going and coming like an endless ribbon. Flowers are thrown from one to the other. They pass through the air like balls, striking fresh faces, bouncing and falling into the dust, where an army of youngsters pick them up.

A thick crowd is standing on the sidewalks looking on and held in check by the mounted police, who pass brutally along pushing back the curious pedestrians as though to prevent the common people from mingling with the rich.

In the carriages, people call to each other, recognize each other and bombard each other with roses. A chariot full of pretty women, dressed in red, like devils, attracts the eyes of all. A gentleman, who looks like the portraits of Henry IV., is throwing an immense bouquet which is held back by an elastic. Fearing the shock, the women hide their eyes and the men lower their heads, but the graceful, rapid and obedient missile describes a curve and returns to its master, who immediately throws it at some new face.

The two young women begin to throw their stock of flowers by handfuls, and receive a perfect hail of bouquets; then, after an hour of warfare, a little tired, they tell the coachman to drive along the road which follows the seashore.

The sun disappears behind Esterel, outlining the dark, rugged mountain against the sunset sky. The clear blue sea, as calm as a mill-pond, stretches out as far as the horizon, where it blends with the sky; and the fleet, anchored in the middle of the bay, looks like a herd of enormous beasts, motionless on the water, apocalyptic animals, armored and hump-backed, their frail masts looking like feathers, and with eyes which light up when evening approaches.

The two young women, leaning back under the heavy robes, look out lazily over the blue expanse of water. At last one of them says:

"How delightful the evenings are! How good everything seems! Don't you think so, Margot?"

"Yes, it is good. But there is always something lacking."

"What is lacking? I feel perfectly happy. I don't need anything else."

"Yes, you do. You are not thinking of it. No matter how contented we may be, physically, we always long for something more — for the heart."

The other asked with a smile:

"A little love?"

"Yes."

They stopped talking, their eyes fastened on the distant horizon, then the one called Marguerite murmured: "Life without that seems to me unbearable. I need to be loved, if only by a dog. But we are all alike, no matter what you may say, Simone."

"Not at all, my dear. I had rather not be loved at all than to be loved by the first comer. Do you think, for instance, that it would be pleasant to be loved by — by — "

She was thinking by whom she might possibly be loved, glancing across the wide landscape. Her eyes, after traveling around the horizon, fell on the two bright buttons which were shining on the back of the coachman's livery, and she continued, laughing: "by my coachman?"

Madame Margot barely smiled, and said in a low tone of voice:

"I assure you that it is very amusing to be loved by a servant. It has happened to me two or three times. They roll their eyes in such a funny manner — it's enough to make you die laughing! Naturally, the more in love they are, the more severe one must be with them, and then, some day, for some reason, you dismiss them, because, if anyone should notice it, you would appear so ridiculous."

Madame Simone was listening, staring straight ahead of her, then she remarked:

"No, I'm afraid that my footman's heart would not satisfy me. Tell me how you noticed that they loved you."

"I noticed it the same way that I do with other men — when they get stupid."

"The others don't seem stupid to me, when they love me."

"They are idiots, my dear, unable to talk, to answer, to understand anything."

"But how did you feel when you were loved by a servant? Were you — moved — flattered?"

"Moved? no, flattered — yes a little. One is always flattered to be loved by a man, no matter who he may be."

"Oh, Margot!"

"Yes, indeed, my dear! For instance, I will tell you of a peculiar incident which happened to me. You will see how curious and complex our emotions are, in such cases.

"About four years ago I happened to be without a maid. I had tried five or six, one right after the other, and I was about ready to give up in despair, when I saw an advertisement in a newspaper of a young girl knowing how to cook, embroider, dress hair, who was looking for a position and who could furnish the best of references. Besides all these accomplishments, she could speak English.

"I wrote to the given address, and the next day the person in question presented herself. She was tall, slender, pale, shy-looking. She had beautiful black eyes and a charming complexion; she pleased me immediately. I asked for her certificates; she gave me one in English, for she came, as she said, from Lady Rymwell's, where she had been for ten years.

"The certificate showed that the young girl had left of her own free will, in order to return to France, and the only thing which they had had to find fault in her during her long period of service was a little French coquettishness.

"This prudish English phrase even made me smile, and I immediately engaged this maid.

"She came to me the same day. Her name was Rose.

"At the end of a month I would have been helpless without her. She was a treasure, a pearl, a phenomenon.

"She could dress my hair with infinite taste; she could trim a hat better than most milliners, and she could even make my dresses.

"I was astonished at her accomplishments. I had never before been waited on in such a manner.

"She dressed me rapidly and with a surprisingly light touch. I never felt her fingers on my skin, and nothing is so disagreeable to me as contact with a servant's hand. I soon became excessively lazy; it was so pleasant to be dressed from head to foot, and from lingerie to gloves, by this tall, timid girl, always blushing a little, and never saying a word. After my bath she would rub and massage me while I dozed a little on my couch; I almost considered her more of a friend than a servant.

"One morning the janitor asked, mysteriously, to speak to me. I was surprised, and told him to come in. He was a good, faithful man, an old soldier, one of my husband's former orderlies.

"He seemed to be embarrassed by what he had to say to me. At last he managed to mumble:

"'Madame, the superintendent of police is downstairs.'

"I asked quickly:

"'What does he wish?'

"'He wishes to search the house.'

"Of course the police are useful, but I hate them. I do not think that it is a noble profession. I answered, angered and hurt:

"'Why this search? For what reason? He shall not come in.'

"The janitor continued:

"'He says that there is a criminal hidden in the house.'

"This time I was frightened and I told him to bring the inspector to me, so that I might get some explanation. He was a man with good manners and decorated with the Legion of Honor. He begged my pardon for disturbing me, and then informed me that I had, among my domestics, a convict.

"I was shocked; and I answered that I could guarantee every servant in the house, and I began to enumerate them.

"'The janitor, Pierre Courtin, an old soldier.'

"'It's not he.'

"'A stable-boy, son of farmers whom I know, and a groom whom you have just seen.'

"'It's not he.'

"'Then, monsieur, you see that you must be mistaken.'

"'Excuse me, madame, but I am positive that I am not making a mistake.

"'As the conviction of a notable criminal is at stake, would you be so kind as to send for all your servants?"

"At first I refused, but I finally gave in, and sent downstairs for everybody, men and women.

"The inspector glanced at them and then declared:

"'This isn't all.'

"'Excuse me, monsieur, there is no one left but my maid, a young girl whom you could not possibly mistake for a convict.'

"He asked:

"'May I also see her?'

"'Certainly.'

"I rang for Rose, who immediately appeared. She had hardly entered the room, when the inspector made a motion, and two men whom I had not seen, hidden behind the door, sprang forward, seized her and tied her hands behind her back.

"I cried out in anger and tried to rush forward to defend her. The inspector stopped me:

"'This girl, madame, is a man whose name is Jean Nicolas Lecapet, condemned to death in 1879 for assaulting a woman and injuring her so that death resulted. His sentence was commuted to imprisonment for life. He escaped four months ago. We have been looking for him ever since.'

"I was terrified, bewildered. I did not believe him. The commissioner continued, laughing:

"'I can prove it to you. His right arm is tattooed.'

"'The sleeve was rolled up. It was true. The inspector added, with bad taste:

"'You can trust us for the other proofs.'

"And they led my maid away!

"Well, would you believe me, the thing that moved me most was not anger at having thus been played upon, deceived and made ridiculous, it was not the shame of having thus been dressed and undressed, handled and touched by this man — but a deep humiliation — a woman's humiliation. Do you understand?"

"I am afraid I don't."

"Just think — this man had been condemned for — for assaulting a woman. Well! I thought of the one whom he had assaulted — and — and I felt humiliated — There! Do you understand now?"

Madame Margot did not answer. She was looking straight ahead, her eyes fastened on the two shining buttons of the livery, with that sphinx-like smile which women sometimes have.

# ROSALIE PRUDENT

There was a real mystery in this affair which neither the jury, nor the president, nor the public prosecutor himself could understand.

The girl Prudent (Rosalie), servant at the Varambots', of Nantes, having become enceinte without the knowledge of her masters, had, during the night, killed and buried her child in the garden.

It was the usual story of the infanticides committed by servant girls. But there was one inexplicable circumstance about this one. When the police searched the girl Prudent's room they discovered a complete infant's outfit, made by Rosalie herself, who had spent her nights for the last three months in cutting and sewing it. The grocer from whom she had bought her candles, out of her own wages, for this long piece of work had come to testify. It came out, moreover, that the sage-femme of the district, informed by Rosalie of her condition, had given her all necessary instructions and counsel in case the event should happen at a time when it might not be possible to get help. She had also procured a place at Poissy for the girl Prudent, who foresaw that her present employers would discharge her, for the Varambot couple did not trifle with morality.

There were present at the trial both the man and the woman, a middle-class pair from the provinces, living on their income. They were so exasperated against this girl, who had sullied their house, that they would have liked to see her guillotined on the spot without a trial. The spiteful depositions they made against her became accusations in their mouths.

The defendant, a large, handsome girl of Lower Normandy, well educated for her station in life, wept continuously and would not answer to anything.

The court and the spectators were forced to the opinion that she had committed this barbarous act in a moment of despair and madness, since there was every indication that she had expected to keep and bring up her child.

The president tried for the last time to make her speak, to get some confession, and, having urged her with much gentleness, he finally made her understand that all these men gathered here to pass judgment upon her were not anxious for her death and might even have pity on her.

Then she made up her mind to speak.

"Come, now, tell us, first, who is the father of this child?" he asked.

Until then she had obstinately refused to give his name.

But she replied suddenly, looking at her masters who had so cruelly calumniated her:

"It is Monsieur Joseph, Monsieur Varambot's nephew."

The couple started in their seats and cried with one voice — "That's not true! She lies! This is infamous!"

The president had them silenced and continued, "Go on, please, and tell us how it all happened."

Then she suddenly began to talk freely, relieving her pent-up heart, that poor, solitary, crushed heart — laying bare her sorrow, her whole sorrow, before those severe men whom she had until now taken for enemies and inflexible judges.

"Yes, it was Monsieur Joseph Varambot, when he came on leave last year."

"What does Mr. Joseph Varambot do?"

"He is a non-commissioned officer in the artillery, monsieur. Well, he stayed two months at the house, two months of the summer. I thought nothing about it when he began to look at me, and then flatter me, and make love to me all day long. And I let myself be taken in, monsieur. He kept saying to me that I was a handsome girl, that I was good company, that I just suited him — and I, I liked him well enough. What could I do? One listens to these things when one is alone — all alone — as I was. I am alone in the world, monsieur. I have no one to talk to — no one to tell my troubles to. I have no father, no mother, no brother, no sister, nobody. And when he began to talk to me it was as if I had a brother who had come back. And then he asked me to go with him to the river one evening, so that we might talk without

470

disturbing any one. I went — I don't know — I don't know how it happened. He had his arm around me. Really I didn't want to — no — no — I could not — I felt like crying, the air was so soft  — the moon was shining. No, I swear to you — I could not — he did what he wanted. That went on three weeks, as long as he stayed. I could have followed him to the ends of the world. He went away. I did not know that I was enceinte. I did not know it until the month after — "

She began to cry so bitterly that they had to give her time to collect herself.

Then the president resumed with the tone of a priest at the confessional: "Come, now, go on."

She began to talk again: "When I realized my condition I went to see Madame Boudin, who is there to tell you, and I asked her how it would be, in case it should come if she were not there. Then I made the outfit, sewing night after night, every evening until one o'clock in the morning; and then I looked for another place, for I knew very well that I should be sent away, but I wanted to stay in the house until the very last, so as to save my pennies, for I have not got very much and I should need my money for the little one."

"Then you did not intend to kill him?"

"Oh, certainly not, monsieur!"

"Why did you kill him, then?"

"It happened this way. It came sooner than I expected. It came upon me in the kitchen, while I was doing the dishes. Monsieur and Madame Varambot were already asleep, so I went up, not without difficulty, dragging myself up by the banister, and I lay down on the bare floor. It lasted perhaps one hour, or two, or three; I don't know, I had such pain; and then I pushed him out with all my strength. I felt that he came out and I picked him up.

"Ah! but I was glad, I assure you! I did all that Madame Boudin told me to do. And then I laid him on my bed. And then such a pain griped me again that I thought I should die. If you knew what it meant, you there, you would not do so much of this.

I fell on my knees, and then toppled over backward on the floor; and it griped me again, perhaps one hour, perhaps two. I lay there all alone — and then another one comes — another little one — two, yes, two, like this. I took him up as I did the first one, and then I put him on the bed, the two side by side. Is it possible, tell me, two children, and I who get only twenty francs a month? Say, is it possible? One, yes, that can be managed by going without things, but not two. That turned my head. What do I know about it? Had I any choice, tell me?

"What could I do? I felt as if my last hour had come. I put the pillow over them, without knowing why. I could not keep them both; and then I threw myself down, and I lay there, rolling over and over and crying until I saw the daylight come into the window. Both of them were quite dead under the pillow. Then I took them under my arms and went down the stairs out in the vegetable garden. I took the gardener's spade and I buried them under the earth, digging as deep a hole as I could, one here and the other one there, not together, so that they might not talk of their mother if these little dead bodies can talk. What do I know about it?

"And then, back in my bed, I felt so sick that I could not get up. They sent for the doctor and he understood it all. I'm telling you the truth, Your Honor. Do what you like with me; I'm ready."

Half of the jury were blowing their noses violently to keep from crying. The women in the courtroom were sobbing.

The president asked her:

"Where did you bury the other one?"

"The one that you have?" she asked.

"Why, this one — this one was in the artichokes."

"Oh, then the other one is among the strawberries, by the well."

And she began to sob so piteously that no one could hear her unmoved.

The girl Rosalie Prudent was acquitted.

# REGRET

Monsieur Saval, who was called in Mantes "Father Saval," had just risen from bed. He was weeping. It was a dull autumn day; the leaves were falling. They fell slowly in the rain, like a heavier and slower rain. M. Saval was not in good spirits. He walked from the fireplace to the window, and from the window to the fireplace. Life has its sombre days. It would no longer have any but sombre days for him, for he had reached the age of sixty-two. He is alone, an old bachelor, with nobody about him. How sad it is to die alone, all alone, without any one who is devoted to you!

He pondered over his life, so barren, so empty. He recalled former days, the days of his childhood, the home, the house of his parents; his college days, his follies; the time he studied law in Paris, his father's illness, his death. He then returned to live with his mother. They lived together very quietly, and desired nothing more. At last the mother died. How sad life is! He lived alone since then, and now, in his turn, he, too, will soon be dead. He will disappear, and that will be the end. There will be no more of Paul Saval upon the earth. What a frightful thing! Other people will love, will laugh. Yes, people will go on amusing themselves, and he will no longer exist! Is it not strange that people can laugh, amuse themselves, be joyful under that eternal certainty of death? If this death were only probable, one could then have hope; but no, it is inevitable, as inevitable as that night follows the day.

If, however, his life had been full! If he had done something; if he had had adventures, great pleasures, success, satisfaction of some kind or another. But no, nothing. He had done nothing, nothing but rise from bed, eat, at the same hours, and go to bed again. And he had gone on like that to the age of sixty-two years. He had not even taken unto himself a wife, as other men do. Why? Yes, why was it that he had not married? He might have done so, for he possessed considerable means. Had he lacked an opportunity? Perhaps! But one can create opportunities. He was indifferent; that was all. Indifference had been his greatest drawback, his defect, his vice. How many men wreck their lives through indifference! It is so difficult for some natures to get out of bed, to move about, to take long walks, to speak, to study any question.

He had not even been loved. No woman had reposed on his bosom, in a complete abandon of love. He knew nothing of the delicious anguish of expectation, the divine vibration of a hand in yours, of the ecstasy of triumphant passion.

What superhuman happiness must overflow your heart, when lips encounter lips for the first time, when the grasp of four arms makes one being of you, a being unutterably happy, two beings infatuated with one another.

M. Saval was sitting before the fire, his feet on the fender, in his dressing gown. Assuredly his life had been spoiled, completely spoiled. He had, however, loved. He had loved secretly, sadly, and indifferently, in a manner characteristic of him in everything. Yes, he had loved his old friend, Madame Sandres, the wife of his old companion, Sandres. Ah! if he had known her as a young girl! But he had met her too late; she was already married. Unquestionably, he would have asked her hand! How he had loved her, nevertheless, without respite, since the first day he set eyes on her!

He recalled his emotion every time he saw her, his grief on leaving her, the many nights that he could not sleep, because he was thinking of her.

On rising in the morning he was somewhat more rational than on the previous evening.

Why?

How pretty she was formerly, so dainty, with fair curly hair, and always laughing. Sandres was not the man she should have chosen. She was now fifty-two years of age. She seemed happy. Ah! if she had only loved him in days gone by; yes, if she had only loved him! And why should she not have loved him, he, Saval, seeing that he loved her so much, yes, she, Madame Sandres!

If only she could have guessed. Had she not guessed anything, seen anything, comprehended anything? What would she have thought? If he had spoken, what would she have answered?

And Saval asked himself a thousand other things. He reviewed his whole life, seeking to recall a multitude of details.

He recalled all the long evenings spent at the house of Sandres, when the latter's wife was young, and so charming.

He recalled many things that she had said to him, the intonations of her voice, the little significant smiles that meant so much.

He recalled their walks, the three of them together, along the banks of the Seine, their luncheon on the grass on Sundays, for Sandres was employed at the sub-prefecture. And all at once the distinct recollection came to him of an afternoon spent with her in a little wood on the banks of the river.

They had set out in the morning, carrying their provisions in baskets. It was a bright spring morning, one of those days which intoxicate one. Everything smells fresh, everything seems happy. The voices of the birds sound more joyous, and-they fly more swiftly. They had luncheon on the grass, under the willow trees, quite close to the water, which glittered in the sun's rays. The air was balmy, charged with the odors of fresh vegetation; they drank it in with delight. How pleasant everything was on that day!

After lunch, Sandres went to sleep on the broad of his back. "The best nap he had in his life," said he, when he woke up.

Madame Sandres had taken the arm of Saval, and they started to walk along the river bank.

She leaned tenderly on his arm. She laughed and said to him: "I am intoxicated, my friend, I am quite intoxicated." He looked at her, his heart going pit-a-pat. He felt himself grow pale, fearful that he might have looked too boldly at her, and that the trembling of his hand had revealed his passion.

She had made a wreath of wild flowers and water-lilies, and she asked him: "Do I look pretty like that?"

As he did not answer — for he could find nothing to say, he would have liked to go down on his knees — she burst out

475

laughing, a sort of annoyed, displeased laugh, as she said: "Great goose, what ails you? You might at least say something."

He felt like crying, but could not even yet find a word to say.

All these things came back to him now, as vividly as on the day when they took place. Why had she said this to him, "Great goose, what ails you? You might at least say something!"

And he recalled how tenderly she had leaned on his arm. And in passing under a shady tree he had felt her ear brushing his cheek, and he had moved his head abruptly, lest she should suppose he was too familiar.

When he had said to her: "Is it not time to return?" she darted a singular look at him. "Certainly," she said, "certainly," regarding him at the same time in a curious manner. He had not thought of it at the time, but now the whole thing appeared to him quite plain.

"Just as you like, my friend. If you are tired let us go back."

And he had answered: "I am not fatigued; but Sandres may be awake now."

And she had said: "If you are afraid of my husband's being awake, that is another thing. Let us return."

On their way back she remained silent, and leaned no longer on his arm. Why?

At that time it had never occurred to him, to ask himself "why." Now he seemed to apprehend something that he had not then understood.

Could it?

M. Saval felt himself blush, and he got up at a bound, as if he were thirty years younger and had heard Madame Sandres say, "I love you."

Was it possible? That idea which had just entered his mind tortured him. Was it possible that he had not seen, had not guessed?

Oh! if that were true, if he had let this opportunity of happiness pass without taking advantage of it!

He said to himself: "I must know. I cannot remain in this state of doubt. I must know!" He thought: "I am sixty-two years of age, she is fifty-eight; I may ask her that now without giving offense."

He started out.

The Sandres' house was situated on the other side of the street, almost directly opposite his own. He went across and knocked at the door, and a little servant opened it.

"You here at this hour, Saval! Has some accident happened to you?"

"No, my girl," he replied; "but go and tell your mistress that I want to speak to her at once."

"The fact is madame is preserving pears for the winter, and she is in the preserving room. She is not dressed, you understand."

"Yes, but go and tell her that I wish to see her on a very important matter."

The little servant went away, and Saval began to walk, with long, nervous strides, up and down the drawing-room. He did not feel in the least embarrassed, however. Oh! he was merely going to ask her something, as he would have asked her about some cooking recipe. He was sixty-two years of age!

The door opened and madame appeared. She was now a large woman, fat and round, with full cheeks and a sonorous laugh. She walked with her arms away from her sides and her sleeves tucked up, her bare arms all covered with fruit juice. She asked anxiously:

"What is the matter with you, my friend? You are not ill, are you?"

"No, my dear friend; but I wish to ask you one thing, which to me is of the first importance, something which is torturing my heart, and I want you to promise that you will answer me frankly."

She laughed, "I am always frank. Say on."

"Well, then. I have loved you from the first day I ever saw you. Can you have any doubt of this?"

She responded, laughing, with something of her former tone of voice.

"Great goose! what ails you? I knew it from the very first day!"

Saval began to tremble. He stammered out: "You knew it? Then . . ."

He stopped.

She asked:

"Then?"

He answered:

"Then — what did you think? What — what — what would you have answered?"

She broke into a peal of laughter. Some of the juice ran off the tips of her fingers on to the carpet.

"What?"

"I? Why, you did not ask me anything. It was not for me to declare myself!"

He then advanced a step toward her.

"Tell me — tell me . . . . You remember the day when Sandres went to sleep on the grass after lunch . . . when we had walked together as far as the bend of the river, below . . ."

He waited, expectantly. She had ceased to laugh, and looked at him, straight in the eyes.

"Yes, certainly, I remember it."

He answered, trembling all over:

"Well — that day — if I had been — if I had been — venturesome — what would you have done?"

She began to laugh as only a happy woman can laugh, who has nothing to regret, and responded frankly, in a clear voice tinged with irony:

"I would have yielded, my friend."

She then turned on her heels and went back to her jam-making.

Saval rushed into the street, cast down, as though he had met with some disaster. He walked with giant strides through the rain, straight on, until he reached the river bank, without thinking where he was going. He then turned to the right and followed the river. He walked a long time, as if urged on by some instinct. His

478

clothes were running with water, his hat was out of shape, as soft as a rag, and dripping like a roof. He walked on, straight in front of him. At last, he came to the place where they had lunched on that day so long ago, the recollection of which tortured his heart. He sat down under the leafless trees, and wept.

## A SISTER'S CONFESSION

Marguerite de Therelles was dying. Although she was-only fifty-six years old she looked at least seventy-five. She gasped for breath, her face whiter than the sheets, and had spasms of violent shivering, with her face convulsed and her eyes haggard as though she saw a frightful vision.

Her elder sister, Suzanne, six years older than herself, was sobbing on her knees beside the bed. A small table close to the dying woman's couch bore, on a white cloth, two lighted candles, for the priest was expected at any moment to administer extreme unction and the last communion.

The apartment wore that melancholy aspect common to death chambers; a look of despairing farewell. Medicine bottles littered the furniture; linen lay in the corners into which it had been kicked or swept. The very chairs looked, in their disarray, as if they were terrified and had run in all directions. Death — terrible Death — was in the room, hidden, awaiting his prey.

This history of the two sisters was an affecting one. It was spoken of far and wide; it had drawn tears from many eyes.

Suzanne, the elder, had once been passionately loved by a young man, whose affection she returned. They were engaged to be married, and the wedding day was at hand, when Henry de Sampierre suddenly died.

The young girl's despair was terrible, and she took an oath never to marry. She faithfully kept her vow and adopted widow's weeds for the remainder of her life.

But one morning her sister, her little sister Marguerite, then only twelve years old, threw herself into Suzanne's arms, sobbing: "Sister, I don't want you to be unhappy. I don't want you to

479

mourn all your life. I'll never leave you — never, never, never! I shall never marry, either. I'll stay with you always — always!"

Suzanne kissed her, touched by the child's devotion, though not putting any faith in her promise.

But the little one kept her word, and, despite her parents' remonstrances, despite her elder sister's prayers, never married. She was remarkably pretty and refused many offers. She never left her sister.

They spent their whole life together, without a single day's separation. They went everywhere together and were inseparable. But Marguerite was pensive, melancholy, sadder than her sister, as if her sublime sacrifice had undermined her spirits. She grew older more quickly; her hair was white at thirty; and she was often ill, apparently stricken with some unknown, wasting malady.

And now she would be the first to die.

She had not spoken for twenty-four hours, except to whisper at daybreak:

"Send at once for the priest."

And she had since remained lying on her back, convulsed with agony, her lips moving as if unable to utter the dreadful words that rose in her heart, her face expressive of a terror distressing to witness.

Suzanne, distracted with grief, her brow pressed against the bed, wept bitterly, repeating over and over again the words:

"Margot, my poor Margot, my little one!"

She had always called her "my little one," while Marguerite's name for the elder was invariably "sister."

A footstep sounded on the stairs. The door opened. An acolyte appeared, followed by the aged priest in his surplice. As soon as she saw him the dying woman sat up suddenly in bed, opened her lips, stammered a few words and began to scratch the bed-clothes, as if she would have made hole in them.

Father Simon approached, took her hand, kissed her on the forehead and said in a gentle voice:

"May God pardon your sins, my daughter. Be of good courage. Now is the moment to confess them — speak!"

Then Marguerite, shuddering from head to foot, so that the very bed shook with her nervous movements, gasped:

"Sit down, sister, and listen."

The priest stooped toward the prostrate Suzanne, raised her to her feet, placed her in a chair, and, taking a hand of each of the sisters, pronounced:

"Lord God! Send them strength! Shed Thy mercy upon them."

And Marguerite began to speak. The words issued from her lips one by one — hoarse, jerky, tremulous.

"Pardon, pardon, sister! pardon me! Oh, if only you knew how I have dreaded this moment all my life!"

Suzanne faltered through her tears:

"But what have I to pardon, little one? You have given me everything, sacrificed all to me. You are an angel."

But Marguerite interrupted her:

"Be silent, be silent! Let me speak! Don't stop me! It is terrible. Let me tell all, to the very end, without interruption. Listen. You remember — you remember — Henry — "

Suzanne trembled and looked at her sister. The younger one went on:

"In order to understand you must hear everything. I was twelve years old — only twelve — you remember, don't you? And I was spoilt; I did just as I pleased. You remember how everybody spoilt me? Listen. The first time he came he had on his riding boots; he dismounted, saying that he had a message for father. You remember, don't you? Don't speak. Listen. When I saw him I was struck with admiration. I thought him so handsome, and I stayed in a corner of the drawing-room all the time he was talking. Children are strange — and terrible. Yes, indeed, I dreamt of him.

"He came again — many times. I looked at him with all my eyes, all my heart. I was large for my age and much more precocious than — any one suspected. He came often. I thought only of him. I often whispered to myself:

"'Henry-Henry de Sampierre!'

481

"Then I was told that he was going to marry you. That was a blow! Oh, sister, a terrible blow — terrible! I wept all through three sleepless nights.

"He came every afternoon after lunch. You remember, don't you? Don't answer. Listen. You used to make cakes that he was very fond of — with flour, butter and milk. Oh, I know how to make them. I could make them still, if necessary. He would swallow them at one mouthful and wash them down with a glass of wine, saying: 'Delicious!' Do you remember the way he said it?

"I was jealous — jealous! Your wedding day was drawing near. It was only a fortnight distant. I was distracted. I said to myself: 'He shall not marry Suzanne — no, he shall not! He shall marry me when I am old enough! I shall never love any one half so much.' But one evening, ten days before the wedding, you went for a stroll with him in the moonlight before the house — and yonder — under the pine tree, the big pine tree — he kissed you — kissed you — and held you in his arms so long — so long! You remember, don't you? It was probably the first time. You were so pale when you came back to the drawing-room!

"I saw you. I was there in the shrubbery. I was mad with rage! I would have killed you both if I could!

"I said to myself: 'He shall never marry Suzanne — never! He shall marry no one! I could not bear it.' And all at once I began to hate him intensely.

"Then do you know what I did? Listen. I had seen the gardener prepare pellets for killing stray dogs. He would crush a bottle into small pieces with a stone and put the ground glass into a ball of meat.

"I stole a small medicine bottle from mother's room. I ground it fine with a hammer and hid the glass in my pocket. It was a glistening powder. The next day, when you had made your little cakes; I opened them with a knife and inserted the glass. He ate three. I ate one myself. I threw the six others into the pond. The two swans died three days later. You remember? Oh, don't speak! Listen, listen. I, I alone did not die. But I have always been ill. Listen — he died — you know — listen — that was not the worst. It was afterward, later — always — the most terrible — listen.

"My life, all my life — such torture! I said to myself: 'I will never leave my sister. And on my deathbed I will tell her all.' And now I have told. And I have always thought of this moment — the moment when all would be told. Now it has come. It is terrible — oh! — sister —

"I have always thought, morning and evening, day and night: 'I shall have to tell her some day!' I waited. The horror of it! It is done. Say nothing. Now I am afraid — I am afraid! Oh! Supposing I should see him again, by and by, when I am dead! See him again! Only to think of it! I dare not — yet I must. I am going to die. I want you to forgive me. I insist on it. I cannot meet him without your forgiveness. Oh, tell her to forgive me, Father! Tell her. I implore you! I cannot die without it."

She was silent and lay back, gasping for breath, still plucking at the sheets with her fingers.

Suzanne had hidden her face in her hands and did not move. She was thinking of him whom she had loved so long. What a life of happiness they might have had together! She saw him again in the dim and distant past-that past forever lost. Beloved dead! how the thought of them rends the heart! Oh! that kiss, his only kiss! She had retained the memory of it in her soul. And, after that, nothing, nothing more throughout her whole existence!

The priest rose suddenly and in a firm, compelling voice said:

"Mademoiselle Suzanne, your sister is dying!"

Then Suzanne, raising her tear-stained face, put her arms round her sister, and kissing her fervently, exclaimed:

"I forgive you, I forgive you, little one!"

# COCO

Throughout the whole countryside the Lucas farn, was known as "the Manor." No one knew why. The peasants doubtless attached to this word, "Manor," a meaning of wealth and of splendor, for this farm was undoubtedly the largest, richest and the best managed in the whole neighborhood.

The immense court, surrounded by five rows of magnificent trees, which sheltered the delicate apple trees from the harsh wind of the plain, enclosed in its confines long brick buildings used for storing fodder and grain, beautiful stables built of hard stone and made to accommodate thirty horses, and a red brick residence which looked like a little chateau.

Thanks for the good care taken, the manure heaps were as little offensive as such things can be; the watch-dogs lived in kennels, and countless poultry paraded through the tall grass.

Every day, at noon, fifteen persons, masters, farmhands and the women folks, seated themselves around the long kitchen table where the soup was brought in steaming in a large, blue-flowered bowl.

The beasts-horses, cows, pigs and sheep-were fat, well fed and clean. Maitre Lucas, a tall man who was getting stout, would go round three times a day, overseeing everything and thinking of everything.

A very old white horse, which the mistress wished to keep until its natural death, because she had brought it up and had always used it, and also because it recalled many happy memories, was housed, through sheer kindness of heart, at the end of the stable.

A young scamp about fifteen years old, Isidore Duval by name, and called, for convenience, Zidore, took care of this pensioner, gave him his measure of oats and fodder in winter, and in summer was supposed to change his pasturing place four times a day, so that he might have plenty of fresh grass.

The animal, almost crippled, lifted with difficulty his legs, large at the knees and swollen above the hoofs. His coat, which was no longer curried, looked like white hair, and his long eyelashes gave to his eyes a sad expression.

When Zidore took the animal to pasture, he had to pull on the rope with all his might, because it walked so slowly; and the youth, bent over and out of breath, would swear at it, exasperated at having to care for this old nag.

The farmhands, noticing the young rascal's anger against Coco, were amused and would continually talk of the horse to Zidore, in order to exasperate him. His comrades would make sport with him. In the village he was called Coco-Zidore.

The boy would fume, feeling an unholy desire to revenge himself on the horse. He was a thin, long-legged, dirty child, with thick, coarse, bristly red hair. He seemed only half-witted, and stuttered as though ideas were unable to form in his thick, brute-like mind.

For a long time he had been unable to understand why Coco should be kept, indignant at seeing things wasted on this useless beast. Since the horse could no longer work, it seemed to him unjust that he should be fed; he revolted at the idea of wasting oats, oats which were so expensive, on this paralyzed old plug. And often, in spite of the orders of Maitre Lucas, he would economize on the nag's food, only giving him half measure. Hatred grew in his confused, childlike mind, the hatred of a stingy, mean, fierce, brutal and cowardly peasant.

When summer came he had to move the animal about in the pasture. It was some distance away. The rascal, angrier every morning, would start, with his dragging step, across the wheat fields. The men working in the fields would shout to him, jokingly:

"Hey, Zidore, remember me to Coco."

He would not answer; but on the way he would break off a switch, and, as soon as he had moved the old horse, he would let it begin grazing; then, treacherously sneaking up behind it, he would slash its legs. The animal would try to escape, to kick, to get away from the blows, and run around in a circle about its rope, as though it had been enclosed in a circus ring. And the boy would slash away furiously, running along behind, his teeth clenched in anger.

Then he would go away slowly, without turning round, while the horse watched him disappear, his ribs sticking out, panting as a result of his unusual exertions. Not until the blue blouse of the young peasant was out of sight would he lower his thin white head to the grass.

As the nights were now warm, Coco was allowed to sleep out of doors, in the field behind the little wood. Zidore alone went to see him. The boy threw stones at him to amuse himself. He would sit down on an embankment about ten feet away and would stay there about half an hour, from time to time throwing a sharp stone at the old horse, which remained standing tied before his enemy, watching him continually and not daring to eat before he was gone.

This one thought persisted in the mind of the young scamp: "Why feed this horse, which is no longer good for anything?" It seemed to him that this old nag was stealing the food of the others, the goods of man and God, that he was even robbing him, Zidore, who was working.

Then, little by little, each day, the boy began to shorten the length of rope which allowed the horse to graze.

The hungry animal was growing thinner, and starving. Too feeble to break his bonds, he would stretch his head out toward the tall, green, tempting grass, so near that he could smell, and yet so far that he could not touch it.

But one morning Zidore had an idea: it was, not to move Coco any more. He was tired of walking so far for that old skeleton. He came, however, in order to enjoy his vengeance. The beast watched him anxiously. He did not beat him that day. He walked around him with his hands in his pockets. He even pretended to change his place, but he sank the stake in exactly the same hole, and went away overjoyed with his invention.

The horse, seeing him leave, neighed to call him back; but the rascal began to run, leaving him alone, entirely alone in his field, well tied down and without a blade of grass within reach.

Starving, he tried to reach the grass which he could touch with the end of his nose. He got on his knees, stretching out his neck and his long, drooling lips. All in vain. The old animal spent the whole day in useless, terrible efforts. The sight of all that green food, which stretched out on all sides of him, served to increase the gnawing pangs of hunger.

The scamp did not return that day. He wandered through the woods in search of nests.

The next day he appeared upon the scene again. Coco, exhausted, had lain down. When he saw the boy, he got up, expecting at last to have his place changed.

But the little peasant did not even touch the mallet, which was lying on the ground. He came nearer, looked at the animal, threw at his head a clump of earth which flattened out against the white hair, and he started off again, whistling.

The horse remained standing as long as he could see him; then, knowing that his attempts to reach the near-by grass would be hopeless, he once more lay down on his side and closed his eyes.

The following day Zidore did not come.

When he did come at last, he found Coco still stretched out; he saw that he was dead.

Then he remained standing, looking at him, pleased with what he had done, surprised that it should already be all over. He touched him with his foot, lifted one of his legs and then let it drop, sat on him and remained there, his eyes fixed on the grass, thinking of nothing. He returned to the farm, but did not mention the accident, because he wished to wander about at the hours when he used to change the horse's pasture. He went to see him the next day. At his approach some crows flew away. Countless flies were walking over the body and were buzzing around it. When he returned home, he announced the event. The animal was so old that nobody was surprised. The master said to two of the men:

"Take your shovels and dig a hole right where he is."

The men buried the horse at the place where he had died of hunger. And the grass grew thick, green and vigorous, fed by the poor body.

# THE AGE FOR LOVE
## BY PAUL BOURGET

When I submitted the plan of my Inquiry Upon the Age for Love to the editor-in-chief of the Boulevard, the highest type of French literary paper, he seemed astonished that an idea so journalistic — that was his word — should have been evolved from the brain of his most recent acquisition. I had been with him two weeks and it was my first contribution. "Give me some details, my dear Labarthe," he said, in a somewhat less insolent manner than was his wont. After listening to me for a few moments he continued: "That is good. You will go and interview certain men and women, first upon the age at which one loves the most, next upon the age when one is most loved? Is that your idea? And now to whom will you go first?"

"I have prepared a list," I replied, and took from my pocket a sheet of paper. I had jotted down the names of a number of celebrities whom I proposed to interview on this all-important question, and I began to read over my list. It contained two ex-government officials, a general, a Dominican father, four actresses, two café-concert singers, four actors, two financiers, two lawyers, a surgeon and a lot of literary celebrities. At some of the names my chief would nod his approval, at others he would say curtly, with an affectation of American manners, "Bad; strike it off," until I came to the name I had kept for the last, that of Pierre Fauchery, the famous novelist.

"Strike that off," he said, shrugging his shoulders. "He is not on good terms with us."

"And yet," I suggested, "is there any one whose opinion would be of greater interest to reading men as well as to women? I had even thought of beginning with him."

"The devil you had!" interrupted the editor-in-chief. "It is one of Fauchery's principles not to see any reporters. I have sent him ten if I have one, and he has shown them all the door. The Boulevard does not relish such treatment, so we have given him some pretty hard hits."

"Nevertheless, I will have an interview with Fauchery for the Boulevard," was my reply. "I am sure of it."

"If you succeed," he replied, "I'll raise your salary. That man makes me tired with his scorn of newspaper notoriety. He must take his share of it, like the rest. But you will not succeed. What makes you think you can?"

"Permit me to tell you my reason later. In forty-eight hours you will see whether I have succeeded or not."

"Go and do not spare the fellow."

Decidedly. I had made some progress as a journalist, even in my two weeks' apprenticeship, if I could permit Pascal to speak in this way of the man I most admired among living writers. Since that not far-distant time when, tired of being poor, I had made up my mind to cast my lot with the multitude in Paris, I had tried to lay aside my old self, as lizards do their skins, and I had almost succeeded. In a former time, a former time that was but yesterday, I knew — for in a drawer full of poems, dramas and half-finished tales I had proof of it — that there had once existed a certain Jules Labarthe who had come to Paris with the hope of becoming a great man. That person believed in Literature with a capital "L;" in the Ideal, another capital; in Glory, a third capital. He was now dead and buried. Would he some day, his position assured, begin to write once more from pure love of his art? Possibly, but for the moment I knew only the energetic, practical Labarthe, who had joined the procession with the idea of getting into the front rank, and of obtaining as soon as possible an income of thirty thousand francs a year. What would it matter to this second individual if that vile Pascal should boast of having stolen a march on the most delicate, the most powerful of the heirs of Balzac, since I, the new Labarthe, was capable of looking forward to an operation which required about as much delicacy as some of the performances of my editor-in-chief? I had, as a matter of fact, a sure means of obtaining the interview. It was this: When I was young and simple I had sent some verses and stories to Pierre Fauchery, the same verses and stories the refusal of which by four editors had finally made me decide to enter the field of journalism. The great writer was traveling at this time, but he had replied to me. I had responded by a letter to which he again replied, this time with an invitation to call upon him. I went I did not find him. I went again. I did not find him that time. Then a sort of timidity prevented my returning to the charge. So I had never met him. He knew me only as the young Elia of my two epistles. This is what I counted upon to extort from him the favor of an interview which he certainly would refuse to a mere newspaper man. My plan was simple; to present myself at his house, to be received, to conceal my real occupation, to sketch vaguely a subject for a novel in which there should occur a discussion upon the Age for Love, to make him talk and then when he should discover his conversation in print — here I began to feel some remorse. But I stifled it with the terrible phrase, "the struggle for life," and also by the recollection of numerous examples culled from the firm with which I now had the honor of being connected.

The morning after I had had this very literary conversation with my honorable director, I rang at the door of the small house in the Rue Desbordes-Valmore where Pierre Fauchery lived, in a retired corner of Passy. Having taken up my pen to tell a plain unvarnished tale I do not see how I can conceal the wretched feeling of pleasure which, as I rang the bell, warmed my heart at the thought of the good joke I was about to play on the owner of this peaceful abode.

Even after making up one's mind to the sacrifices I had decided upon, there is always left a trace of envy for those who have triumphed in the melancholy struggle for literary supremacy. It was a real disappointment to me when the servant replied, ill-humoredly, that M. Fauchery was not in Paris. I asked when he would return. The servant did not know. I asked for his address. The servant did not know that. Poor lion, who thought he had secured anonymity for his holiday! A half-hour later I had discovered that he was staying for the present at the Château de Proby, near Nemours. I had merely had to make inquiries of his publisher. Two hours later I bought my ticket at the Gare de Lyon for the little town chosen by Balzac as the scene for his delicious story of Ursule Mirouet. I took a traveling bag and was prepared to spend the night there. In case I failed to see the master that afternoon I had decided to make sure of him the next morning. Exactly seven hours after the servant, faithful to his trust, had declared that he did not know where his master was staying, I was standing in the hall of the château waiting for my card to be sent up. I had taken care to write on it a reminder of our conversation of the year before, and this time, after a ten-minute wait in the hall, during which I noticed with singular curiosity and *malice* two very elegant and very pretty young women going out for a walk, I was admitted to his presence. "Aha," I said to myself, "this then is the secret of his exile; the interview promises well!"

The novelist received me in a cosy little room, with a window opening onto the park, already beginning to turn yellow with the advancing autumn. A wood fire burned in the fireplace and lighted up the walls which were hung with flowered cretonne and on which could be distinguished several colored English prints representing cross-country rides and the jumping of hedges. Here was the worldly environment with which Fauchery is so often reproached. But the books and papers that littered the table bore witness that the present occupant of this charming retreat remained a substantial man of letters. His habit of constant work was still further attested by his face, which I admit, gave me all at once a feeling of remorse for the trick I was about to play him. If I had found him the snobbish pretender whom the weekly newspapers were in the habit of ridiculing, it would have been a delight to outwit his diplomacy. But no! I saw, as he put down his pen to receive me, a man about fifty-seven years old, with a face that bore the marks of reflection, eyes tired from sleeplessness, a brow heavy with thought, who said as he pointed to an easy chair, "You will excuse me, my dear confrère, for keeping you waiting." I, his dear confrère! Ah! if he had known! "You see," and he pointed to the page still wet with ink, "that man cannot be free from the slavery of furnishing copy. One has less facility at my age than at yours. Now, let us speak of yourself. How do you happen to be at Nemours? What have you been doing since the story and the verses you were kind enough to send me?"

It is vain to try to sacrifice once for all one's youthful ideals. When a man has loved literature as I loved it at twenty, he cannot be satisfied at twenty-six to give up his early passion, even at the bidding of implacable necessity. So Pierre Fauchery remembered my poor verses! He had actually read my story! His allusion proved it. Could I tell him at such a moment that since the creation of those first works I had despaired of myself, and that I had changed my gun to the other shoulder? The image of the Boulevard office rose suddenly before me. I heard the voice of the editor-in-chief saying, "Interview Fauchery? You will never accomplish that;" so, faithful to my self-imposed role, I replied, "I have retired to Nemours to work upon a novel called The Age for Love, and it is on this subject that I wished to consult you, my dear master."

It seemed to me — it may possibly have been an illusion — that at the announcement of the so-called title of my so-called novel, a smile and a shadow flitted over Fauchery's eyes and mouth. A vision of the two young women I had met in the hall came back to me. Was the author of so many great masterpieces of analysis about to live a new book before writing it? I had no time to answer this question, for, with a glance at an onyx vase containing some cigarettes of Turkish tobacco, he offered me one, lighted one himself and began first to question, then to reply to me. I listened while he thought aloud and had almost forgotten my Machiavellian combination, so keen was my relish of the joyous intimacy of this communion with a mind I had passionately loved in his works. He was the first of the great writers of our day whom I had thus approached on something like terms of intimacy. As we talked I observed the strange similarity between his spoken and his written words. I admired the charming simplicity with which he abandoned himself to the pleasures of imagination, his superabundant intelligence, the liveliness of his impressions and his total absence of arrogance and of pose.

"There is no such thing as an age for love," he said in substance, "because the man capable of loving — in the complex and modern sense of love as a sort of ideal exaltation — never ceases to love. I will go further; he never ceases to love the same person. You know the experiment that a contemporary physiologist tried with a series of portraits to determine in what the indefinable resemblances called family likeness consisted? He took photographs of twenty persons of the same blood, then he photographed these photographs on the same plate, one over the other. In this way he discovered the common features which determined the type. Well, I am convinced that if we could try a similar experiment and photograph one upon another the pictures of the different women whom the same man has loved or thought he had loved in the course of his life we should discover that all these women resembled one another. The most inconsistent have cherished one and the same being through five or six or even twenty different embodiments. The main point is to find out at what age they have met the woman who approaches nearest to the one whose image they have constantly borne within themselves. For them that would be the age for love.

"The age for being loved?" he continued. "The deepest of all the passions I have ever known a man to inspire was in the case of one of my masters, a poet, and he was sixty years old at the time. It is true that he still held himself as erect as a young man, he came and went with a step as light as yours, he conversed like Rivarol, he composed verses as beautiful as De Vigny's. He was besides very poor, very lonely and very unhappy, having lost one after another, his wife and his children. You remember the words of Shakespeare's Moor: 'She loved me for the dangers I had passed, and I loved her that she did pity them.'

"So it was that this great artist inspired in a beautiful, noble and wealthy young Russian woman, a devotion so passionate that because of him she never married. She found a way to take care of him, day and night, in spite of his family, during his last illness, and at the present time, having bought from his heirs all of the poet's personal belongings, she keeps the apartment where he

494

lived just as it was at the time of his death. That was years ago. In her case she found in a man three times her own age the person who corresponded to a certain ideal which she carried in her heart. Look at Goethe, at Lamartine and at many others! To depict feelings on this high plane, you must give up the process of minute and insignificant observation which is the bane of the artists of to-day. In order that a sixty-year-old lover should appear neither ridiculous nor odious you must apply to him what the elder Corneille so proudly said of himself in his lines to the marquise:

"'Cependant, j'ai quelques charmes
Qui sont assez eclatants
Pour n'avoir pas trop d'alarmes
De ces ravages du temps.'

"Have the courage to analyze great emotions to create characters who shall be lofty and true. The whole art of the analytical novel lies there."

As he spoke the master had such a light of intellectual certainty in his eyes that to me he seemed the embodiment of one of those great characters he had been urging me to describe. It made me feel that the theory of this man, himself almost a sexagenarian, that at any age one may inspire love, was not unreasonable! The contrast between the world of ideas in which he moved and the atmosphere of the literary shop in which for the last few months I had been stifling was too strong. The dreams of my youth were realized in this man whose gifts remained unimpaired after the production of thirty volumes and whose face, growing old, was a living illustration of the beautiful saying: "Since we must wear out, let us wear out nobly." His slender figure bespoke the austerity of long hours of work; his firm mouth showed his decision of character; his brow, with its deep furrows, had the paleness of the paper over which he so often bent; and yet, the refinement of his hands, so well cared for, the sober elegance of his dress and an aristocratic air that was natural to him showed that the finer professional virtues had been cultivated in the midst of a life of frivolous temptations. These temptations had been no more of a disturbance to his ethical and spiritual nature than the academic honors, the financial successes, the numerous editions that had been his. Withal he was an awfully good fellow, for, after having talked at great length with me, he ended by saying, "Since you are staying in Nemours I hope to see you often, and to-day I cannot let you go without presenting you to my hostess."

What could I say? This was the way in which a mere reporter on the Boulevard found himself installed at a five-o'clock tea-table in the salon of a château, where surely no newspaper man had ever before set foot and was presented as a young poet and novelist of the future to the old Marquise de Proby, whose guest the master was. This amiable white-haired dowager questioned me upon my alleged work and I replied equivocally, with blushes, which the good lady must have attributed to bashful timidity. Then, as though some evil genius had conspired to multiply the witnesses of my bad conduct, the two young women whom I had seen going out, returned in the midst of my unlooked-for visit. Ah, my interview with this student of femininity upon the Age for Love was about to have a living commentary! How it would illumine his words to hear him conversing with these new arrivals! One was a young girl of possibly twenty — a Russian if I rightly understood the name. She was rather tall, with a long face lighted up by two very gentle black eyes, singular in their fire and intensity. She bore a striking resemblance to the portrait attributed to Froncia in the Salon Carré of the Louvre which goes by the name of the "Man in Black," because the color of his clothes and his mantle. About her mouth and nostrils was that same subdued nervousness, that same restrained feverishness which gives to the portrait its striking qualities. I had not been there a quarter of an hour before I had guessed from the way she watched and listened to Fauchery what a passionate interest the old master inspired in her. When he spoke she paid rapt attention. When she spoke to him, I felt her voice shiver, if I may use the word, and he, he glorious writer, surfeited with triumphs, exhausted by his labors, seemed, as soon as he felt the radiance of her glance of ingenuous idolatry, to recover that vivacity, that elasticity of impression, which is the sovereign grace of youthful lovers.

"I understand now why he cited Goethe and the young girl of Marienbad," said I to myself with a laugh, as my hired carriage sped on toward Nemours. "He was thinking of himself. He is in love with that child, and she is in love with him. We shall hear of his marrying her. There's a wedding that will call forth copy, and when Pascal hears that I witnessed the courtship — but just now I must think of my interview. Won't Fauchery be surprised to read it day after to-morrow in his paper? But does he read the papers? It may not be right but what harm will it do him? Besides, it's a part of the struggle for life." It was by such reasoning, I remember, the reasoning of a man determined to arrive that I tried to lull to sleep the inward voice that cried, "You have no right to put on paper, to give to the public what this noble writer said to you, supposing that he was receiving a poet, not a reporter." But I heard also the voice of my chief saying, "You will never succeed." And this second voice, I am ashamed to confess, triumphed over the other with all the more ease because I was obliged to do something to kill time. I reached Nemours too late for the train which would have brought me back to Paris about dinner time. At the old inn they gave me a room which was clean and quiet, a good place to write, so I spent the evening until bedtime composing the first of the articles which were to form my inquiry. I scribbled away under the vivid impressions of the afternoon, my powers as well as my nerves spurred by a touch of remorse. Yes, I scribbled four pages which would have been no disgrace to the Journal des Goncourts, that exquisite manual of the perfect reporter. It was all there, my journey, my arrival at the chateau, a sketch of the quaint eighteenth century building, with its fringe of trees and its well-kept walks, the master's room, the master himself and his conversation; the tea at the end and the smile of the old novelist in the midst of a circle of admirers, old and young. It lacked only a few closing lines. "I will add these in the morning," I thought, and went to bed with a feeling of duty performed, such is the nature of a writer. Under the form of an interview I had done, and I knew it, the best work of my life.

What happens while we sleep? Is there, unknown to us, a secret and irresistible ferment of ideas while our senses are closed to the impressions of the outside world? Certain it is that on awakening I am apt to find myself in a state of mind very different from that in which I went to sleep. I had not been awake ten minutes before the image of Pierre Fauchery came up before me, and at the same time the thought that I had taken a base advantage of the kindness of his reception of me became quite unbearable. I felt a passionate longing to see him again, to ask his pardon for my deception. I wished to tell him who I was, with what purpose I had gone to him and that I regretted it. But there was no need of a confession. It would be enough to destroy the pages I had written the night before. With this idea I arose. Before tearing them up, I reread them. And then — any writer will understand me — and then they seemed to me so brilliant that I did not tear them up. Fauchery is so intelligent, so generous, was the thought that crossed my mind. What is there in this interview, after all, to offend him? Nothing, absolutely nothing. Even if I should go to him again this very morning, tell him my story and that upon the success of my little inquiry my whole future as a journalist might depend? When he found that I had had five years of poverty and hard work without accomplishing anything, and that I had had to go onto a paper in order to earn the very bread I ate, he would pardon me, he would pity me and he would say, "Publish your interview." Yes, but what if he should forbid my publishing it? But no, he would not do that.

I passed the morning in considering my latest plan. A certain shyness made it very painful to me. But it might at the same time conciliate my delicate scruples, my "amour-propre" as an ambitious chronicler, and the interests of my pocket-book. I knew that Pascal had the name of being very generous with an interview article if it pleased him. And besides, had he not promised me a reward if I succeeded with Fauchery? In short, I had decided to try my experiment, when, after a hasty breakfast, I saw, on stepping into the carriage I had had the night before, a victoria with coat-of-arms drive rapidly past and was stunned at recognizing Fauchery himself, apparently lost in a gloomy reverie that was in singular contrast to his high spirits of the night before. A small trunk on the coachman's seat was a sufficient indication that he was going to the station. The train for Paris left in twelve minutes, time enough for me to pack my things pell-mell into my valise and hurriedly to pay my bill. The same carriage which was to have taken me to the Château de Proby carried me to the station at full speed, and when the train left I was seated in an empty compartment opposite the famous writer, who was saying to me, "You, too, deserting Nemours? Like me, you work best in Paris."

The conversation begun in this way, might easily have led to the confession I had resolved to make. But in the presence of my unexpected companion I was seized with an unconquerable shyness, moreover he inspired me with a curiosity which was quite equal to my shyness. Any number of circumstances, from a telegram from a sick relative to the most commonplace matter of business, might have explained his sudden departure from the château where I had left him so comfortably installed the night before. But that the expression of his face should have changed as it had, that in eighteen hours he should have become the careworn, discouraged being he now seemed, when I had left him so pleased with life, so happy, so assiduous in his attentions to that pretty girl. Mademoiselle de Russaie, who loved him and whom he seemed to love, was a mystery which took complete possession of me, this time without any underlying professional motive. He was to give me the key before we reached Paris. At any rate I shall always believe that part of his conversation was in an indirect way a confidence. He was still unstrung by the unexpected incident which had caused both his hasty departure and the sudden metamorphosis in what he himself, if he had been writing, would have called his "intimate heaven." The story he told me was "per sfogarsi," as Bayle loved to say; his idea was that

I would not discover the real hero. I shall always believe that it was his own story under another name, and I love to believe it because it was so exactly his way of looking at things. It was apropos of the supposed subject of my novel — oh, irony! — apropos of the real subject of my interview that he began.

"I have been thinking about our conversation and about your book, and I am afraid that I expressed myself badly yesterday. When I said that one may love and be loved at any age I ought to have added that sometimes this love comes too late. It comes when one no longer has the right to prove to the loved one how much she is loved, except by love's sacrifice. I should like to share with you a human document, as they say to-day, which is in itself a drama with a dénouement. But I must ask you not to use it, for the secret is not my own." With the assurance of my discretion he went on: "I had a friend, a companion of my own age, who, when he was twenty, had loved a young girl. He was poor, she was rich. Her family separated them. The girl married some one else and almost immediately afterward she died. My friend lived. Some day you will know for yourself that it is almost as true to say that one recovers from all things as that there is nothing which does not leave its scar. I had been the confidant of his serious passion, and I became the confidant of the various affairs that followed that first ineffaceable disappointment. He felt, he inspired, other loves. He tasted other joys. He endured other sorrows, and yet when we were alone and when we touched upon those confidences that come from the heart's depths, the girl who was the ideal of his twentieth year reappeared in his words. How many times he has said to me, 'In others I have always looked for her and as I have never found her, I have never truly loved any one but her.'"

"And had she loved him?" I interrupted.

"He did not think so," replied Fauchery. "At least she had never told him so. Well, you must now imagine my friend at my age or almost there. You must picture him growing gray, tired of life and convinced that he had at last discovered the secret of peace. At this time he met, while visiting some relatives in a country house, a mere girl of twenty, who was the image, the haunting image of her whom he had hoped to marry thirty years before. It was one of those strange resemblances which extend from the color of the eyes to the 'timbre' of the voice, from the smile to the thought, from the gestures to the finest feelings of the heart. I could not, in a few disjointed phrases describe to you the strange emotions of my friend. It would take pages and pages to make you understand the tenderness, both present and at the same time retrospective, for the dead through the living; the hypnotic condition of the soul which does not know where dreams and memories end and present feeling begins; the daily commingling of the most unreal thing in the world, the phantom of a lost love, with the freshest, the most actual, the most irresistibly naïve and spontaneous thing in it, a young girl. She comes, she goes, she laughs, she sings, you go about with her in the intimacy of country life, and at her side walks one long dead. After two weeks of almost careless abandon to the dangerous delights of this inward agitation imagine my friend entering by chance one morning one of the less frequented rooms of the house, a gallery, where, among other pictures, hung a portrait of himself, painted when he was twenty-five. He approaches the portrait abstractedly. There had been a fire in the room, so that a slight moisture dimmed the glass which protected the pastel, and on this glass, because of this moisture, he sees distinctly the trace of two lips which had been placed upon the eyes of the portrait, two small delicate lips, the sight of which makes his heart beat. He leaves the gallery, questions a servant, who tells him that no one but the young woman he has in mind has been in the room that morning."

"What then?" I asked, as he paused.

"My friend returned to the gallery, looked once more at the adorable imprint of the most innocent, the most passionate of caresses. A mirror hung near by, where he could compare his present with his former face, the man he was with the man he had been. He never told me and I never asked what his feelings were at that moment. Did he feel that he was too culpable to have inspired a passion in a young girl whom he would have been a fool, almost a criminal, to marry? Did he comprehend that through his age which was so apparent, it was his youth which this child loved? Did he remember, with a keenness that was all too sad, that other, who had never given him a kiss like that at a time when he might have returned it? I only know that he left the same day, determined never again to see one whom he could no longer love as he had loved the other, with the hope, the purity, the soul of a man of twenty."

A few hours after this conversation, I found myself once more in the office of the Boulevard, seated in Pascal's den, and he was saying, "Already? Have you accomplished your interview with Pierre Fauchery?"

"He would not even receive me," I replied, boldly.

"What did I tell you?" he sneered, shrugging his big shoulders. "We'll get even with him on his next volume. But you know, Labarthe, as long as you continue to have that innocent look about you, you can't expect to succeed in newspaper work."

I bore with the ill-humor of my chief. What would he have said if he had known that I had in my pocket an interview and in my head an anecdote which were material for a most successful story? And he has never had either the interview or the story. Since then I have made my way in the line where he said I should fail. I have lost my innocent look and I earn my thirty thousand francs a year, and more. I have never had the same pleasure in the printing of the most profitable, the most brilliant article that I had in consigning to oblivion the sheets relating my visit to Nemours. I often think that I have not served the cause of letters as I wanted to, since, with all my laborious work I have never written a book. And yet when I recall the irresistible impulse of respect which prevented me from committing toward a dearly loved master a most profitable but infamous indiscretion, I say to myself, "If you have not served the cause of letters, you have not betrayed it." And this is the reason, now that Fauchery is no longer of this world, that it seems to me that the time has come

for me to relate my first interview. There is none of which I am
more proud.

www.ingramcontent.com/pod-product-compliance
Lightning Source LLC
Chambersburg PA
CBHW070540030726
47505CB00001B/106